D0908488

3 1232 00051 9027

6901

MARVELS OF
ANCIENT ROME

THE EAST END OF THE ARCH OF CONSTANTINE
Water Colour by Samuel Prout. London, Victoria and Albert Museum

MARVELS OF ANCIENT ROME

BY

MARGARET R · SCHERER

RESEARCH FELLOW · THE METROPOLITAN
MUSEUM OF ART

EDITED AND WITH A FOREWORD
BY CHARLES RUFUS MOREY

NEW YORK AND LONDON · MCMLV

PUBLISHED BY THE PHAIDON PRESS

FOR THE METROPOLITAN MUSEUM OF ART

MADE IN GREAT BRITAIN
PRINTED BY GEO. GIBBONS LTD · LEICESTER

CONTENTS

    Page

Foreword BY CHARLES RUFUS MOREY   V

Acknowledgements   VII

Introduction: Mirrors of Rome   I

The Capitol   37

The Palatine   49

The Roman Forum   63

Triumphal Arches   75

The Basilica of Constantine or Maxentius   77

The Colosseum   80

The Golden House of Nero   90

The Baths of Caracalla   94

The Baths of Diocletian   98

The Forum of Nerva   101

The Forum and Column of Trajan   103

Ruins in the Colonna Gardens   107

The Theatre of Marcellus   112

Page

Unidentified Temples by the Tiber   115

The House of Crescentius   116

The Pantheon   118

The Pyramid of Cestius   122

Hadrian's Tomb: the Castle of Sant' Angelo   125

The Vatican Obelisk   129

Statues that were never buried   133

PLATES   143

Notes   367

Chronological List of Dates   395

Sources of Photographs   403

List of Plates   405

Index   413

FOREWORD

*T*HE *theme of this book, the reader will find, is* Roma sparita, *an expressive Italian phrase which might best be rendered in English by 'the Rome that used to be.' Its author is not lacking in respect toward the archaeologists and their learned reconstruction of the ancient city, but it is Rome of the Middle Ages, the Renaissance, and the Romantic Movement that has intrigued her more, and impelled her to confront the present aspect of the city's historic sites and monuments with what they looked like long ago.*

And before they were divested, as the archaeologists desired, of their patient accumulation, over centuries, of picturesque debris (so fertile of herbage and flowers that two whole monographs have been written on the flora of the Colosseum), or before their transformation at the hands of medieval barons and renaissance princes. However much we may admire the skill with which the scholars can re-make ancient Rome, and people it, as Lanciani does in his fascinating books, with authentic Romans, the net result of such resurrection is to meet ourselves again, so up-to-date do these Romans seem who planned and inhabited the imperial city. They lived in flats, went to the theatre (with tickets), piped their houses, had central hot-air heating, a fire-department, and police. An interesting result of the reconstruction of the ancient Roman Forum is to bring to light another of the many facets of the genius of Julius Caesar. He was, among other things, a city-planner, who not only rearranged the Forum, but seems to have initiated the master-plan of that magnificent avenue of imperial forums which opened up easy and monumental communication between the old southern city and its new extensions into the Campus Martius and the Esquiline. He was, in fact, a person with whom one could talk in contemporary terms about circulation of crowds, sewage disposal, zoning laws, fire hazards, and water-supply. The reconstructed models of the Rome he dreamed of, realized in the imperial age, are products of endless research and learning, but all in all they bear a remarkable likeness to Washington, D.C.

The writer of this foreword confesses to a nostalgia for the other Rome 'that used to be', and its 'marvels'. He belongs to a generation that knew the city before the monument to Victor Emmanuel inserted its huge whiteness into the mellow tone of weathered travertine and rose-and-yellow plastered walls which is the normal Roman colouring, and responsible, he suspects, for the jewelled beauty of its summer twilights. Nor, when he was young and a student in Rome, had the Fascist antiquarians as yet denuded the ancient buildings of their secular accretions and left them naked skeletons of brick and concrete. Admirable and efficient in the last degree as museum pieces, they have somehow lost their age. Who, gazing at the present dismal shell of the Mausoleum of Augustus, can dream of the golden epoch of the Empire and its founder?

In truth, the word Rome *has overtones which time alone has added, reimbursing what it took away. The overtones are all time's contribution: spots recalling old tragedies, such as that doorway across the Corso from the Café Aragno where an Orsini once ran a Colonna through in a quarrel; the flavour of papal Rome in the verses of Gioacchino Belli, evoked by the statue standing at the entrance to his beloved, noisy, proletarian Trastevere; the deep tranquillity one can find in the churches and gardens of the Aventine; the old oak passed as you come down the Janiculum, where Tasso sat.*

The undertone, persistent and ubiquitous, is of course the hoary antiquity of the city, the oldest great city that still retains its grandeur. But its antiquity is enriched by what men have thought and written about it, and the beauty they have found in it to paint and draw. The reader is led by this book through the city's accumulated past, through Rome la grande *of the medieval troubadours, the ruined capital of the world that stirred the imagination of the Renaissance, the Mecca of romantic poets, painters, and sculptors, inspiration of Byron and Shelley, Hawthorne and Longfellow. It is of time-encumbered Rome that Miss Scherer writes, when*

'Over all
Was spread the mantle of compassionate age,
Veiling disintegration with a pall
Of clinging ivy, moss, and saxifrage.'

C. R. Morey

ACKNOWLEDGMENTS

THIS book is a work of collaboration; I shall never know exactly how many have helped, directly or indirectly, in its preparation, but to one and all I owe the deepest gratitude. Whatever errors may remain are due to none of my co-workers and critics, but solely to my own human frailty.

Two men have been most largely responsible for whatever pleasure the book may afford: Francis Henry Taylor, Director of the Metropolitan Museum, who gave it his encouragement from the beginning and made possible the photography and the months of selecting and checking fresh material in Rome; and Charles Rufus Morey of Princeton, whose emphasis on the continuity between the ancient and the medieval world has long been an inspiration to many. As Cultural Attaché at the American Embassy during my stay in Rome, he made possible and pleasant most of the special photography of Roman monuments; as editor, during the revision of the text, he made freely available his rich store of knowledge gathered through a long and intimate acquaintance with the city.

My thanks are due, as well, to the members of the Metropolitan Museum's staff who have tirelessly called my attention to all matters concerned with Rome. They are extended especially to Walter Hauser and Stuart M. Shaw for their generous sharing of knowledge gained from architectural training and from residence in Rome; to Lillian Green for unfailing help in many kinds of need; to Marcia Harty for guidance through the mazes of indexing; to Albert Ten Eyck Gardner for invaluable suggestions concerning American artists who worked in Rome; to Marjorie J. Milne for translations from Poggio Bracciolini; to A. Hyatt Mayor and Alice Newlin for their help in locating old prints; to Alice Franklin and Mary Kinsella for similar guidance among old photographs; to the staff of the Museum's library, without which the work could not have been carried on; to Edward Milla and Thomas McAdams for skilful photographing of material in the Museum's collections; and to Marshall B. Davidson for his editorial advice and his guiding hand throughout. Finally, I am deeply grateful to the Trustees of the Museum for making possible the publication of the book.

Among others in the United States, my deepest thanks are due to Edgar P. Richardson, Director, and John S. Newberry, Jr., Curator of Graphic Arts of the Detroit Institute of Arts, for help in assembling material from that museum's collections, especially its unique group of drawings by Thomas Cole; to Henry Sayles Francis, Curator of Prints and Drawings of the Cleveland Museum of Art; and to Otto Wittman, Jr., Assistant Director of the Toledo Museum of Art, for many helpful suggestions; to Edna Donnell for her guidance through the rich store of drawings in Cooper Union; to W. G. Constable, Curator of Paintings in the Museum of Fine Arts, Boston, for suggestions concerning material there; to Helen

Willard for advice concerning that in the Fogg Art Museum at Harvard; to the late Henry Wadsworth Longfellow Dana for making freely available the notebooks and journals of his grandfather and grandmother; to Mrs. Marie de Mare for information concerning the paintings of her grandfather, George Peter Alexander Healy, in Rome; to Van Wyck Brooks and George S. Hellman for aiding in the search for probably non-existent Roman drawings by Washington Irving; to Hildegarde Hawthorne Oskinson and Louise Hall Tharp for similar aid in seeking Roman drawings by Sophia Peabody Hawthorne; to Dr. Charlotte Weidler; to Helmut von Erffa of Rutgers University for helping in the search for possible sketches of Roman monuments by Benjamin West; to Mrs. Ralph Catterall of the Valentine Museum, Richmond, for procuring a photograph of Moses Ezekiel's studio in the Baths of Diocletian; to Mary Alves of *Life Magazine* for kind assistance; to Edward Coykendall and Mrs. Louis P. Church for the photographs of Vanderlyn's *Arch of Titus* and Cole's *Protestant Burying-ground* in their respective collections; to Ernest Nash for permitting me to choose freely from his wide and well-documented collection of photographs of Rome; to Aldo M. Mazio, Italian Consul-General in New York, and the members of his staff, for much checking of current information; to Lino Lipinsky de Orlov for many suggestions; to the staff of the Frick Art Reference Library, the New York Society Library, the Print Room of the New York Public Library, and Avery Architectural Library at Columbia University for their patience in answering interminable questions and making available their rich collections; to Theodore Heinrich, of Monuments, Fine Arts and Archives, for assuring me of the safety of Marten van Heemskerck's sketchbook and for many valuable suggestions; and, finally to Anne O'Hare McCormick of *The New York Times* for the spark of enthusiasm which helped to revive a flagging spirit.

To many whom I knew in Rome my debt is very great. My thanks belong in special degree to Dr. Albert William Van Buren, Professor Emeritus of Archaeology at the American Academy in Rome, for his tireless reading and criticism of the classical sections of the text and for his generous introductions to his friends among the scholars and archaeologists of Rome; to Marion Elizabeth Blake, Fellow of the American Academy, for her advice concerning construction and for the sharing of her own feeling for the living past of Rome; to Laurance P. Roberts, Director, and to the staff of the American Academy for their kindness in making me feel at home and for their help through the mazes of appointments and correspondence in a foreign tongue; and to Frank E. Brown of Yale University and the Academy's School of Classical Studies for helpful suggestions. My gratitude is especially due to the Academy's Librarian, Colonel Peter de Daehn, and his assistant, Inez Longobardi, who not only guided me in the use of the Academy's own library, but also helped me with regard to other institutions in the city, such as the Gabinetto delle Stampe and the Biblioteca Nazionale Centrale; to the staff of the United States Information Service in Rome; and to Dr. Isabella Panzini, who, as Mr. Morey's invaluable assistant at the American Embassy, helped to make smooth my path. I am most grateful, also, to Prince Colonna for permission to photograph the ancient ruins in the Colonna Gardens on the Quirinal.

Among those in charge of antiquities, museums, and other national services of Rome, my deepest thanks are due to Professor Antonio Maria Colini, Director of the Musei Communale di Roma and of the excavations of the Capitol and other monuments, as well as to his colleague, Professor Carlo Pietrangeli; to Professor Pietro Romanelli, Superintendent of Antiquities in the Forum and Palatine; to Professor Salvatore Aurigemma, Director of the Museo Nazionale Romana, for permission to photograph there and for checking information concerning the history of the Baths of Diocletian; to Professor Carlo d'Aloisio da Vasta, Director of the Modern Section of the Museo di Roma, for permission to photograph material in its collection; most especially to Professor Vito Coppola, Director of the Gabinetto Fotografico Nazionale, without whose co-operation the necessary photographs might never have been secured at all; to Professor Maurizio Borda, who acted as interpreter; and to the Gabinetto's photographer, Angelo Carletti, who recorded the eternal magic of sunlight and cloud as well as the shape and texture of Roman monuments. Besides these, I am also indebted to John Ward Perkins, Director of the British School in Rome, for the use of that school's library; to Vera Cacciatore, Librarian of the Keats-Shelley Memorial, for much help especially in locating the grave of that Charles Mills whose name still haunts the site of the old Villa Palatina; to Virginia Vacca for providing a photograph of the painting of Moses Ezekiel on his studio balcony in the Baths of Diocletian, and to Anita Vedder for the treasured gift of her father's drawing of the Baths of Caracalla.

There are others, met, as it were, in passage and forming a link between the United States and Rome, to whom I am deeply grateful: Dorothy Robathan of Wellesley College, who helped me both in this country and in Rome; Eva Maria Sanford of Sweet Briar College, who gave me permission to use her translation from the work of Alcuin; Theodor Mommsen of Princeton, who gave me many valuable suggestions and criticisms on points of history and helped me to secure several of my most valued photographs; Mason Hammond of Harvard and Henry T. Rowell of Johns Hopkins, who aided me greatly in the course of their work as directors of the summer sessions of the American Academy in Rome; Laura B. Voelkel, who secured photographs for me at the first summer session after the war; Zebulon Vance Hooker and Albert Ezekiel Rauh for information concerning Moses Ezekiel; and John Bayley of Cambridge, whose collection of photographs is a treasure house of beauty.

Finally, my thanks are also due in a large measure to the unknown men and women of Rome—the custodians of public monuments and museums, the gardeners, the drivers of *carrozze*, taxis, and buses, who rescued me many times when lost; and the restaurant keepers and dispensers of coffee and ices, who refreshed both body and spirit and, by their kindness, made it impossible to remain an alien in Rome.

New York, 1953

INTRODUCTION: MIRRORS OF ROME

Plates 1–56

'HER very ruin shows how great Rome was.' For a thousand years men have rung the changes on this theme, with words, with pencil, with brush or burin, or with the camera. Through the dark centuries while the old order crumbled and the Roman peace was but a memory, these mighty ruins have remained the outward and visible signs of that underlying spiritual continuity of religion, of language, and of law, by which Rome bridged the gap between the ancient and the modern world and built a new civilization based upon the old. The changing yet continuous panorama of history is everywhere apparent in the varied fortunes of these monuments and what men have seen in them. In themselves they form a commentary upon time.

We know the monuments of ancient Rome from their surviving ruins, from descriptions, and from pictorial recording over many centuries. Those that remain are their own best records, though even here descriptions and portraits left by artists who knew them in different aspects may explain or amplify. By far the most numerous of such memorabilia are coins (Figure 1), on which the buildings are conventionalized, to be sure, but dated. Sometimes, too, there are reliefs (Plates 1, 2, 61, 106), showing in their backgrounds buildings either real or fanciful, but suggesting, in any case, how the men of ancient Rome visualized the city in its prime. These reliefs, despite arbitrary proportions and perspective, have something of the opulent quality which marked the civilization of Rome's world empire. Less beautiful, but unique as a record of ancient days, is the famous Marble Plan, or *Forma Urbis* (Plates 3–4), whose fragments still show, in rough ground plan, the structures in various sections of the city early in the third century A.D., but make no attempt to represent their actual appearance. Its closest parallels in written records are the *Notitia* and the *Curiosum*, fourth-century catalogues of the city's buildings based on an earlier original now lost.

Coins and broken fragments and ruined brick and stone may suggest a cheerless picture of Rome over the ages. But they have always as background a natural beauty of sunshine and soft air and wide-arched sky as unchanging as the interpretations of her monuments are mutable; as much a 'marvel' of Rome today as in the years of her ancient glory. The city's 'golden air' mists the pages of Henry James; to Gilbert Chesterton there was no city 'in which the sky seemed so significant as in Rome'. And more than fifteen centuries ago the Gallo-Roman Rutilius Namatianus, saying farewell to 'that dear scene', had felt that 'a fairer tract of sky and a serene expanse marks the clear summits of the Seven Hills. There 'tis lasting sunshine: the very daylight which Rome makes for herself seems purer than all else.'

Rutilius Namatianus, last of the classical Latin poets, said his farewell to Rome in A.D. 416, only six years after her first capture in eight centuries by a foreign foe. This sack by the Goths under Alaric in 410 was followed by the Vandals' raid under Genseric in 455. The traditional 'Fall of Rome' in 476 simply marked the deposition of the last Western emperor by the Teuton *condottiere* Odoacer. There was no sudden, formal break with the Eastern emperor at Constantinople, or New Rome. Theodoric, king of the Ostrogoths, who revered the ancient city and her civilization, tried to establish an Italian state which should carry on the Roman tradition. After his death in 526, however, the Eastern emperor Justinian slowly reconquered Italy at great cost. Rome was captured and recaptured five times in eighteen years and her far-reaching aqueducts were cut by besieging forces. Soon after the middle of the sixth century the city, ravaged and exhausted, finally came under the control of the Eastern emperor, to be administered for almost two centuries and a half by the Exarch of Ravenna as part of the eastern or Byzantine empire.

During these troubled centuries the popes or bishops of Rome, into whose care more and more responsibilities fell as civic agencies lapsed, gradually gained in authority. It was, indeed, largely the genius of Pope Gregory the Great (590–604) which made it possible for Rome to recover from the disastrous Gothic wars. The popes and the city they represented grew restive presently under Byzantine rule, which tended to subordinate both the Church and the ancient capital of the West. Leo III turned to the Frankish king, Charlemagne, as the strongest orthodox counter-force and crowned him Roman Emperor on Christmas Day of the year 800. From this recognition of the Germanic kings of France instead of the Byzantine emperors as the protectors of Rome, grew the medieval Holy Roman Empire, and as a far-off result of strife between the emperors and the popes, the later claims of French and Hapsburg rulers to interfere in Italian affairs.

The Eternal City had long since become the goal of Christian pilgrims, who carried to their homes tales of her ancient as well as her Christian 'marvels'. Such a pilgrims' saying, dating from Charlemagne's early years perhaps, is that linking the Colosseum, or the colossal statue which had once stood near it, with the fall of Rome and of the world. The emperor's emphasis on the learning of the ancient world revived nostalgic interest in the city's past. Charlemagne's great scholar, Alcuin, has left one of the earliest in the long series of medieval laments for her vanished glory:

'Rome, once head of the world, the world's pride, the city of gold,
Stands now a pitiful ruin, the wreck of its glory of old.'

Though the literature of Rome persisted despite waning empire and crumbling walls, there is a gap, reflecting the decline of classic art, in the pictorial record of her monuments after the fourth century. A picture of Rome which belonged to Charlemagne and was described by his biographer, Einhard, may have been done during his time or may have been a survival from late Roman days. Einhard simply says that among the emperor's treasures was a silver table, 'round in shape, inscribed with a picture of Rome', which was bequeathed to the Bishopric of Ravenna. Since this table has long since been lost it is impossible to tell its date, but its influence may have been felt in the popularity of round panoramic views in the Middle Ages.

A circular plan is believed to have accompanied the oldest surviving pilgrims' guide to Rome, the *Einsiedeln Itinerary*, compiled by an eighth-century Swiss monk, which lists the pagan and Christian 'marvels' to be seen along different routes. By the time this document was discovered in the seventeenth century in the Swiss monastery of Einsiedeln, the plan had disappeared and it is left to scholars to ponder whether it may have suggested or been suggested by the shape of Charlemagne's picture.

With Charlemagne, Rome was once more firmly bound to the West, but this connection only added to her trials. The centuries immediately following the emperor's coronation were among the darkest of her history. Islam was at her gates. In the ninth century the Saracens came so close that they plundered the great churches of Saint Peter and Saint Paul. Worse yet, popes and emperors, mutually jealous, locked forces in a struggle which tore the city into factions. This struggle accelerated the transformation of ancient Rome, cosmopolitan mistress of the world, into a provincial medieval city. Probably the most destructive sack in her history was due to this contest between popes and emperors; in 1084 one of two rival popes called in the Normans from Sicily to expel the emperor, and let loose an orgy of fire and plunder unequalled by those of Goths and Vandals. But more than to wars and sacks and earthquakes and fires, the destruction of Rome's monuments was due to plundering by her own citizens, too crushed by misfortune to do more than take their building materials from the easiest and most available sources — the crumbling edifices about them.

The disastrous eleventh century finally wore to a close; the twelfth brought a renaissance of interest in the Roman past on the part of the Romans themselves. To the early part of the century belongs Hildebert of Tours' famous lament, echoing that of Alcuin and setting a pattern for those to come:

> 'Rome, thy grand ruins, still beyond compare,
> Thy former greatness mournfully declare,
> Though time thy stately palaces around
> Hath strewed, and cast thy temples to the ground.'

A little later in the same century appeared the great medieval guide to Rome, the *Mirabilia Romae*, or Marvels of Rome. The first version of this guide was probably written about 1150. Like the *Einsiedeln Itinerary* the *Mirabilia* mingled pagan and Christian 'marvels'; unlike the *Itinerary*, it never lapsed into complete obscurity. In many expanded and differing versions, together with books related to it or based upon it, this guide coloured the thinking of the Middle Ages concerning Rome and influenced even the early Renaissance. In its twelfth-century form it contained a short classified list of monuments, a group of legends, pagan and Christian, and an account of sights to see in walking from Saint Peter's into the city and back.

The *Mirabilia* was a timely book, written at a crucial period in Roman history and perhaps for a specific purpose—to celebrate or to inspire a revival of Roman freedom by pointing out the glories of the past. The Romans had finally recovered from the terrible Norman sack and had gained a short breathing space in the long contest between Empire and Papacy. In 1143 they established a Roman Senate among the ruins of the Capitol and proclaimed their city an independent republic, following the ancient pattern which Italian cities to the north had already revived. The phrase 'in the time of the Consuls and Senators' runs through the *Mirabilia* like the 'once upon a time' of fairy tale.

The book's spirit is summed up in its Conclusion: 'These and many more temples and palaces of emperors, consuls, senators, and prefects were in the time of the heathen within this Roman city, even as we have read in old chronicles, and have seen with our eyes, and have heard tell of ancient men. And moreover, how great was their beauty in gold, and silver, and brass, and ivory, and precious stones, we have endeavoured us in writing, as well as we could, to bring back to the remembrance of mankind.'

This republican movement, probably best remembered for its association with Arnold of Brescia, lover of antiquity as well as of liberty, ended in failure. But the name of the Senate remained, though it usually consisted of one or two appointed Senators, and the dream of liberty was not forgotten.

Closely related to the *Mirabilia* in time and inspiration are the *Graphia aureae urbis Romae*, or Account of the Golden City of Rome, and a description by the Englishman, Master Gregory, which is devoted even more completely to antiquities than either of the others. Master Gregory was the chief source for the work of another Englishman, Ranaulf Higden, whose *Polychronicon*, or world history, dates from the fourteenth century.

Picture plans of Rome which seem related to the *Mirabilia* appear in various manuscript chronicles. These maps present the city in the spirit of the *Mirabilia* and other medieval guides as a collection of isolated 'marvels'. The enveloping atmosphere, the sense of interrelated objects which ancient Roman artists conveyed, has vanished completely, and buildings appear in crudely drawn elevation, scattered upside down or lying upon their sides as space and the artist's fancy directed. Probably the earliest of such plans is that in a world history compiled by Paulinus the Minorite early in the fourteenth century (Plate 5). This plan, now in the Library of Saint Mark's, Venice, has no direct connection with the text of the book, except that passages from the *Mirabilia* appear opposite it and the marginal notes on the plan seem to be condensed from the *Mirabilia's* lists of monuments. Another version of the plan, perhaps a slightly later copy, is in the Vatican Library. The golden seal of Ludwig of Bavaria (Plate 6), done at the time of his coronation as Holy Roman Emperor in 1328, compresses the city's marvels into a circle, reminiscent, perhaps, of Charlemagne's round picture.

More sophisticated and skilful in rendering but equally in the spirit of the *Mirabilia* and *Graphia*, upon both of which it draws for iconography, is the view of Rome in Fazio degli Uberti's *Dittamondo* (Plate 7), a description of the world written between 1350 and 1367. Here Rome is 'the widowed city', abandoned by the popes, who had forsaken her to live in Avignon; toyed with by the emperors, who avoided the responsibility of rule; and roused to futile revolt, about the middle of the century, by Cola di Rienzi. It is the city of Dante, who had appealed to an indifferent emperor:

> 'Come and behold thy Rome, who calls on thee,
> Desolate widow, day and night with moans,
> "My Caesar, why dost thou desert my side?" '

Petrarch used the same imagery in addressing the emperor Charles IV in 1350: 'Picture to yourself the Genius of the city of Rome, presenting herself before you. Imagine a matron, with the dignity of age, but with her grey locks dishevelled, her garments rent, and her face overspread with the pallor of misery: and yet with an unbroken spirit, and unforgetful of the majesty of former days, she addresses you as follows: "Lest thou shouldst angrily scorn me, Caesar, know that once I was powerful and performed great deeds. I ordained laws and established the divisions of the year. I taught the art of war. . . . But then, I know not why, unless it is not fitting that the works of mortals should prove themselves immortal, my magnificent structure fell a prey to sloth and indulgence." '

Fazio degli Uberti, imitating Dante's journey with Vergil in the *Divine Comedy*, represented himself as accompanied by Solinus, a Roman geographer of about the third century A.D., who pointed out the sights of the journey. In Rome the widowed city herself became their guide, addressing them in words that recall the *Mirabilia*:

> 'Come hither and thou shalt see
> How fine my castles were, my towers,
> My mighty palaces and my triumphal arches.'

Fazio follows the pattern which Dante and Petrarch had set in his description of 'widowed Rome':

> 'I saw her face wet with the tears of woe.
> I saw her raiment torn and undone,
> And her widow's garb, threadbare and tattered.
> Yet in spite of these her appearance,
> Honest and dignified, showed her noble race.'

Meanwhile, the art of painting on a larger scale was reviving here and there throughout Italy. By the late thirteenth century a few scattered monuments of Rome, such as Hadrian's Tomb and the Vatican obelisk, chosen because of their relationship to Saint Peter's to typify the city, had been painted in the cross-vaulting of the Upper Church of Saint Francis at Assisi, perhaps by Cimabue's hand. Time-worn and half-ruined as this painting is, there is in it something of that roundness and solidity and simplicity of mass which had once belonged to the art of ancient Rome.

But the painting of isolated 'marvels' was carried over for a time in such a large-scale work as Taddeo di Bartolo's circular view of Rome (Plate 8), painted in 1413–1414 on the ceiling of the chapel of the Palazzo Pubblico in Siena. Taddeo may have followed some older source, perhaps one done in the tradition of Charlemagne's round silver table or the Emperor Ludwig's golden seal. Its resemblance to the round view of the

FIG. I.   MONUMENTS SHOWN ON ROMAN COINS

London, British Museum

Top left: THE TEMPLE OF JUPITER CAPITOLINUS. Sestertius of Vespasian (A.D. 69–79).

The temple of Jupiter is shown as Vespasian restored it, following the old plan, but on a larger scale. It has six Corinthian columns across its portico and, in the pediment, the figure of Jupiter, flanked by those of Juno and Minerva, who were also worshipped here. The figures at the sides of Jupiter may represent these goddesses. Jupiter is also seated, with a goddess on each side, within the portico.

Top right: THE CIRCUS MAXIMUS. Sestertius of Trajan (A.D. 98–117).

The Circus Maximus at the southern foot of the Palatine hill appears on Trajan's coin as he rebuilt it. It is surrounded by a colonnaded portico and has, of course, the *spina*, or low wall, running lengthwise along its centre, on top of which appears the obelisk which Augustus brought from Heliopolis in Egypt. At each end of the *spina* are conical *metae* or goal posts, about which chariots turned.

Below: THE COLOSSEUM. Sestertius of Titus (A.D. 79–81).

The Colosseum appears on the coin of Titus much as it must have looked when that emperor opened it, still unfinished, in A.D. 80. It is shown in tilted perspective, so that there is a view of the interior filled with spectators at the games.

   At the left stands the tall fountain called the *Meta Sudans*, 'the sweating *meta*', from the fact that it resembled in shape the *meta* of a circus; *sudans* refers to the splashing water which issued from its top and covered the conical centre.

FIG. 2.   CIRCULAR VIEW OF ROME
(*The south is at the top*)
From the 'Très Riches Heures de Jean de France, Duc de Berry', 1412–1416
Illumination by Pol de Limbourg (French). Chantilly, Musée Condé

The general plan is so like that of the view by Taddeo di Bartolo (Plate 8) as to suggest a common original. There are fewer buildings here and some differences, but the locations are similar enough to make the same key usable for both.

Pol de Limbourg shows his unfamiliarity with Rome in a number of details. The Colosseum, near the statue of Marcus Aurelius, resembles a tower. Some of the classic ruins have northern forms. The Palatine, to the right of the Colosseum, is a mass of Gothic structures, a combination of castle and cathedral. The Theatre of Marcellus, below the Palatine, is disproportionately large and has a dome. The Pantheon, below the central Capitol hill, is very small. And the space toward the left, where the Marble Horses stood, is left blank, as is that within the outlines of Marcus Aurelius' statue.

city in the Duc de Berry's *Book of Hours* (Figure 2), painted about the same time, is so close as to suggest a common original.

In Taddeo's painting, despite the city's compression to fit the circular space and the oblique tilting of the section about Saint Peter's to make it seem larger and more important in the eyes of pilgrims, the relationship of locations has become remarkably accurate. Allowing for the difference in orientation, with the south at the top, it is surprisingly easy to find many of Taddeo's buildings on modern maps turned upside down.

By the middle of the fifteenth century, painting had recaptured much of the full, firm modelling of ancient days and had advanced far beyond them in scientific perspective and proportion. General views of Rome and her famed monuments now began to emerge as unified landscape compositions, the isolated marvels being subordinated to the whole.

Such a landscape composition is Benozzo Gozzoli's *Saint Augustine Leaving Rome for Milan* (Plate 9). The 'marvels' are here, in a somewhat scrambled grouping, but the city appears from a distance as a unified view. So it must have looked indeed to those approaching old Saint Peter's from the north along the pilgrim roads, or leaving it with a last backward glance on their return. It is typical of the reasoned renaissance approach that the subject should be so chosen and arranged that the saint is plausibly shown journeying north from Rome to Milan, so that the famous first view seen by most pilgrims and tourists until the coming of railroads is the inevitable background. The beauty of natural setting has returned to painting, and Benozzo paints *con amore* the trees that rise along the slopes, or here and there above a garden wall, and a glimpse of the western hills.

Rome by the mid-fifteenth century was the head of a cultural as well as a spiritual world, for the popes had become lavish patrons of the arts. From the days of Cimabue and Giotto in the late thirteenth century leading artists had been called to Rome for papal commissions, but the fifteenth century saw them summoned for longer and longer periods. Fra Angelico, brought from his cloister in Florence to work in the Vatican, had died in Rome ten years before Benozzo Gozzoli painted his view of the city. From the fifteenth century well through the nineteenth, Rome remained the goal of artists and her ruins left a deep impress on their style and subject-matter. But though Rome was a home for artists, the artists themselves were seldom Romans. As the Empire had once drawn her statesmen and creative workers from the imperial provinces, so Rome of the Renaissance drew her artists and scholars from other cities to serve the papal court.

The fifteenth century saw also the beginning of the new archaeology which was slowly to replace the legends of the *Mirabilia* as a source of information both in literature and in art. Poggio Bracciolini's *De Varietate Fortunae* (Vicissitudes of Fortune) written before 1431, opened a new epoch in the interpretation of Roman monuments. Instead of the delightful but credulous wonder of the medieval guide, Poggio's book combined first-hand observation with study of neglected or hitherto unknown classical writings. Flavio Biondo carried still further the scientific study of Roman topography. His *Roma Instaurata* (Rome Restored), completed in 1446, was the first attempt to describe Roman antiquities with suggestions for their restoration. Flavio used not only the usual classical literary sources but also the late antique regional catalogues, the *Notitia* and *Curiosum*, in his evocation of ancient Rome. His *Roma Triumphans* seeks to recreate the social and religious life as well as the antiquities of the classic city and his *Historiarum ab inclinato Romano Imperio Decades III* (History of the Decline of the Roman Empire) was a forerunner of Gibbon's *Decline and Fall*.

It was the work of these early renaissance scholars that laid the foundations for a new concept of history, including a transitional or 'middle age' between the fall of the Roman Empire and later times. The division of history into ancient, medieval, and modern periods, however, was not fully established until the seventeenth century. The ancient Roman reckoning of time as before and after the founding of Rome in 753 B.C. had lasted until the sixth century A.D. and even later in some countries. Men of the Middle Ages in general considered, not without foundation, that their civilization was a continuation of imperial Rome—*Rome la grande*— carried on by the coronation of Charlemagne in Rome and the succeeding Holy Roman Empire.

Petrarch, however, on the borderline between the Middle Ages and the Renaissance, in a letter to his friend Giovanni Colonna in 1341 noted the growing recognition of a definite break between pagan and Christian times: 'Those things which happened before the name of Christ was celebrated and venerated in Rome, we reckoned as ancient; all that has occurred since that epoch to the present time, as modern.'

The sixteenth century dawned brilliantly for Rome as the centre of the High Renaissance. During its first quarter both Raphael and Michelangelo were busy there, the one at work on the frescoes of the Vatican apartments and the other on the ceiling of the Sistine Chapel. Raphael was also placed in charge, by Leo X, of the removal of material from ancient monuments, in order to minimize the destruction of 'antique marbles, without regard to the inscriptions which are engraven thereon'. Such a safeguard was especially necessary since as architect he was also charged with securing stones for the new building of Saint Peter's.

After this bright flowering early in the century, Rome became once more a pawn in the struggle between foreign powers. The French kings and the Spanish Hapsburgs both claimed one or more of the Italian states as their rightful inheritance by descent or marriage. Their claims, in some cases, went back to situations created by the medieval struggles between Empire and Papacy; now, once more, both sides exerted pressure upon the popes. Fierce warfare broke out between Francis I of France and the Hapsburg emperor Charles V of Spain, in the course of which the imperial forces captured the city in 1527 and plundered it more mercilessly than in any sack save that of the Normans in 1084.

Again the city recovered, this time with no long period of decline. The Rome which rallied from this disaster was never again quite so gay, quite so pagan, as in the days of Julius II and Leo X. The city of the popes which emerged after the middle of the century was the baroque Rome of the Counter Reformation, whose buildings, sculpture, and painting alike were keyed to produce an exciting, dramatic, spectacular effect, meant for the service of the Christian religion but oddly harmonious with the more elaborate monuments of the ancient pagan capital.

Monuments spared by the sack were imperilled by the triumph which Charles V celebrated in Rome in 1536, on the pretext of his victory over the Turks in Tunisia the year before. For this occasion Paul III, then pope, had many changes made in the Forum through which the procession marched on its way to the Capitol, and a fresh wave of discovery— and destruction—passed over the city.

Meanwhile, as Rome became more and more the centre of the artistic as well as of the religious world, artists had begun those delightful, detailed sketches of her monuments which are the clearest and perhaps the most beautiful record of their appearance from the late fifteenth century onward. Among the earliest of these was a pupil or follower of Ghirlandaio, usually called the Anonymus Escurialensis from the name of the collection in which his sketchbook is preserved (Plate 11).

The drawings in this sketchbook, though done about 1491, betray a lingering trace of the Middle Ages in their tight outlines and meticulous detail. Occasionally, too, they suffer from an incomplete mastery of problems in perspective, already solved by leading painters of the time. But the artist observed keenly and drew firmly. The result is an outstanding document, of both topographical and artistic importance, showing

Roman monuments as they looked on the eve of the New World's discovery.

The sketchbook of the Netherlander, Marten van Heemskerck (Plate 12), is outstanding among sixteenth-century drawings of Roman ruins. Van Heemskerck came to Rome in 1532, twelve years after Raphael's death, and remained there until 1535 or 1536, about the time Michelangelo began work on his *Last Judgment* in the Sistine Chapel. The emotions which drew him like so many others to the Eternal City, and his activities there, were recorded by his younger contemporary Carl van Mander: 'He went to Rome, for which place he had had a strong desire for a long time. . . . He made drawings from antiques and from the works of Michelangelo. He made many sketches of ancient ruins, architectural details, and interesting remains of ancient works that may be seen in great abundance in this city.' Northern fidelity to detail and a bold simplicity and grace acquired from Italy combine to make Van Heemskerck's drawings among the most accurate and the most attractive records of Roman monuments in the days of the Renaissance.

Three strangers from the north put into immortal words the spell of renaissance Rome, as Van Heemskerck expressed it in line. The French poet, Joachim du Bellay, who lived in the city from 1553 to 1556, wrote the sonnet sequence, *The Antiquities of Rome*; Spenser translated it into haunting Elizabethan verse as the *Ruines of Rome*:

> 'Thou stranger, which for Rome in Rome here seekest,
> And nought of Rome in Rome perceiv'st at all,
> These same olde walls, olde arches, which thou seest,
> Olde palaces, is that which Rome men call.
> Behold what wreake, what ruine, and what wast,
> And how that she, which with her mightie powre
> Tam'd all the world, hath tam'd herselfe at last,
> The prey of Time, which all things doth devowre.
> Rome, living, was the world's sole ornament,
> And dead, is now the world's sole moniment.'

Later in the same century Montaigne's essays reveal the renaissance reverence for Rome and the French cultural and political ties rooted in Roman Gaul and strengthened by Charlemagne and the French kings. With a nostalgia reminiscent of Rutilius Namatianus and Cassiodorus, he wrote in his essay *Of Vanity*: 'I was familiar with the affairs of Rome long before I was with those of my own house. . . . I knew the Capitol and its position before I knew the Louvre, and the Tiber before the Seine.' And again, '. . . This same Rome that we see deserves our love, having been so long and by so many ties allied with our own crown: the only common and universal city.'

It is in the works of the late fifteenth and the sixteenth century, especially in such drawings as those of the Anonymus Escurialensis and Marten van Heemskerck, that the artists' records begin to show the difference in ground-level between ancient and modern Rome, which excavations have so abundantly revealed. Aside from buildings which have collapsed or have been torn down, there are many which remained for centuries partly or entirely buried beneath the accumulation of soil and debris, while new structures and new streets rose above and hid them. In this city of alternating dry and rainy seasons, whose lower sections suffered from floods when the Tiber overflowed, it has been estimated that dust and rain alone would raise the level more than an inch a year. To this natural rise in level the Romans added by crushing and filling in the lower stories of buildings to provide foundations for later ones. This custom, begun even in ancient times, continued through the centuries. The levelling of the surface of the Forum for the triumphal procession of Charles V in 1536 probably accounted for much of the change between the drawings done by the Anonymus Escurialensis and those of various artists in the second half of the sixteenth century.

The introduction of printed pictures in the fifteenth century added another type of artistic record and greatly increased the number of views of Rome and her antiquities. It did not, however, increase their accuracy, for prints were often copied from earlier drawings and therefore do not show the actual condition of monuments at the time of printing. Also, the convenience and economy of reprinting from old blocks put a premium on their use long after they were out of date.

The oldest known printed view of Rome appeared in 1490 in the *Supplementum Chronicorum Orbis* (Supplement to the Histories of the World) by Giovanni Filippo Foresti of Bergamo (Plate 13). It is a combination of panoramic landscape with the type of plan painted by Taddeo di Bartolo, and seems to be related to a late fifteenth-century painting on cloth, now in the Ducal Palace at Mantua. Both may have followed some older source. As the printed view is much compressed and crowded, it is fortunate that the Mantua painting shows the buildings in the same general form but more correctly located. The arrangement followed in this painting and early woodcut was continued for more than half a century, long after some of the monuments shown had been destroyed or altered.

By the early sixteenth century the production of printed plans and pictures of Rome had become a flourishing business, often attracting capital from other lands. One of its most successful figures was Antoine Lafrère of Burgundy, known in Italy as Antonio Lafreri, who came to Rome about 1540 and eventually got almost a monopoly of the copper engraving business there. His *Speculum Romanae Magnificentiae* (Mirror of Roman Magnificence), published as separate plates, contains the work of many years and many men, and records the early stages of classical antiquarianism. The *Speculum*'s map of Rome in 1557 (Plate 14) is one of the first to be a true picture map rather than a collection of 'marvels'.

The prolific foreign etcher, Etienne Du Pérac, came to Rome from France about 1559 and made numerous drawings and etchings, which were published in 1575 under the title *Vestigi dell' Antichità di Roma* (Remains of Roman Antiquities). Du Pérac interpreted the ruins with considerable freedom in some of his drawings; furthermore, as radical changes had sometimes taken place in a structure between the date of his drawing and the date of publication, the etchings do not always show the condition of the monuments in 1575. A noteworthy example of this is his etching of the central hall of the Baths of Diocletian (Plate 158), done from a drawing made before Michelangelo had converted it into the church of Santa Maria degli Angeli, but dated 1575, after the hall had become a church.

Outstanding among the many Italians who recorded Roman antiquities in the sixteenth century are the members of the Sangallo family and Giovanni Antonio Dosio. Especially valuable is such a drawing as that looking into the central hall of the Baths of Caracalla (Plate 149) which shows this monument not long before its remaining marble decorations were torn away. Engravings from many of Dosio's drawings were published in 1569 in the *Aedificiorum illustrium reliquiae* (Remains of Famous Buildings).

Guidebooks and archaeological handbooks multiplied with the spread of printing. The *Mirabilia* was printed and reprinted many times and new works sprang up to meet the new situation. Among such new guides prepared in the light of renaissance antiquarianism, one of the best was the *Antiquities of Rome* by Raphael's friend, Andrea Fulvio, which marked the first real advance over the work of Flavio Biondo in the fifteenth century. Careful and critical, too, in the light of information then available, was much of the work of Bartolommeo Marliani, which appeared later in the sixteenth century. Marliani is also remembered as an early fighter in one of the long and bitter archaeological disputes which have enlivened

Roman antiquarianism from the Renaissance to the present. The traditional site of the Roman Forum, running roughly east and west below the north face of the Palatine hill, had been accepted until the middle of the sixteenth century, for it contained many well-preserved and documented monuments. But with all the enthusiasm of an amateur archaeologist, Pirro Ligorio, a Neapolitan architect, then propounded the theory that it ran north and south between the Palatine and Capitoline hills. Marliani vigorously defended the old east–west site, but Ligorio won many followers in his own time and later, and succeeded in complicating a hitherto simple situation for several centuries.

Less dependable than Marliani's works were such popular illustrated guides as those of Prospero Parisio and Girolamo and Giovanni Franzini, published in the sixteenth and seventeenth centuries. These guides discuss the monuments learnedly, to be sure, using the terminology of ancient Rome, but the disciplined enthusiasm of the early Renaissance all too often disintegrates into classical fairy tales, no less fanciful than the marvels of the *Mirabilia*. Like it, they are valuable as reflections of a time when a detailed if specious explanation was frequently more welcome than an inconclusive if honest striving for accuracy. An outstanding book for the well-instructed traveller dates from the end of the century. Bernard de Montfaucon, French scholar and monk, wrote his *Diarium Italicum* as the result of a tour in Italy in 1698–1699. Published in Paris in Latin in 1702, it was translated into English twice in the next quarter-century. Montfaucon not only observed and reported perceptively what he himself saw, but delved into works at that time comparatively little known. His book includes many passages from the sixteenth-century Italian, Flaminio Vacca, and a long excerpt from a version of the *Mirabilia*. This, through John Henley's English translation of Montfaucon's book in 1725, seems to have had a strong influence on the style of Nichols' *Marvels of Rome* in 1889.

Rome in the seventeenth century began to take on the baroque appearance which it kept until comparatively recent years. New streets were opened, the water-supply was increased, and for the first time since ancient days the hills again became residential sections. Although classic ruins suffered somewhat during these changes, it was chiefly the buildings of medieval Rome that vanished before the baroque style, with its monumental planning and its emphasis on contrast and surprise.

Baroque Rome continued to draw many of her most noted artists from outside Italy. Rubens left comparatively few works representing Roman monuments, but he visited the city twice between 1601 and 1606. A

Landscape with Ruins of the Palatine in the Louvre is a very free treatment of this famous scene; another rather similar painting is known now only through an engraving. In Rome during these first years of the century the great Fleming knew the German, Adam Elsheimer, who played a considerable part in the development of classical landscape paintings with Roman ruins; he knew too Paul Brill from Antwerp, who had been influenced strongly by Elsheimer and carried on his tradition. Paul's older brother, Matthaeus (Plate 187), had died in Rome in 1583. Two outstanding painters who lived and worked in the city slightly later in the century were French: Nicolas Poussin (Plates 15–16) and Claude Lorrain (Plates 17–18, 103). In his training days Claude had worked with Paul Brill's follower, Agostino Tassi. Poussin's firmly modelled, sculpturesque forms show the influence of the classical enthusiasm surrounding him as well as the dramatic formality of the baroque. Another element appears in the work of Claude Lorrain: the atmospheric beauty of the Roman scene. He could paint the Roman Forum accurately enough when he chose, but he was more interested in the sunset light that flooded it. Naturally enough the drawings of both men were much closer to nature than their finished paintings, in which the monuments were apt to be generalized and regrouped to form ideal classical landscapes.

The seventeenth century saw also official recognition by France of Rome's cultural influence in the creation of the French Academy. Founded in 1666 by Louis XIV as part of his general plan for the encouragement of the arts, this academy not only enabled talented artists to study in Rome at state expense, but also set the pattern for later academies founded by other nations.

The desire for pictures of ruins, real or imaginary, and for scenes drawn from Roman history increased steadily in the eighteenth century, keeping pace with a romantic interest in the ancient world. Excavations at Herculaneum, begun in 1738, and at Pompeii, in 1748, roused both scholarly and popular enthusiasm throughout the western world and were followed by the beginning of scientific archaeology in Rome. The early excavations at Herculaneum and the life, art, and monuments of Rome and other Italian cities were observed by the Frenchman, Charles de Brosses, on a tour in 1739. His delightful *Letters on Italy,* based on the visit, were not published, however, until 1799, years after his death. Critical interest in classical art and history found literary expression in the work of Winckelmann, pioneer among art historians; in Lessing's epoch-making *Laokoön;* and in Gibbon's *History of the Decline and Fall of the Roman Empire,* conceived in 1764 among the ruins of the Roman Capitol.

The Roman past was used, also, as propaganda by the revolutionary intellectuals of France to strengthen their case for a republican government, although, ironically enough, most of the works that inspired them came from a period of despotic empire.

Although the characteristic contribution of the eighteenth century to the painting of the Roman scene was the landscape with ruins fantastically arranged, Antonio Canaletto, who visited Rome in 1719 for a stay of several years, was comparatively accurate. Best known for his views of his native Venice and those of London painted during a sojourn in England, he did, however, produce a number of delicately rendered paintings and engravings of Rome and her monuments (Plate 104).

Outstanding among the painters of the more imaginary landscapes with ruins were Giovanni Paolo Pannini of Piacenza (Plates 19–20, 115, 195) and Hubert Robert of Paris (Plates 21–22). Pannini, who may have studied with the stage designer Ferdinando Galli Bibiena in Piacenza, came to Rome about 1717 and was later invited to teach perspective in the French Academy there. His work combined a formal antiquarian approach with the theatrical magnificence so characteristic of baroque art. Hubert (known also in France as Robert of the Ruins) came to Rome in 1754 and studied at the French Academy, where he was strongly influenced by Pannini. To the accuracy of detail and strong classical feeling absorbed from his teacher he added something of the atmospheric quality of Claude Lorrain's work, a characteristic French delicacy and lightness, and an interest in the contrast of ancient ruins with contemporary life that prefigured the dawn of romanticism. In the work of both men actual monuments were usually accurately drawn but regrouped and interspersed with fanciful or composite structures, not with the intent to deceive, but for the satisfaction of romantic taste or the artist's fancy. The combination of Italian landscape and ruins with scenes from everyday life was still more noticeable in the paintings of Joseph Vernet, whose *genre* pictures were popular souvenirs for the wealthy traveller.

The eighteenth century saw also a continually growing demand for engravings and etchings of Roman scenes and monuments, less expensive and more easily housed than paintings. Giovanni Battista Falda's work in the seventeenth century (Plate 73) was followed by that of Giuseppe Vasi (Plates 99, 116). In 1786 Goethe noted, on his first visit to Rome, the influence of such pictures in producing a sense of familiarity with places far away: 'All the dreams of my youth I now beheld realized before me: the subjects of the first engravings I ever remember seeing (several views of Rome were hung up in an ante-room of my father's house) stand

bodily before my sight.' These Roman views, he noted later in his auto-
biographical *Truth and Poetry*, were 'by predecessors of Piranesi', and
doubtless included some by Vasi.

Giovanni Battista Piranesi (Plates 23–24, 138, 164, 194), who worked in
Rome from about 1740 to his death in 1778, was undoubtedly the most
widely known among eighteenth-century etchers of Roman monuments.
Smollett, the English novelist, writing of the various engravings to be
found in Rome, noted: 'The most celebrated are the plates of Piranesi,
who is not only an ingenious architect and engineer but also a learned
antiquarian, though he is apt to run riot in his conjectures.' At the century's end the painter Pierre de Valenciennes, with French perfection of
phrase, characterized the work of this fantastic baroque genius: 'Piranesi
did not tell the history but the romance of Rome. . . . He pictured Rome a
wonderful city such as the imagination of one excited mind might conceive without any rational knowledge of archaeology.' Nevertheless,
despite riotous fancy and frequent disregard of proportion and probability
Piranesi's etchings are often scrupulously exact in detail.

Toward the end of the eighteenth century the artists who dominated
the Roman scene were sculptors rather than painters. Antonio Canova,
the Venetian who settled in Rome in 1779, though essentially classical in
his rendering of form, was not untouched by the growing romantic movement. This rising tide of emotional interpretation, however, passed by
Bertel Thorwaldsen, the Dane who worked in the city from 1797 to his
death in 1838 and whose fame drew artists from all Europe and from the
New World as well (see Plate 36).

But perhaps the most outstanding personality to visit Rome in these
years—or, indeed, in the course of the whole century—was neither a
painter nor a sculptor but a poet. Goethe, archetype of all northerners who
have responded to the lure of Italy, had longed to visit this homeland of
classic culture for years before he was able to realize his dream. He came
to Rome for some months in 1786 and returned in 1787 after a stay in
Naples and Sicily. The direct record of his experience lies in his sketches
(Plate 26), his correspondence, his *Italian Journey*, his *Roman Elegies*, and his
Truth and Poetry. His nostalgic memories of the sunny land have haunted
men's minds ever since, in Mignon's song from *Wilhelm Meister*, written
a few years after his return to Germany:

> 'Know'st thou the land where flowering lemons grow,
> And through dark leaves the golden oranges glow?'

The far-reaching indirect result of Italy's classic culture on his later work seems to be prophetically suggested by Tischbein's portrait of the poet in the Roman Campagna in 1787 (Plate 25).

Eighteenth-century Rome drew her visitors not from European lands alone. Americans, too, began to take their place among those who, in Cassiodorus' words, found Rome 'unfriendly to none, since she is foreign to none'. Before the New World colonies had separated from the mother country, their citizens had shared the English enthusiasm for Roman culture and Roman monuments. The sons of well-to-do families, especially from southern plantations, had travelled to Italy as part of the Grand Tour essential for an English gentleman's education.

American artists, too, soon followed the example of their fellows overseas. Benjamin West spent three years in Italy, chiefly in and about Rome, before he settled in London in 1763. Several anecdotes told by his early biographer, John Galt, suggest that the city welcomed him as warmly as has ever been her wont. There is his widely quoted remark about the Apollo Belvedere, 'How like he is to a young Mohawk warrior'. There is also the story of an old *improvisatore*, singer of extemporaneous songs, who, upon hearing that West was an American, 'immediately unslung his guitar, and began to draw his fingers rapidly over the strings', finally beginning his song with 'the darkness which for so many ages veiled America from the eyes of Science'; invoking 'the fancy of his auditors to contemplate the wild magnificence of mountain, lake, and wood, in the new world'; and ending: 'Rejoice then, O venerable Rome, in thy divine destiny, for though darkness overshadows thy seats, and though thy mitred head must descend into the dust, as deep as the earth that now covers thy ancient helmet and imperial diadem, thy spirit, immortal and undecayed, already spreads towards a new world.'

John Singleton Copley spent some months in Rome in 1774–1775, and painted there his fellow-countrymen, Mr. and Mrs. Ralph Izard of South Carolina (Plate 27), indicating their presence in the city by the old device of placing a well-known Roman monument (the Colosseum) in the background. Both West and Copley were essentially painters in the British tradition who chanced to be born west of the Atlantic. Study in Rome was, to them, as to their English fellows, largely a means toward satisfying British taste and achieving success in England.

But in Washington Allston Italian influence for its own sake became apparent. Able, because of independent means, to paint what he wished, and highly susceptible to his surroundings, he was strongly influenced both by Italy's beauty and by the colour and atmosphere of Roman and Venetian painters and of the French who followed them. The three-and-a-half years he spent in Italy from 1804 to 1808, chiefly in and about Rome, added to his natural romantic love of the 'wild and marvellous' a serene, idyllic note, a flowing line and classic grace not unlike the quality of Claude Lorrain. Like Claude, too, Allston painted, not so much specific monuments as atmospheric landscapes flooded with dreamy light and adorned with fanciful ruins.

Allston influenced American romantic painting rather by his compelling personality than by his actual work, which was comparatively small in volume. His pliable genius did not permit a consistent development of his art; but his personality was outstanding and pervasive. Friendly, urbane, always ready to aid and advise young artists, he helped to forge the links of understanding between the ancient culture of Rome and the growing traditions of the New World. Among his friends he numbered Coleridge, Wordsworth, Southey, Canova, Thorwaldsen, Vanderlyn (Plate 28), Sully, Irving, Bryant, Longfellow, and Lowell; with some of them he shared long hours of artists' talk in the cafés of Rome. Years later, perhaps in 1836, a young American painter, James Freeman, listened to Vanderlyn's description of the gatherings at the Caffè Greco in the Via Condotti near the Spanish Steps, popular then as now for morning and evening coffee (see Plate 35). 'One day Vanderlyn met me at the Greco', wrote Freeman in *Gatherings from an Artist's Portfolio*, many years later, 'and said, "Thirty years ago I was on this very spot", and, pointing to different seats, observed, "there sat Allston opposite me; that was Turner's corner; here, on my left, sat Fenimore Cooper; and there, I was told, Sir Joshua Reynolds and West sat." '

Irving wrote of the pleasure of seeing the city with Allston: 'We had delightful rambles together about Rome and its environs, one of which came near to changing my whole course of life. We had been visiting a stately villa, with its gallery of paintings, its marble halls, its terraced gardens set out with statues and fountains, and were returning to Rome about sunset. The blandness of the air, the serenity of the sky, the transparent charm which hangs about an Italian landscape, had derived additional effect upon being enjoyed in the company of Allston, and pointed out by him with the enthusiasm of an artist. . . . Suddenly the thought presented itself: "Why might I not remain here and turn painter?" . . . I promised myself a world of enjoyment in his society, and in the society of several artists with whom he had made me acquainted, and pictured forth a scheme of life, all tinted with the rainbow hues of youthful promise.'

Irving's notebooks for England and Wales and parts of the Continent are often illustrated by entertaining sketches, but, oddly enough, none of

Rome are known. Perhaps he found the pleasure of absorbing it through Allston's eyes too engrossing to allow time for sketching.

Generation after generation of Americans reacted to Rome in Irving's fashion. Beauty of nature, beauty of men's work, the magic of the past, the companionship of kindred minds and tastes—all these Rome had to offer the traveller, the artist, and the writer, who followed the footsteps of Allston and came to Rome seeking with unconscious nostalgia the homeland in Europe of a common culture.

The spread of the romantic movement, that many-sided force expressed in philosophic thought, in politics, and in all the arts, was diverted somewhat by the French Revolution and its counter-force, the Napoleonic Wars. These upheavals kept Europe in turmoil from the late eighteenth century through the early years of the nineteenth. The romantic movement had begun in England soon after the middle of the century and had found quick acceptance in France in Rousseau's doctrine of 'back to nature' and the revolutionists' belief in the dignity of the individual. Eighteenth-century painting showed its influence in nostalgic mood, in picturesque contrasts of old with new, of ancient ruins with contemporary life. The violence of the Revolution, however, and the anti-English feeling that attended the Napoleonic struggles, almost stifled for a time the Continent's development of reflective, idyllic individualism; over Napoleon's France and the lands she influenced passed a wave of more formal, grandiose classicism, suited to the conqueror's imperial ideal.

The international give and take, the easy travel and exchange of ideas, which had been so characteristic of the eighteenth century, were seriously impaired during these war-torn years. At no time, however, did Rome cease to be a centre for visitors from all nations, and books dealing with its monuments continued to be in demand.

The Scotch traveller, Joseph Forsyth, detained for years on the Continent by order of Napoleon, wrote during this period of restraint one of the popular travel books of the early nineteenth century, *Remarks on Antiquities, Arts, and Letters During an Excursion in Italy in the Years 1802 and 1803*. About the same time the Englishman, John Chetwode Eustace, compiled his *Journal of a Classical Tour through Italy*, which was to wring bitter complaints from Byron's circle. How ready Rome herself was to display her monuments may be gathered from the title of Angelo Dalmazonni's English volume of 1803: *The Antiquarian; or The Guide for Foreigners to Go the Rounds of the Antiquities of Rome*. The closing sentences of the author's preface make this readiness even clearer: 'I think, that whoever is furnished with this book, even without an antiquarian will be well satisfied with the guide, and instructive account of it. However if any Gentleman wishes to have my personal attendance, I shall be glad to do myself the honour of serving him.' Among German travel books from the same years were the dramatist August von Kotzebue's *Erinnerungen von einer Reise . . . nach Rom und Neapel*, published in Germany in 1805 and in London in 1807, as *Travels through Italy*; Ludwig Herman Friedländer's *Ansichten von Italien während einer Reise in der Jahren 1815 und 1816*, translated into English in 1820 as *Views in Italy during a Journey in 1815 and 1816*; and Elisa von der Recke's *Tagebuch einer Reise durch Deutschland und Italien, 1804–1806*, the diary of a journey through Germany and Italy.

Two outstanding French writers on Rome in the early nineteenth century were creative authors. Mme de Staël was inspired by a Roman visit of 1804–1805 to write her popular romance, *Corinne*, filled with descriptions of Roman scenes and monuments interpreted with all the 'sensibility' fashionable in her day. This was translated into English in 1807, within a year of its Paris publication, and had several fresh translations during the century. It also appeared, at a rather later date, in German. Her compatriot, Stendhal (Henri-Marie Beyle), also began his romantic interpretations of Rome in Napoleon's time, his *Journal d'Italie* appearing in 1811 and *Rome, Naples et Florence* a few years after the emperor's fall. Notes made during these early years were also the basis for his *Promenades dans Rome*, not published, however, until 1829.

Not until after Napoleon's final defeat in 1815 did the Englishmen who immortalized the romantic dream of Rome come to her sun-warmed hills. The poets of these years following the emperor's exile have become identified with Rome throughout the English-speaking world and, through translation, in all lands where men's minds have been attuned to the romantic view of the city and its ruins.

The Rome of Byron, Shelley, and Keats, though nominally ruled by the popes, was directly or indirectly dominated by Austria from Napoleon's fall in 1815 until the middle of the century. For a brief time in 1798–1799 her citizens, fired by the example of the French Revolution, had proclaimed a Roman Republic. This was soon abolished by Napoleon, who first restored the papal power and then, in 1809, incorporated Rome and all the papal states with France. The old Holy Roman Empire, which had expired quietly in 1806 under pressure from Napoleon, was not restored when the French emperor was exiled, but the Hapsburgs, as successors to his power in Rome, exerted an authority which was considerably resented by the Romans and criticized bitterly by the foreign visitors who thronged the city when travel became easy once again.

George Gordon, Lord Byron, was in Rome less than four weeks in the spring of 1817. Yet his descriptions in the third act of *Manfred*, written there, and in the fourth canto of *Childe Harold*, composed within a few months after his departure, have coloured the traveller's thoughts of Rome for more than a century, taking their place among the immortal commonplaces of English literature. It is difficult to think of a time when Rome had not been called 'Niobe of Nations'—though the aptness of that phrase is now gone—or 'city of the soul'.

Percy Bysshe Shelley was in Rome a little longer than Byron, visiting it first in the fall of 1818 and returning early in the following year. Although renaissance Rome was the setting for his tragedy of *The Cenci*, his poems contain few mentions of the ancient city except for the famous descriptions of the Pyramid of Cestius in *Adonais*. Yet his name is indissolubly linked with Rome; through his lament for Keats and its exquisite prose preface; through his description of the writing of *Prometheus Unbound* 'upon the mountainous ruins of the Baths of Caracalla' (Plate 30); through his letters; and through his own burial in the Protestant Cemetery by the ancient pyramid (Plate 198). 'The first aspect of Italy enchanted Shelley', wrote his wife in later years; 'it seemed a garden of delight placed beneath a clearer and brighter heaven than any he had lived under before. He wrote long descriptive letters during the first year of his residence in Italy [1818–1819], which, as compositions, are the most beautiful in the world. . . . The charm of the Roman climate helped to clothe his thoughts in greater beauty than they had ever worn before; and as he wandered among the ruins, made one with nature in their decay, or gazed on the Praxitelean shapes that throng the Vatican, the Capitol, and the palaces of Rome, his soul imbibed forms of loveliness which became a portion of itself.'

John Keats was too near his end to write of Rome when he reached the city late in 1820, yet in death his name was bound with it more closely than the names of many who have filled volumes with its lore. This link was partly the work of Joseph Severn, the friend who comforted his last days, but chiefly that of Shelley, with his passionate defence of the dead poet and description of his burial place. When, a year later, Shelley too was laid to rest in that same Protestant Cemetery in the shadow of the pyramid, the bond between the two and the city was complete. Their memory is fittingly united now in the Keats-Shelley Memorial, the house by the Spanish Steps where Keats died in 1821.

From these years illumined by the English romantic poets comes an interesting comparison between the city as evoked by a poet and as described by an intelligent tourist with a keen power of observation and sense of humour. Charlotte Eaton's *Rome in the Nineteenth Century*, a series of letters written during a stay covering much of the years 1817 and 1818, describes the antiquities and life of Rome at almost the same time as Byron's short visit. The two saw the scene with a similar romantic appreciation; even in their phraseology there is sometimes a striking resemblance; but the Englishwoman noted many a detail and nuance which the poet either did not observe or chose to ignore. Mrs. Eaton, though almost forgotten now, was well appreciated in her day. In the 1840's George Stillman Hillard, writing one of the most nearly comparable of American travel books, noted of Mrs. Eaton's volume: 'Before the days of Murray, there was not a better guide-book in English to the sights of Rome; and it will still be found an agreeable and instructive companion both there and at home.'

In these early golden days of peace, painters as well as poets and sculptors thronged from other lands to Rome; her sunshine and picturesque charm and her wealth of paintings as well as ancient monuments gave her still a peculiar appeal. But the forerunners of the new movement in painting no longer cared essentially for ruins; they were experimenting instead with still more universal themes, on which the romanticists had already touched—the significance of ordinary life, the effects of atmosphere and light which were to lead before many years to the French Impressionists and to shift the centre of painting from Rome to Paris. The English were the leaders here; the French brought the movement to its full flowering.

Turner, the Englishman, was already deep in studies of light and atmosphere when he first visited Rome in 1819. Most of his delicate drawings of the city done at this time (Plate 112) are accurate topographical sketches of Rome and her monuments as Byron, Shelley, and Keats saw them. A few paintings done at the same time (Plates 31, 134) suggest the city's colour and light as well. Both drawings and paintings of this period have the added interest of being among the last works to show certain ancient monuments just before the considerable alterations which took place in the 1820's. That Turner was by no means exclusively interested in topography even in his views of Rome is evident from a picture done after his second visit to the city in 1828–1829. In the *Palace and Bridge of Caligula*, a few actual remnants on the Palatine and in the Forum serve merely to state the theme of an imaginative composition, a brilliant and timeless harmony of colour.

Some of the monuments painted by Turner, such as the Colosseum and Arch of Titus, had already been changed considerably before Corot reached Rome in 1825. The French artist's representations of the massive structures he saw about him (Plates 32, 135, 202) have a solid simplicity and clarity not to be found in his later and softer grey-green idylls of the northern countryside. The city's intense light was a revelation to him; as he painted it, this light was not the serene, soft radiance of Claude Lorrain. It was strong, almost violent, a form in itself rather than an enveloping atmosphere.

Both Turner and Corot occasionally treated the Roman scene in the more consciously picturesque manner, selecting or arranging their compositions to appeal to the imagination and the memory. This was especially true of Turner's delightful vignettes for the de-luxe edition of Rogers' *Italy* published in 1830. Samuel Prout's popular water-colours and drawings (Frontispiece, Plate 33), while topographically accurate and detailed, were avowedly picturesque, meant to attract the eye and the pocketbook of the homeward-bound or nostalgic traveller. Prout, who has been aptly called a 'master of dilapidation', dwelt lovingly on each time-worn stone and broken column, while adding as a note of piquant contrast some attractive scene from Roman life of his time.

German artists, who came to Rome increasingly in the late eighteenth and first half of the nineteenth century, found several avenues of approach to the city's life and monuments. To some, Rome meant classical landscape in the tradition of Poussin and Claude; to others, the search for an inner harmony between classic beauty of form and medieval Christian tradition; to still others, of course, it meant chiefly the picturesque blending of the ancient and the contemporary, of ruins and the fresh life led within their shadow.

Asmus Jakob Carstens, who came to Rome in 1792 and devoted himself to figure painting and literary themes, was a leader in the classic style. In 1795 he was joined by the Tyrolese Joseph Anton Koch, who served as a link between the classic and the romantic movements. After Carstens' early death Koch worked chiefly on heroic landscapes in the tradition of Claude, with generalized though sometimes recognizable Roman ruins and picturesque groups of men, women, and animals, sometimes contemporary, sometimes derived from medieval story. His etchings (Plate 34) are at once closer to actuality than his paintings and more romantic in treatment, with a touch of that fantasy so highly developed among many German artists of the medieval revival. Perhaps even more important than the considerable body of his work was his influence upon other artists. Karl Philipp Fohr (Plate 35) and Franz Hörny, whose *Rome in the Renaissance* strangely prefigures the English Pre-Raphaelite movement, were among his pupils. Karl Rottmann and Ludwig Richter, though widely divergent in their aims, considered him a master. And among his friends he counted such diverse men as Thorwaldsen and the German Nazarenes.

Friedrich Overbeck was the leader of this German group in Rome, who received their name partly because of their intense religious interests and partly because of the long hair affected by some of their members. Overbeck, in revolt against the classical formalism taught in Germany, came to Rome in 1810 and, with a few friends, formed a group dedicated to the revival of the Christian influence in art. This brotherhood of Saint Luke, which had already been drawn together in Vienna, lived a communal life in Rome in the abandoned monastery of Sant' Isidoro on the Pincian hill. Franz Pforr was one of the original founders; Peter Cornelius, Philipp Veit, the brothers Wilhelm and Rudolph von Schadow, and Julius Schnorr von Carolsfeld were among the many associated with it. Friedrich Olivier (Plate 136) also studied under Overbeck. Though the Nazarenes emphasized religious subjects and themes from Christian epic and history, many of their members naturally painted the life and monuments of Rome. Franz Catel, for instance, though intimately associated with the group, became more and more a painter of popular Roman *genre* pictures, from the sale of which he acquired considerable wealth. Aside from their preoccupation with religious work, another fact tended to lessen the interest of the Nazarenes in the remains of Rome itself. This was the number of delightful hill towns nearby which recalled to these lovers of the Middle Ages the legend-haunted crags and castles of Germany. Olevano and Tivoli, crowning their small, steep hills, appear again and again in the sketches and paintings of this group.

The life of the brotherhood may sound aloof and ascetic, but contemporary accounts as well as Fohr's drawing (Plate 35) are evidence of social gatherings in the cafés of Rome, especially the Greco. 'After a good breakfast in the Café Greco, the rendezvous of all the German artists in the city', Ludwig Friedländer set out in 1815 to see the sights of Rome. James Freeman described it more fully some years later. 'The place was resorted to,' he wrote, 'not because of its superior appointments and fame, for it was decidedly one of the smallest, darkest, and untidiest of restaurants; its central position and superior coffee were its chief attractions, added to which a greater freedom of speech was permitted without a strict surveillance of the police, whose spies found their way into all reunions of society. . . . The walls and windows were toned down . . . into asphaltum dinginess, the smoke penetrating into every nook and corner, and keeping the atmosphere so thickly charged with it that it was difficult either to see or breathe. Added to this were the commingling of a dozen languages and dialects, and a variety of costumes, physiognomy, and gesticulation peculiar to Russians, Poles, Hungarians, Danes, Swedes, Spaniards, French, Dutch, English, and other mixed races and eccentric characters.'

As the Germans gathered about Overbeck, so did the Danes about Thorwaldsen, their most famous figure, though they formed no such organized group as that of Overbeck's circle. Detlev Blunck has left an entertaining glimpse of the Danish group in the tavern of *La Gensola* in 1837 (Plate 36). One of those at the table there was Ernst Meyer, creator of such delightful Roman *genre* scenes as the *Public Letter Writer* (Plate 37); another was Wilhelm Marstrand, whose *October Festival* (Plate 38) records one of the picturesque celebrations which fascinated visitors from distant lands. Other Danes who painted with gusto Roman monuments and Roman life were Christoffer Eckersberg, Constantin Hansen, and Jorgen Sønne. To this Scandinavian group the young Danish author, Hans Christian Andersen, then unknown, attached himself in 1834. The immediate result of this visit to Rome was his first successful book, *The Improvisatore*. Though sentiment and narrative contributed much to its popularity at the time, its enduring quality lies in descriptions filled with the evanescent charm of a passing day. With the freshness of observation and diction that later characterized his fairy tales, Andersen noted not only such outstanding sights as the Colosseum, 'like a vast mass of rock' and the Palatine, crowned with black cypresses and pines, 'demon-like and huge', but also the teeming life that surged about them. His young hero's first song dealt with a bacon shop where 'amid beautiful garlands of laurel hung the white buffalo-cheeses, like great ostrich eggs'; where sausages 'reared up like columns, sustained a Parmesan cheese, shining like yellow amber'; and where, 'in an evening . . . the red glass-lamps burned before the images of the Madonna in the wall among sausages and ham'.

To such a cosmopolitan yet picturesque society, to a life totally different from anything they had known across the Atlantic, Americans came in ever-increasing numbers. A period of peace, the improvement of transportation, and a wider distribution of wealth led more and more citizens of the New World to travel for pleasure as well as study. Though the professional guidebook as we know it today was a development of Europe, American writers were at work early to supply the increasing demand for travel books. Theodore Dwight, Connecticut educator and author, published in 1824 his *Journal of a Tour in Italy in the Year 1821*.

Aside from valuable comments on the condition of Roman monuments at that time, Dwight's book contributes sympathetic descriptions and anecdotes from the city's life.

Henry Wadsworth Longfellow's slender prose volume, *Outre-Mer*, appeared in 1835, but the exquisite description, *Rome in Midsummer* (Plate 113), dates from 1828 when the poet visited the city during his first European journey preparatory to teaching modern languages. Unlike Irving, he never considered the career of an artist; like many another traveller he enlivened his notebooks with occasional sketches by the way (Plate 39). So too did Frances Elizabeth Appleton (Plate 40), whom he met in Europe and later married.

James Freeman, on the other hand, who settled in Rome to paint, is remembered today for his slim volumes, *Gatherings from an Artist's Portfolio*. Some of these pleasant reminiscences of fact not unmixed with fancy, date from the year of his arrival in 1836, though the two parts of the book were published respectively in 1877 and 1883.

Perhaps the most widely quoted travel book of its time, and still delightful reading, was *Six Months in Italy*, by George Stillman Hillard, New England lawyer and man of letters, and a friend of Longfellow. Based on a trip in 1847–1848, the book won instant success upon its publication in 1853. The reason is immediately apparent: in its ability to create an atmosphere and interpret a sensitive stranger's reaction to 'the grandeur and mystery of the Eternal City', Hillard's book takes its place among haunting pictures of *Roma sparita*, vanished Rome, with Story's *Roba di Roma* and the work of Henry James.

Beyond question, however, Hawthorne's *Marble Faun* was, in English-speaking lands, the most widely read of nineteenth-century books dealing with Rome. Shortly after its publication in England in 1860 under the title *Transformation*, a friend wrote him: 'I suppose no one will visit Rome without a copy of it in his hand.' This was precisely the case. Combining the long and delightful descriptions of his *Italian Notebooks* with the interest of a romantic love story, shadowed by the clouds of mystery and violence in a foreign land, the book became at once almost as necessary equipment for seeing the city as Murray's guide. Tourists not only visited the spots which Hawthorne described; they saw them through the eyes of his characters; with Hilda and Miriam and Kenyon they stood in the Colosseum by moonlight, gazed at the statue of Marcus Aurelius on the Capitol, shuddered at the fateful precipice of the Tarpeian Rock whence the unhappy Faun hurled the mysterious villain, and watched the clouds pass to and fro above the great opening of the Pantheon's dome.

Artists came to Italy from across the Atlantic as they had come for centuries from the rest of Europe. Many were painters, but they no longer came to learn a manner or technique of painting; the centres for such training were already shifting. They came rather to the wellsprings of western art, to that Latin land through which there had flowed into the West its ancient inheritance from Greece and from which had spread the quickening spirit of the Renaissance. They were quick to feel the wonder of its past; they were even quicker, perhaps, to respond to its present beauty.

Sculptors reaped the most immediate practical benefits, for here were patrons attracted by the fame of Thorwaldsen and of the English sculptor, John Gibson, ready to buy statues they would never have considered at home. Here, too, was a plentiful supply of good and inexpensive marble-cutters, such as existed in no other land. Material conditions could scarcely have been more favourable, but the results were disappointing. The gap between the artist's intent and the craftsman's execution all too often led to lifelessness in the finished product. This danger seems to have affected untrained American talent even more than that of Europeans schooled in the classical tradition. Indeed, this declining tradition itself was not the best in which to develop a vigorous group of sculptors coming from a very different kind of life. Yet, if the works of Thomas Crawford, Harriet Hosmer, William Henry Rinehart, William Wetmore Story, and Moses Ezekiel seem remote today, these sculptors played an important part in the relationship between Rome and nineteenth-century America. Harriet Hosmer has become a legend as the centre of a group of women active in the artistic life of Rome. The Rinehart scholarships for American sculptors studying in Paris and Rome still keep green the memory of a gentle artist's love for the Old World and the New as well as for his art. The studios of Crawford, Story, Ezekiel (Plates 159, 160) and others were centres of pleasant social life. Crawford's son, Marion, carried on the tradition of this life in his romantic novels of Rome and his *Ave Roma Immortalis*. In his lifetime Story's interests were divided between the law, for which he was trained at Harvard, the art of sculpture, which he prac-tised with considerable success in Rome, and his writing, which expressed a romantic side not apparent in his solidly classical sculpture. It was almost inevitable that Hawthorne's American hero in Rome should be a sculptor, that his studio should be modelled after Story's, that the statue described there should be Story's *Cleopatra*, and that the heroines, Miriam and Hilda, should be drawn from Harriet Hosmer's group. Story's own volume, *Roba di Roma*, remains a haunting word picture of *Roma sparita*, the 'vanished Rome' of the days just before the papal city became the capital of united Italy. 'The golden air, as I look over its pages, makes a mist,' Henry James wrote of it in later years.

Painters and writers, able to practise their arts with less expenditure of money than sculptors and with less dependence on other hands, were less hampered by circumstances and tradition and freer to take inspiration from a slant of light or the shadow of a cloud. Landscape painters, of course, were strongly attracted by the deep, mellow colours, the tempered intensity of light, and the endless combinations of the works of nature and of man which formed irresistible compositions on every side. Even portrait and figure painters were drawn to landscape in this land, or at least to sketching picturesque scenes. Samuel F. B. Morse, still primarily interested in painting rather than in the telegraph, turned aside in 1830 from the portraits that furnished his living to paint his *Chapel of the Virgin at Subiaco*. As a pupil of Allston, of course, it is not surprising that he should have delighted in this serene landscape. Daniel Huntington, Morse's pupil, painter of portraits and religious subjects, was also strongly attracted by the Roman landscape in the forties; and in the fifties and sixties such portrait painters as William Page and George Peter Alexander Healy were touched by the spell of Roman light and Roman monuments. Elihu Vedder, too, though best known for his fanciful excursions into the fields of mythology and literature, painted a few delightful Roman views when he first visited Italy in the fifties (Plate 154), and more when he settled there a decade later.

In the Italian countryside, American painters saw at first hand the beauty they had admired in the landscapes of Claude Lorrain. The artists of the romantic Hudson River School, America's first recognized group of landscape painters, were with few exceptions men from the northern, north-middle, or midwestern states, to whom the Roman light and the teeming life and colour of Mediterranean lands were a revelation. Thomas Cole, pioneer of the group, who was already well trained in his art when he first saw Italy in 1831, delighted in the combination of this gracious beauty with the handiwork of men. Describing the hill country north of Rome he lovingly pointed out the effects of changing lights on its 'distant villages and towers', implying its contrast with the wilder mountains that he loved in his homeland or in the quiet England in which he had been born. His descriptions exemplify his typically romantic axiom that an artist should 'walk with nature as a poet'. If he wrote much of Rome itself, little is now known except for one exquisite description of the Colosseum and a shorter passage on the Pantheon. 'The things that most affect me, in

Rome', he wrote in a letter of 1832, 'are the antiquities. None but those who have seen the remains can form an idea of what Ancient Rome was.' His sketchbooks, however, are filled with drawings of the city's monuments (Plate 41) and of the wide Campagna which spread between the city and the hills; some of these he translated into such paintings as the *Roman Aqueduct* (Plate 43).

The Campagna, especially that section south of Rome through which the Claudian Aqueduct passes along the Appian Way and thence up into the hills, was a favourite haunt of artists and authors alike. Among many fine descriptions, two are outstanding; one in Story's *Roba di Roma*, begun in 1862, and one included in Henry James' *Transatlantic Sketches* of 1875.

'Over these long unfenced slopes', wrote Story, the complete romantic, 'one may gallop on horseback for miles without let or hindrance, through meadows of green smoothness on fire with scarlet poppies—over hills crowned with ruins that insist on being painted, so exquisite are they in form and colour, with their background of purple mountains—down valleys of pastoral quiet, where great *tufa* caves open into subterranean galleries leading beyond human ken; or one may linger in lovely secluded groves of ilexes and pines, or track the course of swift streams overhung by dipping willows, and swerving here and there through broken arches of antique bridges smothered in green . . . or sit beneath the sun-looped shadows of ivy-covered aqueducts, listening to the song of hundreds of larks far up in the air, and gazing through the lofty arches into wondrous deeps of violet-hued distances.'

Henry James' description has a more solid structure beneath its romantic atmosphere; his period of elaborate style for its own sake had not yet begun. 'The landscape here has two great features', he wrote of the Campagna, 'close before you on one side is the long, gentle swell of the Alban Mountains, deeply, fantastically blue in most weathers, and marbled with the vague white masses of their scattered towns and villas. It is hard to fancy a softer curve than that with which the mountain sweeps down from Albano to the plain; it is a perfect example of the classic beauty of line in the Italian landscape—that beauty which, when it fills the background of a picture, makes us look in the foreground for a broken column couched upon flowers, and a shepherd piping to dancing nymphs.' In painting, these descriptions are paralleled by Cole's *Roman Aqueduct* (Plate 43) and Inness' *Italian Landscape, Roman Campagna* (Plate 44).

Sooner or later most of the men associated with the Hudson River group came to Rome. Asher Durand, best known for his carefully detailed paintings of sunny New World fields and hills, was in Rome in the forties, as was also Jasper Cropsey, painter of the Hudson country. Sanford Gifford was there for the first time in the mid-fifties and again in later years. Healy painted Gifford with Longfellow and the poet's daughter Edith at the Arch of Titus in 1869 (Plate 123). Gifford's own view of Tivoli, its hills, cascades, and ancient ruins enveloped in a rosy autumn haze, is dated 1879. George Loring Brown, in his time perhaps the most celebrated American landscape painter in Europe, spent some years in Rome in the fifties and sixties, while Albert Bierstadt, later to become a pioneer painter of the Rockies, passed the winter of 1857–1858 in the city, where he painted landscapes and *genre* scenes such as the *Portico of Octavia* (Plate 47). In 1868–1869 Frederic E. Church, last of the great Hudson River men and the only pupil whom Cole himself had taught, spent some time in and about Rome on his return journey from Syria and Palestine. Panoramic views of then comparatively remote places, such as the Aegean Sea and the Andes, are more representative of his work, but his small sketches of Roman scenes and ruins (Plate 42) have a boldness and freedom of handling lacking in his large canvases.

George Inness, beginning in the tradition of the Hudson River School, went on to a broader, less detailed style. The *Italian Landscape* of 1858 (Plate 44) marks a period of transition. Inness' first visit to Italy, when he spent considerable time in and near Rome, was made in 1847–1848, but he returned often. The greater part of his Roman work belongs to his last residence there, from 1870 to 1874.

While painters, sculptors, and writers drew their inspiration from the city, historians were busy as well, carrying on the great tradition of Gibbon and consolidating Rome's position as a centre of scholarship. Niebuhr's *Roman History* was published between 1811 and 1832; Mommsen's, from 1854 to 1856. Between 1855 and 1872 Ferdinand Gregorovius wrote his monumental and delightful *History of the City of Rome in the Middle Ages*, conceiving the idea, as he noted in his *Roman Journals*, during a 'view of the city as seen from the bridge leading to the island of the Tiber'. During these same years the French Jean Jacques Ampère was weaving a web of mingled history and poetic interpretation in his *Histoire romaine à Rome* unfinished at his death in 1864, and its posthumous second part, *L'Empire romain à Rome*. He had already disclosed the pattern of his thought in *La Grèce, Rome et Dante* in 1848: 'To compare is to comprehend. You choose an object—no matter what—observe how it has been regarded by different men at different times, and a whole portion of human history passes before you.' In a more restrictedly historical vein the Englishman, Thomas Hodgkin, described the early medieval period in his *Italy and Her*

Invaders, published from 1885 to 1899. Narrower in scope than Gregorovius' *History*, Hodgkin's work deals at great length with 'the changes by which classical Italy . . . became that Italy of the Middle Ages'.

During this period of intensive scholarship and rapidly growing travel, modern guidebooks came into being, to spread still more widely a general knowledge of the Eternal City. These guides, complete with lists of hotels, restaurants, and places of amusement as well as sights to be seen, began with the increase of travel after the Napoleonic Wars. John Murray, third of the British firm of Murray which had published the works of Scott and Byron, set out for the Continent in 1829, 'unprovided,' as he later wrote, 'with any guide excepting a few manuscript notes about towns and inns'. This situation he set about to remedy. The first edition of his *Handbook for Central Italy* appeared in 1843; by the time Hillard made his tour in 1847, he commented that 'there is not an innkeeper who does not turn pale at the name of Murray'. The German Baedeker followed the Murray tradition; early in the First World War the Scot, Findlay Muirhead, who had worked on the Baedeker staff, began the English Blue Guide series. Augustus Hare's *Walks in Rome* was a development of Murray's guides. Having written some of the Murray handbooks, Hare put into his popular 'Walks' series the wealth of quotations and associations for which there had been no place in the more compact volumes. Heterogeneous as some of this material may seem, it is of endless value, not only as a key to what has been said of Roman monuments over almost two thousand years but also as to what the more reflective and widely read tourist of the nineteenth century wanted to know concerning them. The need for the book was evidently real; first published in 1870, it had gone through twelve editions on both sides of the Atlantic by the early eighties and reached its twenty-first in 1923.

By the time Hare first wrote, Rome was changing so rapidly that it was necessary to revise the volumes frequently. It was this changing Rome, more changeless, though, than he could have known, that Story described in passages of the *Roba di Roma* that might have been written to accompany the paintings of Ernst Meyer, Bierstadt, or Roesler-Franz. The opening chapter records his return in 1856 for his third visit to the city: 'We plunge into long, damp, narrow, dirty streets. . . . Yet—shall I confess it? they had a charm for me. Twilight was deepening into dark as we passed through them. Confused cries and loud Italian voices sounded about me. Children were screaming,—men howling their wares for sale. Bells were ringing everywhere. Priests, soldiers, *contadini*, and beggars thronged along. The *Trasteverini* were going home, with their jackets hanging over one shoulder. Women, in their rough woollen gowns, stood in the doorways, bare-headed, or looked out from windows and balconies, their black hair shining under the lanterns. Lights were twinkling in the little cavernous shops, and under the Madonna shrines far within. . . .

'It was dirty, but it was Rome; and to any one who has long lived in Rome even its very dirt has a charm which the neatness of no other place ever had. . . . Fancy for a moment the difference for the worse, if all the grim, browned, rotted walls of Rome, with their peeling mortar, their thousand daubs of varying grays and yellows, their jutting brickwork and patched stonework, from whose intervals the cement has crumbled off, their waving weeds and grasses and flowers, now sparsely fringing their top, now thickly protruding from their sides, or clinging and making a home in the clefts and crevices of decay, were to be smoothed to a complete level, and whitewashed over into one uniform and monotonous tint. What a gain in cleanliness! what a loss in beauty!'

In this second half of the nineteenth century, while artists, architects, historians, and travellers were busy each in his own way, Rome passed through the political upheavals which produced the modern capital. Left under Austrian domination after Napoleon's downfall, her citizens rebelled when the European revolutions of 1848 swept the Continent. Under the leadership of Garibaldi and Mazzini they declared their city a republic in 1849, but neither France nor Austria would permit the movement to succeed. France, though herself a republic at the time, moved to forestall Austria and restored the nominal papal power in 1850, under French protection, leaving to Austria the rest of Italy.

The northern state of Piedmont, with its expanded title of Sardinia, alone kept its revolutionary constitution. Count Cavour, leader of the movement there, maintained a steady pressure for a united kingdom free from foreign domination, which was finally achieved in 1861 with Victor Emmanuel of Savoy, king of Sardinia, as ruler of united Italy.

The kingdom's capital was first at Florence, Rome remaining separate under papal rule. In 1870, however, the French garrison finally withdrew, and before the end of the year a plebiscite made Rome a part of united Italy, and its capital. The Piedmont constitution of 1848 was the basis for that of the new kingdom and continued in force, at least nominally, even through the Fascist rule of 1922–1943. The present republic was voted in 1946; its new constitution went into effect on January 1, 1948.

This *Roma sparita*, dear alike to artists and travellers, was recorded for later eyes by both painters and early photographers. There was, indeed, but a fine line of distinction between the academically trained painter of the time and the photographer; each was bent on reproducing reality in the popular romantic mood and the work of each amplified that of the other. Outstanding among the painters who at this moment devoted themselves to portraying the vanishing Rome, was Ettore Roesler-Franz, Roman-born of Teutonic stock. Near the century's end he began the series of pictures in which the moment's transitory charm lives on in its moods of gray cloud and silver rain as well as its golden sun (Plate 45). Though a comparatively young man in the 1870's, he must have shared the feeling of the ageing Gregorovius, who had just completed his *History of Rome in the Middle Ages*. The historian wrote in his *Journal* for January, 1873: 'Building is proceeding at a furious pace. . . . Almost every hour witnesses the fall of some portion of ancient Rome. New Rome belongs to the new generation, while I belong to the ancient city, in whose spell-bound silence my history arose. Were I to come to Rome now for the first time, I neither should nor could conceive the idea of such a work.'

The 'mirror of Rome' in the last hundred years has been largely that of photography (Plates 46, 48–56), though painters have by no means abandoned her streets and her Campagna. The new art of photography began its revolutionary course between the eighteen-thirties and the eighteen-fifties; when the first great wave of excavation began on a national scale soon after 1870 there was at hand, therefore, a considerable body of photographic record, invaluable today as a portrait of the vanishing city.

Though Rome's face has changed almost continuously throughout the ages, as does that of any city where men have lived for so long a stretch of time, it has been altered more since 1870 than in the course of many centuries before. It is this fact that gives such inestimable value to the photographs of the ten or fifteen years just before that date and, indeed, to many taken considerably later. For the alteration of the city falls into two main periods: one from 1870 to about the turn of the century and one from about 1922 until the Second World War.

Scientific excavation, the uncovering and studying of monuments for the sake of the knowledge to be derived from them, began in Rome about the end of the eighteenth century. The rise of a disciplined interest in antiquity was due largely to the German art historian Winckelmann, at that time papal Commissioner of Antiquities. For many years, however, the scale of operation was small. The first of these excavations was, as might be expected, in the Roman Forum, where a part of the Basilica Julia was uncovered in 1788 by the Swedish ambassador to Rome. Early in the nineteenth century, in Napoleon's time, parts of the west end of the Forum were excavated under the direction of Carlo Fea, who worked intermittently from 1801 to about 1817. Then, after a lull of ten years, the work was undertaken again, under Antonio Nibby, in 1827. Though the project was still limited in scope, by 1834 the picturesque appearance of the Forum had suffered enough to trouble Louis I, king of Bavaria, noted German patron of the arts, who wrote of it:

'Everywhere rents in the earth, till the eye beholds nothing but chaos!
    Beautiful as it was once—now not a trace of it left!
Artists have nothing to say, archaeologists rule as they please here,
    Blind to all but one side, caring for nought but their own.'

On the Palatine the gardens which the Farnese had laid out in the sixteenth century above the buried palaces of the emperors had been rifled for treasure by the dukes of Parma early in the eighteenth century, and had then been left to moulder in quiet neglect. In 1860 they were bought by Napoleon III of France, in the hope that the excavators had not been too thorough. Although he was essentially seeking for buried treasure, Napoleon put the work of excavation under the direction of the capable Pietro Rosa, who carried it out with care.

When the new government of Italy took charge of all excavations, buying the Farnese Gardens from Napoleon in 1870, Rosa was made head of excavations both there and in the Forum. From 1878 to 1880 the exploration was carried on by his successor, Giuseppe Fiorelli, and was then taken over until 1885 by Rodolfo Lanciani, best known in England and America through his popular as well as scholarly books on Rome. During this period of great activity the Forum was laid bare from end to end and the successors of the trees planted along its length for the triumphal procession of Charles V in 1536 were removed from the eastern end, as they had been long before from the western. During a lull in the work, from 1885 to 1898, while the wreckage of excavation lay about neglected, Zola, in his romantic *Rome*, called the Forum 'a city's cemetery, where old exhumed stones are whitening'. Work was begun again in 1898 and carried on patiently and exhaustively by Giacomo Boni, especially on the Palatine, but the First World War and its immediate aftermath slowed its progress.

The second great period of excavation began under Mussolini's government soon after 1922; accompanied by an amount of demolition which obliterated whatever interfered with its progress; it returned to the light the remnants of imperial Rome and displayed them in imposing settings. Two great thoroughfares were opened through the heart of the city: the Via dei Trionfi, now once more called by its old name, Via di San Gregorio, which runs along the side of the Palatine to the Colosseum; and the Via dell' Impero, now Via dei Fori Imperiali, running from the

Colosseum to the seat of the Mussolini government in the Palazzo Venezia, near the monument of Victor Emmanuel. The forums of Caesar, of Augustus, of Nerva, and of Trajan, were excavated; the Theatre of Marcellus was cleared of its time-honoured shops; the Mausoleum of Augustus of its fittings as a concert hall.

None now can remember Rome as she looked before 1870. Those who lament her as she was before the 1920's may find comfort in Hillard's reflections on the Forum over a century ago:

'Those who can remember the Forum as it was at the beginning of the present century, before any excavations had been made, are now but few in number; but the changes caused by these excavations were looked upon, at the time, with no favour by artists; and this feeling was shared with them by the common people in Rome. What was gained to knowledge, say they, was lost to beauty. Formerly, there was a certain unity and harmony in the whole scene. The mantle of earth, which for centuries had been slowly gathering around the ruins, had become a graceful and appropriate garb. Trees and vines and green turf had concealed the rents and chasms of time; and a natural relation had been established between the youth of nature and the decay of art. But the antiquarians had come, and with their pickaxes and shovels had hacked and mangled the touching landscape as surgeons dissect a dead body. . . . The beauty of the Forum had vanished forever. No more would peasants come here to dance the saltarello; nor artists, to sketch. The antiquarians had felled the tree that they might learn its age by counting the rings in the trunk. They had destroyed that they might interrogate.

'In words like these, the artists and sentimentalists of forty years since lamented what they called the desecration of the Forum. They were not all right; nor yet wholly wrong. Each one will judge of their regrets by his own taste and temperament. Time has since done much to repair the disfigurement of which they then complained.'

Time has again done much, and Roman archaeologists have, since Hillard's day, taken beauty into consideration, filling in many of the gaping holes their predecessors left and planting laurel and wistaria and oleander in place of the trees and vines and shrubs which had been weeded out. They may yet prove that beauty and truth are not incompatible.

Nor is the artist's city dead—the city of old streets filled with gay and many-coloured life and heavy with the sense of their accumulated past. It lives on west of the Tiber in Trastevere's steep and narrow ways, where, as the sun dips behind the houses, men and women surge out to eat and drink and make merry at tables set before the doors; in those dark streets, too, on the river's eastern side, where time-blackened palaces rise like cliffs, and around any turn may lie a fallen column, a huge marble foot, a battered statue, or a half-hidden courtyard where water splashes in some mossy fountain. Most persistently of all, perhaps, it lives in the flash of colour and gaiety when festivals and processions of the Church follow the Madonna through the streets as once they did the triumphal cars of conquerors, or the statues of the gods during the Roman games. Nothing can take from this living and eternal city her twofold spell of continuity and change. 'Here all moments of history confront us; past and present cry aloud together.'

THE CAPITOL

Plates 57–73

'THIS hill with its leafy crown,' wrote Vergil of the Capitol two thousand years ago, '. . . is a god's home: my Arcadians believe they have looked on Jove himself, while his right hand shook the darkening aegis and summoned the storm clouds.' It is a little hill, this, to have been a great god's home and to have ruled the world. Its highest peak is about 168 feet above the plain at its western foot; its greatest length, about 500 yards; yet it has given its name to seats of government throughout the western world.

In Vergil's day the word Capitol was applied both to the hill and to Jupiter's temple gleaming on its southern summit. The men of ancient Rome explained the name by a legend shaped to fit the city's history. When their ancestors dug the foundations for the first temple there in the sixth century B.C. they unearthed a human head (*caput*), an event which the augurs interpreted as an omen that Rome would become head of all Italy. The name Capitolium was further explained as derived from *caput Tollii*, 'head' of a mythical hero, 'Tollius'. Softened now to the Italian *Campidoglio*, the name was used at first to refer only to the southern summit, earlier called the Tarpeian Mount, where the temple stood. This old term presently passed out of common use but it remained a literary convention in such classic phrases as 'Tarpeian Jove', chief deity of the temple. Capitolium soon was used to designate the entire hill, including the northern summit, known as the Arx, or fortified citadel. On this peak there stood also the temple of Jupiter's queen, Juno Moneta. Juno's temple housed the offices of Rome's early mint and from her surname came the English word money, and its counterparts in other languages.

The lower saddle of land between the summits was known in ancient times as the Asylum from the tradition that Romulus offered refuge there to fugitives who joined his band. Today, beneath the Capitol piazza which occupies part of the Asylum, lie the shattered ruins of a temple of Vejovis, the anti-Jove of the lower world, buried for centuries, but visible, since excavations in the 1930's, in subterranean tunnellings suggesting the dark realm sacred to the god.

Like other Mediterranean powers, Rome began as a city state. When she acquired an empire, the city and her Capitol remained the official

(37)

military and religious centre of the Roman world. Religion being closely
related to the state, the Senate sat by preference in consecrated places,
though not in temples erected in honour of deified emperors. Its first
meeting of the year was in Jupiter's temple, the centre of national worship, sacred to the king of gods and men and lord of storms. On the
Capitol emperors and magistrates held solemn sacrifices in the open
space before the temple's great portico, beneath the enthroned statues of
Jupiter, Juno, and Minerva in the pediment. From this temple the images
of the gods were carried down into the city, much as the Virgin's figure,
robed in white and blue, is now carried through the streets of Rome from
church to church or as the saints are paraded on their holy days. And to
this temple victorious emperors and generals brought home the spoils of
war, riding in triumphal procession through the Forum and up the winding road to the Capitol in precisely the opposite direction from today's
approach.

The term 'golden Capitol' came both from the temple's wealth of
dedicated treasure and from its gleaming ornament. The roof was
covered with tiles of gilded bronze, the doors with golden plate, and
gilded statues added to the shining splendour.

Long after the Empire had begun to wane and Constantine had moved
the seat of imperial government to Constantinople, the Capitol's fame
lived on. In A.D. 356, when Constantinople had been the centre of empire
for a quarter of a century, the soldier-historian, Ammianus Marcellinus,
though he knew the eastern cities well, marvelled at 'the sanctuaries of
Tarpeian Jove, so far surpassing [all else] as things divine excel those of
earth'. At the end of the fourth century the gold plates were stripped from
the temple's doors by Stilicho, Vandal general of Emperor Honorius; yet
the Capitol remained a symbol of eternity, as it had been four hundred
years before, when Vergil had measured his own fame by the ages through
which men of Roman race 'shall dwell upon the Capitol's unshaken rock'.

The temple survived Alaric's sack in 410 only to suffer severely in 455
when the Vandals, as the Byzantine historian Procopius wrote, 'plundered also the temple of Jupiter Capitolinus and tore off half the roof.
Now this roof was of bronze of the finest quality, and since gold was laid
over it exceeding thick, it shone as a resplendent and wonderful spectacle'.
Yet in the sixth century Cassiodorus, Theodoric's great councillor, could
still write: 'To stand on the lofty Capitol is to see all other works of the
human intellect surpassed.'

When the great temple disappeared, whether catastrophe caused its
destruction or it was torn down by human hands, no record tells. With all

the other monuments of the Capitol except the massive Tabularium it was engulfed in silence. Centuries of night closed so deeply about the 'head of the world' that the very locations of its buildings became confused and lost. Some of the temple's fragments were found long afterward, when the Caffarelli family built their palace on its desolate site in the 1540's. Many were destroyed; some were used by sculptors for the beauty of their marble. Flaminio Vacca, sculptor and amateur archaeologist of the late sixteenth century, spoke of several fragments found on the Capitol being re-used in this fashion.

Before long the temple's site was so completely forgotten that many believed it had stood upon the hill's other summit. Even Gibbon, eighteenth-century historian of the Roman Empire, accepted the view that its ruins lay beneath the church of Santa Maria in Aracoeli; not until the late nineteenth century did excavation disclose its true site. Most of the remains to be seen today were found during the last quarter of that century or shortly after the First World War, when the Caffarelli Palace was being transformed into the present New Museum, an extension of the Conservatori.

The greater part of the huge platform which supported the temple, built late in the sixth century B.C., lies beneath the various buildings of the southern summit. In several places, however, its stones have been restored to light—*ritornate in luce*, as the Italian phrase melodiously expresses it. One section of this platform may be seen below the level of the floor in a gallery of the New Museum; an angle is visible in the nearby Piazzetta della Rupe Tarpeia and the opposite corner in the Via del Tempio di Giove, formerly the Via di Monte Tarpeo (Plate 58). A great stretch of masonry belonging to the podium of the temple forms part of a wall in the gallery called the Passagio del Muro Romano at the southern end of the Conservatori Museum; a parallel wall of this podium stands open to the light of day in the New Museum's garden, once garden of the Caffarelli Palace (Plate 59). Here dark and fragrant cedars of Lebanon throw luminous patterns of light and shade against the gray volcanic stone, their heavy branches swinging slowly when a breeze steals into this green and sheltered place deep among foundations built almost twenty-five hundred years ago.

Little else remains of the temple which once rose high above this great platform to glitter under the brilliant sun of Rome—a fragment of fluted column in the Caffarelli garden; a few bits of carving built into the pedestal of the statue of Cola di Rienzi in the triangle between the two flights of steps which lead, respectively, to Santa Maria in Aracoeli and to the Capitol square; and the great pieces of richly carved cornice (Plate 60) discovered under the foundations of houses and now lying on the grass along the Salita delle Tre Pile, the drive which winds up the hill below the Conservatori. These, like the other marble fragments, are probably remnants of the temple as re-built by Domitian after A.D. 80.

The medieval mind could play all the more freely with the Capitol because destruction had overtaken it so completely; its very disasters afforded a clear field for fancy. By the middle of the twelfth century the typical medieval description of the Capitol in its glory appeared in the *Mirabilia urbis Romae*, the standard guidebook to the pagan as well as the Christian 'marvels of Rome'. The entire hill seemed to the medieval imagination one magnificent fortress filled with wonders. The *Mirabilia*'s description echoes the words of ancient writers with an overtone of eastern fantasy: 'The Capitol was the head of the world, where the consuls and senators abode to govern the Earth. The face thereof was covered with high walls and strong, rising above the top of the hill, and covered all over with glass and gold and marvellous carved work. . . . Within the fortress was a palace all adorned with marvellous works in gold and silver and brass and costly stones, to be a mirror to all nations. . . . And it was therefore called Golden Capitol, because it excelled in wisdom and beauty before all the realms of the whole world.'

One of the greatest wonders of the Capitol, which was itself ranked among the Seven Wonders of the World, was a magic device called the Salvation of Rome. The shifting currents of medieval legend gave this more than one form, but usually it was regarded as a group of statues, said by some to be the work of Vergil, whom the Middle Ages had transformed from poet to magician. 'In the temple of Jupiter and Moneta in the Capitol,' says the *Mirabilia*, 'was an image of every kingdom in the world, with a bell about his neck, and as soon as the bell sounded, they knew that the kingdom was rebellious.' The *Mirabilia* does not say that Vergil was the maker of the statues; that story came later. Other places, too, were said to house them; the Pantheon, the Colosseum, or even the Lateran. But usually their home was the Capitol, 'head of the world'.

The actual Capitol of medieval times was very different from this glittering, magic wonder. Its southern summit was bare. Where Jupiter's temple had once raised its gilded roof, cloth dyers now spread their drying racks (Plate 63). Nearby was the gallows, which gave the neighbourhood an unsavoury reputation. Goats browsed there undisturbed, giving still another name to the once mighty mount of Jove—*Monte Caprino*, Hill of Goats.

But Romans of the early Middle Ages had at least one stronghold upon 'the Capitol's unshaken rock'. At the edge of the Asylum, used then as a market and meeting-place, a baronial family had fortified the only surviving monument of ancient Rome left standing on the hill—the Tabularium overlooking the Forum. Built of grey, volcanic stone, the lower floors of this old Record Office (Plates 64, 65) had defied time and disaster from the days of the old Republic in the first century before Christ.

In 1143, tired of being pawns in the long struggle between popes and emperors, the Romans broke into revolt. Their first step was to meet on the Capitol, there to re-establish their ancient Senate and revive their ancient Republic. Precisely where they met is not recorded. But when, a few years later, they built their first simple Senator's Palace, it rested upon the Tabularium's lower floors (Plate 64). Perhaps this was merely because it was the strongest site upon the hill, but it is tempting to think that the builders dimly knew the link with the old Republic of twelve centuries before.

The Senator's Palace presently took on the name of Capitol, sharing it with the hill as Jupiter's temple had done long before. The magistrates for whom it was built became, all too soon, senators in name only, but they were obliged to hold some meetings there, and the building was a centre for many other activities. When Petrarch was crowned on the Capitol in 1341 with the laurel symbolic of triumph in the art of poetry, he received the wreath in the Audience Hall of the Senator's Palace. Nor could Romans entirely forget that the Capitol had once been the centre of far more than a local city government. In 1347 Cola di Rienzi, dreaming that Rome might once more be the capital of all Italy, gathered his revolutionary assembly in the old Palace. And near it, seven years later, when the dream had failed, he met violent death at the hands of the Roman people who had once acclaimed him.

The century of Rienzi was that of 'widowed Rome', a city in rebellion against both popes and emperors, forsaken by both and pleading for the return, sometimes of one and sometimes of the other.

The fifteenth century saw the return of the popes to Rome and also the dawn of the Renaissance with its humanistic revival of interest in antiquity. This revival brought new laments for Rome's vanished glory, although the renaissance city, whose popes drew to her the ranking artists of the time, was now no unfit successor to the imperial state. Rome had not yet seen the full flowering of the Renaissance when, some time before 1431, Poggio Bracciolini, humanist of Florence, recorded what he could see of Rome's ancient monuments from the Capitol. Sitting somewhere on the hill, looking across the Forum and the city's ruins, he meditated on the contrast of past and present:

'How greatly does this Capitol differ from that which Vergil describes as "Now golden, where once throve the tangled wood". This line is reversed to "Once golden, now with thorns and brambles spread! . . ."'

'This Capitol hill, once the head of the Roman Empire, the citadel of the earth, which so many kings have feared, so many emperors ascended in triumph, which has been enriched by the spoils of so many nations— this spectacle of the world, how is it fallen, how changed from its former state. Vines cover now the benches of the senators, which have become a waste heap and a dunghill. . . . The public and private buildings, founded for eternity, lie prostrate now, nude and broken like the limbs of a gigantic decaying corpse.'

More had fallen or had been destroyed before Marten van Heemskerck made his drawing (Plate 63) a century later, but in essentials the artist saw the Capitol much as Poggio had described it.

The Middle Ages had revived the Senate and created the Senator's Palace, the hidden nucleus of the building which stands today. It remained for Michelangelo and those who carried out his plans to give the building its present form. The great square where markets had been held in the Middle Ages was levelled off and a road built up to it from the western side, finally completing the change of approach from ancient days.

Under the popes, affairs of importance to the papal state—and therefore all affairs of an international nature—were conducted from the papal offices. But many civic matters were left, as they are today, for action on the Capitol. Plays were presented there on festival days, such as the celebration of the traditional birthday of Rome on April 21st or the reception of distinguished visitors. The various academies of art and literature which sprang up toward the end of the Renaissance held special fêtes and meetings there. The custom of crowning poets on the Capitol had been kept up at intervals since Petrarch's day. The year 1776 saw the crowning of a poetess—Corilla, famous in her day for improvised poetry, though now remembered chiefly as the original of Madame de Staël's popular heroine, Corinne.

Before the middle of the eighteenth century, when the French painter Hubert Robert sketched it (Plate 66), the Capitol piazza had taken on the form it has today. The glory of Renaissance and baroque had waned, but papal Rome, in the last full century of its unique existence, was still the goal of artists, the centre of learned academies, a city which retained to the last the elegance and long perspective of the eighteenth century.

Gibbon, when he conceived the idea of his immortal *History of the Decline and Fall of the Roman Empire*, saw the Capitol as Robert drew it. 'It was at Rome, on the 15th of October, 1764,' he wrote, 'as I sat musing amidst the ruins of the Capitol, while the bare-footed fryars were singing Vespers in the temple of Jupiter, that the idea of writing the decline and fall of the City first started to my mind.' In another *Journal* he tells the story somewhat differently, narrowing the setting to 'the Church of the Zoccalanti or Franciscan fryars . . . on the ruins of the Capitol' (Santa Maria in Aracoeli). It matters little that the historian, as we now know, mused above the ruins of Juno's rather than of Jupiter's temple. Had he known this he might have been even more deeply stirred by the continuity of history through which one queen of heaven succeeded another and Mary's hymns were sung where Juno had so long been worshipped.

But beneath the surface elegance and reason, change fermented. The Revolution which began in France with a wave of popular republicanism swept southward into Italy where it united with a native longing for national unity and independence. This was a revolution doomed from its beginning. French forces were occupying Rome when, in 1798, the Roman Republic was proclaimed and a Tree of Liberty planted in the Capitol square in the presence of four hundred French dragoons. Napoleon's empire soon overwhelmed the republic, but the idea of freedom did not die.

Again, in 1848, revolution began in France and swept through Europe, and again it led to a short-lived republic in Rome. On February 5th, 1849, a Roman Assembly gathered once more on the Capitol to go in solemn procession to its meeting place in the Chancery Palace. Here, at one in the morning on February 9th it voted to establish a Roman Republic. The next step was to proclaim it from the Capitol. Margaret Fuller, friend of Emerson, crusader for liberty, and one of the group of Americans who remained in Rome throughout this stormy period, wrote her impressions of that day: 'At last the procession mounts the Campidoglio. It is all dressed with banners. The tricolor surmounts the palace of the senator; the senator himself has fled. The deputies mount the steps, and one of them reads in a clear, friendly voice . . . The Fundamental Decrees of the Constitutional Assembly of Rome.' These deprived the Church of temporal power and declared that 'the form of government of the Roman State shall be a pure democracy, and will take the glorious name of Roman Republic.' In the pauses between the articles 'the great bell of the Capitol gave forth its solemn melodies; the cannon answered; while the crowd shouted: *Viva la Republica! Viva Italia!*' At night the buildings of the *Campidoglio* were lit in celebration of the new government (Plate 68).

But the time was not yet ripe for Italian independence. The rest of Europe, as usual, would not let Italy alone; France and Austria combined to overthrow the republic in the summer of 1849 despite Garibaldi's heroic defence of Rome. Yet the wave of national feeling, though halted, could not be turned back. The principle of republic versus monarchy was of less importance at the time than that of national unity and freedom. As a result the kingdom of Sardinia, the only state in Italy to keep its constitution of 1848, became the champion of a united Italy. In 1861 the Italian territories, with the exception of Rome which remained under papal rule, united under Victor Emmanuel II of Piedmont and Sardinia; in 1870, his shrewd statesman, Count Cavour, seized the opportunity provided by the fall of the French Empire of Napoleon III to move upon the Eternal City. The papal troops made only a token resistance and on October 2, by popular vote, Rome was united with the rest of Italy and became once more its capital. The result of this plebiscite was announced from the Capitol. But when the next year the government officially moved from Florence to Rome, the national seat was established in the papal palace on the Quirinal, leaving the Capitol hill the seat of Roman city government.

Today, the Senator's Palace resting upon the Record Office of two thousand years ago is the city hall of Rome. The Forum and the Palatine are venerable shrines, but empty of modern life save for tourists and workmen busy returning to the light more remnants of the ancient city. But on the Capitol the gold and purple city flag still flies above the Palace staircase when the council is in session and city officials constantly come and go in the clear sunlight of the square.

As the centre of Rome's civic life the Capitol still spans the centuries. No period has passed without leaving its traces on this hill; here, more than in most places even in this Eternal City, 'all moments of history confront us'. This little hill is itself a living monument to Time. From the stairway of the Senator's Palace, on June 16, 1946, the flag of the Roman Republic of 1849 welcomed the proclamation of the present Republic of Italy. But these two republics graze only the surface of time in Rome. Beneath the sixteenth-century façade of the Senator's Palace is hidden the nucleus remaining from the palace built for the Republic of 1143; that in its turn rests upon the great stones of the Tabularium, the work of a republic which had been dead almost a century before the birth of Christ. And on April 21, in the square around the ancient statue of the Emperor Marcus Aurelius, the Romans still celebrate the birth of their city in 753 B.C. (Plate 69).

Centuries have mellowed the stones of the Tabularium as they have softened *Capitolium* to *Campidoglio*. Under the Italian sun even ruins seem less austere and desolate and the past more near at hand than in greyer northern lands. On this pleasant hill, as hot afternoon turns to welcome evening, the 'Golden Capitol' glows again. The sunlight slanted through the cooling air gilds once more the horse of Marcus Aurelius and deepens into orange the honey-coloured walls of the Senator's Palace. Offices close and the hill grows quiet. Alone in the centre of the square, miraculously preserved in bronze through so many and such disastrous centuries, the emperor returns in eternal silence the salutes of legions that have been dust for eighteen hundred years.

The Capitol's northern summit, where Juno's temple stood in ancient times, had been crowned for centuries by Mary's church (Plates 70–71). When the south end of the hill lay in desolation, religion had kept this summit alive. Santa Maria in Aracoeli was an important church in the Middle Ages, so important that the city magistrates often met here as, in ancient days, the Senate had convened in pagan temples. The city held this church under its special protection and placed here its first municipal clock, transferred in the eighteenth century to the Capitol tower. Here, at Christmas time, is set up Rome's most famous *Presepe* or Nativity Group, with its richly jewelled Holy Child. And here the Roman children still come, between Christmas and Epiphany, to recite verses and 'sermons' in praise of the *bambino Gesù.*

This present church, where Gibbon mused on his *History of the Decline and Fall,* dates from the Middle Ages—probably the thirteenth and fourteenth centuries. An older building which it replaced may have been built late in the sixth century. The flight of steps which leads up to the church today was a thank-offering to the Madonna for deliverance from the plague of 1348—the only public work done in Rome during the popes' exile in Avignon. The stairway which led in pagan times from the Forum, on the other side of the hill, up to Juno's temple, is immortalized in Ovid's phrase, 'Where high Moneta lifts her steps sublime'.

The ancient name of this church, Saint Mary in the Capitol, belongs to the time when Christianity was recently victorious over paganism, when the Queen of Heaven had not long before replaced the queen of the gods on her sacred hill. The present name of the church, Santa Maria in Aracoeli, or Saint Mary at the Altar of Heaven, which came into use about the thirteenth century, is explained by one of the most famous legends of Christian Rome. As the *Mirabilia* tells it, the Roman Senators were overcome by the virtues of Augustus, 'seeing him to be of so great beauty that none could look into his eyes, and of so great prosperity and peace that he had made all the world to render him tribute'. Therefore they 'said unto him: We desire to worship thee, because the godhead is in thee; for if it were not so, all things would not prosper with thee as they do. But he, being loth, demanded a delay, and called unto him the Sibyl of Tibur [the modern Tivoli], to whom he rehearsed all that the Senators had said. She begged for three days' space, in the which she kept a straight fast; and thus made answer to him after the third day: These things, sir emperor, shall surely come to pass:

> Token of doom: the Earth shall drip with sweat;
> From Heaven shall come the King for evermore,
> And present in the flesh shall judge the world.

And the other verses that follow:

'And anon . . . the heaven was opened, and a great brightness lighted upon him; and he saw in heaven a virgin, passing fair, standing upon an altar, and holding a man-child in her arms, whereof he marvelled exceedingly; and he heard a voice from heaven . . . saying, This is the altar of the Son of God. The emperor straightway fell to the ground, and worshipped the Christ that should come. This vision he showed to the Senators, and they in likewise marvelled exceedingly. The vision took place in the chamber of the emperor . . . where now is the church of Saint Mary in the Capitol.' Tradition says that one of the many ancient columns in the church came from 'the chamber of Augustus'—a story derived from the phrase *a cubiculo Augustorum*, the title of a servant attached to the imperial bedchamber, which appears in the inscription on its base.

Here is the familiar medieval emphasis on the divine direction of history that had ordained the simultaneous birth of Christianity and the Roman Empire. Such a legend is a popular development of the pronouncement of the great pope, Leo I, in the fifth century: 'That the working of unspeakable grace might be spread abroad throughout the whole world, Divine Providence prepared the Roman Empire.'

Nowhere in Rome are the successive layers of time more clearly visible than at the foot of Mary's church on the Capitol. Here ancient, medieval, and renaissance Rome have met together; the pagan and the Christian world confront each other in the shadow of the present.

At the foot of the steps is a 'marvel' unseen for centuries, an ancient apartment house or insula of the first century A.D. (Plates 72–73) brought to light by the excavations of the Mussolini era. Though rare now, such houses far outnumbered detached private homes in imperial Rome; one of them, the Insula of Felicula or Felicles, was ranked, in the fourth century after Christ, as one of the sights of the city.

Unlike the single houses, which faced inward upon courts and turned blank walls to the outer world, these apartment houses, even when they had courtyards, faced outward upon the street. Often their ground floors were divided into small shops facing directly upon it, as in this building. Here the two lower floors now lie below the level to which the present street has risen in the course of centuries.

Accustomed as the world has grown to the solidity of Roman construction, it comes as a shock to realize that then as now commercial housing was often scamped and poorly done. Big apartment houses often had foundations too shallow and too narrow and walls too thin to carry the weight of five or six stories. The emperors tried to control the height of these buildings, Augustus setting a limit of seventy feet, but in imperial Rome, as in large cities today, a builder had to choose between going up into the air or out into the suburbs.

Faulty construction often made such houses a menace. Ancient writers complain of their frequent collapse and of the many fires which swept them. Wooden beams supporting the heavy floors of the upper stories combined with the use of open braziers for heating to make fire a constant hazard. Juvenal, writing early in the second century A.D., complained of the construction of Roman apartments in comparison with buildings in smaller places: 'Who at cool Praeneste, or at Volsinii amid its leafy hills, was ever afraid of his house tumbling down?... But here we inhabit a city propped up for the most part by slats; for that is how the landlord patches up the cracks in the old wall, bidding the inmates sleep at ease under the ruin that hangs above their heads.' Nothing points out this danger so well as the fact that the only wheeled traffic which had perpetual permission to use the narrow streets during the day was the contractor's cart engaged in wrecking houses in order to rebuild them in better condition.

Wheeled vehicles, barred from the streets by day to prevent congestion of traffic, filled the nights with a din to which such houses, opening on the streets, were especially vulnerable. Juvenal complained also about the noisy nights. 'Most sick people here in Rome,' he wrote, 'perish for want of sleep, the illness itself having been produced by food lying undigested on a fevered stomach. For what sleep is possible in a lodging? Who but the wealthy get sleep in Rome? There lies the root of the disorder. The crossing of wagons in the narrow, winding streets, the slanging of drovers when brought to a stand ... make sleep impossible.'

The satirist, however, was probably not typical of the general crowd of Romans of his time, who doubtless accepted this confusion as matter-of-factly as Romans today.

The remains of these nameless, ordinary apartments were quickly forgotten amid the ruin of more famous and spectacular buildings. How long the Capitol insula was inhabited or when the first church was built within its walls no one can tell, but as early as the thirteenth century the church of San Biagio di Mercatello stood there. Carlo Fontana partially demolished San Biagio in 1665 to build the baroque church of Santa Rita da Cascia on its site. Santa Rita, in its turn, was torn down in 1927, and reconstructed near the Theatre of Marcellus. When it was gone the sunlight shone once more upon the walls of the ancient apartment house and the bell-tower of San Biagio embedded in them, and lit up the painted Man of Sorrows, remnant of the medieval church's decoration, enshrined beneath a little pent roof which the excavators built.

The house which sheltered so many Romans eighteen hundred years ago now looks quiet and remote. The neighbourhood was undoubtedly noisier in ancient days, when the surrounding streets were narrow and crowded with buildings edging up the Capitol hill. But nowhere along a Roman street is life far away. Just around the corner of Victor Emmanuel's monument is the Piazza Venezia, where buses start and stop and start again as traffic snarls in a jumble of taxis and motor-cycles and pedestrians. Juvenal would feel at home in this tumult, which must at least equal any made by 'crossing of wagons' or 'slanging of drovers brought to a stand'. After a sleep of centuries the noise of Rome, like her ruins, has come to life again. But this is a noise of the day. Wheeled traffic, unlike that of ancient times, is lighter by night, and even the high-strung satirist might sleep now in peace.

THE PALATINE

Plates 74–99

IF the Capitol is a centre of activity, the Palatine is a hill for dreams. When its emperors forsook the imperial buildings there, more than sixteen hundred years ago, the palaces still stood intact, rich with facings of many-coloured marbles, bright with paintings and gold. But soon their history grew as dim as the fading frescoes on their deserted walls. Through the dark centuries that followed, one fact only remained clear: here, on this mount which the ancient Romans knew as *Palatium*, stood the remnants of those great structures called after the hill itself, which gave the name 'palace' to stately buildings throughout the world.

Here, too, centuries before the first palaces were even dreamed, was the birthplace of Rome. In a thicket at the Palatine's foot, tradition says, the kindly wolf suckled Rome's founders, Romulus and Remus; and about this hill Romulus built the walls of the city's first settlement, when the Romans were a simple shepherd folk with no thought of a fortified citadel or a shining temple to Jupiter on the Capitol. Archaeology bears out the tradition that here were the oldest habitations of the Eternal City.

Kings known to history came and went, but though the breezy Palatine was a desirable place of residence, there is no indication that they lived there. By the first century before Christ, however, the hill had its famous inhabitants. Cicero lived there, and Catiline, whom Cicero's orations sent into exile. And here, in 63 B.C., was born Octavius, Julius Caesar's great-nephew, whom the world knew later as Augustus. Because Augustus lived on the Palatine the hill began to take on its character of 'the imperial mount'. Augustus' own house was modest; he kept it so from policy as well as taste. But his successors had no such scruples. They built and re-built, taking over private property with a high hand until the hill became practically one labyrinthine palace. Often they deliberately crushed and filled in their predecessors' buildings to use as foundations for their own. To give themselves more room they extended the surface of the hill by the mighty substructures of brick and concrete which are its most prominent features today, as they have been for centuries.

Rome and the Palatine ceased to be the centre of the imperial court when Diocletian, late in the third century A.D., divided the empire into eastern and western parts. Milan first and then Ravenna became the seat

(49)

of the western government. A still worse blow to the hill's prestige came when Constantine removed the capital of the briefly reunited empire to Constantinople in 330. Yet for a long time the palaces were kept in repair, ready for infrequent imperial visits. Through Claudian's welcoming poem to Honorius in 404 echoes the wistful longing of the Romans for their emperors' return:

'Of a truth no other city could fitly be the home of the world's rulers; on this hill is majesty most herself, and knows the height of her supreme sway; the palace, raising its head above the forum that lies at its feet, sees around it so many temples and is surrounded by so many protecting deities. . . . The eyes are dazed by the blaze of metal and blink out-wearied by the surrounding gold.'

Six years later, in 410, Alaric sacked the city—a disaster less utterly overwhelming, however, than it first appeared to the horrified Roman world. The palaces, or at least parts of them, were still fit for habitation, and later in the century the Ostrogothic ruler Theodoric repaired them. Although Ravenna was the official centre from which the eastern em-perors governed Italy, the Byzantine governor Narses lived on the Palatine as late as 570 and died there at a ripe old age, according to the ninth-century chronicler Agnellus of Ravenna. Soon after his death dark-ness falls over the Palatine except for mentions of churches which had crept in among its decaying buildings and indications that repairs were made as late as 680. Time and the hands of men stripped the imperial halls of their marble facings, overthrew them, and filled their chambers with debris, leaving only a few bare walls standing above ground and a labyrinth of buried rooms beneath.

The most impressive view of the hill today is from the south, looking across the desolate site of the ancient Circus Maximus toward the sub-structures built by Severus (193–211), though begun by Domitian a century before (Plate 75). Though these substructures are merely under-pinning, meant to widen the ground area of the hill, and are far from the present entrance to the Palatine, they afford the only chance for com-parison between its appearance today and in past centuries. Almost no other recognizable early views of ruins on the Palatine are known and very few could exist. Before the end of the sixteenth century these sub-structures and the remnants of building above them were not only the most outstanding features of the hill but among the few ancient structures still unburied there.

Between today's photograph and Etienne Du Pérac's etching done almost four hundred years ago (Plates 75–76), the main mass of these great

arches has changed but little. Seen from their foot or from the hilltop of
the Janiculum across the Tiber, they seem as much the work of nature
as of man. By day the immense piers of brick rise stark and brown beneath
their crown of pines and cypresses. Moonlight pales them to a ghostly
radiance. And on a night when lightning flares across the wide sky they
leap out suddenly against the darkness like gigantic skeletons articulated
by no human hands. Then indeed Jupiter Tonans, the Thunderer, seems
to speak as he did long ago to Numa, king of Rome, when he hurled a
brazen shield from heaven as a pledge of empire amid crashing thunder
peals.

Besides its palaces, the Palatine had temples famed in ancient times.
Of these, that dedicated to Cybele, the Great Mother, is best identified.
Excavated in the 1870's, though known considerably earlier, its grey
stone platform and truncated columns have a look of immemorial age as
they stand beneath a thick ilex grove near the southwest corner of the hill.
One of the oldest shrines on the Palatine, it was built before marble came
into use in Rome. The location of the temple of Apollo, so lyrically described by Propertius, though many a battle of scholars has been fought
about it, is now generally identified with the large podium approached
by a monumental staircase southeast of Cybele's temple. Where the
temples of Vesta, of Jupiter the Victorious, and other deities once stood is
still in question.

The complex of ruins on the Palatine has discouraged many a visitor,
and the varying array of names applied to the palaces has added to the
bewilderment. Yet these names need not clash with enjoyment; they are
merely convenient ways of identifying the different parts of a maze of
structures.

On the northwest corner of the hill overlooking the Roman Forum
stand the ruins known as the Palace of Tiberius (Plates 94, 96, 98) from
the emperor who began it. The rest of the imperial buildings are often
called, as a whole, the Augustan Palace, though this name is usually
reserved for the residential palace (Plate 85) which Domitian, third of the
Flavian emperors, built on the southeastern part of the hill. Flavian
Palace, a name met frequently, is sometimes used both of this and of
Domitian's official or state palace in the centre (Plate 87). More generally,
however, it is applied to the official palace only, and is so used here.

By the Middle Ages, differences between the various palaces had been
forgotten. The hill was occupied by churches and their gardens, nestled
among the spreading ruin. Medieval men, in general, spoke of only one
palace on this hill—the Greater Palace, or *Palazzo Maggiore*. This was 'the

Palace of the Monarchy of the Earth, wherein is the capital seat of the whole world', wrote the compiler of the *Graphia Aureae Urbis Romae*, the Description of the Golden City of Rome, in the twelfth or thirteenth century. The *Mirabilia* calls it simply 'The Greater Palace in the Pallantean Hill'. The authors of both books probably meant the whole complex of ruins which, by then, were crumbling into one tangled labyrinth. Medieval views (Plates 5, 62) show a generalized mass labelled *palatium maius* or *Palazzo Maggiore*, with rows of conventionalized arches which probably represented the substructures of Septimius Severus.

These, looking much as they do today, rise in the background of Marten van Heemskerck's drawing (Plate 77), though the foreground emphasis is on one of Rome's completely vanished 'marvels', the Septizonium. This was a great façade built by Severus to screen the substructures from travellers approaching from the south along the Via Appia and to impress, his chronicler says, those coming to Rome from the emperor's native Africa. What other purpose it may have served is unknown. Its very name is a puzzle; if ever it had seven floors, as the term implies, all but three had disappeared before any artist drew it. It may, perhaps, have been dedicated to the seven planets. Medieval Romans saw in it some connection with the heavens, for besides calling it 'the Seven Floors' they referred to it as 'the temple of the Sun and Moon'. So thoroughly did the workmen of Sixtus V carry out its final destruction in 1588–1589 that it is likely to remain one of archaeology's unsolved problems.

When, in the sixteenth century, Roman nobles and princes of the Church began to build villas and lay out gardens in the centre and on the northern side of the Palatine, this southeastern angle with the immense arches surrounding it remained in the hands of churches and convents. So, comparatively unchanged by casual excavators, it slept in quiet until the more thorough explorations of the late nineteenth century.

The romantic spirit in which this century began took special delight in stressing the mystery of ruins just as scientific archaeology was preparing to dispel it. The early years of excavation, indeed, increased the public bewilderment, for theories and identifications changed almost overnight, and each had its passionate defenders. Through most of the century the name 'Palace of the Caesars' was as vague as 'Greater Palace' had been in the Middle Ages, meaning sometimes the buildings of Severus, sometimes the Palace of Tiberius, and sometimes all the buildings on the hill.

Romantic feeling for the Palatine found its perfect expression in the Fourth Canto of *Childe Harold*, written in 1817 shortly after Byron's brief Roman visit in the spring of that year:

'Cypress and ivy, weed and wallflower grown
Matted and massed together, hillocks heaped
On what were chambers, arch crushed, column strown
In fragments, choked up vaults, and frescoes steeped
In subterranean damps, where the owl peeped
Deeming it midnight:—Temples, baths, or halls
Pronounce who can: for all that Learning reaped
From her research hath been, that these are walls—
Behold the Imperial Mount! 'Tis thus the mighty falls.'

A paragraph of prose is devoted to precisely the same conclusion by one of the most entertaining travel writers of the time. The Englishwoman, Charlotte Eaton, though unknown to fame, was possessed of an inquiring mind and an observant eye as well as a romantic fancy. 'I have made repeated visits to this hill,' she wrote in *Rome in the Nineteenth Century*, the outcome of a long visit in 1817 and 1818. 'I have spent whole days upon it: I have been there with the most renowned antiquaries, professional and unprofessional: I have read and thought and inquired about it; and all I have gained by puzzling my own brains, and those of other people, is the simple fact I knew at first—that it is covered with the walls of the Palace of the Caesars.'

The very guidebooks of the nineteenth century shared the romantic fondness for the vague and picturesque. Murray's *Handbook* for 1869 led visitors to the Palace of the Caesars 'from the side of the Circus Maximus, through a house on the Via de' Cerchi', to the substructures of Severus with the enticing statement that 'these magnificent ruins, clothed in ivy and other creeping plants, diversified by laurels and ilex, will supply the artist with varied combinations for his pencil'. (Plate 79.)

Enchantment lingers still beneath these arches in this quiet corner of the Palatine. Steep paths, slippery with pine needles, lead down into the deep shadows (Plate 80), where golden broom clings to the old bricks and fills the air with its honey scent. And by the same paths the visitor climbs up again to the ruins of the baths which Severus built above, and to the great curved wall of Domitian's exedra overlooking the Stadium. There is no easy entrance now 'through a house on the Via de' Cerchi' and no quick way to reach the shadow of these arches. But the very walls which bar entrance from today's noisy thoroughfares help to guard the remnants of romantic peace.

On the hill above, the convent of Saint Bonaventura stands beside the Baths of Severus (Plate 81), its high-perched garden with the famous palm looking toward their towering ruins as it has for centuries. Saint

Bonaventura's garden (Plate 82) is one of the few now remaining from the many which once filled the hill. In 1836 Frances Elizabeth Appleton, who was later to be Longfellow's wife, described these gardens ecstatically in her *Journal*: 'Passed a lovely morning most enchantingly wandering about the Palace of the Caesars. Flowers and green boughs were nodding in the wind from every broken wall and tall weeds and luxurious vegetation made the ground "one emerald". I had not been here before and was fascinated with the picturesqueness of the ruins. . . . After I had sketched and gazed till I was nearly sunstruck we rambled about the rest of the ruins of this Mount Palatine once all a palace now a most picturesque kitchen garden with here and there a jagged mass of brick looming up like a huge tombstone of the Past.'

Westward, beyond the Baths of Severus, rise the walls enclosing the sunken Stadium, named from the resemblance of its shape to the race track of a Roman circus (Plates 83–84). Though some sports may have been held here it is more likely that Domitian built it as a garden for his residential palace. The wall nearest the baths is broken by a curved box or exedra, once surrounded by a two-storied portico. Similar porticoes ran about the inner walls, making a pleasant shade where members of the imperial family or court could walk to watch the fountains playing in the garden or whatever activities might be going on. Only the stumps of brick columns, their marble facings long since re-used or burnt for lime, remain now to mark the line of the colonnade. The upper walls of the Stadium are gone, except at the ends and in the imperial box. On the lower floors of the exedra are still some faded paintings in blue and red, and in the semicircular corridor which runs behind it are glimpses of a vaulted ceiling beautifully coffered.

Some time near the end of the ancient empire or early in the Middle Ages changes were made in the Stadium's interior. Someone built a portico across it at right angles to its sides, and traces of the old columns still remain in the grass which now fills the enclosure. Someone, perhaps Theodoric, built an oval enclosure at its southern end. Though the Stadium's high walls have always stood erect, its sunken garden gradually became filled with the ruins of ages. Casual explorations by those who excavated in the Farnese Gardens beneath the Palace of Tiberius early in the eighteenth century left here comparatively little trace. The excavations of the late nineteenth century, however, uncovered its ancient level; since then time has carpeted it with grass where scarlet poppies wave.

If masses of ancient wall still stand on the southeastern corner of the Palatine, this is less true of the centre of the hill. Here the builders of the

Renaissance, laying out gardens and building villas, dug into or demolished much of the remaining ruins in search of rare marbles or works of
art, and then filled in and levelled off for their own uses. The eighteenth
century saw a fresh wave of excavation here, followed by some more or
less accurate restorations. And here today, especially in Domitian's residential palace, active excavation is still going on in rooms that have lain
buried for centuries.

The site of much of this residential palace lay comparatively unexplored
from the second half of the sixteenth century until the early nineteenth,
because it was continuously occupied. The Villa Palatina, on part of
whose site the Palatine Museum now stands, was begun soon after the
middle of the sixteenth century and grew in size from time to time, incor-
porating ancient walls into its new structure. It has been called by the
names of many owners from the time the Mattei bought it about 1560.
The Spada and Magnana families owned it after the Mattei, and in the
last quarter of the eighteenth century it belonged to the French abbé
Rancoureuil, who did considerable excavation and much damage. In
1818 it came into the possession of the eccentric Scot, Charles Andrew
Mills, whose name still lingers about the site. He covered it with a sham
Gothic façade (Plate 86) in the high romantic style and decorated it
with the symbols of the United Kingdom, the Tudor rose, the Scottish
thistle, and the Irish shamrock. In 1856 the property came into the
hands of the nuns of the Order of the Visitation and was closed to visitors;
in 1906 it was taken over by the Italian Government and excavation
begun.

Demolition of the villa began in 1927, and as a result blinding light now
plays upon fragments of the emperor's bare brick walls, long hidden by those
of later days. But the old stone pines are being handled tenderly, and in
time the scars of excavation will heal here as they have done already in the
Stadium, so that it will be possible to enjoy both the remains of the
imperial palaces and the beauty of the Palatine.

Domitian's residential palace was built around two peristyles or colonnaded open courts, both laid bare now to their old levels. About the lower
courtyard (Plate 85) rise bare walls, denuded long ago of all decoration.
Fragments of their upper levels, now considerably restored, have always
stood above ground, many of them actually incorporated in the walls of
the Villa Palatina. The lower stories, though explored by the Abbé Rancoureuil in the late eighteenth century, lay almost entirely buried until
after 1927 (Plate 86). Of the few underground rooms which could earlier
be seen, Rodolfo Lanciani wrote in the 1890's: 'The shimmering light

which falls through masses of ivy from an opening in the middle of the ceiling makes these ruins very picturesque.'

These remnants of imperial Rome in the Villa Palatina gardens were proudly shown to select visitors by Charles Mills and doubtless by many another owner. Marguerite, Countess of Blessington, noted in her *Journal* in 1828 that she had seen 'in the beautiful villa of Mr. Mills, on the Mount Palatine. . . . Some most interesting fragments of antiquity . . . mingled with trees and flowering plants.' In the same year she met there Madame Letitia Bonaparte, mother of Napoleon. 'There was something highly scenic in the whole scene,' she wrote. 'Here was the mother of a modern Caesar, walking amidst the ruins of the palace of the ancient ones, lamenting a son whose fame had filled the four quarters of the globe.'

North and west of Domitian's residence lies the official or Flavian Palace, also bare and sundrenched in the centre. But the excavations are older here and along the edges there are grass and trees and vines. A few tall masses of this palace wall have always stood, spared by builders of long ago (Plate 87). The fragments of marble and the stumps of columns grouped about them have been unearthed and arranged in the course of successive excavations.

Underfoot here lie buried rooms of older times, dating from the days of the Republic to those of Nero. These rooms were filled and levelled off to serve as foundations for new buildings above, in a process beginning with Nero's *Domus Transitoria*, built to connect the Palatine with the emperor's other properties. When this was burned in A.D. 64, Nero replaced it by later construction on the site, which formed a small part of the vast Golden House, extending to well over the neighbouring hills. Later emperors in their turn destroyed the Golden House and built above it, so that the foundations beneath Domitian's palace are a labyrinth of buried chambers, crushed centuries ago. Some of these rooms have been known since the excavations by the duke of Parma in 1724; some were found then but later closed up and almost forgotten; and some remained seemingly unknown until comparatively recent times.

Under the basilica of the Flavian Palace itself (Plate 87) is one of the most interesting rooms, a hall probably dating from Caligula's time, and called, from motifs used in its decoration, the 'Hall of Isis'. On its walls remnants of scenes from mythology and Roman legend may still be traced in the thick darkness by the fitful light of incandescent lanterns. Below its vaulted roof, painted with an almost baroque design of wavy bands of blue and rose with spirals of golden ribbons, is the frieze of sacrificial vessels, lotus, and sacred asps of Egypt which suggested the name of

Isis, whose mystery cult Caligula revived in Rome. A curving brick wall, which cuts ruthlessly through the hall, belonged to Nero's *Domus Transitoria*.

The paintings of this room, discovered in 1724, were drawn by several artists, and were engraved and printed by George Turnbull, together with copies of other ancient frescoes, in two books. But despite the interest the pictures had created at the time, the room was forgotten by all except a few devotees of Roman antiquities until it was re-excavated in 1912.

South of the basilica are two other underground rooms, belonging to the *Domus Transitoria*, which were also discovered in 1724 but remained visible throughout the nineteenth century under the name of 'Baths of Livia'. These are not the same as the half-buried chambers once called the 'House of Livia' but now generally known as the House of Augustus. Charlotte Eaton spoke of seeing here by 'the glimmering of some wax tapers . . . the gilded ceiling of these splendid dungeons still shining in the passing ray, and painted with figures designed with exquisite taste and correctness'. Today these rooms, like the 'Hall of Isis' and the still earlier Republican chamber, the 'Hall of the Griffins', discovered in the 1930's, are kept covered for protection and shown only by special arrangement.

Considerably farther to the south and west, and closer to the Palace of Tiberius than to that of Domitian, lies a little half-buried house discovered in 1869. It has borne the names of Livia, widow of Augustus and mother of Tiberius, and of Germanicus, father of Caligula, but is now believed to have been the modest dwelling of Augustus himself, preserved unharmed as a State monument through the building orgies of later emperors. The frescoes of mythological scenes upon its walls are among the best-known ancient paintings in Rome, though exposure to the light has dimmed their colours sadly.

The dividing line between the Palace of Tiberius and the other palaces on the hill runs roughly parallel with the modern road leading up from the Forum (Plate 87). No remnants of the upper stories now stand on the site of the Palace of Tiberius, but a few feet above the level of the present Farnese Gardens a low ridge marks the line of the half-subterranean Cryptoporticus built by Nero (Plate 88) as a link between the Palatine and his Golden House and enlarged by the addition of cross branches. Openings high up in the massive vaults let in a cool, dim light as grateful now on a summer day as when the imperial household used it as a passageway between the buildings on the hill. Who else may have used it since, or for how long, remains a field for fascinating conjecture. Something at least has long been known of some buried chambers beneath these gardens, for

Bernard de Montfauçon wrote of them late in the seventeenth century: 'All the hill is full of subterraneous passages, the Entrance into which is purposely stopt up.' Whether he meant the Cryptoporticus or some of the corridors in the Palace of Tiberius, or simply spoke in general of all the substructures beneath the Farnese Gardens, is a matter for speculation.

Most of the rooms in this palace, begun by Tiberius and extended by his successors, especially Domitian, still lie buried beneath the gardens. Those which can be seen today are shut off from the light not only by the earth above their vaults but also by the massive substructures built in front of them toward the Forum (Plates 94, 96, 98). Caligula, successor of Tiberius, began these substructures, and later emperors extended them so far that they must have almost completely darkened the rooms behind, unless they were lit by interior courts. Long ago, at least as early as the mid-sixteenth century when the Farnese family levelled the ground above them, the great brick arches were filled with earth to more than half their height, while above them spread, in all their glory, the gardens which were fit successors to the palaces on the imperial hill (Plates 90–91).

The Farnese began these gardens about the middle of the sixteenth century, when Cardinal Alessandro II, kinsman of Pope Paul III, bought the site of the Palace of Tiberius and much of that covered by the Flavian Palace. Having dug for works of art and demolished considerable remnants of ancient masonry, they employed the best architects and gardeners of the day to lay out the gardens which were among the sights of renaissance and baroque Rome. Extending from the top of the hill well into the Forum, they contained no palace but were dotted with pavilions and towers. The retaining wall at their foot ran through the middle of the ancient House of the Vestals, and its high terraces covered these ruins and those of many buildings on the hillside. The casino opposite the great entrance gate which Vignola built was squarely in front of the northern entrance to Nero's Cryptoporticus. All that remained visible of the Palace of Tiberius were the immense arches of the substructures (Plates 96, 98) which supported the northwest corner of the gardens and perhaps a few fragments of crumbling wall.

These gardens passed presently to Farnese kin, the dukes of Parma, in whose hands they remained until they were inherited by the Bourbons of Naples in 1731. It was during the last years of their ownership, between 1720 and 1730, that the dukes of Parma excavated the centre of the hill in search of buried works of art and discovered the painted rooms beneath the Flavian Palace.

The gardens soon lapsed into sad and long-continued decay. Ludwig Friedländer wrote of them in 1815, in his *Ansichten von Italien* (Views in Italy): 'The villa with the gardens (*orti Farnesiani*) which was built here by pope Paul III, is nearly a ruin again, and the gardens, once so renowned, are almost turned into a wilderness; yet they still offer some fine views and prospects. Through weeds and shrubs, we cut our way to some small subterraneous chambers, which are said to have formed a part of Livia's baths.' In almost the same terms Charlotte Eaton described them about two years later: 'The casinos of popes mouldering upon the palaces of Roman emperors—pigs and peasants inhabiting a corner of these splendid ruins—cabbages and artichokes flourishing above them—fragments of precious marbles and granites, of carved cornices and broken alabaster, scattered among the mould,—while the eye wanders over a confused array of long corridors, nameless arcades, unknown vaults, forgotten chambers, and broken arches.'

The sense of abandonment and decay is strong, too, in Theodore Dwight's *Journal* for 1821, with a suggestion, however, of the growing interest in excavation. 'We were allowed, though with a bad grace,' he wrote, 'to traverse the Farnesian Gardens. . . . Our path up the hill was the main alley through the vineyards. The ground was perfectly bare, excepting only the leafless vines, and the slight frames and sticks by which they were supported. The soil had at first the appearance of being thickly scattered with gravel; but this proved to be owing to vast quantities of bricks, marble, stones, and pottery, broken into small bits and mingled by a long course of cultivation. It seemed no very incredible thing, when we reflected what piles of buildings had in former ages occupied the grounds: for the earth was filled with an indiscriminate and incalculable mass of ruins. Here one naturally thinks of subterranean apartments, and undiscovered treasures hid beneath the ground; for in a place so teeming with memorials of former times, a stranger thinks he could not rest until the dark interior is exposed to view; and quite unsatisfied with what he sees upon the surface, feels that he would gladly lend his strength to lay open the foundations of the immortal Mons Palatinus.'

Antiquarians and topographers reported, from time to time, more and more alluring glimpses of buried rooms in the 'dark interiors', and interest in exploration grew. In 1860 the emperor Napoleon III bought the Farnese Gardens for excavation, putting the architect Pietro Rosa in charge. The new Italian State bought them from him in 1870 and continued the excavations to the great benefit of knowledge but at the cost, eventually, of almost complete destruction of the gardens. Neither

Napoleon, whose chief aim was the discovery of works of art, nor the State, primarily interested in uncovering the imperial palaces, found such a wealth of 'undiscovered treasure' as they may have hoped. But they did reveal much of the structural grandeur of the imperial hill.

In the 1860's Pietro Rosa cleared the earth from the arches over the *Clivus Victoriae*, or Street of Victory (Plate 96), which ran along the hillside above the Forum. More than any other spot on the hill these dark substructures now stir the imagination with their glimpses of black and hidden rooms where feet may not at present enter. As early as 1869, when Helen Hunt Jackson visited the Palatine, she was struck by the contrast between these dark arches, the barren excavations in the Flavian Palace, and the planting of the Farnese Gardens, where Napoleon III had evidently done some tidying. 'I had all along anticipated seeing ruins grander than any other except the Colosseum,' wrote the American authoress. 'As I saw them from the distance they looked imposing, and looked wild and overgrown. . . . But what do you think you see when the gate is first opened? . . . You see a broad walk and a sort of *café*-like building, and very much landscape garden, nice little beds, such as you might see in Brooklyn or Springfield, bushels of roses, and white thorn and box borders; if you are like me, you stand stock-still and burst out laughing, and say "Where is the Palace of the Caesars?" and then your archaeologist leads you along, up and up, into great spaces, some of them floored with mosaic, some of them bare earth. . . . However,' she continued, 'when I was fairly underground, walking along an old street, many feet beneath the landscape garden, and looking into stuccoed room after room, and up steep stone staircases . . . I found my usual faith and reverence reviving.' By the end of the 1880's little was left of the Farnese Gardens except the ilex grove at the northwestern corner, with its marvellous view across the Forum to the Capitol, and the casino, the 'café-like building', with its double staircase and fountain (Plates 91, 93-94).

In the remnants of the garden peace now broods, save for the disturbing sense of buried history in the still-unopened rooms of the palace below, where excavators long to penetrate. Here, on the hill above the ancient vaults, roses and orange trees strike notes of brilliant colour, stone pines shade the casino's walls, ivy mantles them, and glossy-leaved oleanders fill the air with their spicy smell. Under the central baroque arch the old fountain still drips over emerald moss and lichens to splash into a grotto below. Through the opened archway of the right-hand staircase (Plate 93), cool darkness beckons into Nero's Cryptoporticus. And toward the Capitol a pathway leads past walls of crumbling brick, under the arches of the

Palace of Tiberius, along the *Clivus Victoriae*, and down a steep ramp to the church of Santa Maria Antiqua (Plate 97) at the edge of the Forum.

This church, dedicated to Mary, was one of the first to creep into the buildings abandoned by the emperors. It was founded about the early sixth century in part of a huge brick structure just below the Palace of Tiberius on the northern border of the Forum. The identity of this building is still a problem. Known for a long time as 'the library of the temple of Augustus', it may have formed a monumental approach to the Palatine. In the ninth century the church had to be abandoned as unsafe; perhaps the gigantic ruins poised on the hill above had been dangerously weakened by the earthquake of 847. In its place the worshippers built another church for the Virgin, *Santa Maria Nova*, New Saint Mary's, in the ruins of the temple of Venus and Rome at the east end of the Forum, leaving to the abandoned church the name of Santa Maria Antiqua, or Old Saint Mary's. Early in the seventeenth century the new church was rebuilt and re-dedicated to Santa Francesca Romana.

The site of Old Saint Mary's on the edge of the Forum was reputed in the Middle Ages to be a haunted spot. The *Mirabilia* describes it as 'a place that is called Hell, because of old time it burst forth there; and brought great mischief upon Rome; where a certain noble knight, to the intent that the city should be delivered after the responses of their gods, did on his harness and cast himself into the pit, and the earth closed; so the city was delivered.'

This was a medieval version of the ancient Roman legend of Marcus Curtius, told about another part of the Forum. As Livy tells the tale: 'The ground gave way, at about the middle of the Forum, and, sinking to an immeasurable depth, left a prodigious chasm. This gulf could not be filled with the earth which everyone brought and cast into it, until admonished by the gods, they began to inquire what it was that constituted the chief strength of the Roman People; for this the soothsayers declared that they must offer up, as a sacrifice to that spot, if they wished the Roman Republic to endure. Thereupon Marcus Curtius, a young soldier of great prowess, rebuked them, so the story runs, for questioning whether any blessing were more Roman than arms and valour. A hush ensued, as he turned to the temples of the immortal gods which rise above the Forum, and to the Capitol, and stretching forth his hands, now to heaven, and now to the yawning chasm and to the gods below, devoted himself to death. After which, mounted on a horse caparisoned with all possible splendour, he plunged fully armed into the gulf; and crowds of men and women threw offerings and fruits in after him.' The traditional site of the gulf described by Livy was in the western part of the Forum, not far from the foot of the Capitol hill, where its location is still marked by an irregular pavement, surrounded by a border, in front of the Basilica Julia.

Some time in the Middle Ages, probably in the thirteenth century, when danger from falling ruins was evidently over, the church of *Santa Maria libera nos a poenis inferni*, Saint Mary Deliverer from the Pains of Hell, was built near this haunted spot. Early in the seventeenth century this church, known in Italian as Santa Maria Liberatrice, was given the baroque front which appears in Vasi's etching (Plate 99). In 1702, when digging for marbles in the debris behind the church, excavators discovered part of Santa Maria Antiqua, had drawings made of some of its ancient frescoes, and filled it up again. The old church remained almost entirely buried until Santa Maria Liberatrice was, in turn, demolished in 1900–1901 in order to uncover the older buildings and the ramp leading up to the Palace of Tiberius on the hill.

Santa Maria Antiqua was probably built into the imperial pile in the very century when the Middle Ages were closing in on Rome. Medieval men were slow to recognize an abrupt break between their own times and the ancient world and felt themselves still a part of the Roman Empire. But one of the sixth century's most far-sighted statesmen, Cassiodorus, minister to Theodoric, seems to have sensed the moment of fundamental change, when the Church rather than the State became the guardian of the intellect as well as of the soul. At the beginning of the Gothic wars in 535 Cassiodorus was planning, with Pope Agapetus I, a Christian university in Rome, modelled on the universities of the pagan empire. A scant five years later, when the forces of the Emperor Justinian were slowly reducing Rome to a dependency of the Byzantine East, Cassiodorus withdrew from the Eternal City and founded, in southern Italy, two monasteries where his monks could copy, before it was too late, the great works of ancient times.

From the shadow of Santa Maria Antiqua, founded in a pagan building when the tide was turning toward the Middle Ages, it is but a step to the site most thickly peopled with memories of the city's ancient, pagan past— the Roman Forum.

THE ROMAN FORUM

Plates 100–120

'I NEED no ivory temple for my delight,' wrote Propertius in Augustus' day, 'enough that I can see the Roman Forum.' Here, from immemorial times, had been the meeting place of a civilization that was always positive. This Forum, so quiet in its ruins now, was filled with activity from the dawn of recorded history. Around its edges butchers, fruit-sellers, and money-lenders had their stands; in its centre were held public meetings and religious ceremonies closely bound up with the city's practical life. If the past haunts the Forum, it is a past filled with less sinister figures than those which linger in the shadows of the Palatine above.

Nowhere in Rome has more human drama been crowded into so little space. Here, according to tradition, the men of Romulus had snatched as brides the maidens of the Sabine tribes. Here, too, was set the tragic, stirring tale of the centurion Virginius, and his daughter, Virginia, whom he stabbed with a knife from a nearby butcher's shop to save her from a tyrant's claim. Here legend placed the ancient story of Marcus Curtius' leap into the unfathomable gulf yawning below the Capitol. Here Antony showed the Romans the body of the murdered Caesar and read them his will. Here, too, roused to fury by this sight and by the dead Caesar's generosity, the people burned his body in their most honoured spot as a final tribute to his memory. And along the Forum's Sacred Way, from the Arch of Titus up the Capitol hill, passed the triumphal processions of emperors and generals, returning victorious from the wars.

The Forum's activities probably took place at first entirely in the open air. Later shops and temples were built and the great basilicas along the edges, which combined halls for courts and assemblies with space for shops. Throngs too large for these basilicas were addressed from the rostra, special platforms built for this purpose, or from the steps of the Forum's temples. The Senate met in these temples, as well as in others throughout Rome, but its special home was in the Forum, in the Senate House, consecrated to Victory (Plate 107).

Julius Caesar, city planner as well as warrior and statesman, gave the Forum the general shape it preserves today. One of the most arresting spots in its whole area is the altar before the temple dedicated there by the

Senate to mark the place where his body was burned in 44 B.C. (Plate 100, No. 9).

As power grew more and more concentrated in the hands of the emperors and their officials, public activities in the Forum became less important. But the place remained as unique in Roman memory as when Cicero had called it 'the Forum in which all justice is preserved'. The emperors built larger and more elaborate forums for business and amusement, but this remained 'the Forum' or 'the Forum of the Romans', by virtue of its age and associations.

As Christianity gradually conquered paganism, the temples of the Forum were closed by imperial edicts, though these edicts were disregarded from time to time. For a while some of the temples were safeguarded as public monuments or kept for various uses. But the Gothic wars of the sixth century so drained the city's resources that it would have been impossible to keep the old buildings in good repair, even had any considerable group wanted to preserve the remnants of paganism. The temples which survived did so largely because they were transformed into churches or because they were too massive to be pulled down easily for building material. The earthquake of 847, which damaged the Colosseum, probably hastened their destruction.

During the centuries of slow decay and active pillage, the ground-level of the Forum rose with the debris of fallen structures and the washing down of earth and ruin from the surrounding hills, until traffic was almost completely blocked, and papal processions had to find other ways than the old triumphal road. The few remaining columns of the ancient temples were buried, sometimes half their height; the crumbling ruins were robbed of stone and brick to be burnt for lime or re-used in humbler buildings.

Such was the Forum's state in the first years of the fifteenth century, when interest in antiquity was reviving with the early Renaissance. Some time before 1431 Poggio Bracciolini the humanist, wrote wistfully: 'The Roman Forum, the most celebrated place in the city, where the people assembled and laws were made, and the nearby Comitium, where magistrates were chosen, are now deserted through the malignance of Fortune. The one is given over to swine and cattle; the other is enclosed as a vegetable garden.'

In 1536 the Forum was partially cleared to provide a triumphal way for the Hapsburg Emperor, Charles V, in celebration of his victory over the Turks in Tunisia the year before. Unfortunately, the preparation of this triumphal road gave a fresh impetus to the plundering of the ruins, against which Raphael had already protested. After this clearing, the Forum, once more passable for traffic, was drawn again into the active life of Rome. When the excavators of the sixteenth century had finished their search for antiques, quiet settled once more about the Forum, but it was no longer a quiet of death. The lowing of cattle and the shouts of drovers now filled the air, for the Forum was again used as a market. Indeed, its classic name was almost forgotten and it was known then, and for long afterward, as the *Campo Vaccino*, or Cow Pasture, from the animals herded and sold there. Its very site, questioned by Ligorio in the sixteenth century, long remained a subject of antiquarian argument. Fortunately there were always men of plain common sense who, refusing to be drawn into fine-spun argument, kept to the old site while accepting the new name, and said with the seventeenth-century Englishman, John Raymond: 'The *Campo Vaccino* was heretofore the *Forum Romanum.*'

The eighteenth century saw a revival of interest in antiquity unequalled since the early Renaissance, which stimulated the desire for scholarly excavations. Late in the century such excavations were begun in the Forum, and for a hundred and fifty years its ruins were laid bare, down even to graves of the eighth century B.C. or earlier, below its ancient paving stones. During the last century and a half more has been learned of the Forum's buildings than was known during the thousand years before; yet even today scholars feel certain of less than many a Roman boy of ancient times.

Throughout the centuries three groups of columns and one lone shaft have been landmarks of the Forum. Most of these, at the western end, close below the Capitol, mark the sites of the temples of Saturn and of Vespasian. The eight grey and red granite columns of the portico of Saturn's temple stand almost at right angles to the Senator's Palace (Plate 100, No. 4). This was one of the Forum's oldest temples, although the columns which stand today are late. An inscription above them states that the temple was restored by vote of the Senate after a fire, probably that of A.D. 284, which swept the Forum. The Senate had a special interest in this temple, where the steep *Clivus Capitolinus* wound up the Capitol, for it had its treasury here. The writer of the *Mirabilia* had these facts clearly in mind when he referred to the 'public Treasury, that was the temple of Saturn', beside the 'Triumphal Arch, whence was the ascent into the Capitol'. Later generations which had lost the tradition called it by many names, such as the 'Temple of Concord' and the 'Temple of Fortune.'

Close by the Temple of Saturn stand the three corner columns of the Temple of Vespasian (Plate 100, No. 5). Called for centuries 'Temple of

Jupiter Tonans', this temple's columns, with their sharp flutings, their rich Corinthian capitals, and their elaborately carved frieze above, were the delight of artists. Titus and Domitian built the temple late in the first century A.D. and dedicated it to Vespasian, their father. Titus died and was deified before it was completed; he may have shared the dedication.

The anonymous monk of the eighth century who copied the inscriptions preserved at Einsiedeln left the clue which finally solved the temple's identity. Much more of the temple was evidently standing then, for the inscription stated clearly that the building had been dedicated to Vespasian and restored by the emperors Severus and Caracalla. Today all that remains is part of the last word, 'restored'—(R)ESTITVER.

Between Vespasian's temple and the Arch of Severus rises the Column of Phocas (Plate 100, No. 6) which has stood erect ever since it was set up in A.D. 608, the last monument erected in the Forum in what might still be considered ancient times. Its identity was completely lost until the excavations of the early nineteenth century uncovered its base with a dedication to ' . . . our lord, Phocas, the eternal emperor'. It was a sign of the fallen fortunes of Rome that the citizens set up no new column to honour this upstart Byzantine Emperor of the East, but one carved long before and put to a new use. By one of the world's pleasant ironies this column is best known throughout the English-speaking world through two lines of poetry far from accurate. Its base had been uncovered and the inscription read in 1813; Charlotte Eaton referred to its identity in 1817 as common knowledge among visitors. But Byron, who was in Rome the same year as Mrs. Eaton, was not noted for close attention to specific facts; even when he knew them, he often preferred the suggestion of mystery. The sober facts are cold beside his apostrophe:

> 'Tully was not so eloquent as thou,
> Thou nameless column with the buried base!'

The third group of columns (Plate 100, No. 1) is midway between the Capitol and the Arch of Titus. These three parallel fluted shafts of the Temple of Castor which appear in the foreground of Marten van Heemskerck's drawing (Plate 102), in that of Claude Lorrain (Plate 103), and in Canaletto's painting (Plate 104), are perhaps the most outstanding of the three groups. They rise in comparative isolation near the end of the old Republican Forum, and the richness of their Corinthian capitals and carved entablature has made them, like the three of Vespasian's temple, a favourite subject for artists. These columns do not belong to the first temple there, or even to the one Cicero called 'that famous and glorious memorial of the past . . . which stands where the nation may see it daily'.

Tradition says that the first Temple of Castor was vowed by the Romans in 496 in return for his aid and that of his brother Pollux at the Battle of Lake Regillus, and that it was built in 484 B.C. The existing columns probably belong to the rebuilding by Tiberius in A.D. 6, forty-nine years after Cicero's death. Following their pattern of associating temples and state offices, the Romans housed the imperial bureau of weights and measures in this temple's high foundations, open now to public gaze. When the temple fell, no one knows; by the fifteenth century evidently only these columns were standing, for a nearby street was called after them the 'Street of the Three Columns'. In the seventeenth, eighteenth, and much of the nineteenth century they were believed to belong to the Temple of Jupiter Stator, the Steadier, who rallied the wavering Romans in the war which followed the rape of the Sabine women.

Another landmark of the Forum today is the round Temple of Vesta (Plates 105–106), east of the Temple of Castor. Unseen for centuries, but now partially restored, it was probably lying buried beneath heaped earth when Van Heemskerck made his panoramic drawing of the Forum (Plate 102). This was one of Rome's most venerable shrines. Here burned the perpetual fire sacred to Vesta, guardian of the hearth, tended by the Vestal Virgins, the most severely disciplined, the most privileged, and the most highly honoured among Roman women. Here, too, was kept the Palladium, the image of Pallas Athena fallen from heaven, which Aeneas was said to have brought from burning Troy and passed on to his descendants, the founders of Rome.

In shape the temple followed the pattern of some far older and more primitive shrine, as Ovid stated clearly in his *Fasti* two thousand years ago: 'The buildings which now you see roofed with bronze you might then have seen roofed with thatch, and the walls were woven of tough willows. . . . Yet the shape of the temple, as it now exists, is said to have been its shape of old, and it is based on a sound reason. Vesta is the same as the Earth; under both of them is a perpetual fire.' Plutarch, a little later, took issue with this philosophy and explained that the temple was built, 'not in imitation of the shape of the earth . . . but of the entire universe, at the centre of which the Pythagoreans place the element of fire.' Actually its shape probably followed the tradition of the primitive Romans' round huts, like the little thatched house so long cherished on the Palatine as the home of Romulus.

However the shape be explained, the temple was unique in containing no statue of its goddess, which may have been kept in a small shrine nearby. It was not, indeed, a regularly consecrated temple, and was guarded by a taboo so strict that no man except the Pontifex Maximus was allowed to enter, and women only during the June festival of the goddess.

The temple was closed by imperial decree in 394 and the remaining Vestals were driven from their house, the near-by Atrium Vestae. When the temple fell into ruin is unknown. The twelfth century knew it in some form, for the *Mirabilia*, in describing the Forum, states: 'There is the temple of Vesta, where it is said that a dragon coucheth below, as we read in the life of Saint Silvester.' This was the correct location, for it placed the temple near the church of Santa Maria Liberatrice, associated with the story of the dragon. Before 1489 the ruins had evidently been buried for some time, as there is mention of their discovery in that year. Sixty years later, in 1549, they were rediscovered, still fairly complete, and then burned for lime or used by the builders of Saint Peter's. After this the temple's very site seems to have become uncertain, though its shape, described by so many Latin authors, was remembered and its name given to round buildings still standing, such as the little circular temple by the Tiber, which has been called by so many names. The foundations and scattered fragments of the temple in the Forum were again discovered in the 1870's and 80's, and in the 1930's the building was partially reconstructed from pictures on coins and from a relief in the Uffizi (Plate 106). The fragments which remain belong to the reconstruction by the wife of Septimius Severus after the fire of A.D. 191.

The sites of the temples of Vesta and of Castor have been closely coupled since very ancient times. The story of the founding of Castor's temple was old when Dionysius of Halicarnassus retold it in the first century before Christ. At the battle of Lake Regillus, wrote Dionysius, after the Romans had implored the help of the Twin Brothers, Castor and Pollux, there appeared 'two men on horseback, far excelling in both beauty and stature those our human stock produces.' Encouraged by this omen the Romans rallied to victory. 'In the late afternoon, two youths are said to have appeared in the same manner in the Roman Forum attired in military garb, very tall and beautiful and of the same age, themselves retaining on their countenances . . . the look of combatants, and the horses they led being all in a sweat. And when they had each of them watered their horses and washed them at the fountain which rises near the temple of Vesta . . . they related how the battle had gone and that the Romans were the victors. And it is said that after they left the Forum they were not seen again by anyone, though great search was made for them.' Convinced that these were Castor and Pollux, the fabulously skilled horsemen whose aid the army had besought, the Romans built them a temple close by the place where they had watered their steeds.

Two thousand years after Dionysius' day, Macaulay's *Lays of Ancient Rome* put the name of Vesta on every school-child's lips:

'And on rode these strange horsemen,
  With slow and lordly pace;
And none who saw their bearing
  Durst ask their name or race.
On rode they to the Forum,
  While laurel-boughs and flowers
From house-tops and from windows,
  Fell on their crests in showers.
When they drew nigh to Vesta,
  They vaulted down amain,
And washed their horses in the well
  That springs by Vesta's fane.
And straight again they mounted,
  And rode to Vesta's door;
Then, like a blast, away they passed,
  And no man saw them more.'

The 'well that springs by Vesta's fane' was the fountain of Juturna, nymph of healing waters, still fed by springs from the foot of the Palatine.

Westward from Vesta's temple the triumphal Arch of Septimius Severus (Plate 107) closes the end of the Forum. Outstanding as the columns of the ancient temples are, the most impressive monuments of the Forum are this arch and that of Titus just beyond its eastern boundary. These two arches and the Temple of Antoninus and Faustina are the only monuments of this area which have kept their ancient names throughout the centuries, for these alone have retained their inscriptions unburied and readable.

The Arch of Severus was erected by the Senate in A.D. 203 to commemorate the emperor's successful wars against the Parthians and Arabs and it is decorated with scenes from these campaigns. Originally its inscription bore the names of the emperor's two sons, Geta and Caracalla, as well. Later, when Caracalla had his brother murdered, he removed Geta's name and filled the vacant spaces with additional titles for his father and himself. Today the ancient bronze letters are gone, but their matrices and rivet holes still show the wording of both the original inscription and the changes, testifying mutely to a murder seventeen centuries ago. During the Middle Ages the arch was divided between two owners. The church of Saints Sergius and Bacchus held the southern part; the northern was used by a noble Roman family as part of a fortress, one of whose towers still appears in Du Pérac's etching (Plate 108).

Between the Arch of Severus and the Tabularium is the concrete core of the platform on which once stood the Temple of Concord. Nothing else remains of this building in which the Senate met so often except a few architectural fragments, most of which are kept in the Tabularium.

At right angles to the Arch of Severus, on what was once the ancient Comitium or open space for public assemblies, stands the double church dedicated to Saint Martina, a virgin martyr, and Saint Luke, Evangelist and patron of painters (Plate 107). It was founded in honour of Saint Martina in the seventh century, among the ruins of an annex to the Senate House, the *Secretarium Senatus*; an upper church was added in 1640 and dedicated to their patron Luke by the artists of Rome. Church and triumphal arch together suggest the essential harmony of baroque and imperial Roman styles, with their marriage of column, dome, and arch, their balance of the horizontal and the vertical, and their delight in ornament. The Middle Ages had reared few magnificent structures in the Eternal City, in comparison with the cathedrals and guild halls of northern lands, and much of what was built then in Rome was destroyed by the architects of later times. The Rome of the popes was a baroque city, gorgeous and dramatic, in which emperors of ancient Rome would assuredly have felt at home.

Beside this lavishly decorated church the severely plain Senate House of yellowish brick (Plate 107) stands in sharp contrast. Yet no sumptuous monument touches the imagination more deeply than this building, small and now so unadorned.

Shortly before his death, Julius Caesar began a new Senate House on this site to replace the older one nearby. Though the Senate met in various temples, this was its own special home, dedicated, as was essential for a senatorial meeting place, to a deity. The patron of the Senate House was the goddess of Victory, whose statue Augustus set in its main hall when he finished Caesar's building. Domitian, late in the first century A.D., and Diocletian, two hundred years later, rebuilt the Senate House on this same site, centred always about the altar of Victory, where senators swore loyalty to the Empire and opened their sessions with offerings of wine and incense. So closely was this altar connected with the Roman state and the Roman state religion that it was almost inevitably the centre of one of the last open battles waged between paganism and Christianity.

Until nearly the end of the fourth century paganism, despite imperial decree and popular acceptance of Christianity, had a majority in the patrician and conservative Senate. The altar of Victory, first removed by imperial edict in 357, had been restored by Julian the Apostate, Constantine's nephew, during his brief attempt to revive the old religion. In 382 the Emperor Gratian again ordered its removal as part of an aggressive campaign against paganism, during which he refused the office of Pontifex Maximus, automatically bestowed upon the emperors, and forbade the use of State funds for pagan ceremonies.

Four times the pagan party of the Senate, meeting within these walls, petitioned for the altar's restoration. Symmachus, its leader, described Rome herself as a venerable matron pleading with the emperor: 'Most excellent princes . . . pity and respect my age, which has hitherto flowed in an uninterrupted course of piety. Since I do not repent, permit me to continue in the practice of my ancient rites. Since I am born free, allow me to enjoy my domestic institutions. This religion has reduced the world under my laws. These rites have repelled Hannibal from the city, and the Gauls from the Capitol.'

Though his predecessors were adamant, the altar was restored in 392 by the short-lived Emperor Eugenius. About 394, however, it was removed forever and the official triumph of Christianity was complete. When, in 410, Alaric the Visigoth sacked Rome, the remaining pagan element was quick to link this disaster with neglect of the old gods. To this, the new faith replied with one of the masterpieces of Christian literature—Saint Augustine's *City of God*, the Eternal City of the spirit rather than that of this world. Two centuries later the Senate House, with little external change, became the Christian church of Sant' Adriano.

Next to the Senate House there stood, in ancient times, the Basilica Aemilia, whose marble colonnades and rich carvings made Pliny class it among the three most beautiful buildings in the world. Some of its walls were still standing in the sixteenth century, but were then torn down, with only a few drawings left to suggest their lavish decoration. Lately some rediscovered and restored fragments have been set up on the excavated site and a few exquisitely carved reliefs removed to shelter.

Beside this basilica, toward the east, still stands the Temple of Antoninus and Faustina (Plates 109–110), whose greyed-white *cipollino* columns have, since the Middle Ages, housed the church of San Lorenzo in Miranda. For more than fifty years, guidebooks have declared that the present 'modern' or 'hideous' baroque church of 1602 is about to be demolished, but as this has not yet been done, it may be hoped that the picturesque contrast will remain as evidence of Rome's changing continuity.

The temple was erected by the Senate in honour of the deified empress
Faustina, wife of Antoninus Pius, after her death in A.D. 141. Twenty
years later, when the emperor himself had gone to join the gods, his
name was added to the inscription and the temple rededicated to both.
But even this enduring inscription could not prevent men of a later time
from sometimes confusing this emperor with his adopted son and successor, Marcus Aurelius Antoninus, married to another Faustina, daughter
of the first. To Christian antiquarians, no doubt, Marcus Aurelius seemed
a more fitting deity, if human deities there must be, because of the
nobility of his Stoic *Meditations*. Neither Faustina, according to most
standards, was worthy of deification, but the tradition of divine honours
to the imperial family was by now firmly established.

Separated from the Temple of Antoninus and Faustina by a clump of
deep green laurel trees and oleanders, rose and white, stands a little round
building (Plates 109–110) whose identity remains one of Rome's unsolved
problems. It has been called by many names but none has remained completely satisfying. It first emerged into the light of history when it was
consecrated, between 526 and 530, together with the large hall behind
it to which it formed a vestibule, as the church of Saints Cosmas and
Damian. The vestibule may not have been much more than two centuries old when it was consecrated to these twin Arabian physicians, for its
construction suggests that it was built early in the fourth century, in the
time of Maxentius or Constantine.

In the Middle Ages it was probably associated with the name of
Romulus the Founder, as were all the buildings in this neighbourhood.
The *Mirabilia* refers to 'the church of Saint Cosmas, that was the temple
of Asylum'. The Basilica of Constantine beyond it was then known as 'the
temple of Romulus', a name transferred by the seventeenth century to
the little round vestibule. Later it was called after another Romulus, the
son of Maxentius, who may have begun the building as a *heroon* or hero's
shrine in memory of his dead son. Originally the round building had a small
oblong room at each side, which jutted out closer to the Sacred Way. The
tall *cipollino* columns which still stand belonged to the portico of one of
these rooms.

In the seventeenth century, when baroque façades were being added to
so many buildings of ancient times, the front of this little vestibule was
remodelled and it was also given the cupola it has today. The surface of
the Forum had risen here, too, and the old bronze doors, which were
well below the ground-level, were taken out and reset higher up. In
1879–1880, however, when the Forum was being excavated, the baroque

façade was removed—though the cupola was left—and these doors, their ancient automatic lock still functioning, were replaced near their old level.

The large hall behind this little building (Plate 109), which forms the main church of Saints Cosmas and Damian today, is also puzzling. It is older than its vestibule, and was perhaps built at different periods. The only certainty about it at present is that it was probably some structure belonging to the Forum of Peace on which it faced. On the wall overlooking this forum Septimius Severus attached the Marble Plan of Rome, found in fragments at its foot. Christians have worshipped here for more than fourteen hundred years, while from the apse in its massive wall, Christ, in classic Roman robes, has looked down from a Byzantine pattern of gold-edged clouds against a deep blue sky, and Peter and Paul have presented to Him the saints for whom the church was named. In this old mosaic the realistic human qualities and rounded form of ancient Roman art are passing, and in their place are dawning the formal composition and flat, stylized designs of the Byzantine East.

The Arch of Titus (Plates 120–123) at the *Summa Sacra Via*, the highest point of the Sacred Way, now spans the eastern entrance to the Forum. A worn ancient pavement leads down from it past the Temple of Antoninus and Faustina. Between the arch and the Basilica of Constantine stands the church of Santa Francesca Romana, the medieval church of Santa Maria Nova (Plate 131), founded in the ruins of the temple of Venus and Rome, rebuilt several times, and finally rededicated to Santa Francesca, who had been revered here for years in the place where she was buried. Behind the baroque façade rises the bell tower of Saint Mary's, adding a medieval note to the span of centuries.

At times in the sunlit hush of the Forum today one regrets the loss of that everyday activity, whether of ancient Romans or of cattle and their drovers, which marked the place through so many centuries. Yet the Forum has a life of its own, though it is not as clearly linked as the Capitol with both past and present. Today, from behind a mass of masonry or a clump of laurels, come the voices of workmen setting up some fragment which may have lain unknown years beneath the earth. Tourists, their noses in guidebooks, pursue eternally their search for facts eternally liable to change, or sit happily in a golden dream upon a marble step on which Augustus may have stood. Day after day artists, young and old, singly or in groups, sketch the ruins as they have done for so many centuries. And from the oleanders by Faustina's temple, when friendly feet pass quietly along the Sacred Way, may come one of Rome's cherished cats, tail erect, to rub ankles or to bask in the sun upon some carved marble of days long gone.

Time and the hands of men are healing the scars of excavation which made Zola, more than half a century ago, call the Forum 'a long, clean, livid trench'. In some places this barrenness persists today; in others ivy and wistaria and roses veil a shattered column, or oleanders and white-spiked acanthus soften the outline of a ruined wall. Caesar and Augustus and Cicero and Antony are links with a memorable and moving past, but a new and kindly beauty of the present is stealing through the Forum—a beauty which changes as the hours pass. On a May morning cloud shadows sweep darkly across the ancient paving of the Sacred Way. As evening comes, the setting sun behind the Capitol gilds the flutings and rich ornaments of its fallen monuments (Plate 117) and lights the Arch of Titus rising in stately simplicity at its eastern end (Plate 119). And at night when the moon rides high and white across the deep sky, the stone pines and ilexes of the Palatine rise sharp and black above the Forum, stately guardians of a gracious sleep.

TRIUMPHAL ARCHES

Plates 120–127

THREE of the great triumphal arches which were among Rome's unique contributions to architecture stand today: the Arch of Severus at the west end of the Forum (Plate 107), the Arch of Titus at its eastern end (Plate 120), and the Arch of Constantine beyond it (Plate 124). Strangely enough, little is recorded in ancient literature about these three; more is known of those which have disappeared. The three which remain, however, have kept their identity through the centuries because of clearly readable inscriptions.

By the Middle Ages such arches had become outstanding 'marvels' from the imperial past. The *Mirabilia* defined them as 'Arches Triumphal . . . the which were made for an Emperor returning from a triumph, and whereunder they were led with worship by the senators, and his victory was graven thereon for a remembrance to posterity.' This definition gives a vivid picture of the pageantry of imperial Rome and was undoubtedly in the minds of those who cleared the way for the triumphal procession of Charles V in 1536 from the Arch of Titus through the Forum and the Arch of Severus. It is not, however, completely accurate. The permanent arches probably replaced temporary structures which were erected for the actual procession of a general or emperor after a successful war. In some cases the finished arch was so constructed that no procession could pass under it. That of Severus, for instance, was approached by steps; no road led under it in ancient times; the road did not run beneath but beside the Arch of Constantine.

The Arch of Titus does span the Sacred Way, but though it commemorates the capture of Jerusalem in A.D. 70, the victor never saw it completed; it was erected some time after his death in 81. It is not mentioned in ancient literature, but a late Roman relief shows it with the title ARCUS IN SACRA VIA SUMMA, 'Arch at the summit of the Sacred Way'.

Its medieval name 'Arch of the Seven Lamps', or, as the *Mirabilia* puts it, 'Arch of the Seven Lamps of Titus and Vespasian', comes from the famous relief on one of its inner faces showing the seven-branched candlestick and other spoils from the temple at Jerusalem carried in triumph through Rome (Plate 122). A later version adds 'where is Moses his candlestick having seven branches, with the Ark'. The oblong object

(75)

carried in this relief is not, however, the Ark but the golden table of the shewbread used in the temple ritual.

In the Middle Ages the Arch of Titus was included in the fortress of the Frangipani family and had a room built into its upper story. Much of this structure was removed in the fifteenth century but some still appears in Van Heemskerck's drawing (Plate 121). When the supporting buildings at the sides were taken down in 1821, the centre was found to be so weakened that the architect Valadier rebuilt the lost ends in travertine. The original inscription still remains on the eastern side, which appears in the drawing; Valadier copied it for the side facing the Forum.

East of the Arch of Titus and close by the Colosseum stands the Arch of Constantine (Plate 124), which recalls, perhaps more than any other monument in Rome except the Senate House, the victory of Christianity. It was erected about A.D. 315 in honour of Constantine's victory over his rival Maxentius at the Milvian Bridge near Rome in 312—the victory which, according to tradition, led to the emperor's recognition of Christianity the next year. It was just before this battle, so the story goes, that he beheld the vision of the cross with the motto 'In this sign thou shalt conquer'. The inscription extols not only the emperor's greatness of mind but also 'the inspiration of the Deity' (unnamed), but since deity had, by this time, become an imperial attribute, nothing concerning the emperor's religion then can be gathered from this statement. Like the Arch of Titus, that of Constantine passes unnoticed in existing classical literature.

Though harmonious in its general conception, Constantine's arch is largely made up of fragments from earlier monuments. Among these older parts are the round medallions on the two long sides; all the reliefs of the upper story and of the middle passage; and the free-standing figures, now considerably restored, which are above the columns. Of Constantine's time, and of much cruder workmanship, are the narrow bands of relief above the side arches and on the ends, those on the bases of the columns, and the delightfully designed round medallions on the ends showing the setting moon and the rising sun.

In the Middle Ages and Renaissance this was sometimes popularly called the *arcus Thracius* or *Arco de Trasio* from the free-standing figures of the Thracian or Dacian prisoners above the columns, which Constantine borrowed from some monument of Trajan's. The *Mirabilia*, however, gives it the old name, 'Arch of Constantine by the Amphitheatre', keeping for both it and the Colosseum the terms used by Romans of antiquity.

THE BASILICA OF CONSTANTINE OR MAXENTIUS

Plates 128–131

THREE immense vaults of the Basilica of Constantine or Maxentius (Plate 128) dominate the Forum's northeastern end. Little is known of the early days of this building; it came too late into the ancient world to find a place among the great descriptions in Latin literature, though it is mentioned briefly in several writings of the fourth and fifth centuries, including the *Notitia* or Regionary Catalogue. Maxentius began it during his brief period of power from A.D. 306 to 312, on a site which excavation has shown to have been occupied at various times by private houses, part of the portico of Nero's Golden House, and markets and storehouses.

As first planned, it had a nave and two aisles running lengthwise approximately east and west, parallel to the Roman Forum and opening eastward through an arched portico toward the Colosseum. At the west end of the nave, opposite this entrance, was a large apse where, in the fifteenth century, were found parts of a colossal statue of Constantine, now in the Conservatori Museum.

Constantine changed this plan by adding another entrance at the south side so that the building opened on the Forum as well as toward the Colosseum. He also built another apse opposite this entrance, in the central compartment of the north aisle, which, like its southern counterpart, was divided into three barrel-vaulted sections, each large enough to contain a good-sized building.

It is this north aisle, with Constantine's apse, which towers impressively beyond the Forum today. Part of the western end wall, with the apse of Maxentius, also stands, and here and there jagged fragments of masonry which belonged to the great piers of the nave still rise from the high platform on which the basilica rests.

The building was of brick-faced concrete, the interior walls panelled with marble, the brick coffering of its vaults covered with stucco. Fluted marble columns with richly carved Corinthian capitals originally stood against the piers, apparently carrying the weight of the massive cross-vaulting of the nave, though this was actually borne by the piers themselves. The last of these marble columns, one of which still appears in place in prints and drawings of the sixteenth century, was taken away in

(77)

the seventeenth and set up in the Piazza of Santa Maria Maggiore to bear the statue of the Virgin.

Just when the nave and south aisle collapsed is unknown. Probably they were badly damaged by the earthquake of the ninth century and perhaps by a later one as well. By the Middle Ages the mass of ruin was a giant quarry for building materials; as it began to emerge from the realm of legend into that of record, the remnant was in use for such purposes as hay lofts, cattle sheds, drill grounds, and a riding school.

The building was far too large to be converted easily into a church; its central nave was over 262 feet long, more than 97 feet wide, and almost 115 feet high. It would have required the genius and technical resources of a Michelangelo to make use of it, as he later did the central hall of the Baths of Diocletian, but by his time the basilica was in the same state of ruin as today. The barrel vaulting of its aisle, however, was one of Bramante's inspirations for the plan he proposed for the new Saint Peter's.

The great ruin has gone by various names throughout its long history. Most early records call it simply the New Basilica, but by the sixth century its true identity was so far forgotten that it was referred to as the 'Temple of Rome' and later as the 'Temple of Romulus'. By the fifteenth century it was known as the 'Temple of Peace,' from the actual but long-since-vanished temple which stood nearby in Vespasian's forum of that name. With the name went the associations of the real Temple of Peace. The basilica was believed to have been built by Vespasian and to have housed the plunder of the temple at Jerusalem and innumerable other treasures. It was called 'the Temple of Peace' well into the nineteenth century. In Rome today it is better known by the name of Maxentius, who began it, than by that of Constantine, who completed it.

John Evelyn's *Diary* for 1644 gives a typical gentleman's glimpse of the ruin as it was known in the seventeenth century:

'We went into the *Campo Vaccino*, by the ruins of the Temple of Peace, built by Titus Vespasianus, and thought to be the largest as well as the most richly furnished of all the Roman dedicated places: it is now a heap rather than a temple, yet the roof and *volto* continue firm, showing it to have been formerly of incomparable workmanship.' Evelyn adds the surprising statement, contradicted by his own dating of it in Vespasian's time: 'This goodly structure was, none know how, consumed by fire the very night, by all computation, that our Blessed Saviour was born.'

Almost two centuries later the American traveller, Theodore Dwight, described the ruin as it appeared to the romantic visitor:

'Nearly opposite to us on the other side of the Forum were the remains of the Temple of Peace, which are supposed to have formed for the time the vestibule of Nero's house; and here we were struck with astonishment, having never seen such wide and noble arches. . . . The remaining arches of the Temple of Peace have been left exposed to the sunshine and rain, hallowed however in the eyes of the people by a small cross elevated at the top, among the shrubbery with which it is crowned, to preserve them from dilapidation, though cattle often wander to its shade from the Forum (which in Italian bears the name of Cow-Pasture), and lie quietly down in the inmost recesses of the temple.'

The basilica's great vaults have been put to a new use since 1933; a use which would undoubtedly have pleased the dwellers in ancient Rome as much as it does her citizens and visitors today. On spring afternoons and summer nights, concerts by orchestra and chorus are held in its great area (Plate 131), the musicians stationed beneath an inconspicuous shell built into Constantine's apse. Besides the crowds which can be seated on chairs and benches, adventurous climbers find superior accommodations on the tops of the ruined piers, and black-frocked priests listen from the roof of the neighbouring church of Saints Cosmas and Damian. The vaults are lit by night with an orange glow, which throws their deep coffering into strong relief. Beyond the arches of the portico the Colosseum gleams in silver floodlight, while the façade of Santa Francesca Romana and sometimes the buildings in the Forum as well stand out red or green or orange against the blue-black sky.

THE COLOSSEUM

Plates 132–141

THE Colosseum was a 'marvel' of Rome when it was new, almost nine-teen hundred years ago, partly because of its size and partly because the circumstances under which it was built made it one of the world's great 'gallery plays'. 'Here, where the far-seen Amphitheatre lifts its mass august,' wrote Martial, 'was Nero's mere.' Vespasian had drained the artificial lake in the gardens of Nero's Golden House and begun upon its site this vast theatre for the games and spectacles dear to Roman hearts, which his son Titus was to finish. Nero, last emperor of the line of Caesar and Augustus, had died by his own hand, hated by the people and the army and declared a public enemy by the Senate. Within a year, the Roman legions nominated three successors, also doomed to quick and violent deaths. Vespasian, the final candidate, was more fortunate. A popular general, who was waging a successful siege against Jerusalem when he was chosen emperor, he returned to Rome and set about the task of blotting out the evil memory of Nero.

A man of humble birth and shrewd common sense, without the legendary glamour of the Julian dynasty, he, together with Titus, suc-ceeded in building up the prestige of the new imperial line, largely through a far-reaching programme of public works by which the people were given back as recreation centres much of the land which Nero had confiscated for his own pleasures. Suetonius echoed the popular response to this policy in a remark concerning Titus, probably written within half a century of that emperor's death: 'He took away nothing from any citizen. He respected others' property, if anyone ever did. . . . And yet he was second to none of his predecessors in munificence.'

The Colosseum was practically ready for use when Vespasian died in A.D. 79. Titus opened it, still unfinished, in A.D. 80, with magnificent gladiatorial games and naval contests for which the arena was flooded. It was completed by Domitian, Titus' brother and successor, but had to be restored several times because of fires due to lightning.

Standing isolated beyond the Forum, in the low spot between the Palatine, Esquiline, and Caelian hills, this new amphitheatre was easily accessible from the heart of the ancient city, yet isolated enough to permit the easy movement of crowds. It could seat about forty-five thousand, and probably had standing room for about five thousand more in its upper gallery. Its great oval shell was about one-third of a mile in circumference, its longer axis measuring about 617 feet, its shorter about 512. The long axis, whose entrances were used for processions, runs parallel with the Roman Forum, roughly southeast and northwest. The imperial seats were at the south side, facing along the shorter axis, to give a closer view of the spectacles. Immense awnings, handled by sailors from the imperial fleet, sheltered the spectators.

Though the exterior of the great building is impressive by reason of its severe and solid bulk, its outstanding feature was its perfect adaptation to the handling of large and potentially unruly crowds. Seventy-six of its eighty arcades were numbered; the tickets bore corresponding numbers, so that holders could find their way directly to their seats from the appropriate entrance without crowding the corridors. It was a structure to delight the practical Vespasian and the architectural engineers who had built it.

The Colosseum's builders followed much the same principle as that employed in steel construction today, except that for the skeleton framework of piers and arches they used hard travertine stone. The outer walls are of the same stone; the inner ones are composed of several kinds of stone and concrete, with or without brick facings. Metal cramps reinforced the joining of the stones; the holes now so noticeable in the walls were made in the centuries following the decline of Rome by those who dug out these cramps for their metal or for the lead which was sometimes used with them.

The tradition that Christians by the thousands were martyred in the arena grew up in comparatively late times. Some may have suffered here during various persecutions, but, needless to say, not in those of Nero's day, as the site was then the emperor's lake. The last gladiatorial games were held in the Colosseum in A.D. 404; emperors from the time of Constantine had tried to stop them without success. The last recorded animal sports are mentioned in 523.

The ancient Romans called this building the Flavian Amphitheatre from the family of Flavius to which Vespasian and his sons, Titus and Domitian, belonged. The present name came into use some time during the early Middle Ages. The first-known mention of the amphitheatre as the Colosseum is in an eighth-century Latin work traditionally ascribed to the English monk and historian, Bede. The writer of this work quotes a current Saxon pilgrim's proverb: *Quandiu stabit Coliseus, stabit et Roma; quando cadet Coliseus, cadet et Roma; quando cadet Roma, cadet et mundus*, which today is best known through Byron's translation in *Childe Harold*:

> 'While stands the Coliseum, Rome shall stand;
> When falls the Coliseum, Rome shall fall:
> And when Rome falls—the world.'

Some have held that this proverb referred not to the amphitheatre but to the colossal bronze statue of Nero which stood nearby, remodelled by later emperors as a sun god. No one knows just when this colossus fell—the last known reference to it in ancient times was in A.D. 354 when it was mentioned as the 'crowned colossus' in connection with a spring festival of garland sellers along the Sacred Way. It had probably disappeared by Bede's time, for the eighth-century Einsiedeln *Itinerary* did not mention it, although its fame lingered throughout the Middle Ages. It seems more likely that such a proverb would grow up about an immense and enduring building than about a statue which was only one of several of its kind in Rome, and that the building was first called 'colossal amphitheatre' and then 'colosseum' because of its great size.

The Colosseum was damaged by earthquakes in the fifth and sixth centuries, again in 847, and perhaps in the fourteenth century as well. Originally it was entirely surrounded by a double arcade, but in the course of these earthquakes the outer ring of arches fell along the whole southwestern side, forming a mountainous quarry which for centuries furnished building material for the palaces and churches of Rome.

Such plundering stopped in the eighteenth century, and early in the nineteenth the popes began to strengthen the broken ends of the walls with buttresses. Unbroken though it looks from its least damaged side, less than half of the great building stands today.

Medieval tradition played strange tricks with the purpose and appearance of the Colosseum. The early form of the *Mirabilia* simply mentions it, saying, 'Before the Colosseum was the temple of the Sun'—referring, perhaps, to the nearby Temple of Venus and Rome. A later version embellished this simple statement to read: 'The Colosseum was the temple of the Sun, of marvellous greatness and beauty, disposed with many diverse vaulted chambers, and all covered with an heaven of gilded brass, where thunders and lightnings and glittering fires were made, and where rain was shed through slender tubes. Besides this there were the Signs supercelestial and the planets *Sol* and *Luna*, that were drawn along in their proper chariots.' Here there seem to be confused echoes of the 'old chronicles' to which the twelfth-century compiler of the *Mirabilia* referred. One of these may have been the description by Suetonius of Nero's Golden House, written about half a century after that emperor's death: 'There were dining rooms with fretted ceilings of ivory, whose panels could turn and shower down flowers and were fitted with pipes for sprinkling the guests with perfumes. The main banquet hall was circular and constantly revolved day and night, like the heavens.' The Middle Ages, from whatever source they had their information, took the *Mirabilia's* description literally and pictured the Colosseum with a dome.

The ruins of the ancient building have seen many uses. There are records of mystery plays held there in the fifteenth and sixteenth centuries. In 1490 the Confraternity of the Gonfalone, a group of citizens vowed to charitable works, produced in the Colosseum the first of its Passion Plays—a mystery in seven acts in the Roman dialect. Arnold of Harff, a German visitor to Rome in 1497, wrote of seeing: 'A magnificent ancient palace, called the Colosseum, round in shape, vaulted and with various orders of architecture, and having in its centre a round open space surrounded by steps which made it possible to ascend to the upper part. In ancient times, they say, men sat on these steps to watch combats between gladiators and wild beasts. I saw there, on Holy Thursday, the Passion of Jesus Christ. Living men represented the Flagellation, the Crucifixion, the Death of Judas, and so forth. Those who took part were youths of well-to-do families and everything was conducted with great order and decorum.'

Considerable disorder was reported from time to time, however, and the plays were finally abolished under Paul III (1534–1549) because they had become too secular to be countenanced by the Church.

The use of the Colosseum for religious spectacles did not prevent the popular imagination from peopling it with the devils who were always ready to take over pagan monuments. A bull is said to have been sacrificed in the Colosseum to appease the demons during a pestilence in 1522; Benvenuto Cellini tells the classic tale of sorcery there in his *Autobiography*.

In 1534 he and a renegade Sicilian priest decided to consult the demons which were said to haunt the place. 'We went together to the Coliseum,' he wrote, 'and there the priest, having arrayed himself in necromancer's robes, began to describe circles on the earth with the finest ceremonies that can be imagined.' The ceremonies having brought little result (they saw only several legions of devils that night) they returned again and were well rewarded. 'In a short space of time the whole Coliseum was full of a hundredfold as many as had appeared upon the first occasion.' The boy who served as a medium 'shrieked out in terror that a million of the fiercest men were swarming round and threatening us. He said, moreover, that four huge giants had appeared, who were striving to force their way into the circle' and again that 'the whole Coliseum is in flames, and the fire is advancing on us'. When the devils were finally routed and the party was going home, the boy 'kept saying that two of the devils he had seen in the Coliseum were gambolling in front of us, skipping now along the roofs and now upon the ground'.

Meanwhile the popes had entertained various plans for the Colosseum. Sixtus V proposed to turn it into a cloth manufactory, for which he had Fontana prepare drawings, but at the pope's death in 1590 this idea was abandoned. Clement IX in the seventeenth century stored saltpetre in it for use in a neighbouring gunpowder factory.

In 1744 Benedict XIV moved to put an end to both plundering and superstitious practices by consecrating the arena to the memory of the Christians martyred there, whose numbers tradition had now brought into the thousands. He also set up the central cross and its stations, which appear in so many pictures of the late eighteenth and nineteenth centuries. These were removed for excavations in the eighteen-seventies, but the cross was renewed in 1927.

By the nineteenth century the broken walls were in danger of collapse; more stone had been brought down by an earthquake in 1703. Pius VII began the work of strengthening and supporting them by buttressing the outer wall of the east end between 1805 and 1807. Leo XII erected a similar support for the outer wall of the west end in 1825, and Gregory XVI and Pius IX continued the work in 1845 and 1852. Leo XII's great western buttress of 1825, which appears in the views most widely known, has become so familiar as to seem an integral part of the structure. Turner's drawings and paintings of 1819 are among the last well-known pictures to show the old, vertical crumbling edge instead of the present smooth and sloping line. This new buttress must have been barely completed when Corot painted his views of the Colosseum in 1825 and 1826 (Plates 130, 135).

Excavation had begun early in the century and was continued for many years, until the whole area of the arena, originally covered with removable wooden flooring and later filled with the earth and debris of centuries, was finally laid bare, revealing the dens where beasts were kept for performances and the chambers which housed the mechanical contrivances used in the elaborate settings of spectacles.

Despite consecration and excavation the Colosseum had a bad reputation after nightfall, and from time to time it was closed at dusk or patrolled by guards. One hazard against which no guard could avail was the 'Roman fever', believed to haunt its shadows after sunset. Lovers of the romantic moonlit peace of the great ruin were quick to blame this on the excavators, who had opened long-closed vaults and, it was said, disarranged the ancient drainage. Yet in spite of its ill-repute, visits to the Colosseum by night grew more and more popular in the nineteenth century, moonlight and meditation replacing Cellini's spectral flames and demons.

In 1787, as the romantic movement was taking shape, Goethe had written: 'Of the beauty of a walk through Rome by moonlight, it is impossible to form a conception, without having witnessed it. All single objects are swallowed up by the great masses of light and shade, and nothing but grand and general outlines present themselves to the eye. . . . Peculiarly beautiful at such a time is the Coliseum. At night it is always closed; a hermit dwells in a little shrine within its range, and beggars of all kinds nestle beneath its crumbling arches.'

Twenty years later Byron's descriptions shaped the nineteenth-century conception of the Colosseum by moonlight. Of these two descriptions, that in the third act of *Manfred* was written in Rome. The original draft of the act, finished in March of 1817, did not contain this passage. Then, in late April and May, the poet visited Rome and there re-wrote this part, adding the soliloquy in which his hero recalls:

> '. . . upon such a night
> I stood within the Coliseum's wall,
> 'Midst the chief relics of almighty Rome;
> The trees which grew along the broken arches
> Waved dark in the blue midnight, and the stars
> Shone through the rents of ruin; from afar
> The watch-dog bayed beyond the Tiber; and
> More near from out the Caesars' palace came
> The owl's long cry, and, interruptedly,
> Of distant sentinels the fitful song
> Begun and died upon the gentle wind.
> . . . .
> And thou didst shine, thou rolling moon, upon
> All this, and cast a wide and tender light,
> Which softened down the hoar austerity
> Of rugged desolation, and filled up,
> As 't were anew, the gaps of centuries;
> Leaving that beautiful which still was so,
> And making that which was not, till the place
> Became religion, and the heart ran o'er
> With silent worship of the great of old,—
> The dead, but sceptred sovereigns, who still rule
> Our spirits from their urns— . . . .'

The fourth canto of *Childe Harold*, written in the summer of 1817 after Byron had been gone from the city for some weeks, was drawn from emotion freshly recollected:

> 'Arches on arches! as it were that Rome,
> Collecting the chief trophies of her line,
> Would build up all her triumphs in one dome,—
> Her Coliseum stands; the moonbeams shine
> As 't were its natural torches, for divine
> Should be the light which streams here, to illume
> This long-explored but still exhaustless mine
> Of contemplation; and the azure gloom
> Of an Italian night, where the deep skies assume
>
> Hues that have words, and speak to ye of heaven,
> Floats o'er this vast and wondrous monument,
> And shadows forth its glory. There is given
> Unto the things of earth, which Time hath bent,
> A spirit's feeling, and where he hath leant
> His hand, but broke his scythe, there is a power
> And magic in the ruined battlement,
> From which the palace of the present hour
> Must yield its pomp, and wait till ages are its dower.
>
> A ruin—yet what ruin! from its mass
> Walls, palaces, half-cities, have been reared;
> Yet oft the enormous skeleton ye pass,
> And marvel where the spoil could have appeared.
> Hath it indeed been plundered, or but cleared?
> Alas! developed, opens the decay,
> When the colossal fabric's form is neared:
> It will not bear the brightness of the day,
> Which streams too much on all years, man, have reft away.'

Probably few visitors in the next hundred years stood in the Colosseum by moonlight without at least some dim memory of Byron's lines. Certainly they were in Longfellow's mind when he wrote of the Colosseum at midnight in 1828:

'Silence, and the quiet moonbeams, and the broad, deep shadows of the ruined wall. . . . At length I came to an open space where the arches above had crumbled away, leaving the pavement an unroofed terrace high in air. From this point, I could see the whole interior of the amphitheatre spread out beneath me, half in shadow, half in light, with such soft and indefinite outline that it seemed less an earthly reality than a reflection in the bosom of a lake. . . . I did not conjure up the past, for the past had already become identified with the present.'

Hawthorne, however, found the famous spectacle less impressive than he had imagined it. The moonlight which 'filled and flooded the great empty space,' he wrote in *The Marble Faun*, 'glowed upon tier above tier of ruined, grass-grown arches, and made them even too distinctly visible. The splendour of the revelation took away that inestimable effect of dimness and mystery by which the imagination might be assisted to build up a grander structure than the Coliseum, and to shatter it with a more picturesque decay. Byron's celebrated description is better than the reality.'

Henry James' American heroine of the seventies, Daisy Miller, was typical of a generation whose minds had been steeped in such descriptions. Lingering 'at midnight in the Colosseum with a gentleman' she risked her reputation and her health because, as she retorted to her critics, 'I was bound to see the Colosseum by moonlight. I wouldn't have wanted to go home without *that*. . . . Well, I *have* seen the Colosseum by moonlight— that's one thing I can rave about.' It was in keeping with the etiquette and tradition of the time and place that this 'child of nature and of freedom' should die of a fever contracted at her midnight tryst and be buried 'in the little Protestant cemetery, by an angle of the wall of imperial Rome, beneath the cypresses and the thick spring-flowers.'

As for Winterbourne, dispassionate observer of her innocent tragedy, he himself stood in the Colosseum by night murmuring 'Byron's famous lines out of *Manfred*' until he remembered that 'the air of other ages, coldly analysed was no better than a villainous miasma.'

The moonlight and the flowers of the Colosseum were almost equally celebrated in the nineteenth century (Plates 136–139). In 1813 Antonio Sebastiani published his *Flora Colisea*, listing 261 species. By 1855 Richard Deakin's classic *Flora of the Colosseum* noted 420 species growing from the fertile ancient dust. Among these were figs, cherries, and pears; elms and caper trees; grapes, ivy, clematis, and roses; hyacinths, narcissus, gentians, daisies, and cyclamen; acanthus, thyme, rosemary, and sage; marigolds, violets, larkspur, and anemones; saxifrage, pimpernel, and strawberries. The ruin had already been weeded to some extent by the French in 1812, but the flowers had evidently returned in full force by Deakin's time. In 1869 they so strongly impressed Longfellow on his last

Roman visit that he wrote of them in his unfinished poem, *Michel Angelo*:

> '. . . A thousand wild flowers bloom
> From every chink, and the birds build their nests
> Among the ruined arches, and suggest
> New thoughts of beauty to the architect.'

In 1870–1871, however, Pietro Rosa, director of excavations, fearing the effect of roots upon ancient stones, had the ruin weeded thoroughly. Gregorovius noted in his *Roman Journals* for June 18,1871: 'Rosa has shaved even the Colosseum—that is to say, has cleared away all the plants that made it so beautiful.' Yet even today an occasional anemone or mourning bride or cluster of caper blossoms hides in remote crevices and grass continually finds its way among the paving stones.

The romantic appeals of flowers and moonlight blend in Thomas Cole's description, written in 1832:

'From the great multitude of wondrous things, I would select the Colosseum as the object that affected me the most. It is stupendous, yet beautiful in its destruction. From the broad arena within, it rises around, arch above arch, broken and desolate, and mantled in many parts with the laurustinus, the acanthus, and numerous other plants and flowers, exquisite both for their colour and fragrance. It looks more like a work of nature than of man; for the regularity of art is lost, in a great measure, in dilapidation, and the luxuriant herbage, clinging to its ruins as if to "mouth its distress", completes the illusion. Crag rises over crag, green and breezy summits mount into the sky.

'But he who would see and feel the grandeur of the Colosseum must spend his hour there, at night, when the moon is shedding over it its magic splendour. Let him ascend to its higher terraces, at that pensive time, and gaze down into the abyss.'

Cole's painting, *Interior of the Colosseum*, in a private collection in America, does not, however, suggest the softening profusion of flowers. It has rather the stark severity described in another passage: 'The mighty spectacle, mysterious and dark, opens beneath the eye more like some awful dream than an earthly reality,—a vision of the valley and shadow of death. . . . As I mused upon its great circumference, I seemed to be sounding the depth of some volcanic crater, whose fires, long extinguished, had left the ribbed and blasted rocks to the wild-flower and the ivy.'

In recent years the Colosseum has slept, for the most part, in undisturbed and excavated quiet, except for religious processions and occasional assemblies. Electricity has dimmed the mystery of its moonlight, though floodlights (Plate 141) give it a spectacular grandeur in keeping with the temperament of those who thronged it long ago. But by day its travertine walls present a timeless panorama of eternally changing colour, varying with the weather and the hour from ash-grey to gold or to a rose intense enough, at sunset, to rival the Alpine glow.

In 1951 the ancient amphitheatre welcomed an audience to a recreation markedly different from its bloody spectacles of long ago. The Sunday afternoon of October 7 saw the first of a series of concerts which continued into the fall and winter season (Plate 140). The orchestra and singers from the opera were installed opposite the imperial seats, and a temporary wooden floor was laid above part of the great arena. The concert, a commemoration of the fiftieth anniversary of Verdi's death, was not an artistic success, for the acoustics were poor. But the listeners were enthusiastic, partly because of the music, partly because of their affection for favourite singers, and partly, perhaps, because they felt that same spell of the past which touched Arnold of Harff more than four hundred years ago.

THE GOLDEN HOUSE OF NERO

Plates 142–147

BENEATH the surface of the Esquiline hill, close by the Colosseum, lie the remnants of Nero's fabled Golden House, crushed and buried by his successors in their campaign to obliterate his memory. The Baths of Trajan, built above its ruins early in the second century A.D., were part of this campaign, which had begun with the erection of the Colosseum on the site of Nero's lake and the hasty building of the Baths of Titus nearby. Martial echoed the feeling of the time when he wrote of the dedication of these two: 'Rome has been restored to herself, under thy governance, Caesar; that is now the delight of the people which was once a master's.'

Nero began his Golden House after the fire of A.D. 64 had destroyed much of Rome. With its gardens and porticoes it covered not only part of the Palatine but also much of the Esquiline and Caelian hills, stretching across the low-lying site of the Colosseum and around to the Forum on which its vestibule opened. This vestibule, wrote Suetonius, 'was large enough to contain a colossal statue of the emperor a hundred and twenty feet high and it was so extensive that it had a triple colonnade a mile long.' The palace received the name 'Golden House' from the amount of gilding used in its decoration. On its walls and ceilings the famous painter Fabullus was kept so fully occupied that Pliny said 'the golden Palace of Nero was the prison house of this artist's work.'

The palace was still unfinished when Nero died in A.D. 68. One of his short-lived successors set aside funds to carry it on and Vespasian and Titus lived in it for a little while, but they were more concerned with restoring the grounds to public use than with housing themselves magnificently. The actual palace buildings had never covered the Colosseum's site.

A fire in A.D. 104 damaged the Golden House so severely that Trajan felt no compunction about levelling part of the site, filling in the lower floor as a foundation, and building his baths above. Possibly he meant to do this had there been no fire. The vestibule opening on the east end of the Forum was finally destroyed by Hadrian in A.D. 121, before he built the Temple of Venus and Rome on a portion of its location. After this the palace appears no more in the history of the ancient world, but is left to the legends of the Middle Ages.

When the long darkness began to lift in the twelfth century, these buried rooms seem to have been forgotten, though the name of Nero haunted Rome. The *Mirabilia* and the *Graphia* located his palace at such different places as the Lateran and the circus across the Tiber near Saint Peter's. The medieval tower of the Milizie was popularly known as the place from which Nero watched Rome burn, and the great ruined Temple of the Sun or Serapis on the Quirinal was often called the *Frontispizio di Nerone*, Façade of Nero.

The ruined Baths of Trajan above the actual Golden House were long named the Baths or Palace of Titus. The underground rooms there, belonging to the Golden House, were finally discovered late in the fifteenth century, when the reviving interest in ancient times and art spurred on the search for antiquities. Artists flocked to study the new-found paintings (Plates 142–143) although the rooms were filled with debris and earth to the springing of their vaults. The earliest known sketches from these paintings are those of the anonymous artist of the *Codex Escurialensis*, about 1491. Early in the sixteenth century Raphael and his assistant, Giovanni da Udine, were so enchanted by the light and fantastic paintings and the delicate stucco reliefs that the master employed the same type of decoration for the Vatican *loggie* which were painted under his direction in 1517–1519 (Plate 145). As Nero's buried rooms were called caves or grottoes, the style of their decoration was called 'grotesque'—a term usually applied today to the fantastic and incongruous forms associated with medieval carvings.

High up on the walls near the great arch which spans the long corridor in the eastern wing of the Golden House (Plate 142), generations of artists have written or scratched their names, sometimes with dates. The earliest date is 1495, accompanied by an almost unreadable name. Giovanni da Udine's name is there, Domenichino's, and that of Carl van Mander of Holland, who so vividly described Marten van Heemskerck's delight in Rome. Many artists of the sixteenth century and later have left sketches of the decorations they saw here and in other buried rooms.

No thorough excavation of the Golden House was made in these early days. The Roman art dealer, Mirri, who published a collection of engravings from its paintings in 1776, had to have sixteen rooms partially excavated in order to have drawings made for his engravers. More scientific excavation of part of the palace began in the early nineteenth century and fresh excavations are still going on.

Charlotte Eaton left an enthusiastic description of the rooms she was able to see in 1817–1818:

'The Thermae and Palace of Titus,' she wrote, 'were built within the ruins, and on the site of the wide-spreading buildings and pleasure-grounds of Nero's Golden Palace. . . . We entered a damp and dark corridor, the ceiling of which is still adorned with some of the most beautiful specimens that now remain of the paintings of antiquity. Their colouring is fast fading away, and their very outline, I should fear must be obliterated at no very distant period, so extreme is the humidity of the place, and so incessantly does the water-drop fall. By the light of a few trembling tapers elevated on the top of a long bending cane, we saw, at least twenty feet above our heads, paintings in arabesques, executed with a grace, a freedom, a correctness of design, and masterly command of pencil that awakened our highest admiration, in spite of all the disadvantages under which they were viewed. Insensible of the penetrating damps and chilling cold, we continued to stretch our necks with admiring the Faun, the Nymph, the Bacchante, the Mercury, the Loves and Graces, the twining flowers and fantastic groups of gay imagery, which the classical imagination of the Roman painter had assembled seventeen centuries ago.'

Mrs. Eaton's comment suggests the worst drawback of the decorative scheme—the use of motifs so light and small in scale that their delicate detail can scarcely be seen in rooms of such great height.

Besides employing the foremost painters to decorate his palace walls, Nero enriched it with movable sculpture as well. Many of these pieces remained there during the reigns of Vespasian and Titus, but Trajan later moved some of them to his baths above.

The Elder Pliny, shortly before his death in A.D. 79, noted in his *Natural History* one of the most famous of the statues there: 'The Laocoön, which stands in the palace of the Emperor Titus, a work to be preferred to all that the arts of painting and sculpture have produced. Out of one block of stone the consummate artists, Agesandros, Polydoros, and Athenodoros of Rhodes made, after careful planning, Laocoön, his sons, and the snakes marvellously entwined about them.'

This group, perhaps a Roman copy of a Hellenistic work of the second century B.C., represents the punishment of Laocoön, Apollo's disobedient priest at Troy, crushed, with his sons, by monstrous serpents sent by the angry god (Plate 146).

After Pliny's reference, more than fourteen centuries of silence closed about the group. Then, in 1506, a Roman gentleman by the name of de Fredis, digging out inconvenient ancient walls in his vineyard in the neighbourhood of the Baths of Trajan and probably in the buried rooms of the Golden House itself, came upon this marble comparatively undamaged. It was recognized immediately from Pliny's description.

Julius II claimed it for a jewel of the papal collection, and Rome celebrated a festival in its honour. The leading sculptors of the day, including Michelangelo, examined it, and though they concluded that Pliny had been wrong in thinking it wrought from one block of marble, they agreed that it was 'most excellent and deserving of every praise'. Discovered just at the beginning of that baroque movement which was so near akin to the art of imperial Rome, it exercised a profound influence upon the work of sculptors and painters alike and helped to shape their style.

Among various poems celebrating its discovery, one by Cardinal Sadoleto records vividly the feeling with which scholars welcomed the statue:

> 'From heaped-up mound of earth and from the heart
> Of mighty ruins, lo! long time once more
> Has brought Laocoön home, who stood of old
> In princely palaces and graced thy halls,
> Imperial Titus. Wrought by skill divine
> (Even learned ancients saw no nobler work),
> The statue now from darkness saved returns
> To see the stronghold of Rome's second life.'

For more than two centuries the group remained a centre of interest. It was discussed at length by Winckelmann in his pioneer studies in art history (1764); it furnished theme and title for Lessing's study of the principles underlying the various forms of art (1766), and it supplied Goethe with the subject for his critical essay on the Laocoön (1798).

Eventually its very fame endangered it. When Napoleon, in 1797–1798, demanded from Italy a selection of her most prized works of art, the Laocoön was among those taken. With such treasures as the Apollo Belvedere, the Venus de' Medici, and the bronze horses from Saint Mark's in Venice, it was brought in triumph to Paris and placed in the Louvre. The fate of the looted works was, for a time, uncertain, but after Napoleon's final defeat in 1815 the French restored as much as possible to the former owners. The sculptor Canova, who came to supervise the removal of the treasures belonging to Roman collections, wrote on October 5, 1815: 'We removed this day the two first statues of the world, the Apollo [Belvedere] and the Laocoön.'

Since then the Laocoön has survived a period of adverse criticism as exaggerated as the earlier praise, to be recognized more justly now as a magnificent example of that restless, dynamic baroque element which has appeared again and again in the history of art throughout the ages.

THE BATHS OF CARACALLA

Plates 148–156

THE most imposing Roman baths remaining today are those of Caracalla, south of the Golden House and the Palatine, and those of Diocletian to the north. The Baths of Trajan, probably planned by the architect of his forum, were the model for these later baths.

The Baths of Caracalla, second largest in ancient Rome, are the best preserved of all, and give a clearer idea than any others of these great establishments which once played so important a part in Roman life. The Roman baths were not only bathing places but also immense club houses. Admission to many of them was free, while others collected a small fee. In none of the larger ones, at least, was entrance expensive, though considerable could be spent for extra services or in the shops with which they were equipped. They contained libraries, exhibition halls, lounges, covered promenades, areas for games and exercises, and extensive gardens; everything, in fact, to make the day pass pleasurably. This combination of care for body and mind together was a contribution to civilization lost for centuries after the Empire's decline. The number of baths varied considerably from time to time; by the fourth century A.D. there were probably nearly a thousand, large and small, within the city. Many were open to both men and women, though probably at different hours.

Caracalla opened these baths in A.D. 216; they had probably been begun by his father about 211, and were not finished until some years later. Their alternate name, the Antonine Baths, comes from the family name that Caracalla had borrowed from the great Antonine dynasty of the second century. Like most of the baths built by the emperors, Caracalla's were set in an immense, rectangular walled park, decorated with fountains, flowers, and works of art. The baths themselves opened off a great hall (Plate 153) 183 feet long and 79 feet wide, covered by a cross-vaulting supported by huge masonry piers. This type of hall was the inspiration of the main waiting room of the Pennsylvania Station in New York, which employed similar forms of vaulting, clerestory lighting, ornamental columns, and end colonnades, in a considerably larger space. North of this hall lay the *frigidarium*, or cold bath; south of it, the *calidarium*, or warm bath. At each end was a peristyle open to the sky in the centre but surrounded by a covered portico; these may have been gymnasiums.

(94)

In addition there were many rooms for special baths and treatments, for cooling down, and for dressing. Underground there still remains a network of tunnels and staircases along which slaves scurried to serve the patrons without disturbing them; chutes for the disposal of laundry; and pipes and channels for heat and water. Originally the brick-faced concrete walls were covered with stucco painted to imitate marble and were enriched with marble trimmings. Tall columns of grey granite stood against the piers of the central hall; the only one remaining is now in the Piazza Santa Trinità in Florence. A few fragments of these decorations are still left within the baths, but on the whole there is little except the brick and concrete shell.

The magnificent water supply of ancient Rome was primarily designed for public rather than for private use, and supplying the baths was one of its most important functions. The aqueducts which carried water to Rome from the distant hills were among the foremost responsibilities, at first of the Roman officials and later of the emperors. The water for the Baths of Caracalla was supplied by a branch which that emperor constructed from the Aqua Marcia, an aqueduct built about the middle of the second century B.C. Neglect of the aqueducts would, of course, soon destroy the usefulness of the baths. Early in the sixth century A.D., Theodoric and his minister Cassiodorus were fully aware of the ever-increasing danger of such neglect, for Roman resources and manpower were declining rapidly. Cassiodorus exhorted the custodians of the aqueducts in a form letter which is one of the most illuminating documents of the time:

'Though all the buildings of Rome are wonderful, and one can scarce for this reason say which are the chief among them, we think a distinction may be drawn between those which are reared only for the sake of ornament and those which also serve a useful purpose. . . . In the Aqueducts of Rome we note both the marvel of their construction and the rare wholesomeness of their waters. When you look at those rivers, led as it were over piled-up mountains, you would think that their solid stony beds were natural channels, through so many ages have they borne the rush of such mighty waters. . . . These artificial channels, the work of the ancients, never perish, if reasonable care be taken of their preservation.

'Let us consider how much that wealth of waters adds to the adornment of the City of Rome. Where would be the beauty of our *Thermae*, if those softest waters were not supplied to them?'

Cassiodorus lived to see the damage of the Gothic siege and the beginning of the water shortage which led to the baths' decline and lasted throughout the Middle Ages. The main channel of the Aqua Marcia was cut, with the others, during the siege of 537–538. It was repaired several times and it is not known exactly when its waters ceased to flow. By the tenth century, however, if not earlier, the city was depending for its water on springs, wells, the brook Marrana, and the Tiber. These could furnish household supplies for the shrunken population of medieval Rome, but the baths and other public conveniences which depended on the aqueducts had ceased to function.

The Middle Ages had lost all conception of the busy, closely knit social life of such a city as ancient Rome. To them the rich materials and remains of complicated heating and plumbing arrangements seemed appropriate only to royal dwellings. The early versions of the *Mirabilia* simply note under the heading of *Thermae* the names of the baths which the authors knew, among them the Antonine and those of Diocletian. Later versions expanded their explanations of these rich and mystifying structures: 'There be called *thermae* great palaces; having full great crypts under ground, wherein in the wintertime a fire was kindled throughout, and in summer they were filled with fresh waters; so that the court dwelt in the upper chambers in much delight.'

In spite of their imposing remains, the Baths of Caracalla are not mentioned as often in the Middle Ages as those of Diocletian. From the sixteenth century on, however, there are many references to the works of art found among the ruins of Caracalla's baths, which had the reputation in ancient days of being the most richly adorned of any in the city. Three of the best-known pieces of sculpture now in the National Museum at Naples were discovered here in the 1540's—the group of the bull on which Dirce was bound by Amphion and Zethus, the colossal statue of Flora, and the Hercules Farnese (Plate 152), which ranks close to the Laocoön in influence on later sculpture. Originally belonging to the Farnese family, these statues, like the gardens on the Palatine, passed by inheritance to the rulers of Naples. Other statues, elaborately carved capitals (Plate 151), a great number of architectural carvings, and some fine mosaics were found in and about these baths from the sixteenth well through the nineteenth century.

The spasmodic early excavations made for the purpose of finding works of art were followed in the nineteenth century by more thorough exploration devoted to the study of the baths themselves. The resultant clearing away of the debris of centuries took with it most of the luxuriant growth which had made these baths a rival of the Colosseum. Charlotte Eaton, visiting them in 1818, gave a delightful picture of them in their uncleared state: 'We passed through a long succession of immense halls, open to the sky, whose pavements of costly marbles and rich mosaics, long since torn away, have been supplied by the soft green turf, that forms a carpet more in unison with their deserted state. The wind, sighing through the branches of the aged trees that have taken root in them without rivalling their loftiness, was the only sound we heard; and the bird of prey, which burst through the thick ivy of the broken wall far above us, was the only living object we beheld.' In those days of neglected loneliness, heaps of fallen masonry piled up against the piers made it easy to reach the crumbling stairways leading to their tops, where romantic visitors sometimes climbed to meditate in solitude. It was here that Shelley worked, in the spring of 1819, upon *Prometheus Unbound*, noting in its Preface:

'This poem was chiefly written upon the mountainous ruins of the Baths of Caracalla, among the flowery glades and thickets of odoriferous blossoming trees which extend in ever-winding labyrinths upon its immense platforms and dizzy arches suspended in the air. The bright blue sky of Rome, and the effect of the vigorous awakening spring in that divinest climate, and the new life with which it drenches the spirits even to intoxication, were the inspiration of the drama.'

Though the baths have been weeded more than once since Shelley's day, human hands can never completely restrain the luxuriance of growth in Rome. Here and there today, trees spring from a precarious perch and ivy and flowers wave defiantly, while swifts flit in and out among the broken arches in the cool of morning or when the *ponentino*, or evening west wind of Rome, begins to stir the sun-warmed air.

A new life has come to these once solitary ruins in late years. Since 1937 they have served as the magnificent setting for opera at night during the rainless summer season (Plate 156). The sides of the proscenium arch are the two solitary remaining piers of the circular warm bath which opens from the south side of the central hall. Ramps lead up from the hall to an immense stage, said to be the largest in the world, which affords space for the most elaborate settings and the most spectacular processions.

The steel scaffolding of this stage, which remains in place throughout the year, somewhat mars the picturesque quality of the great hall and its surrounding rooms and closes some of them to visitors. Yet if the romantic peace and luxuriant growth which so delighted the nineteenth century are gone, the magnificent spectacles presented here are in perfect keeping with the ancient Rome which loved imperial display and with the papal city which has welcomed whole-heartedly the pageantry of the Church.

THE BATHS OF DIOCLETIAN

Plates 157–161

THE Baths of Diocletian, the largest in ancient Rome, are, paradoxically, both more and less altered than those of Caracalla. Much of the original vaulting still covers the central hall (Plate 158), resting upon eight ancient columns of red granite topped by rich Corinthian capitals. But this hall has been used as a church for about four hundred years, while other parts of the baths have been turned into cloisters, now included in the Terme Museum, and into a planetarium. One of four round buildings which occupied the corners of the outer enclosure was converted into the church of San Bernardo in 1594 and another has been used as a girls' school.

The baths were built between A.D. 298 and 306. Just when they ceased to function is not certain—probably not long after the aqueducts were cut during the Gothic wars of the sixth century. Like the Baths of Caracalla, which they resemble in plan, they were supplied with water by a branch of the Aqua Marcia. Like these baths, too, their brick-faced concrete structure was originally covered with stucco painted to imitate marble; less is known about the fate of their marble and mosaic decoration, and less has been found here than in Caracalla's baths.

During the Middle Ages these were the most celebrated of all Roman baths. A late version of the *Mirabilia* used them to illustrate the magnificence of baths in general—'as may be seen in the thermae of Diocletian before Saint Susanna' and added: 'In the palace [baths] of Diocletian were four temples, of Aesculapius and Saturn and Mars and Apollo, which are now called the Bushels.' These were the round buildings at the corners of the enclosure walls.

In the fourteenth century, Petrarch described the ruins to his friend Giovanni Colonna, writing of the pleasures they had shared during the poet's early visit to Rome: 'We used, after the fatigue of wandering about the immense city, often to make a halt at the Baths of Diocletian, and sometimes to ascend to the vaulted roof of that once most magnificent edifice; for nowhere is there sweeter air, a wider prospect, more silence and desirable solitude. . . . And wandering among the crumbling walls, or sitting on the roof, the fragments of the ruins beneath our eyes, we used to have much talk on history; I being allowed to be the better versed in ancient, you in modern story.' Du Pérac's etching (Plate 158), more than two hundred years later, suggests that there was among these ruins then something of the same luxuriant growth as that which delighted visitors centuries later in the Baths of Caracalla.

The ruins changed owners several times during the Middle Ages and early Renaissance. In 1091 Pope Urban II granted the baths to Saint Bruno for a monastery of Carthusian monks; again, in the fourteenth century, they were granted by the papal Curia of Avignon for the same purpose. The representation of the baths in fourteenth and fifteenth-century views of Rome (Plates 7, 8), which show eight or ten monastic cells, suggests that a Certosa was actually installed.

In the 1560's Pius IV renewed the idea of a Carthusian convent, and turned the great central hall of the baths into a church. Michelangelo was put in charge of the enterprise, which he carried out with magnificent self-restraint, respecting the ancient structure wherever possible and giving it, in its Christian guise, a feeling essentially harmonious with that of ancient Rome. Diocletian might feel at home today in the church occupying the central hall. Vanvitelli, who reoriented the interior in the eighteenth century, did more damage to the old structure, but could not spoil its essential harmony.

Hawthorne's description in the *French and Italian Notebooks* of the ruinous pile, as he saw it in 1858, stressed the church rather than the ancient baths:

'Today, which was bright and cool,' he wrote, 'my wife and I set forth immediately after breakfast, in search of the Baths of Diocletian, and the church of Santa Maria degli Angeli. . . .

'We turned into the Piazza di Termini, the entrance of which is at this fountain [the fountain of the Esedra]; and after some inquiry . . . we found our way to the portal of Santa Maria degli Angeli. The exterior of this church has no pretensions to beauty or majesty, or, indeed, to any architecture whatever—for it looks like a confused pile of ruined brick-work, with a façade resembling half the inner curve of a large oven. No one would imagine that there was a church under that enormous heap of ancient rubbish. But the door admits you into a circular vestibule, once an apartment of Diocletian's Baths, but now a portion of the nave of the church . . . now, with little change, except of detail and ornament, trans-formed into the body of the church. This space is so lofty, broad, and airy, that the soul forthwith swells out and magnifies itself. . . . It was Michel Angelo who contrived this miracle; and I feel even more grateful to him for rescuing such a noble interior from destruction than if he had originally built it himself.'

In Hawthorne's time the ruins housed not only the churches of Santa Maria degli Angeli and San Bernardo and the Carthusian convent and cloister, but granaries, charitable institutions, and prisons as well. In the last quarter of the century an American sculptor's studio (Plates 159–160) was added to the miscellany which the Italian Government gradually took over for public purposes. Moses Ezekiel's studio, nestled in the southwest angle of the ruin at the right of the present entrance from the Piazza dell' Esedra to the Museo delle Terme, was a gathering place for artists, musicians, and the cosmopolitan society of Rome. It was taken over in 1910 as part of the new National Museum which had been begun in the Carthusian cloisters in 1889. In Ezekiel's time this small chamber near the entrance was divided into two stories; one a lower studio or work room, the other an upper studio for living and entertaining, reached by an inclined plane leading up the outside wall to a balcony overhung by wistaria and white roses. Ezekiel had originally selected his quarters partly from motives of economy and partly from the romantic desire to live in a ruin. When he first established himself there, the neighbourhood of the baths, so busy now, was a 'wide and empty space crossed by deserted roads leading past the vast and solemn ruins'.

Today the circular Piazza dell'Esedra in front of the church still preserves the shape and name of Diocletian's immense exedra in the park south of the *calidarium*. In the semi-circular modern colonnades facing the church, visitors may sit now to eat ices or sip cool drinks and to watch the great jet of water splashing into the modern Fountain of the Naiads from the Aqua Marcia which supplied the baths in Diocletian's time.

THE FORUM OF NERVA

Plates 162–165

BEFORE the Empire had begun, the Roman Forum had become too small for the growing needs of the city. Julius Caesar had diminished its area in giving it the present form; in compensation, he built a second forum, called by his name, not as a market but as a centre for business of other kinds. This Forum Julium, which lay to the north, was the first step in a great plan carried on by later emperors for connecting the Roman Forum with the populous quarter of the Campus Martius, or Field of Mars, to the north. Augustus added another forum north of that of Caesar. Vespasian added his great Forum and Temple of Peace, where the spoils of the Temple of Jerusalem were placed, and in A.D. 97 or 98, the Emperor Nerva dedicated a smaller forum (Plates 162–165), begun by his predecessor Domitian, between those of Augustus and Vespasian, to serve as a passageway northeast to the Esquiline hill. From this use, it is often called the Forum Transitorium.

Little is known of Nerva's forum through written records, but artists have loved it and have drawn it oftener than any other except the Roman Forum itself. The ruins of a considerable part of its buildings stood until the seventeenth century, and the fragments which remain still exhibit rich and delightful decoration.

Aside from foundations and broken bits of columns and carvings, all that is visible today is part of a colonnaded enclosing wall (Plate 162), which once surrounded the forum. Attached to this wall are two Corinthian columns and a fragment of frieze and attic above them. On the attic is a relief of Minerva, Domitian's favourite deity, to whom the forum's temple was dedicated; on the frieze are reliefs showing women busy with the household tasks of which Minerva was patroness. One probably represents Arachne, the mortal who boasted that she was superior to the goddess in the art of weaving and was punished by being transformed into a spider. This beautiful fragment, until recent years enclosed in the walls of comparatively modern buildings, has long been known as the *Colonnacce*.

Minerva's temple stood at the northern end of the narrow forum. Drawings of the fifteenth and sixteenth century show considerable portions of it still standing (Plate 163); even then, however, the *Colonnacce* looked much as it does today.

Master Gregory, who described the temple in the twelfth century, wrote of it: 'The temple of Pallas was once an outstanding building, but it was pulled down with great effort by the Christians, and also fell into ruin because of great age. Since it was impossible to demolish it entirely, what remains is now the grain storehouse of the cardinals. Here is a great heap of broken effigies, and here is a headless image of Pallas, armed, standing on the apex of the pediment, a marvel to beholders.

'This image was much venerated among the ancient Romans. They brought Christians before it, and if they refused to bow the knee and worship Pallas, they were tortured to death. It was before this idol that Hippolytus was brought, with his household, and because he scorned it he was torn to pieces by horses.'

This story of a Christian martyrdom echoes the Greek legend of Hippolytus, son of Theseus, killed by Poseidon's horses because he had scorned Aphrodite for the sake of the chaste huntress, Artemis.

The name 'Temple of Pallas' was kept alive through an account in the *Acts of the Martyrs*. The *Mirabilia*, however, calls the forum and temple 'the Forum of Nerva with his temple of *Divus Nerva*', probably because that emperor's name was prominent in the inscription below the pediment (Plate 163). The image that Gregory describes is clearly not that remaining on the *Colonnacce*, which has its head and is in relief. In 1616 most of the remains of the temple were torn down and used as material for other buildings, especially the great fountain of the Acqua Paolo on the Janiculum, named from Paul V who demolished the ruined temple.

The ground-level about this forum rose in the course of centuries, until today the excavated portions of the *Colonnacce* lie far below the street. The columns were not uncovered to their full depth or the surrounding houses completely removed until the early 1930's.

THE FORUM AND COLUMN OF TRAJAN

Plates 166–173

THE Forum of Trajan, unlike that of Nerva, is better known in literature than in art. Its magnificence, surpassing that of any other group
of buildings in imperial Rome, furnished material for enthusiastic descriptions in ancient times, but so much of it has been ruined and buried
for centuries that only one of its great hemicycles (Plates 166–167), with
the column itself, has been available to artists through the centuries.

Trajan built this last and largest of the forums of ancient Rome early in
the second century A.D., partly to give more room for the increasing needs
of a growing population, but mainly to carry through the plan of his
predecessors of opening southern Rome to the Campus Martius by cutting
through a thin ridge between the Capitol and Quirinal hills. Lying
northwest of the Roman Forum, its main entrance was through a magnificent arch at the end next the Forum of Augustus. In the court inside
stood a gilded equestrian statue of Trajan. Two sides of this court were
closed by immense semi-circular exedrae; one, built on level ground
to the south, disappeared long ago, but that on the northeast, built into
the Quirinal hill, has in great part survived. Beyond this entrance court
lay the colonnaded Basilica Ulpia, called after the emperor, whose full
name was Marcus Ulpius Nerva Traianus. Beyond the basilica another
court was flanked by two libraries, one for Greek and one for Latin works;
between these libraries rose, and rises still (Plate 170), the famous
Column of Trajan. The architect who planned this magnificent group was
Apollodorus of Damascus, who probably built Trajan's baths as well.

In ancient times this forum saw many memorable events. Here slaves
were freed; here the Emperor Hadrian burned the notes of debtors to the
state; here Marcus Aurelius sold at auction the treasures of the imperial
household to defray the costs of war instead of levying more taxes on his
subjects; and here the Emperor Aurelian imitated Hadrian's generosity
by burning the lists of political offenders. A little sanctuary to Liberty,
marked on the Marble Plan, seems once to have stood in the northern
hemicycle, receiving its name, perhaps, from being the place where slaves
were freed.

In the markets which surrounded the great exedrae of the entrance
court all kinds of wares were sold—vegetables, fruit, flowers, fish, and

spices. The fish shops were supplied with running water; the spice shops gave the name of their most important commodity, pepper (*pipera*), to the medieval street, the Via Biberatica, which ran above the northern exedra (Plate 169).

Trajan's forum was one of the wonders of the Roman world. When the Emperor Constantius II visited Rome for the first time in A.D. 356, he marvelled at the many buildings which outshone those of his own capital at Constantinople. 'But when he came to the Forum of Trajan,' wrote the historian Ammianus Marcellinus, 'a construction unique under the heavens, as we believe, and admirable even in the unanimous opinion of the gods, he stood fast in amazement, turning his attention to the gigantic complex about him, beggaring description and never again to be imitated by mortal men. Therefore abandoning all hope of attempting anything like it, he said that he would and could copy Trajan's steed alone, which stands in the centre of the vestibule, carrying the emperor himself. To this prince Ormisda, who was standing near him, . . . replied with native wit: "First, Sire," said he, "command a like stable to be built, if you can." '

The forum evidently escaped without too much damage from the plunderings of Rome in 410 and 455, for early in the sixth century, Cassiodorus wrote: 'However often one sees the Forum of Trajan it always seems a miracle.' Venantius Fortunatus, Bishop of Poitiers, a contemporary of Pope Gregory the Great in the late sixth century, implied that even then the works of Vergil and of living poets were being read aloud in the halls of the forum's libraries.

As early as the eighth century a typically medieval legend began to link the name of this great Gregory with those of Trajan and his forum, which seems not to have been entirely in ruin then. According to this legend, Gregory, walking one day in the forum and marvelling at its greatness, was struck by a relief which showed Trajan dismounting from his horse to grant justice to a poor widow. He wept at the thought of a man capable at once of such magnificent buildings and such compassion being condemned to perdition as a pagan. Upon his return to Saint Peter's he heard a voice from heaven which told him that his prayers for the emperor's salvation had been heeded, but counselled him never again to intercede for unbelievers.

In the course of centuries, medieval and modern buildings enclosed the remaining exedra so that it could not be seen from the street (Plate 168). The French excavated the paving in front of it in 1812, but little was done to make the hemicycle easily visible. As late as 1925 Muirhead's Blue

Guide says of it: 'The remains of one of the great exedrae may be seen at No. 6 Via Campo Carleo, or by passing, with permission, through the bakery at No. 33 Via Alessandrina. One of the smaller semi-circular flanking recesses is now occupied by the Ristorante della Basilica Ulpiana.' This restaurant was in a small exedra opening to the left of the hemicycle.

Extensive excavations begun in 1928 have revealed a labyrinth of halls and shops and storerooms, including a two-story market hall found within the barracks of the Milizie, which lay above the ruins in the direction of the Milizie tower. These, with considerable restoration, are open now as a public monument, somewhat bare and lifeless by comparison with their former picturesque neglect. Though many houses were demolished and whole streets eliminated, other streets still cut across great sections of the forum, while the churches of Santa Maria di Loreto and of the Holy Name of Mary lie above the precinct of the ruined temple which Hadrian built in honour of Trajan at the end of the forum beyond the libraries.

Though most of Trajan's forum lay ruined or hidden for centuries, his column (Plates 170–173), with its spiral bands of relief, has remained a prominent landmark ever since the emperor raised it. The reliefs, showing scenes from Trajan's conquests in Dacia and providing a magnificent record of a Roman army of the second century, were carved after the immense drums were put in place, and done so skilfully that the joinings are almost concealed. In ancient times they could be studied much better than now, for the libraries which flanked the column had two-storied porticoes which brought spectators more nearly to the proper height.

The Middle Ages treated the column with great care. In 1162, during the revival of interest in antiquity which accompanied the republican revolution and produced the *Mirabilia*, the Roman Senate passed a resolution to preserve it 'to the honour of the whole Roman people', providing the death penalty for damage. This care was probably not unconnected with the fact that profitable fees were collected from pilgrims who climbed it for the view from its top. The *Mirabilia's* description gives precisely such details as would appeal to tourists, especially the number of steps their weary feet had climbed: 'The winding pillar of Trajan hath in height one hundred thirty and eight feet, steps in number one hundred fourscore and five, windows forty and five.' Actually, the height, including the base, is about one hundred and twenty-five feet, by modern computation. The number of steps is correct, but only forty-three windows are now listed.

Trajan himself did not design the column as his sepulchre, but the Senate, after his death, decreed that his ashes should rest within it, probably in an urn in the base. Originally the column was crowned by a statue of Trajan, which perished long ago; the statue of Saint Peter which now stands there was erected in 1588. Upon the column which Marcus Aurelius built in imitation of Trajan's there now stands the figure of Saint Paul.

RUINS IN THE COLONNA GARDENS

Plates 174–181

NORTH of the Forum of Trajan, in the Colonna Gardens on the western slope of the Quirinal, the corner of a gigantic pediment (Plate 174) lies as it fell more than three hundred years ago. This fragment, estimated at a hundred tons' weight and said to be the largest block of marble in Rome, is the last certain remnant from the superstructure of what was once the city's largest temple. Parts of its substructures still exist, some serving as retaining walls of the garden's terraces, and between the Colonna property and that of the Gregorian University beside it there still rise the brick foundations of one of the immense double staircases (Plates 176–177) which led up the slope to the temple and the neighbouring Baths of Constantine. Until the early seventeenth century the temple's corner wall and a fragment of its pediment rose high on the edge of the hill. The medieval tower close against it and the structures which lay between the staircase ramps in the Middle Ages were built by the Colonna family when it fortified the ruin long ago. The picturesque contrast between the fragment of classic temple and its medieval surroundings may have been one reason why this was a favourite subject among artists of the Renaissance (Plate 175); they may have been delighted, too, by its connections with the colourful and courageous Colonna family, perhaps the most widely popular in Rome.

The temple which once stood here has probably been called by more varied and more fantastic names than any other monument in the Eternal City. Of late years the choice has narrowed to 'Temple of the Sun' and 'Temple of Serapis', both deities imported from Rome's eastern lands. If it was the Temple of the Sun, it was that built by the Emperor Aurelian (A.D. 270–275) after his victory over Zenobia, queen of fabulous Palmyra in the Syrian desert. If built in honour of Serapis, it was that erected by Caracalla (A.D. 211–217). In either case, it belonged to a time in which influences and religions from the East, including Christianity, were growing steadily stronger in Rome. Caracalla's reign and those of his immediate successors bore the imprint of a succession of eastern women— the Syrian Julias, beautiful, intelligent, masterful, and, on the whole, completely unscrupulous. As wife, mother, or grandmother, these women swayed the emperors through the first third of the century—Julia Domna, wife of Septimius Severus and mother of Caracalla; her sister, Julia Maesa, dominating grandmother of Elagabalus, whom she elevated to the position of emperor; and this Julia's daughter, Julia Soaemias, mother of that profligate young ruler.

The sway of the Julias was over before Aurelian, a man of humble birth, was chosen as emperor because of his military ability. His relation with the East was that of a conqueror whose empire, however, continued to be influenced by the eastern lands that came beneath its rule. The deity worshipped in the great temple which he built was probably a blending of several oriental sun gods whose cults he favoured especially; he had shown great concern at the looting of Palmyra's Temple of the Sun and had commanded its restoration.

In size and perhaps in plan this temple on the Quirinal, whatever its date and origin, showed the influence of the vast stone structures of Egypt and of Syrian Baalbek. Its columns are estimated to be fifty-eight feet high, with capitals more than eight feet.

Darkness shrouds the decay and fall of this great temple to a foreign deity, whether it be the Syrian sun god or the Egyptian Serapis. The last reference to it in antiquity comes from the sixth century, when some of its columns were sent to Constantinople. By the twelfth century the confusion of its names was well under way. The *Mirabilia* refers to it as 'the temple of Jupiter and Diana, that is now called the Emperor's Table [*mensa imperatoris*] over the Palace [baths] of Constantine.' What condition the temple was in or how it received the name of *mensa* is not recorded. Perhaps it was some copyist's error; perhaps it had a significance to the medieval mind unknown today. A slightly later name, *mesa* or *torre di mesa*, has been equally puzzling. Some have thought it merely a contraction of *mensa;* others, that it came from a confusion with *mezzo*, 'half', because half of the Colonnas' medieval tower was hidden by the immense fragment of temple wall.

The temple has also been associated with the 'women's senate house', said to have been built by the Emperor Elagabalus, where his mother and grandmother, Julia Soaemias and Julia Maesa, held unquestioned sway. Here, says the presumably fourth-century author of the *Life of Elagabalus*, in the fanciful collection of *Lives of the Caesars*, the women of Rome met to discuss the order of precedence in social affairs, who might travel in a chariot, who in a litter, and who might 'wear gold and jewels on her shoes'. It was also called the 'tower of Maecenas', and as Suetonius had said that Nero watched Rome burn from this tower, it was but a step to connect the great ruin with Nero. Perhaps its most widely known name in the sixteenth and seventeenth centuries was *Frontispizio di Nerone*, 'façade' or 'pediment' of Nero.

The remnants of this great temple and the immense double staircase which led to it served as a quarry for countless buildings from the time when its marble steps were removed for use in the staircase of Santa Maria in Aracoeli in 1348. Much of its marble went into the building of the Colonna palace, which was begun in the fifteenth century, and much into the construction of other palaces and churches.

The present Colonna palace, begun by the Colonna pope, Martin V (1417–1431), and extended and altered in the seventeenth and eighteenth centuries, lies between the Piazza Santi Apostoli and the Via della Pilotta, on lower ground than the gardens. Four bridges rising from its second story (the first by European numbering) span the Via della Pilotta like flying buttresses and connect the palace with the present garden, which was laid out in the sixteenth century and redesigned in the eighteenth (Plate 178).

These gardens, comparatively easy of access in the nineteenth and early twentieth centuries, were well known to visitors in those more leisurely times. The connection between the actual structure of the Colonna palace and the massive ruin on the hill behind it had a special fascination for one of these travellers, Joseph Forsyth, who composed his *Remarks on Antiquities* while detained on the Continent by the Napoleonic Wars. 'The saloon called the *Galleria* is itself too brilliant a picture,' he wrote, 'for the pictures which it contains. . . . Its pavement is Parian marble laid in the form of tombstones.

'This pavement was sawn out of an ancient pediment, of which there are still two stupendous blocks lying in the palace-garden, without any specific mark that could ascertain their edifice. . . . As these blocks lie on the *Quirinal*, one calls them part of the *Maesa*, another of Heliogabalus's female senate-house. Others assign them to the temple of Health, to that of Mithras, to the tower of Maecenas, to the vestibule of Nero's house. Being found near Constantine's baths, and too beautiful for the sculpture of his age, they had been probably removed, like the materials of his arch, from some noble edifice; and the grandeur of their style would not disgrace the temple of Peace itself.'

Charlotte Eaton and George Hillard have left delightful and very different descriptions. 'The garden hangs on the steep side of the Quirinal Hill,' wrote Mrs. Eaton, 'on the summit of which the broken but massive fragments of an immense pediment of Parian marble, covered with the finest sculpture, repose on the soft green turf, overshadowed by an ancient pine tree. . . . These fragments are called the remains of the magnificent Temple of the Sun, built by Aurelian after his triumphal return to Rome, with Zenobia, the captive Queen of Syria, in his train.'

Hillard, of a more archaeological bent, dwelt upon the classic ruins rather than upon the picturesque setting: 'Here are many interesting ruins and fragments, especially some vaults of the baths of Constantine now used as granaries, and two enormous masses of marble belonging to an edifice of the Corinthian order. The building of which they were a part must have been of stupendous magnitude, and have formed a most conspicuous object, placed, as it was in so commanding a position, yet nothing is known with certainty upon the subject; and antiquaries can only guess that these colossal fragments fell from the temple of the Sun built by Aurelian.'

Charles Platt, writing in the 1890's on Italian gardens, had nothing to say of the temple fragments, but was, of course, interested in the structural use the garden made of the old Roman walls, which he assigned to the Baths of Constantine. 'In the very heart of Rome,' he wrote, 'it is so concealed that one might pass it a hundred times without suspecting its existence. The palace is at the foot of the hill, and is separated from the garden by a sunken street and terraces. The street is crossed by several bridges, and in looking from the palace to the terraces is entirely invisible.

'The hill is very abrupt, and one is led through ilex walks and up stairways along terraces, to the flower garden at its very top. . . . The lower terrace, on a level with the first floor of the palace, is also something of a garden and interesting in itself. It is planted in long tiers, with flowering shrubs bordered by tree-roses, and terminating at the west in a grotto with columns and tall cypresses, and at the east in old statuary half covered with vines and undergrowth.

'The side-hill between this and the upper garden was originally occupied by old Roman baths, and the architect has, wherever possible, allowed the mason-work to remain, sometimes forming the old arches into stairways or terraces, and leaving the old brick walls to be covered with vines.'

Platt's description is true of the gardens of the late eighteenth and nineteenth century and of today. They are less easy of access now, but the visitor, once welcome, is surrounded still by the ancient peace which reigns in all mellowed gardens, especially in those where the remote past and the present lie so harmoniously side by side. Here, where the walls of emperors support the gardens of a family whose history covers more than a thousand years of Rome, time itself seems to stand motionless.

Both here and in the Baths of Constantine the early explorations had been in search of buried works of art. Yet one of the most perfectly preserved masterpieces of ancient sculpture ever discovered came to light by accident less than a century ago, in this complex of tangled foundations where remnants of the temple and of the Baths of Constantine are inextricably confused.

In March of 1885, workmen were digging among the substructures of the Quirinal slope to prepare the foundations of the National Theatre, now vanished in its turn, like the creature of a day. Eighteen feet below the level of an ancient concrete platform they came upon the famous bronze Boxer (Plate 180), now one of the treasures of the Terme Museum. Whether the underground chamber in which it was found belonged to the temple or the baths is uncertain. Time, as usual, did not permit a careful study of the site. The workmen who found the statue at once called Rodolfo Lanciani, then in charge of excavations in Rome. The description of its uncovering in his *Ancient Rome in the Light of Recent Excavations* is one of the great accounts of such a find:

'Being notified at once, we . . . were present when only the head of the figure appeared above ground, and consequently we could follow and study the minutest detail of the discovery. On the opposite page is a drawing from a photograph [Plate 181] taken at the moment of the discovery.

'The most important piece of evidence collected in witnessing and following the removal of the earth in which the masterpiece lay buried is that the statue had not been thrown in there, or buried in haste, but had been concealed and treated with the utmost care. The figure, being in a sitting posture, had been placed on a stone capital of the Doric order, as upon a stool; and the trench, which had been opened through the lower foundations of the temple of the Sun, to conceal the statue, had been filled up with sifted earth, in order to save the surface of the bronze from any possible injury.

'I have witnessed, in my long career in the active field of archaeology, many discoveries; I have experienced surprise after surprise; I have sometimes and most unexpectedly met with real masterpieces; but I have never felt such an extraordinary impression as the one created by the sight of this magnificent specimen of a semi-barbaric athlete, coming slowly out of the ground, as if awakening from a long repose after his gallant fights.'

There might well have passed through Lanciani's mind that day the lines of the *Mirabilia* which record Rome's medieval awakening from the centuries of darkness:

'Old Rome was I, now new Rome shall be praised;
I bear my head aloft, from ruin raised.'

THE THEATRE OF MARCELLUS

Plates 182–185

BOTH in time and space the imperial temple in the Colonna Gardens is far removed from the Theatre of Marcellus, which Julius Caesar planned and Augustus built near the Tiber's bank. To turn from the half-oriental splendour of the late Empire to this solid, utilitarian early building (Plate 182) is to step back two hundred years to simpler times and to cross half the ancient city's width.

The Theatre of Marcellus, almost a century older than the Colosseum, probably inspired the architects of the later, larger structure. Augustus finished the theatre by the Tiber between 13 and 11 B.C. and named it for his dead nephew and son-in-law, who had been his first choice as successor. Less than a third of the massive building stands today, but Vergil's melodious lament for the young prince has survived unimpaired through almost two thousand years: 'Ah, Marcellus, child of pity, couldst thou but have escaped the early death which fate decreed! Give me lilies with full hand; let me scatter purple flowers.'

Like the Colosseum, the Theatre of Marcellus was constructed largely of travertine and had rows of open arcades, one above the other, each with a distinct order of columns and entablature. The original third story of the theatre, however, with its Corinthian pilasters, has been almost entirely destroyed and replaced by later masonry. Unlike the Colosseum, where spectacles were held in the central arena entirely surrounded by rows of seats, the theatre followed the usual Greco-Roman plan, with a stage at the end next the Tiber. From the upper rows of seats facing it there was an excellent view across to the river and to the hills behind Trastevere.

The citizens of ancient Rome themselves began the destruction of this theatre. In the late Empire the performances held upon the stage were much less popular than the gladiatorial sports, games, and races of the Colosseum and Circus Maximus. The Theatre of Marcellus seems to have been in bad condition as early as the fourth century, for there is a record of some of its stone being removed about A.D. 370 to repair the Pons Cestius, the modern Ponte San Bartolommeo, which connects the river bank opposite the theatre with the Tiber Island.

The destruction seems to have continued until the twelfth century. By this time the noble families of Rome were busy fortifying usable ruins as strongholds in their wars against each other, the popes, or the emperors. The mass of ruins formed by the destruction of the stage and seats in the interior of the theatre made a hilly foundation for the fortress of the Pierleoni family, while the encircling wall gave added protection. This family was of Jewish extraction, though converted Christians, and it may be because of this that the Jews of Rome, when they expanded from their original location across the Tiber, from the twelfth century on, settled around the Theatre of Marcellus to form the famous Roman Ghetto, where their modern synagogue still stands. By the fourteenth century the fortress-theatre came into the hands of the Savelli family, who built a palace in it in the sixteenth century after designs by Baldassarre Peruzzi. The sorry state of the triglyphs and dentils in the Doric frieze of the lower story is evidence of the mutilation the theatre has undergone through the centuries.

Life here in the early nineteenth century was delightfully described in a letter by the historian, Niebuhr, then Prussian ambassador to the Papal Court:

'Nicolovius will remember the theatre of Marcellus, in which the Savelli family built a palace. My house is half of it. It has stood empty for a considerable time, because the drive into the courtyard (the interior of the ancient theatre) rises like the slope of a mountain upon the heaps of rubbish. . . . The apartments in which we shall live are those over the colonnade of Ionic pillars forming the third story of the ancient theatre, and some, on a level with them, which have been built out like wings on the rubbish of the ruins. These enclose a little quadrangular garden, which is indeed very small, only about eighty or ninety feet long, and scarcely so broad, but so delightful! It contains three fountains—an abundance of flowers; there are orange-trees on the wall between the windows and jessamine under them.'

At least as early as the sixteenth century and probably long before, space had been rented in the lower arcades for use as shops (Plate 185). The shops were cleared away between 1927 and 1932 and the arcades re-opened as in ancient times. This clearing has given a better chance to study the construction, but has weakened that sense of continuity of which Hawthorne wrote in his *French and Italian Notebooks*:

'. . . I soon struck upon the ruins of the theatre of Marcellus, which are very picturesque, and the more so from being closely linked in, indeed identified with, the shops, habitations, and swarming life of modern Rome. The most striking portion was a circular edifice, which seemed to have been composed of a row of Ionic columns, standing upon a lower row of Doric, many of the antique pillars being yet perfect; but the inter-vening arches built up with brickwork, and the whole once magnificent structure now tenanted by poor and squalid people, as thick as mites within the round of an old cheese.' Although much of the ancient ruin has been cleared, a few apartments still nestle snugly into the modern upper floors above the walls of Augustus.

UNIDENTIFIED TEMPLES BY THE TIBER

Plates 186–187

EARLY in date, and closer to the Tiber than the nearby Theatre of Marcellus, are two small temples of unknown identity, built in the low-lying district by the river which was the ancient cattle market, or Forum Boarium. Heavy traffic thunders past them along the river's bank, but plots of grass and flowers enclose the ancient temples of time-blackened stone, while a medieval church and a baroque fountain add their note of continuity and change.

The rectangular temple, only a corner of which is visible in either photograph or drawing, was built of native tufa and travertine in the days of the Republic, before Augustus had made common the use of marble. Long called the 'Temple of Fortuna Virilis', and sometimes that of 'Mater Matuta', it has been thought lately that it may have been a temple to Portunus, guardian of this section which was the Tiber port. Actually, however, its name is still unknown. It owes its excellent preservation to the fact that it was converted in the ninth century into the church of Santa Maria Egiziaca, Saint Mary the Egyptian. It was restored to its ancient condition in the twenties of this century.

The true name of the round temple is equally lost in mystery, though, because of its shape, it has long been commonly but mistakenly called the 'Temple of Vesta'. Its marble columns and walls belong to the time of Augustus, though its foundations may be earlier. Originally it had the entablature proper to its Corinthian columns, but this disappeared some time in the Middle Ages and was replaced by the present conical roof. This temple too owes its preservation to its use as a church. In the twelfth century it was known as Round Saint Stephen's. The *Mirabilia* explains that 'the Round Saint Stephen's was the temple of Faunus' and identifies Faunus as 'the idol that spake to Julian and beguiled him'. This 'idol', according to legend, was a pagan image, said by some to be Mercury, which spoke to Julian the Apostate, Constantine's nephew, and tempted him to the pagan faith. In the sixteenth century the church was called Santo Stefano delle Carrozze, from the wagon-shops nearby; still later, about 1700, it was renamed Santa Maria del Sole, Saint Mary of the Sun.

THE HOUSE OF CRESCENTIUS

Plates 188–189

NEAR the Tiber, north of the unidentified temples, stands the stump of a ruined tower, a survival from a type of fortified dwelling common in medieval Rome. This House of Crescentius (Plate 188) is decorated with carved fragments from ancient Roman structures set into medieval brickwork, whose surface is enlivened by half-columns of the same material.

These nameless and forgotten fragments of ancient Rome were probably put together by a twelfth-century Roman who wished to command the bridge across the Tiber at this point, the now ruined Ponte Rotto, or Broken Bridge, remnant of the ancient Pons Aemilius. A long inscription in medieval Latin on the exterior of the house tells all that is known of its builder. The exaggerated phrases raise more questions than they answer:

'Nicholas, to whom this house belongs, well knew that the glory of the world was vanity. He was induced to build this dwelling, less by vanity than by the desire to restore the splendour of ancient Rome. Within a beautiful house, be mindful of the grave, and remember that thou hast not long to live in thy dwelling. Death travels hither on wings. No man's life is eternal. Our sojourn is brief and our course light as a feather. Whether thou mayest escape from the wind, lock thy door a hundredfold, and surround thyself with a thousand guards, death nevertheless sits beside thy pillow. Even if thou shuttest thyself in a castle that almost approaches the stars, death will only the more rapidly carry thee—its prey—away. The lofty house towers to the skies. From the foundation to the summit it was raised by the First among the First, the great Nicholas— in order to restore the glory of his fathers. Here stands the name of his father Crescentius and of his mother Theodora. This famous house was built for his beloved child, and given to David, by him who was his father.'

The perpetual conflict of the Middle Ages, and especially of medieval Rome, permeates this inscription. The son of the Church accepts the brevity and vanity of life and worldly glory; the heir of the Roman Empire desires 'to restore the splendour of ancient Rome' and 'the glory of his fathers'. Both thought and phraseology are touched with the wistfulness of the twelfth-century Roman who recalled in the *Mirabilia* the 'temples and palaces of emperors, consuls, senators and prefects' that

(116)

'were in the time of the heathen within this Roman city' and of those medieval Romans who revived the Senate on the Capitol hill.

Benjamin of Tudela wrote in the same century that 'around the part of Rome wherein men dwell, are spread out twenty and four miles of ruins'. This Jewish traveller had an exaggerated impression of the size of the ancient city, but his vivid picture brings to mind the concentration of medieval population in just such places as that in which this tower stood—the low-lying ground along the Tiber or between the hills, where water was easily obtainable. Among the habitations many, no doubt, were such patchworks of old and new as still survive in some medieval churches and in the structure which Nicholas built here. Certainly, throughout the Middle Ages, Rome, like San Gimignano today, was a city of tall towers, such as Benozzo Gozzoli painted in his famous view of *Saint Augustine Leaving Rome for Milan* (Plate 9). Prolonged interior conflicts, foreign conquests, and, most of all, the building programmes of renaissance and seventeenth-century popes destroyed most of them. But the great towers of the Milizie and the Conti still stand, though the Conti's was badly damaged in 1312 and lost the last of its upper stories in the seventeenth century. Smaller towers, however, still rise in unexpected places, and this truncated remnant of that built by 'the First among the First' still guards the approaches to the Ponte Rotto.

This half-demolished tower has been known by other names as well. That of 'House of Rienzi', especially popular in the nineteenth century and still occasionally in use, came from antiquarian attempts to connect some puzzling initials in the inscription with Cola di Rienzi, the fourteenth-century champion of the people. The name 'House of Pilate' has more basis in fact, for this building was used as the setting for the trial of Christ before Pilate in processional Passion Plays, which began at a house in the Via della Bocca della Verità, wended their way through the southern part of the city, stopping to play various scenes, and finally ended with the Crucifixion on Monte Testaccio, a little farther south.

THE PANTHEON

Plates 190–195

IN the Campus Martius, the plain which stretches west from the
Quirinal and Capitol hills to the Tiber, stands the best-preserved of
Rome's ancient temples and the only one which is still used as a place of
worship. This is the Pantheon (Plates 190–191), originally completed or
dedicated, according to its inscription, in 27 B.C., by Augustus' friend,
general, colleague, and son-in-law, Agrippa, victor over Antony and
Cleopatra at Actium. Surrounded by the hum of modern Roman life, its
time-blackened mass, with the forest of dark columns which forms its
portico, confronts the visitor at unexpected moments with a sudden
vision of immemorial age. The narrow streets leading to it seem to deflect
the eye rather than to attract it toward the great building lost in their
labyrinth. To emerge from them into the Piazza della Rotonda, which
surrounds the temple, is a surprise. As Hawthorne wrote almost a
century ago it 'often presents itself before the bewildered stranger, when
he is in search of some other objects'. It seems equally often to withdraw
itself into some hidden world from those who seek it, only to confront them
finally with a closed and secret air.

The temple was dedicated especially to Mars and Venus, the patrons of
the Julian family, to which Caesar and Augustus belonged; statues of these
deities were set among those in the niches of the interior. 'Agrippa, for his
part,' says Dio Cassius the historian, 'wished to place a statue of Augustus
there also and to bestow upon him the honour of having the structure
named after him; but when the emperor would not accept either honour,
he placed in the temple itself a statue of the former Caesar and in the
vestibule statues of Augustus and himself.' The statue of Venus in this
temple, according to Pliny, wore in her ears the cut halves of one of two
famous pearls which had belonged to Cleopatra; the queen had dissolved
and drunk the other, says the author, to win a wager from Antony.

The Pantheon was burned twice; after the second fire, about A.D. 110, it
was completely rebuilt by Hadrian, who, scrupulous about claiming for himself a structure which he had merely rebuilt, had the original inscription
bearing the names of Agrippa and his father copied on the new building.

So, for nearly two thousand years, while the names of emperors have
been almost forgotten, men have read that of a great Roman, humbly

(118)

born, who rivalled Augustus in beautifying the city and in popularity, yet was known in his time for his rare loyalty and modesty. The ancient bronze letters disappeared long ago but their matrices remained, their size making them the most clearly legible of any Roman inscription. The hollows were refilled with modern letters in 1894.

Septimius Severus made repairs in the third century, but on the whole it is Hadrian's brick-faced concrete structure which stands today, with its forest of grey and red granite columns, forty-six feet high, surmounted by Corinthian capitals of time-greyed marble. Bronze tiles once covered the outside of its dome and a bronze cornice still surrounds the circular opening in its centre. Walls and dome stand as in imperial days, but the marble facings of the interior are gone, and of the ancient glitter of bronze only the cornice around the opening in the dome and the bronze-covered doors of the vestibule remain. In 663 the Byzantine emperor Constans II carried away the tiles from the dome, and in the seventeenth century the bronze roof trusses of the portico were melted down and recast, much of the metal being used in cannon to defend the Castle of Sant' Angelo.

The pagan temple was already a Christian church when its shining tiles were removed. In 609 it had been dedicated to Mary and All Saints or Martyrs under the name of *Sancta Maria ad Martyres*. Later it received the name it bears as a church today—Santa Maria Rotonda, or Round Saint Mary's. The *Mirabilia* knew it as both a temple and a church, and tells the story of its pagan founding and Christian dedication with a characteristic blending of truth and fantasy:

'In the times of the Consuls and Senators,' Agrippa, tired and troubled concerning the conduct of a war, fell asleep worn out by thinking. 'And there appeared to him a woman, who said unto him: What doest thou, Agrippa? forsooth, thou art in great thought; and he answered unto her: Madame, I am. She said, Comfort thee, and promise me, if thou shalt win the victory, to make me a temple such as I show unto thee. And he said, I will make it. And she showed him in the vision a temple made after that fashion. And he said: Madame, who art thou? And she said, I am Cybele, the mother of the gods: bear libations to Neptune, which is a mighty god, that he help thee; and make this temple to be dedicated to my worship and Neptune's, because we will be with thee, and thou shalt prevail.'

Agrippa was victorious and 'When he returned to Rome, he built this temple, and made it to be dedicated to the honour of Cybele, mother of the gods, and of Neptune, god of the sea, and of all the gods, and he gave to this temple the name of Pantheon. And in honour of the same Cybele he made a gilded image, which he set upon the top of the temple above the opening, and covered it with a magnifical roof of gilded brass.

'After many ages, pope Boniface, in the time of Phocas, a Christian emperor, seeing that so marvellous temple, dedicated in honour of Cybele, mother of the gods, before the which Christian men were oft-times stricken of devils, prayed the emperor to grant him this temple, that as in the Calends of November it was dedicated to Cybele, mother of the gods, so in the Calends of November he might consecrate it to the blessed Mary, ever-virgin, that is the mother of all saints. This Caesar granted unto him; and the pope, with the whole Roman people, in the day of the Calends of November, did dedicate it; and ordained that upon that day the Roman pontiff should sing mass there . . . and that on the same day all saints, with their mother, Mary ever-virgin, and the heavenly spirits should have festival, and the dead have, throughout the churches of the whole world, a sacrifice for the ransom of their souls.'

The facts in this tale are the names of Agrippa, the founder; of Phocas, the emperor who gave the temple to the Church; of Boniface, the pope who received it; and its dedication to Mary and the Martyrs. According to traditional Church observance, however, the date of its consecration is celebrated on May 13 instead of on All Saints' Day, November 1. The Pantheon has achieved an added fame as the burial place for artists, including Raphael, and for the kings and queens of United Italy.

The Pantheon's glory is its interior (Plates 194–195) with a dome more than one hundred and forty feet in diameter, soaring to an equal distance above the floor, and lighted only by the one great central eye, thirty feet across. No photographs can give as adequate an impression of this interior as Piranesi's etching, Pannini's painting, or the descriptions of Byron, Shelley, and Hawthorne.

'Simple, erect, severe, austere, sublime—
Shrine of all saints and temple of all gods,
From Jove to Jesus—spared and blest by time.'

wrote Byron in the Fourth Canto of *Childe Harold*.

Shelley, least ecclesiastically minded of men, but equally reverent beneath the spell of its proportions and changing moods, wrote to Peacock in 1819:

'It is, as it were, the visible image of the universe; in the perfection of its proportions, as when you regard the unmeasured dome of heaven, the idea of magnitude is swallowed up and lost. It is open to the sky, and its wide dome is lighted by the ever-changing illumination of the air. The clouds of noon fly over it, and at night the keen stars are seen through the azure darkness, hanging immovably, or driving after the driven moon among the clouds.'

Hawthorne, staunch descendant of the Puritans, was also fascinated by its changing lights. 'It was pleasant,' he wrote in his *French and Italian Notebooks*, 'looking up to the circular opening, to see the clouds flitting across it, sometimes covering it quite over, then permitting a glimpse of sky, then showing all the circle of sunny blue. . . . The great slanting beam of sunshine was visible all the way down to the pavement, falling upon motes of dust or a thin smoke of incense imperceptible in the shadow. Insects were playing to and fro in the beam, high up toward the opening. There is a wonderful charm in the naturalness of all this; one might fancy a swarm of cherubs coming down through the opening and sporting in the broad ray.'

THE PYRAMID OF CESTIUS

Plates 196–199

CAPITOL, Palatine, and Forum; arches, baths, and temples; all, till now, have lain well within the limits of the imperial city. But the Pyramid of Cestius (Plates 196–197) is at its boundary; forms, indeed, part of those fortifications which the Emperor Aurelian began in A.D. 272 when the danger of barbarian invasions from the north had made Rome feel the need of walls for the first time in five centuries or more. The long Roman Peace was ending and the Middle Ages drawing near.

The pyramid itself belongs to the earlier and more confident time which dispensed with walls. An inscription which bears the name of Caius Cestius, praetor, and tribune of the people, states that Agrippa was one of the executors who raised this tomb; it must, therefore, have been built before that general's death in 12 B.C. In shape this monument of brick and concrete faced with marble recalls the interest in Egyptian affairs which marked those days when Cleopatra was but lately dead and Egypt a newly acquired Roman province. It was almost three centuries later that Aurelian's wall cut into the pyramid's eastern and western faces; the neighbouring Gate of San Paolo, the old Porta Ostiensis opening on the road to Rome's ancient port, was reconstructed by the Byzantine general Belisarius in the sixth century.

The clearest of inscriptions, however, did not prevent confusion in the Middle Ages. This pyramid, and another which stood near the Vatican until the late fifteenth century, seemed then too imposing to mark the graves of any but great heroes.

The pyramid by the Porta San Paolo thus became the 'Tomb of Remus'; the one near the Vatican was called the 'Tomb of Romulus'. The two appear in most medieval views of Rome, usually labelled *meta Remi* and *meta Romuli* because their forms suggested the pyramidal shape of the *meta* or goal of a circus.

In the fourteenth century even Petrarch referred to the pyramid as the 'Tomb of Remus'. A little later Boccaccio, sceptical concerning its connection with this hero, noted in his *Genealogy of the Gods*: 'People of the present day point out a pyramid built over his body and raised on high in the wall with stone blocks.' But by the early fifteenth century the humanist Poggio was surprised that so learned a man as Petrarch should not have read the name of Cestius in the inscription.

The wall which abuts against the ancient pyramid has survived many a war since Aurelian began it; has been repaired and enlarged by Byzantine generals and popes; and has been threatened by destruction in the name of progress. Its latest damage came from Allied bombing during the Second World War, when fragments struck both the wall and the pyramid. But neither the siege-engines of the Goths nor bombs of the present age have so far wrought lasting damage.

New associations have gathered about the old monument during the last two centuries. More visitors, perhaps, are drawn today to the foot of this pyramid because it looks down upon the Protestant Cemetery (Plates 198–199) than come to it because it is a majestic survival from the days of Augustus.

The regular burial of Protestants beside the pyramid and the Aurelian wall began in the second half of the eighteenth century. The dead who lie so near the grave of this citizen of ancient Rome are of many nations, but the majority from English-speaking lands is so great that it has often been called 'the English Burying-ground'. Many of the tombstones here are silent witnesses to the popularity of Rome as a health resort in the nineteenth century for those ordered to a mild climate, and of the frequent tragic failure of the hopes of those who followed this last resource. The sudden upswing of travel after the close of the Napoleonic Wars is evident, too, in the number of foreign tombstones dated early in this period of comparative peace.

It was in these years that the burial of Keats and Shelley here made the cemetery a shrine for literary pilgrims. Keats came to Rome to die in the winter of 1820–1821 in the house beside the Spanish Steps. His was one of the last graves in the old cemetery, for the great increase of burials here, and the fear that the planting of trees might obstruct the view of the pyramid, led to the closing of the old burying-ground soon afterward. Joseph Severn, who had accompanied Keats from England and stayed by him until his death, secured a place for himself at the same time and so, years later, was laid beside his friend.

More than any other individual, perhaps more than all others together, Shelley spread the fame of this cemetery beside the ancient pyramid. He had visited and loved the quiet place before Keats came to Rome, writing of it to a friend in 1818:

'The English burying-place is a green slope near the walls, under the pyramidal tomb of Cestius, and is, I think, the most beautiful and solemn cemetery I ever beheld. To see the sun shining on its bright grass, fresh when we first visited it, with the autumnal dews, and hear the whispering of the wind among the leaves of the trees which have overgrown the tomb of Cestius . . . and to mark the tombs, mostly of women and young people who were buried there, one might, if one were to die, desire the sleep they seem to sleep.'

In the early summer following the death of Keats, Shelley wrote his famous description of the place in *Adonais*, his lament for the young poet:

'Go thou to Rome,—at once the Paradise,
The grave, the city, and the wilderness;
And where its wrecks like shattered mountains rise,
And flowering weeds, and fragrant copses dress
The bones of Desolation's nakedness
Pass, till the Spirit of the spot shall lead
Thy footsteps to a slope of green access
Where, like an infant's smile, over the dead
A light of laughing flowers along the grass is spread;

'And grey walls moulder round, on which dull Time
Feeds, like slow fire upon a hoary brand;
And one keen pyramid with wedge sublime,
Pavilioning the dust of him who planned
This refuge for his memory, doth stand
Like flame transformed to marble; and beneath,
A field is spread, on which a newer band
Have pitched in Heaven's smile their camp of death,
Welcoming him we lose with scarce extinguished breath.'

The next year, Shelley was drowned in the Gulf of Spezia and in 1823 his ashes were buried in the new cemetery here, close by a buttress of the Aurelian wall and the grey pyramid's 'wedge sublime'.

It is not unfitting that beneath an inconspicuous flat stone in this cemetery there should lie the remains of that Charles Andrew Mills who covered the walls of the old Villa Palatina with a Gothic mask. His name, his age of 86, and the date, 10, iii, 1846, alone recall the eccentric Scot whose memory still haunts the halls where Domitian once held court.

HADRIAN'S TOMB:
THE CASTLE OF SANT' ANGELO

Plates 200–205

THE heart of ancient Rome lay on the east or left bank of the Tiber, where the city had first begun to expand from the Palatine settlement. As it spread out over wider areas it took in the west or right bank of the river, including a district that has always held itself aloof. The name of this section, *Regio Transtiberina*, Region across the Tiber, survives today in that of its southern part, Trastevere, a crowded, colourful, still slightly medieval neighbourhood, whose residents long considered themselves more nearly pure-blooded descendants of the ancient Romans than those of any other part of the city.

Through almost the entire length of the region runs 'the long ridge of the Janiculum', which Martial praised more than eighteen hundred years ago. From this, the highest hill of Rome, never reckoned among the immortal seven, 'wide sheltered reaches look down on the hills, and the flat summit, gently swelling, enjoys to the full a clearer sky, and, when mist shrouds the winding vales, alone shines with its own brightness. . . . On this side may you see the seven sovereign hills and take the measure of all Rome, the Alban hills and Tusculan too, and every cool retreat nestling near the city.'

The northern and southern parts of Transtiberine Rome, throughout imperial days, formed the fourteenth region of the city; its separation into two distinct parts came about through later redistricting. The whole section, only a small part of which was enclosed within Aurelian's wall, was characterized by a sharply contrasting mixture of working-class homes, imperial and patrician gardens, and circuses for games and sports. The gardens which Julius Caesar willed to the people of Rome were in the southern section; the site of the immense tomb which Hadrian built for himself and his successors (Plates 200–201) was probably part of an imperial garden in the northern part. By that time little space was available nearer the centre of the city, and the prudent emperor had no wish to copy the folly of Nero by seizing private property.

Hadrian began the tomb several years before his death in A.D. 138, but it was finished by his successor. Its outer walls are of concrete and stone, once faced with marble; within, is a network of brick walls, ancient and medieval and renaissance. The tomb has been one of the most continuously used and therefore one of the most altered of Roman monuments. Beneath the accumulations of centuries, however, the plan is still clear—a circular core rising from a square podium, later surrounded by fortifications shaped roughly like a five-pointed star. The greatest change in its appearance in recent years has been the freeing of these walls from later buildings which had crept over them.

The last Roman emperor known to have been buried here was Caracalla, who died in A.D. 217. Aurelian (270–275) incorporated the tomb in the city's fortifications; in the bloody period of the sixth century it served as one of the chief fortresses of the Byzantine general, Belisarius, after he had captured the city from the Goths. The fighting was especially severe here when the Goths attempted to recapture Rome in 537, as the contemporary Byzantine historian, Procopius, records:

'The tomb of the Roman Emperor Hadrian stands outside the Aurelian Gate, removed about a stone's throw from the fortifications, a very noteworthy sight. For it is made of Parian marble and the stones fit closely one upon the other, having nothing at all between them. And it has four sides which are all equal, each being about a stone's throw in length, while their height exceeds that of the city wall; and above there are statues of the same marble, representing men and horses, of wonderful workmanship. But since this tomb seemed to the men of ancient times a fortress threatening the city, they enclosed it by two walls, which extend to it from the circuit-wall, and thus made it a part of the wall. And, indeed, it gives the appearance of a high tower built as a bulwark before the gate there.'

The Goths pressed so close to the walls that the defenders were unable to use their ordinary weapons. 'For a short time', Procopius continues, 'consternation fell upon the Romans, who knew not what means of defence they should employ to save themselves, but afterwards by common agreement they broke in pieces the most of the statues, which were very large, and taking up great numbers of stones thus secured, threw them with both hands down upon the heads of the enemy, who gave way before this shower of missiles.'

During the Middle Ages the tomb went by various names, such as 'House' or 'Prison' of Theodoric the Ostrogoth, and 'Castle of Crescentius', referring to its defence by Giovanni Crescentius, a Roman noble, against the Holy Roman Emperor Otto III. The early version of the *Mirabilia* refers to it under the heading 'Castle of Crescentius', saying:

'There is a castle that was the temple of Hadrian . . . a temple built up, of marvellous greatness and beauty; the which was all covered with stones and adorned with divers histories, and fenced with brazen railings round about, with golden peacocks and a bull, of the which peacocks two were those that are at the Basin of the Parvise [the atrium of old Saint Peter's]. At the four sides of the temple were four horses of gilded brass, and in every face were brazen gates.'

The name by which it is still most widely known, the Castle of Sant' Angelo, or Holy Angel, comes from an early legend, according to which Pope Gregory the Great, while conducting a procession to pray for the ending of the plague in Rome in the year 590, beheld the Archangel Michael sheathing his sword above the castle as a token that the pestilence would cease. A fourteenth-century version of the *Mirabilia* notes that this 'is called the Angel's Castle'. The bronze angel which crowns the *Castello* today replaced one of marble in 1752. There is some uncertainty as to when the first angel was erected.

From the late fourteenth century the castle was the special fortress of the popes, who connected it with the Vatican by a covered passage for use in emergency. It has endured many sieges since then, the most terrible being that by the German and Spanish forces of Charles V in 1527. This was the siege in which Benvenuto Cellini, one of its defenders, declared that he himself had shot the Constable de Bourbon, leader of Charles' forces. Early in the twentieth century this ancient tomb and fortress, which had meanwhile been put to use as prison, as barracks, and as storehouse for powder, finally became a museum.

The Angel's Castle has a long history in art, fostered, no doubt, by its nearness to Saint Peter's. It occupied a prominent place in every medieval and renaissance plan, and was one of the first monuments to symbolize the city. As such a symbol it appears in the foreground of one of the earliest medieval views of Rome—the dim, almost unrecognizable, group of conventionalized 'marvels' which accompanies the figure of Saint Mark in a thirteenth-century vault of the upper church of Saint Francis at Assisi. In this time-worn fresco, sometimes attributed to Cimabue, the castle seems to have an angel on its summit. An account of a miracle during the plague of 1348 says that the angel's statue bowed to the Madonna, carried in a procession across the Angel-bridge.

When the new Saint Peter's was completed in the seventeenth century, the contrast of its soaring dome with the grim and heavy mass of the castle created a new composition, especially beloved by artists (Plate 202). The old views of the castle from downstream were not forgotten, but that from above, showing both the castle and Saint Peter's, was spread far and wide by engravings.

A note of festivity runs through pictures of the castle too. Through most of four centuries it was the setting for the most magnificent display of fireworks in a city famed, then as now, for the beauty of such spectacles (Plates 204–205). This was *la girandola*, 'the revolving one', named from the profusion of its radiating rockets and revolving wheels.

The first mention of this display is in 1481, though it may have been shown earlier. It was held on various occasions, such as Easter Monday, the Festival of Saints Peter and Paul at the end of June, the election or coronation of a pope, or on papal anniversaries. Tradition has it that some of the effects were designed by Michelangelo.

From the time of the Roman Republic of 1798–1799 until after the city became the capital of United Italy in 1870, the *girandola* was often shown at other places, such as the Pincian hill or the church of San Pietro in Montorio on the Janiculum. For a few years after 1872 the display was again centred at the castle, though more rarely. Soon, however, the jarring caused by the powder charges damaged some of its frescoed rooms, and the fireworks were regarded as too hazardous for the ancient building. The famous spectacle was held here for the last time in 1887.

THE VATICAN OBELISK

Plates 206–210

IF the east bank of the Tiber dominated the pagan city, the west gradually took the lead in Christian Rome. For this change one man was primarily responsible. Saint Peter's name is as closely interwoven with the Transtiberine section as is that of Agrippa with the Pantheon or of Titus with his triumphal arch across the Sacred Way. And upon the 'rock' of Peter's name the Church of Rome was built.

Ancient tradition fixes the date of Peter's death as A.D. 67, near the end of Nero's reign; the place as the Circus of Gaius and Nero in the Vatican fields, where lay the gardens of the emperor's mother Agrippina; and the spot of his burial as a nearby cemetery.

When the first Christians met their deaths in Nero's circus, scapegoats suffering for the fire which the emperor himself had been accused of setting, an obelisk of red granite stood upon its *spina*, or central dividing wall. Caligula had brought it by ship from Heliopolis some twenty years before and set it up in the circus which Nero finished. Its age cannot be reckoned exactly as it has no inscription.

For more than fifteen centuries this obelisk stood where it had been set up by the emperor (Plate 207), while nearby, to the north, rose first an unknown shrine marking the grave of Peter, then the basilica which the Emperor Constantine built, and finally the great church which stands today. As buildings came and went and all the other obelisks of Rome fell from their ancient places, this one alone remained erect, an object of wonder, of admiration, and of conjecture.

The Middle Ages, which named the ruins of the circus where the obelisk stood 'the Palace of Nero', called the tall granite shaft 'Saint Peter's Needle', and believed that it contained the ashes of Julius Caesar in the globe on its top. The *Mirabilia* says of it:

'Within the Palace of Nero . . . is the basilica that is called Vatican, adorned with marvellous mosaic and ceiled with gold and glass. . . . There is also another temple that was Nero's Wardrobe, which is now called Saint Andrew; nigh whereunto is the memorial of Caesar, that is the Needle where his ashes nobly rest in his sarcophagus, to the intent that as in his lifetime the whole world lay subdued before him, even so in his death the same may lie beneath him for ever. The memorial was adorned in the lower part with tables of gilded brass, and fairly limned with Latin letters; and above at the ball, where he rests, it is decked with gold and precious stones, and there is it written:

"Caesar who once wast great as is the world,
  Now in how small a cavern art thou closed." '

By the middle of the fifteenth century the old basilica which had seen the coronation of Charlemagne and many another emperor had become seriously weakened. Nicholas V proposed to rebuild it according to the original plan of a Latin cross, with three short arms and a longer one to form the nave. He died, however, when the work had been barely begun and it lapsed for fifty years. Then Julius II took up the project and commissioned Bramante to construct a new church according to the plan he had submitted—a Greek cross, having four equal arms, each covered with heavy barrel vaulting, their crossing crowned by a dome. 'I wish,' said Bramante, his mind upon the great buildings of the past he saw about him, 'to erect the dome of the Pantheon on the vaults of the temple of Peace' (the current name of the Basilica of Constantine). The cornerstone for this new structure was laid in 1506, a date which may fairly be called that of the present Saint Peter's beginning.

Unfortunately both Bramante and the pope died before many years and a succession of architects, including Raphael, changed Bramante's designs. Finally, in 1547, Michelangelo was put in charge. He revived the original idea of a Greek cross, but saw only the drum of the great dome complete before his death in 1564. His successor, Giacomo della Porta, completed it in accordance with his master's drawings, shaping the subtle curve which is at once the wonder and the despair of architects today.

It was in Giacomo della Porta's time that Sixtus V decided to have the obelisk moved from its comparatively inconspicuous place near the old sacristy south of the church to a commanding position in front. In 1586 Domenico Fontana supervised the moving, an engineering feat worthy of the energies of the Renaissance and one which created great excitement in Rome and comment throughout Europe (Plate 208). When it was completed, the eighty-two foot shaft, still unbroken, stood upright once more in front of the unfinished church. It was at this time that the globe on its top was replaced by the present cross; this globe, which contained no ashes, rests today in the Conservatori Museum, where one can see upon its surface the holes made by the shots of the soldiers of the Constable of Bourbon when they used it as target during the sack of Rome in 1527.

The new church, meanwhile, continued to grow slowly. In order to use it while work was going on, a partition had been run across it from side to side; for years the new dome towered above the old façade. From 1605 to 1615, when work had been completed as far as this wall, the old front part of the church was demolished and re-built in its present form. By this time the ruling pope, Paul V, had asked his architect, Carlo Maderna, who built the façade, to lengthen the nave, thereby giving more room for processions. As a result the lower part of the dome can be seen from the front only at a considerable distance. This defect has been partly remedied by the building of the present unencumbered approach to Saint Peter's. After the new façade was completed, the dividing wall was re-moved and the people of Rome saw their church as a whole for the first time. The new Saint Peter's was dedicated by Urban VIII on November 18, 1626, the traditional anniversary day of the dedication of the basilica built on the same site by Constantine in the fourth century. In the hundred and twenty years since the laying of the cornerstone in Bramante's day, twenty popes and almost as many architects had watched it rise step by step into one of the new wonders of the world.

It is not only the dome which can be called, with Ampère, a 'work of man that has something of the grandeur of the works of God'. An interior so limitless and varied is like a wide landscape; it cannot be seen as a whole; it has also an atmospheric colour of its own. The air, rather than the surfaces, of the immense enclosed space seems heavy with colour, though the walls are rich with subtle harmonies of marble which an emperor might have envied. And this air draws its varying colour from reflected light, changing from silver-grey to gold and rose and violet as the sunlight comes and goes and fades into the dusk.

But all was not finished with the completion of the church. Through the middle years of the seventeenth century Bernini created as its setting the Piazza of Saint Peter's, with its sweeping double colonnade enclosing the obelisk and the two fountains whose drifting clouds of spray and restless movement are subtly in harmony with the curving baroque porticos. No imperial building had a setting more satisfying than this; there comes to mind from ancient days only the vanished glory of the Forum of Trajan, 'beggaring description and never again to be imitated by mortal man'.

In Saint Peter's Piazza and the church beyond, which can contain more people than the Colosseum seated, the pilgrims of the world find a common home, as did the citizens of ancient Rome in their imperial city. The words of Sidonius Apollinaris, extolling Rome to his fellow Gaul,

Eutropius, come inevitably to the mind: 'The city unique upon earth, where none but the barbarian and the slave is foreign.' But here there is no such qualification; this is a place of meeting, of reunion, of shared celebrations and worship for citizens of the Eternal City of the spirit, 'where there is neither bond nor free'.

STATUES THAT WERE NEVER BURIED

Plates 211–222

ANCIENT Rome was so rich in statues that as late as the sixth century, when their destruction was already under way, Cassiodorus wrote, 'the City has an artificial population almost equal to its natural one.'

Carrying out Theodoric's enlightened policy of protecting Roman antiquities, Cassiodorus appointed guardians for the statues' protection. But the tide of feeling was running against such survivals from the pagan past; two centuries earlier, Lactantius Firmianus, tutor of one of the sons of Constantine the Great, had voiced the Christian belief that such images were often the instruments of demons and that 'there is no religion wherever there is an image'. Their destruction was hastened by plundering invaders and by the melting down of works in bronze for their valuable metal.

Presently the very art of making large sculpture in the round was almost forgotten, and the few great statues which remained must indeed have seemed like denizens from another world. About these surviving figures from a more spacious time, unburied and unforgotten among the ruins of the past, fanciful and elaborate explanations gathered, suited to the hearers of a later day. Most of these figures—the equestrian Marcus Aurelius, a colossal head and hand, one of three river gods, the Horse Tamers of the Quirinal—appear as landmarks in medieval views of Rome (Plates 5, 7, 8).

Most famous of all these unburied statues is the bronze figure of Marcus Aurelius, now in the centre of the Capitol Piazza (Plate 211). But the Middle Ages passed over this philosophic emperor in favour of Constantine, and the statue probably owed its preservation through the centuries when most available bronze was melted down to the belief that it represented the first Christian emperor.

Throughout the Middle Ages the statue stood near the Lateran, the official residence of the popes until their return from exile at Avignon at the end of the fourteenth century. It is shown there in the medieval plans of Rome in the Marciana Library at Venice (Plate 212) and in its probable copy at the Vatican. Van Heemskerck drew it there too (Plate 213). Beside it lie the head and hand of the colossal sun god which stood near the Colosseum—or so the medieval mind felt certain. Some have thought

(133)

that it was brought there from the Caelian hill, while others maintain with equal certainty that it had always stood in the Lateran neighbourhood, in the grounds of the palace of Annius Verus, grandfather of Marcus Aurelius.

The twelfth-century Anglo-Norman poet, Wace, reflected the admiration of medieval visitors for this statue in his *Roman de Rou*, the Romance of Rollo, Robert I, Duke of Normandy. His hero:

'Saw Constantine in Rome display'd
In manly shape, of copper made,
Of copper is the horse also,
No wind nor rain them overthrow.
Such is the fame and the honour
Of Constantine the Emperor.'

Benjamin of Tudela, a Jewish traveller who visited Rome about 1170, noted also 'the Emperor Constantine, who built the city that is called after his name Constantinople, whose image with his horse is of gilded brass'.

Although the statue was commonly known as Constantine in the Middle Ages, it had other names as well—Antony, Septimius Severus, and Theodoric. The *Mirabilia* tells a legend designed to prove that it was none of these. 'There is at the Lateran,' it says, 'a certain brazen horse, that is called Constantine's Horse; but it is not so, for whosoever will know the truth thereof, let him read it here.

'In the time of the Consuls and Senators, a certain full mighty king from the parts of the East came to Italy, and besieged Rome on the side of the Lateran, and with much slaughter and war afflicted the Roman people. Then a certain squire of great beauty and virtue, bold and subtle, arose and said to the Consuls and Senators: If there were one that should deliver you from this tribulation, what would he deserve from the Senate? and they answered and said: What thing soever he shall ask, he shall presently obtain it. Give me, said he, thirty thousand sesterces, and ye shall make me a memorial of the victory, when the fight is done and a horse in gilded brass of the best. And they promised to do all that he asked.'

The squire then set out disguised as a groom, riding without a saddle and lay in wait for the king, who was a dwarf. Presently the king came by, accompanied by his nobles, and the squire seized him and bore him away despite their resistance. The Romans then put the enemy to flight and 'returned glorious to the city; and all that they had promised to the aforesaid squire they paid and performed it, thirty thousand sesterces, and a horse of gilded brass without a saddle for a memorial of him, with the man himself riding thereon, having his right hand stretched forth, that he took the king withal. . . . The king, which was of little stature, with his hands bound behind him, as he had been taken, was also figured by way of remembrance under the hoof of the horse.'

This little figure, probably representing one of the barbarians conquered by the emperor, is now gone, but it appears in medieval figures copied from this famous statue. The emperor sits upon a cloth or pad. The riding saddle, whose absence attracted so much medieval interest, was not used by the Romans until long after the time of Marcus Aurelius; it was probably taken over from the barbarians in the fourth century. The Romans did not use stirrups until even later.

In 1538 the statue was moved from the Lateran, under Michelangelo's direction, but somewhat against his will, to form the central feature of the great piazza he planned for the Capitol (Plate 214). Michelangelo himself is said to have constructed the statue's pedestal. In 1940 an ornamental pavement was laid here, following a plan of Michelangelo's preserved in a contemporary engraving, and the statue now rises from the centre of a star composed of travertine blocks (Plate 57).

Hawthorne's description of the statue in *The Marble Faun* is typical of the reaction of nineteenth-century visitors to Rome: 'The moonlight glistened upon traces of the gilding which had once covered both rider and steed; these were almost gone, but the aspect of dignity was still perfect, clothing the figure as it were with an imperial robe of light. It is the most majestic representation of the kingly character that ever the world has seen. A sight of the old heathen emperor is enough to create an evanescent sentiment of loyalty even in a democratic bosom, so august does he look, so fit to rule, so worthy of man's profoundest homage and obedience, so inevitably attractive of his love.'

Some gilding remains today on the emperor's face and cape and on the horse's head. Popular belief has it that this gilding, gradually transpiring from a store of gold within, will one day cover the statue; this will be the signal for the Judgment Day.

A great bronze head and hand (Plates 212, 215–216) which lay beside the emperor's statue at the Lateran were scarcely less famous in the Middle Ages. According to tradition these had belonged to the statue of the sun god which stood before the Colosseum, mentioned by Martial as the 'wondrous colossus . . . girt with rays'. Nero had erected this originally as a statue of himself, in the vestibule of his Golden House. After his death it was transformed into that of the sun god, and the head may have been changed once, or more than once, in later years, to give it the features of other emperors.

The head from the Lateran seems, beyond reasonable doubt, to be one now in the Conservatori Museum, probably brought to the Capitol in the late fifteenth century when most of the bronzes from the papal collections were transferred there. A colossal left hand on the same scale, and an orb which seems to fit the palm from which it has been detached, are also in the Conservatori collection and probably belonged to the same statue. The head as it now exists appears to be of late workmanship and is thought to represent one of the sons and successors of Constantine the Great, although it has borne many names since it became the subject of inquiry. The Middle Ages, however, accepted both head and hand unquestioningly as those of the great sun god and gave them a colourful history.

The earliest version of the *Mirabilia* says flatly—and incorrectly—that the statue 'stood on the top of the Colosseum,' and does not mention the head and hand by the Lateran. A later version gives the typical medieval story:

'In the midst [of the Colosseum] abode Phoebus, that is the god of the sun, which having his feet on the earth reached unto heaven with his head, and did hold in his hand an orb signifying that Rome ruled over the world.

'But after a space of time the blessed Silvester bade destroy that temple, and in like wise other places, to the intent that the orators [pilgrims offering prayers] which came to Rome should not wander through profane buildings, but shall pass with devotion through the churches. But the head and hands of the aforesaid idol he caused to be laid before his Palace of the Lateran in remembrance thereof; and the same is now called by the vulgar "Samson's Ball".' This name, of course, refers to the orb.

Master Gregory's twelfth-century description states that the image 'was over gilt with gold imperial, shining continually in the darkness, moving equally with the sun'. This idea of movement with the sun seems another echo of Suetonius' account of the revolving ceiling of Nero's banquet hall, met already in the medieval description of the Colosseum. Ranaulf Higden's fourteenth-century *Polychronicon* says much the same, its Roman section being based on Master Gregory. Both of these accounts state that the statue was destroyed by Gregory the Great in the sixth century, not by Silvester in the fourth. Silvester, indeed, could not have destroyed it: the last mention of it in antiquity refers to its coronation in a June festival of A.D. 354, nineteen years after Silvester's death. And no one destroyed the Colosseum, the temple in question.

Though there is little doubt that the head and hand in the Conservatori are those which lay before the Lateran, there is some difficulty of size in identifying them with the ancient colossus before the Colosseum. Pliny says that this statue was one hundred and ten feet high; Suetonius, that it was one hundred and twenty feet, or at least in the neighbourhood of twenty times life size. The head and hand in the Conservatori are only about five times larger than life. Also, there is a slight discrepancy about the hand. Master Gregory and Ranaulf Higden both say that it was a right hand, and it is an unmistakable right hand in the Marciana plan; but the hand in the Museum is a left. However, considering the centuries through which the fragments were thought of as belonging to the famous ancient statue, they may be regarded with all the deference due to long tradition and association.

Among other unburied statues are the colossal river gods which repose at the sides of the staircase to the Senator's Palace today (Plate 217). They appear in drawings by Marten van Heemskerck (Plates 216, 218) and in many early plans of Rome. These lay for centuries on the Quirinal, where they had perhaps adorned the Baths of Constantine. In 1517 they were moved to the Capitol, first to the arcade of the old Conservators' Palace, where Van Heemskerck drew them, and finally, in 1552, to their present place.

The figure at the left, as one faces the Senator's Palace, probably represents the Nile, resting one arm upon a sphinx. The other, leaning upon a rather nondescript animal restored as a wolf, now symbolizes the Tiber, but may once have been meant for the Tigris with a tiger. The figures of the twins, Romulus and Remus, suckled by the wolf, which are under this statue's arm, are later additions.

The *Mirabilia* says of the river gods in their old location:
'On the brow of the hill [the Quirinal] was the temple of Jupiter and Diana, that is now called the Emperor's Table, over the Palace of Constantine. There in the palace was the temple of Saturn and Bacchus, where their idols now lie. Fast by are the Marble Horses.' The 'Palace of Constantine' was the Baths of Constantine. The 'temple of Jupiter and Diana' or 'Emperor's Table', was the great ruin on the Quirinal now generally called the Temple of the Sun or the Temple of Serapis, where the immense block of marble lies in the Colonna Gardens (Plate 174). Master Gregory referred to the statues as 'two old men' and also as 'Solomon and Bacchus'.

The Marble Horses on the Quirinal (Plate 219) mentioned in the *Mirabilia* and many other medieval descriptions as guides for the location of other monuments, appear in almost every medieval view of the city (Plates 7–8). They may have been meant to represent the Dioscuri or twin demi-gods, Castor and Pollux, and from this association and their gesture of checking the rearing steeds, have taken on another popular name, the Horse Tamers. 'Marble Horses', however, was their most common name for centuries, and the hill in their neighbourhood was called from them *Monte Cavallo*, the Horses' Hill.

They were probably made by a Roman artist who followed some Greek original, though for centuries they have borne inscriptions stating that they were the work of Phidias and Praxiteles. The first of these inscriptions, which have been renewed more than once, was probably attached in the very late classic or early medieval times, when nothing was known of these two Greek masters except their fame.

The *Mirabilia* has a typical medieval explanation of the group: 'Hear now to what intent the Horses of Marble were made bare, and the men beside them naked, and what story they tell. . . . In the time of the emperor Tiberius there came to Rome two young men that were philosophers, named Praxiteles and Phidias, whom the emperor, observing them to be of so much wisdom, kept nigh unto himself in his palace; and he said to them, Wherefore do you go abroad naked? who answered and said: Because all things are naked and open to us, and we hold the world of no account, therefore we go naked and possess nothing; and they said: Whatsoever thou, most mighty emperor, shalt devise in thy chamber by day or night, albeit we be absent, we will tell it thee every word. If ye shall do that ye say, said the emperor, I will give you what thing soever ye shall desire. They answered and said, We ask no money, but only a memorial of us. And when the next day was come, they showed unto the emperor in order whatsoever he had thought of in that night. Therefore he made them the memorial that he had promised, to wit, the naked horses, which trample on the earth, that is upon the mighty princes of the world. Meanwhile . . . there be the two men half naked, which stand by the horses, and with arms raised on high and bent fingers tell the things that are to be; and as they be naked so is all worldly knowledge naked and open to their minds'.

Master Gregory's guide calls the group the 'marble horses' and comments upon their 'marvellous size'—they are over eighteen feet high. The men he calls 'calculators' and says that the horses are symbols of their quick-working intelligence.

In the late sixteenth century Sixtus V moved the statues some distance from their ancient location, restored them and their inscriptions thoroughly, and set them up near their present location in the Quirinal Piazza. Sixteenth and seventeenth-century guidebooks added to their descriptions such fancies as that the statues were brought to Nero from Egypt or Armenia, that the men represented Alexander the Great and his father, Philip of Macedonia, and that one of the horses was Alexander's famous Bucephalus.

The statues were rearranged in the late eighteenth century, and an obelisk which had once stood near the Mausoleum of Augustus was set up with them. The marble basin of the fountain, set below them in 1818, came from the Roman Forum, where it stood near the three columns of Castor's temple and was used as a watering trough for the cattle of the *Campo Vaccino*. It shows clearly in Vasi's etching of the church of Santa Maria Liberatrice (Plate 99) at the foot of the Palatine.

The figures have seldom been more pleasingly described than in Hawthorne's *French and Italian Notebooks*:

'Those admirable ancient statues of Castor and Pollux . . . seem to me sons of the morning and full of life and strength. The atmosphere, in such a length of time, has covered the marble surface of these statues with a grey rust, that envelops both the men and horses as with a garment; besides which, there are strange discolorations, such as patches of white moss on the elbows, and reddish streaks down the sides; but the glory of form overcomes all these defects of colour. It is pleasant to observe how familiar some little birds are with these colossal statues,—hopping about on their heads and over their huge fists, and very likely they have nests in their ears or among their hair.'

Another colossal statue, a river god not unlike those by the Senator's Palace, lay throughout the centuries in the very heart of ancient Rome. It rests now in the courtyard of the Capitoline Museum (Plate 221). Its home in the Middle Ages and well through the sixteenth century was in the Via di Marforio (Plate 222), a street which ran between the Roman Forum and the Forum of Augustus. This was often called the 'Forum of Mars' from the temple of Mars Ultor dedicated there; the name of both statue and street is a contraction of 'Mars' Forum'. The *Mirabilia* speaks of the statue as a likeness of the god himself, saying, 'Before Mamertinus his prison was the temple of Mars, where is now his image.' The prison is the ancient Mamertine prison at the foot of the Capitol, where Nero was said to have imprisoned Saint Peter.

The statue was removed from its ancient place in 1587 and, after being set in various locations, among them the portico of the Conservators' Palace on the Capitol, where it figured as a fountain adorned with the bronze ball from the Vatican obelisk, it finally came to rest in the court-yard of the Capitoline Museum in 1592. Its old location was the place where answers were posted to political satires composed in the name of another unburied statue, Pasquino, which still stands by the Palazzo Braschi. This mutilated torso, the remnant of a group showing Menelaus supporting the body of Patroclus, took its name, it is thought, from a nearby tailor noted for his sarcastic remarks. These *pasquinades*, so characteristic of Italian literature in late renaissance and baroque days, recall at times the biting satires of Martial centuries before.

A few other statues, too, have always stood unburied and visible in Rome—notably the bronze Boy Extracting a Thorn from His Foot, and the much-restored Romulus and Remus Suckled by the Wolf—but these, though noted by Master Gregory in the twelfth century, have not had the same frequent and detailed history in either art or literature as those which have been discussed here.

No statue of the most potent deity of all, the goddess of love, is known to have remained unburied in Rome throughout the centuries. Master Gregory, however, tells of one he saw on his visit there, one which impressed him strongly. It stood, he says, near the Marble Horses on the Quirinal, several miles from his hostelry, but so compelling was its beauty that he was drawn to see it three times despite the distance. The goddess was nude, according to his description, as she had appeared to Paris on the occasion of the famous contest with Juno and Minerva for the prize of beauty, and was so subtly made that the blood seemed to flush the cheeks and lips.

The hint of its location has tempted some to wonder whether the statue might have been the Capitoline Venus, found late in the seventeenth century near San Vitale between the Quirinal and the Viminal. There is an unproved tradition that it was discovered immured in a wall; certainly it was in excellent condition, as though it had been carefully preserved. It is tempting to think that someone, after Gregory's time, may have hidden it there to save it from a destruction threatened because too many men had pondered its un-Christian beauty.

The demonic power which such a statue might wield furnished the Middle Ages with a legend which William of Malmesbury told about 1125 in his *Gesta Regum Anglorum*, History of the Kings of England. According to William, a rich young citizen of medieval Rome, going out to exercise with his friends soon after his marriage, placed his wedding ring upon the finger of a bronze statue nearby. When he returned the hand had closed over the ring. Not wishing to attract attention he said nothing at the time, but came back at night to force it off. The hand was unclenched again but the ring was gone.

That night when he went to his bride, something dense and cloudlike came between, which could be felt but not seen, and he heard a voice, saying, 'Embrace me, since you wedded me today! I am Venus, on whose finger you put the ring! I have it, nor will I return it.'

When this had happened time after time the young man sought the aid of a priest skilled in necromancy, who told him to watch by night at a certain place where he would see a band of demons, male and female. When he should see one more corpulent than the rest, riding in a chariot, he should demand his ring. This he did, and the ring was returned—but the priest, who had been reviled by the demon, killed himself soon afterward. In the centuries since the English monk wrote his history this story has reappeared many times in many forms, from Prosper Mérimée's *Venus d'Ille* and William Morris' *Ring Given to Venus*, to Nash and Perelman's libretto of *One Touch of Venus*.

Not until long after William of Malmesbury and Master Gregory wrote were sculptors able once more to create figures which could rival the great works Cassiodorus had described when ancient Rome was not yet utterly cast down:

'Statues of men, showing the muscles swelling with effort, the nerves in tension, the whole man looking as if he had grown rather than been cast in metal. Statues of horses, full of fire, with the curved nostril, with rounded, tightly-knit limbs, with ears laid back—you would think the creature longed for the race, though you know that the metal moves not.'

Through these many and disastrous centuries, the wonder is, not that so few statues escaped destruction or burial, but that these few remained unburied amid the ruins to excite curiosity, awe, or fear in generation after generation.

PLATES

I. THE TEMPLE OF MAGNA MATER ON THE PALATINE

Detail of a Roman relief, first century A.D. Rome, Villa Medici

This relief is one of many built into the garden façade of the Villa Medici on the Pincian Hill. Since Napoleon's time the villa has been the seat of the French Academy.

The temple has been identified by its resemblance to pictures on coins. Remains of the actual temple, first excavated in the 1870's, still stand upon the Palatine.

2. MARCUS AURELIUS PASSING A TEMPLE ON HIS WAY TO
A TRIUMPHAL ARCH

Roman relief, second century A.D. Rome, Conservatori Museum

The temple and arch here may be merely generalized types suggesting the
Roman setting. On the chariot, in relief, are figures of Neptune, Rome enthroned,
and Minerva.

3. FRAGMENT OF THE MARBLE PLAN OR FORMA URBIS SHOWING
THE TEMPLE OF MINERVA ON THE AVENTINE
Early third century A.D. Rome, Municipal Antiquarium

This incised marble map was set by Septimius Severus on the outer wall of a building still standing (Plate 109), which faced upon the Forum of Peace. The first fragments were discovered in the late sixteenth century and others have been found since from time to time. Many are still unidentified, but some, as in this case, are clearly labelled.

This marble plan has its closest literary parallels in the *Notitia* and the *Curiosum*, fourth-century Latin catalogues of the structures in the city's various regions, based on some earlier original now lost. Both map and documents cover wide areas and are summary in treatment. Both include not only outstanding monuments but also the insulae, or blocks of apartment houses, warehouses, and other structures for ordinary use.

4. REPRODUCTIONS OF FRAGMENTS OF THE MARBLE PLAN SET IN A
WALL OF THE COURTYARD OF THE CONSERVATORI MUSEUM

(The south is at the top. The convention which places the north at the top
of a map is comparatively modern)

Photographed 1949

A reconstruction of the plan, with reproductions of many of the pieces, as it appeared in 1949 on a wall of the courtyard of the Conservatori Museum.

The arrangement of the fragments is no longer considered correct but the reconstruction gives a general idea of the ancient plan. The fragment of the preceding illustration can be seen in the section labelled *Mons Aventinus*.

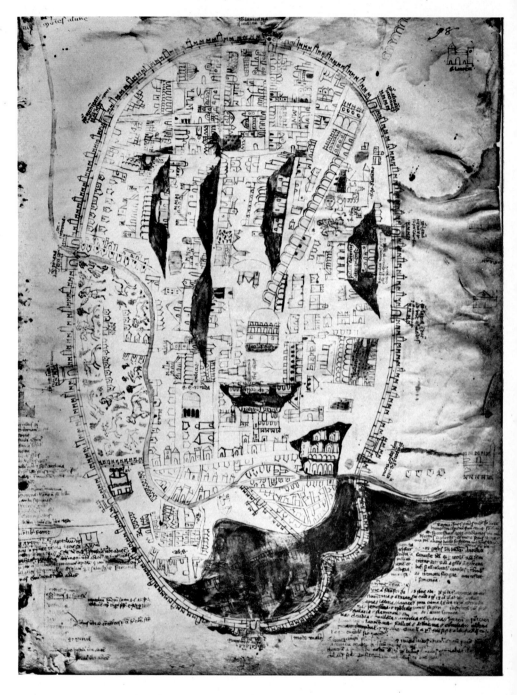

5. THE OLDEST KNOWN MEDIEVAL VIEW OF ROME

(The east is at the top)

From a manuscript of the World History *of Paulinus, about 1320–1328*
Venice, Library of Saint Mark's

In the manuscript illumination opposite, the large hill at the bottom is the Janiculum. Above it at the right is the Porta San Paolo, beside this is the Pyramid of Cestius with its medieval name, 'Tomb of Remus'.

Near the centre, upside down, is the Capitol with the Senator's Palace. Above this is the Colosseum with a dome. To the right of these is the Palatine hill, shown as one huge building called the 'Greater Palace'. To the left of the Capitol is the Pantheon. Above the Pantheon are the medieval tower and palace of the Milizie; above the Capitol is the tower of the Conti, labelled *turris comitis*.

At the upper right an aqueduct runs from the Colosseum beyond the walls. This may be the branch of the Claudian which ran across the Caelian hill. Beside it is the Lateran Palace, or 'Palace of Nero'. Near this is the statue of Marcus Aurelius, moved to the Capitol in 1538 and the colossal head and hand now in the Conservatori Museum, traditionally believed to be those of Nero's Colossus.

At the lower left across the Tiber is Saint Peter's with its obelisk and above it, Hadrian's Tomb. At the extreme left men hunt animals in what may represent an abandoned arena for water sports known as the Vatican Naumachia.

6. CIRCULAR VIEW OF ROME ON THE GOLDEN SEAL OF THE EMPEROR LUDWIG OF BAVARIA, 1328 (The south is at the top). *Dresden, State Archives*

The seal shows a jumble of Roman 'marvels'. At the upper left is the Lateran with Trajan's Column below it; beside it is the Colosseum without a dome. At the right are the Pyramid of Cestius and Arch of Titus. In the centre is the Senator's Palace on the Capitol; below this, the Pantheon. At the bottom are the Tomb of Hadrian and old Saint Peter's, with the pyramid (demolished 1499) called the 'Tomb of Romulus'. The church above it may be Santa Maria in Trastevere.

The inscription is that borne by the imperial seals since 1033: *Roma caput mundi regit orbis frena rotundi*—'Rome, head of the world, holds the reins of the round earth.'

7. ROME BEWAILING HER WIDOWED STATE IN THE FOURTEENTH
CENTURY (The south is at the top)
From a fifteenth-century manuscript of Fazio degli Uberti's Dittamondo
Paris, National Library

In the manuscript illumination opposite, Fazio and his guide, Solinus, lean upon the walls of Rome while the personification of the city, in widow's garb, addresses them. Most of the important monuments are labelled. The churches are: Saint Sebastian's and Saint Paul's at the top, outside the walls; inside, Santa Croce in Gerusalemme and Saint John Lateran; San Pietro ad Vincula below the Lateran; Santa Maria Rotonda (the Pantheon) in the centre; and across the Tiber, Santa Cecilia and Saint Peter's. Several of the city gates are also labelled and a few medieval secular buildings, such as the palace of the Milizie near the centre.

The narrowness of the picture and the space covered by Rome's flowing robes led to the omission of some notable monuments. Rome is seated upon the Palatine and her robes hide the Capitol. Her foot rests on the brook Almo or the Marrana, flowing in through a postern in the city wall above.

At the left is an aqueduct, labelled *le forme*, from *forma*, meaning pipe or conduit; this is probably a branch of the Aqua Marcia (still the principal water supply of Rome) stretching toward the Baths of Diocletian, which it supplied. By a branch of this aqueduct, near the Lateran, stands the equestrian statue of Marcus Aurelius. Between the statue and the figure of Rome is the Colosseum, again shown with a dome. Below it is the Basilica of Constantine, then and for centuries later called the Temple of Peace. Near the city wall at the lower left are the Baths of Diocletian, labelled *Termine*, a corruption of *thermae*, or 'baths'. Near these baths are the Marble Horses or Horse Tamers, standing on the Quirinal hill. The ten little cells may well be those of the Carthusian monks who were to be settled in the Baths of Diocletian in the fourteenth century by permission of Urban V, pope in Avignon. Rome bids her two listeners:

> 'Look upon my marble horses, on those two,
> Which men carved long ago, as thou mayest read.'

Above the horses is the Column of Trajan, called, as often in the Middle Ages, the Column of Hadrian; below is the Column of Marcus Aurelius, labelled Antonine Column, after the emperor's family. Across the Tiber is the Tomb of Hadrian, bearing the name it acquired in the Middle Ages and still keeps—the Castle of Sant'Angelo, or Holy Angel.

8. CIRCULAR VIEW OF ROME, 1413–1414
(The south is at the top)

Painting by Taddeo di Bartolo. Siena, Chapel of the Palazzo Pubblico

Beginning with the Porta Maggiore (No. 1) at the top left, the monuments in the following key have been numbered horizontally, ending with the Ponte Molle (No. 76) at the bottom.

    1. Porta Maggiore. 2. Church of Santa Croce in Gerusalemme. 3. Amphitheatrum Castrense. 4. Basilica of Saint John Lateran. 5. Statue of Marcus Aurelius, now on the Capitol. 6. Baptistery of San Giovanni in Fonte, where, according to tradition, the Emperor Constantine was baptized. 7. Perhaps the church of Santi Quattro Coronati, the 'Four Crowned Martyrs'. 8. Porta Metronia, now closed. The stream Almo (or

Marrana) is shown passing under the walls. 9. Church of San Sebastiano on the Appian Way, beyond the old Porta Appia, now the Porta San Sebastiano. 10. Baths of Caracalla. 11. Church of Santa Balbina(?). 12. Basilica of Saint Paul's Outside the Walls. 13. Pyramid of Cestius, the medieval 'Tomb of Remus'. 14. Colosseum. 15. Arch of Constantine. 16. Palatine hill with the Greater Palace. 17. Church and convent of Santa Prisca(?). 18. Church of San Saba(?). 19. Castle of the Savelli, with Santa Sabina. The round hill behind is Monte Testaccio. 20. Aqueduct: left, perhaps a branch of the Aqua Marcia; right, Aqua Claudia. 21. Basilica of Santa Maria Maggiore, identified by the shape of the apse and tall tower. 22. Basilica of Constantine or Maxentius. 23. Church of Santa Maria in Cosmedin. 24. So-called Temple of Vesta in the Forum Boarium (the church of San Stefano Rotondo in the Middle Ages). 25. The Arch of Janus Quadrifrons in the Forum Boarium. 26. Theatre of Marcellus. 27. Church of Santa Cecilia in Trastevere. 28. Church of San Francesco a Ripa. 29. Baths of Diocletian (with Carthusian cells?). 30. Church of San Pietro in Vincoli. 31. Structure (now demolished) known in the Middle Ages as the *mensa imperatoris* or Emperor's Table, and later as the *Frontispizio di Nerone*, 'Façade of Nero, and the Tower of Maecenas'. 32. Medieval towers of the Milizie and the Conti(?). 33. Church of Santa Susanna. 34. Horse Tamers or Marble Horses on the Quirinal. 35. Church of Santi Apostoli. 36. Column of Trajan. 37. Tower of San Marco or of the Chancellor Malabranca. 38. Church of Santa Maria in Aracoeli on the Capitol. 39. Palace of the Senator on the Capitol. The medieval gallows stands beside it. 40. Tarpeian Rock, from which, in ancient Rome, those convicted of certain crimes were hurled to death. 41. Bridge of Santa Maria, the ancient Pons Aemilius. Its two remaining arches are known as the Ponte Rotto. 42. Bridge of Fabricius. 43. Church of San Giovanni Calibita on the Tiber Island, a site now occupied by the hospital of San Giovanni di Dio. 44. Church of San Bartolommeo. 45. Bridge of Cestius. 46. Church of Santa Maria in Trastevere. 47. Walls of the Gardens of Sallust. 48. Fountain of Trevi. 49. Church of San Marcello. 50. Hadrianeum, formerly called the Temple of Neptune, in the Piazza di Pietra. 51. Pantheon. 52. Castle of the Orsini family by the Campo dei Fiori. 53. Hospital of Santo Spirito. 54. Spur of the Janiculum, included within the walls built by Pope Leo IV after the Saracen invasion of 848 A.D. 55. Saxon gate, rebuilt as the Porta di Santo Spirito by Sangallo in the sixteenth century. 56. Church of San Silvestro. 57. Column of Marcus Aurelius. 58. Probable route from the Vatican to the Capitol. 59. Castle of Giovanni Orsini. 60. Hadrian's Tomb or Castle of Sant' Angelo. 61. Pyramid known in the Middle Ages as the 'Tomb of Romulus', demolished 1499. 62. Vatican. 63. Basilica of Saint Peter. 64. Top of obelisk erected in the Circus of Nero, now in front of Saint Peter's. 65. Porta Pinciana. 66. Pincian Palace. 67. Arch, so-called, of Marcus Aurelius, demolished in 1662 for the enlargement of the Corso 68. Palace of the titular cardinal of San Lorenzo in Lucina, on the site of the Ara Pacis Augusti, and the present Palazzo Fiano. 69. Church of San Lorenzo in Lucina. 70. Church of Sant'Agnese or of Sant'Agostino, or Sant'Apollinare. 71. Church of Santa Maria del Popolo. 72. Porta Flaminia. 73. Mausoleum of Augustus. 74. Bridge of Sant'Angelo. 75. Porta Viridaria. 76. Ponte Molle, the ancient Pons Milvius, where Constantine conquered Maxentius.

9. A PANORAMIC VIEW OF ROMAN 'MARVELS' IN 1465

Detail from a painting, The Departure of Saint Augustine from Rome for Milan, *by Benozzo Gozzoli (Italian). San Gimignano, Church of Saint Augustine*

Here Rome is seen from the north, with the Castle of Sant'Angelo and the Vatican neighbourhood in the foreground. The Column of Trajan and the Pantheon, at the left, mark the eastern limit of the view. On the Capitol hill beyond Trajan's Column rise the church of Santa Maria in Aracoeli and the medieval Senator's Palace.

To the right of Sant'Angelo and the central tree are the pyramidal 'Tomb of Romulus', the old basilica of Saint Peter, with its tall bell tower, and the Palace of the Popes, with its airy gardens at the extreme right.

10. GIULIANO DE' MEDICI, DUKE OF NEMOURS, WITH HADRIAN'S
TOMB IN THE BACKGROUND, ABOUT 1514–1515
Detail from a painting by Raphael (Italian). New York, Metropolitan Museum of Art,
Jules S. Bache Collection

Giuliano, youngest son of Lorenzo the Magnificent of Florence, was probably painted against this background because of its peculiar appropriateness. He had shortly before been appointed Gonfaloniere or standard bearer of the papal forces by his brother, the Medici Pope Leo X. The ancient tomb, for some time a papal fortress, was connected with the Vatican by a partially covered passage for use in emergency. This had been finished not many years before the portrait was painted. The view of the castle is that seen from the Vatican looking along this passage, soon to be used by Clement VII when the city was captured by Charles V and suffered the fearful sack of 1527.

11. THE ROMAN FORUM FROM THE CAPITOL, ABOUT 1491
Drawing by the Anonymus Escurialensis. Madrid, Escorial Collection

At the left is the Arch of Septimius Severus, the pedestals supporting its columns already buried. Through its central arch can be seen a corner of the Basilica Aemilia. To the right are, first, the columns of the portico of the Temple of Saturn and, second, the corner of the Temple of Vespasian.

In the background is a simplified group of buildings represented almost by a system of graphic shorthand. Farthest away is the Colosseum, next to it the bell-tower and façade of a church, apparently that of Saints Cosmas and Damian, and then the portico of the Temple of Antoninus and Faustina, masked by medieval intrusions.

12. GARDEN OF THE CASA GALLI, ROME, WITH ANCIENT SCULPTURE
SURROUNDING MICHELANGELO'S BACCHUS, 1532–1535
Drawing by Marten van Heemskerck (Dutch). Berlin, Print Room

Van Heemskerck's drawing suggests the treasures and rewards which awaited
renaissance artists in Rome. The garden is filled with ancient sculpture collected
by the Galli family, but in the midst stands one of Michelangelo's early statues,
the Bacchus done in 1497, commissioned by the noble Roman banker and
collector, Jacopo Galli, during the young sculptor's first visit to the city.

13. THE EARLIEST KNOWN PRINTED VIEW OF ROME
(The west is at the top)
Woodcut from the Supplementum Chronicorum, *Venice, 1490*
Philadelphia, Free Library, P. A. B. Widener Collection

This view seems to follow the same original as the fifteenth-century painting at
Mantua in which, fortunately, some of the monuments are named. In both, the
space is so crowded that buildings do not always appear in their proper relation-
ships. The Colosseum at the left, for instance, is so close to the Pantheon that the
Column of Trajan and most of the Roman Forum are omitted. Left to right on
the east bank of the Tiber (bottom) outstanding ancient monuments are:

Colosseum; Theatre of Marcellus on the river's bank; the Palatine, its hill shown
smaller than the Colosseum and crowned by a ruined circular building; Baths of Diocletian with the small round buildings called in the *Mirabilia* the 'Bushels'; Marble
Horses on the Quirinal beside the baths; below them one of the two statues of river gods
which then lay on the Quirinal; Pantheon, facing east instead of north; Column of
Marcus Aurelius.

On the west bank of the Tiber (top):

Vatican obelisk; old Saint Peter's with the Belvedere beyond upon the hill; truncated
pyramid, the so-called 'Tomb of Romulus'; Hadrian's Tomb, or Castle of Sant'Angelo,
surmounted by its angel.

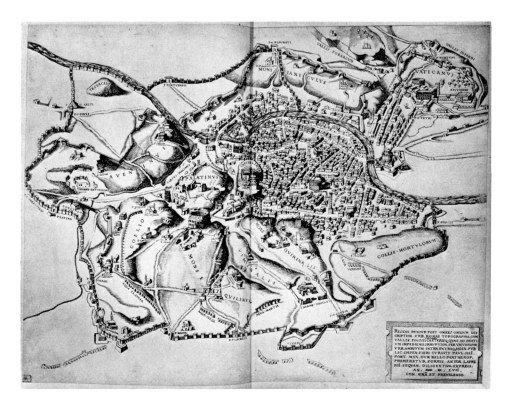

14. MAP OF ROME, 1557
(The west is at the top)

From Lafreri's Speculum, *Rome, 1557. New York, Metropolitan Museum of Art*

This map presents the city from the same point of view as the woodcut of 1490, but it is up to date in details and is a true picture plan rather than a collection of 'marvels' or a panoramic view. Aside from a certain distortion of proportions, due to drawing out the city's shape too long from north to south, this map is a comparatively good guide to the monuments of Rome today.

Many of the buildings, represented in conventionalized form, are clearly labelled. Among those which are unmarked but clearly recognizable are: the Colosseum; the Septizonium, standing as an isolated fragment at the foot of the Palatine hill; the round 'Temple of Vesta' and rectangular 'Temple of Fortuna Virilis' in the Forum Boarium near the Tiber; the Column of Trajan close to the Roman Forum; near it the towering fragment of temple wall on the Quirinal hill, the Castle of Sant'Angelo, and the Vatican obelisk. On Saint Peter's the new dome is rising under Michelangelo's direction.

15. THE PONTE MOLLE IN THE ROMAN CAMPAGNA
Drawing by Nicolas Poussin (French). Paris, École des Beaux Arts

Poussin's drawing of this historic bridge just north of Rome demonstrates his accuracy of observation and his ability to convey the essentials of a scene in simple form. Though it underwent some repairs and alterations in the nineteenth century, the bridge today is immediately recognizable in the drawing of three centuries ago.

Aside from its picturesque quality this bridge has the added interest of age and association. Its four central arches, dating probably from 109 B.C., are among the oldest of any bridge in the neighbourhood of Rome. And it was near this ancient Pons Milvius that the rival emperors, Constantine and Maxentius, fought their decisive battle for control of the Empire in A.D. 312, ending in the defeat of Maxentius and his drowning in the Tiber.

16. ORPHEUS AND EURYDICE, 1659
Painting by Nicolas Poussin (French). Paris, Louvre

The free, vigorous line of Poussin's drawings is softened in his finished pictures; objects are more generalized; the light that veils the paintings blends the objects into the surrounding landscape. In the background of this scene from Greek mythology Poussin has combined several monuments of ancient Rome into one harmonious whole. Just behind the group of Eurydice, Orpheus, and the spell-bound listeners to his song, flows the Tiber. Beyond it, to the left rises the Tomb of Hadrian or Castle of Sant'Angelo. To the right is the medieval tower of the Milizie. Between them stretches a bridge that resembles the Ponte Molle rather than the Ponte Sant'Angelo, which is the actual bridge built by Hadrian as the approach to the mausoleum.

17. THE ROMAN FORUM, OR CAMPO VACCINO
Drawing by Claude Lorrain (French). London, British Museum

This drawing was probably done, at least in part, from nature, though the artist has taken some liberties with the actual scene. The Forum is viewed from the Capitol, looking east toward the Arch of Titus. The three corner columns of the Temple of Vespasian are hidden by the stones on which the drovers sit, though they would have been partially visible. At the left is the Arch of Septimius Severus; the medieval bell tower of the Milizie is behind it. A little beyond the arch is the portico of the Temple of Antoninus and Faustina, with the arches of the Basilica of Constantine suggested behind it. Then comes the lightly indicated vestibule of the church of Saints Cosmas and Damian. Beyond is the Colosseum; then the church of Santa Francesca Romana with its medieval bell tower; to the right appears the Arch of Titus.

In the right foreground stand the columns of the Temple of Saturn; beyond are the three columns of the Temple of Castor near the centre of the Forum. At the right the walls of the Farnese Gardens on the Palatine are dimly suggested.

18. RUINS OF ANCIENT ROME WITH THE BURIAL OF SANTA SERAPIA
Detail from a painting by Claude Lorrain (French). Madrid, Prado Museum

Claude's paintings were less true to actuality than his drawings; here only the Colosseum is by any means exact. But inaccuracies are forgotten in the harmony of that pellucid light of Rome which he was one of the first to interpret.

Serapia was said to have been the slave of the noble Roman lady Sabina, whom she converted to Christianity. When Serapia was martyred about A.D. 126, her mistress buried her in her own tomb; later Sabina herself suffered martyrdom. According to tradition, the famous old church of Santa Sabina on the Aventine was built on the site of her house.

19. LANDSCAPE WITH ROMAN RUINS, 1735
Giovanni Paolo Pannini (Italian). Berlin, Kaiser Friedrich Museum

In this typical example of the imaginary landscape with ruins, Pannini assembled a magnificent collection of actual monuments, which visitors to Rome would wish to see, placed in impossible juxtaposition. At the left the Column of Trajan rises in front of the Colosseum, though actually the two are separated by a considerable distance. At the right the three columns of the Temple of Castor in the middle of the Roman Forum stand close beside the Arch of Constantine, outside the Forum's boundary. In the middle distance is a round temple with a complete entablature which marks it as the so-called Temple of Vesta at Tivoli, some miles outside Rome. On the horizon the point of the Pyramid of Cestius cuts the sky; this pyramid tomb that intersects the southern wall of Rome cannot, and never could, be seen from the Forum or the Colosseum.

As for the statues in the foreground, the Hercules standing at the left, now in the National Museum at Naples, was then in the Palazzo Farnese in Rome. The Dying Gaul nearby was already housed in the Capitoline Museum, which had acquired it from Prince Odescalchi some years before.

20. A GALLERY OF VIEWS OF ANCIENT ROME, 1757
Painting by Giovanni Paolo Pannini (Italian). New York, Metropolitan Museum of Art

Here, in an imaginary baroque gallery, a group of connoisseurs inspects works which range from photographically realistic paintings of Roman monuments to famous pieces of sculpture found in the city, such as the Laocoön, the Dying Gaul, the Hercules Farnese, and the Apollo Belvedere. The paintings suggest the 'big business' of ruin painting in the eighteenth century; the work as a whole illustrates the combination of theatrical quality and careful detail characteristic of Pannini. The objects he represents never were, of course, assembled in any one place.

21. ARCHES OF THE COLOSSEUM

Drawing by Hubert Robert (French). Besançon, Library

This drawing of the Colosseum is much more exact than most of Robert's representations of ancient monuments. His sketches of renaissance and baroque buildings were likely to be considerably more faithful than those of Roman ruins.

Here the Colosseum's lower arches are boarded up or filled with refuse, as they often were, but the upper gallery is peopled by the shadowy presences of long-dead Romans, wrapped in the flowing togas of antiquity.

To Plate 22:

In Robert's painting the actual and the fanciful are combined with a result quite satisfying to the eye though at complete variance with facts. The statue of Marcus Aurelius which stood in Robert's time, as now, isolated in the Capitol Piazza, is painted here beside a round temple resembling the so-called Temple of the Sibyl at Tivoli. The 'portico' which frames these widely separated monuments is a skilfully and plausibly constructed fantasy based on late Roman work. Beneath it leans the relief of the triumphal procession on the Arch of Titus. The laundry hung to dry between the emperor's horse and the arch provides a touch of homely realism for romantic contrast with monumental ruin.

22. PORTICO WITH THE STATUE OF MARCUS AURELIUS

Painting by Hubert Robert (French). Paris, Louvre

23. THE PYRAMID OF CESTIUS, ABOUT 1756

Etching by Giovanni Battista Piranesi (Italian). New York, Metropolitan Museum of Art

This view shows the inner, or northern, face of this pyramid-tomb of a praetor who died late in the first century B.C., with a glimpse of the Wall of Aurelian and the Porta San Paolo beyond.

In its dramatic foreshortening and profusion of fantastic trees and plants, and of humans who seem themselves to be almost a part of the vegetable world, this etching is characteristic of Piranesi's work.

24. FRAGMENTS OF ROMAN RUINS IN THE COLONNA GARDENS
ON THE QUIRINAL, 1762

Etching by Giovanni Battista Piranesi (Italian). New York, Metropolitan Museum of Art

Piranesi's *Campo Marzo*, published in 1762, includes this delightful fantasy of the great fragments of late Roman work still in the Colonna Gardens. Here, lying upside down as it fell, is the huge pediment block from an immense temple (Plates 174–5), whose exact identity is still in question. At the right, impossibly tilted, is a long fragment of frieze carved with scrolls of foliage that still stands in the gardens. This may or may not belong to the same building. At the left, far closer to the spectator than they really are, rise the arches of the ruined staircase ramp (Plates 176–7) that led up the hill to the temple.

The great temple fragment has borne many names throughout the centuries. In his caption, Piranesi calls it by a name that came into favour some time after the Middle Ages: the 'women's senate house', said to have been built by the emperor Elagabalus in the third century A.D.

25. GOETHE IN THE ROMAN CAMPAGNA, 1787
Painting by Johann Heinrich Wilhelm Tischbein (German).
Frankfurt-am-Main, Staedel Institute

The German painter Tischbein, who had lived in Rome for some years before Goethe's visit, acted as the poet's companion and guide during much of his stay. Goethe noted in December, 1786: 'I have often observed Tischbein attentively regarding me; and now it appears that he has long cherished the idea of painting my portrait. His design is already settled, and the canvas stretched. I am to be drawn of the size of life, enveloped in a white mantle, and sitting on a fallen obelisk, viewing the ruins of the Campagna di Roma, which are to fill up the background of the picture.' The portrait was completed the next year.

The obelisk was probably chosen because Goethe developed a strong interest in the traces of Egyptian objects in Rome. Beside it lie fanciful fragments of classic architecture. There is a composite Roman capital and a relief showing Orestes and Pylades brought before Iphigenia in Tauris. This may have been suggested by a sarcophagus relief in the Villa Albani, but the two compositions have little in common. The subject was, however, especially appropriate, as at this time Goethe was working on the final form of his *Iphigenia in Tauris*.

In the background is a somewhat idealized view of the Campagna—a barely suggested line of aqueduct, the Tomb of Caecilia Metella, and what is probably a villa. In the distance is Monte Cavo, with the range of the Alban Hills.

26. THE PALATINE FROM THE VIA DI SAN SEBASTIANO
Drawing by Johann Wolfgang Goethe, 1787. Weimar, Goethe Museum

To Goethe, who longed to master many forms of artistic expression, the artist's Rome had a special appeal. In 1786, soon after his arrival, he noted that 'wherever one goes and casts a look around, the eye is at once struck with some landscape—forms of every kind and style; palaces, ruins, gardens and statuary, distant views of villas, cottages and stables, triumphal arches and columns, often crowding so close together, that they might all be sketched on a single piece of paper.' And again, the next year, he wrote: 'In these lands here you *must* become an artist, you get fuller and fuller every day, and it grows at last a necessity for you to deliver yourself of something.'

Among his many Roman sketches are several of the Palatine, crowned, as he wrote, by 'the ruins of the Palace of the Caesars, which stand there like walls of rock'. This view may have been sketched from that part of the Via di San Sebastiano now included in the Via delle Terme di Caracalla, where it crosses the Via di San Gregorio.

27. MR. AND MRS. RALPH IZARD
WITH THE COLOSSEUM IN THE BACKGROUND, 1774
Painting by John Singleton Copley (American). Boston, Museum of Fine Arts

Copley, one of the first American painters to visit Rome, followed the established tradition for suggesting the city. Not content with placing the Colosseum in the background to indicate the presence of the Izards in Rome, he also showed a reduced version of the marble group known as Orestes and Electra, then in the Villa Ludovisi, now in the National Museum, Rome. Mr. Izard holds a drawing of the group in his hand.

Ralph Izard was typical of the many Americans of his time who, despite sturdy independence and staunch patriotism, remained English gentlemen in spirit. Sent from his father's South Carolina plantation to school in England at the age of twelve, he spent much of his life there, working for compromise and for the preservation of the ties with the mother country.

Upon his return to this country in 1780 he entered the service of the new government as congressman from South Carolina. After the adoption of the Federal Constitution, he was chosen United States Senator from his native state.

To Plate 28:
Vanderlyn's view of the Arch of Titus looks westward beneath the arch toward the Roman Forum, with the bell tower of the Senator's Palace on the Capitol in the background. The medieval structures which had replaced the ancient sides of the arch when it was part of the Frangipani fortress were not removed until 1821.

28. THE ARCH OF TITUS, ABOUT 1805
Painting by John Vanderlyn (American). Collection of Edward Coykendall, Kingston, N.Y.

29. SHELLEY IN ROME
Painting by Joseph Severn (English). Rome, Keats-Shelley Memorial

Joseph Severn, who had accompanied Keats to Rome and stayed with him till his death, remained in the city for some years, first as an art student and later as English Consul. He did this painting while he was in England in 1845, from memory and from sketches and portraits of the poet. While the likeness is unmistakable, the setting is misleading. The painting has sometimes been called *Shelley writing 'Prometheus Unbound' upon the Ruins of the Baths of Caracalla*, and the artist may indeed have intended to suggest this scene, but the baths themselves are not represented.

The right side of the picture is easily identifiable as the top of the substructures of Severus on the Palatine. In the distance is Monte Cavo in the Alban Hills. The generalized ruins upon which Shelley sits, however, are not to be found either on the Palatine or in the Baths of Caracalla, nor do they correspond with any ruins known to exist in his time. The general shape of the masses of masonry is similar to that shown in Towne's drawing of the tops of the piers, as shown in the opposite plate, but that is the extent of the resemblance.

30. THE TOPS OF THE PIERS OF THE BATHS OF CARACALLA, 1781
Drawing by Francis Towne (English). London, British Museum

What Shelley actually saw about him as he wrote was probably much the same as the luxurious wilderness that the English artist Francis Towne had sketched thirty-eight years before. Towne's drawing shows an enchanting scene of level, overgrown arches framed by masses of much higher ruin; just such a picture as Shelley described to his friend, Thomas Love Peacock, in a letter written in March, 1819, while he was working on *Prometheus*:

'Never was any desolation more sublime and lovely. The perpendicular wall of ruin is cloven into steep ravines filled up with flowering shrubs, whose thick, twisted roots are knotted in the rifts of the stones. At every step the aerial pinnacles of shattered stone group into new combinations of effect, and tower above the lofty yet level walls, as the distant mountains change their aspect to one travelling rapidly along the plain. . . . These walls surround green and level spaces of lawn, on which some elms have grown, and which are interspersed toward their skirts by masses of fallen ruin, overtwined with the broad leaves of the creeping weeds. The blue sky canopies it, and is as the everlasting roof of these enormous halls.'

31. THE ARCHES OF CONSTANTINE AND TITUS, 1819
Painting by Joseph Mallord William Turner (English). London, British Museum

Cattle still cluster here beside the Arch of Constantine as they did in the Roman Forum beyond, known then as the *Campo Vaccino*, or Cow Pasture. The painting is, however, not a carefully detailed picturesque rendering of the scene, but a broadly treated study in light and colour.

At the entrance to the Forum stands the Arch of Titus with its single opening, still surrounded by remnants of medieval fortifications. These were removed two years later and Valadier reconstructed the arch, with new sides, in 1822. To the left, near the Palatine, is still another trace of medieval Rome, the *Turris Cartularia*, Archive Tower, once part of the Frangipani fortress, demolished in 1828. At the right are the ruins of the Temple of Venus and Rome, with the church of Santa Francesca Romana beyond.

32. THE CASTLE AND BRIDGE OF SANT'ANGELO, ABOUT 1826–1827
Painting by Jean Baptiste Camille Corot (French). Paris, Louvre

The impact of the afternoon sun striking the massive cylinder of Hadrian's Tomb and the old houses on the west bank of the Tiber is suggested here by the broad, simple masses of light and shade in which Corot composed during his years at Rome and for some time afterward.

Late in the nineteenth century the old houses were removed in order to widen the river's bed and strengthen its banks. At that time two new arches replaced the small ones at the ends of the bridge which Hadrian built to give access to his tomb, later the castle of the popes.

33. VIEW IN THE FORUM, ROME, SECOND QUARTER OF THE
NINETEENTH CENTURY

Water-colour by Samuel Prout (English). Bristol City Art Gallery, England

Here, at the west end of the Forum, Roman women with the picturesque head-dresses which had almost vanished by the century's end, add a note of gaiety and grace to the massive, time-stained ruins. In the foreground stands the Column of Phocas; in the background, the medieval Palace of the Senator, rebuilt in later days, rises above the ancient Republican Tabularium on the Capitol slope. At the left are the columns of the Temple of Saturn; in the centre, those of the Temple of Vespasian; at the right, part of the Arch of Septimius Severus.

34. RUINS OF THE PALACE OF THE CAESARS IN ROME, AFTER 1810
*Etching by Joseph Anton Koch (German). Rome, Library of the American Academy
in Rome*

Koch's etching, one from a series of twenty Roman views, is far less fantastic than
the standard eighteenth-century classical landscape with ruins. Like the work of
Piranesi, however, it is carefully composed to please the eye and to appeal to the
imagination. With its romantic emphasis on the picturesque and on sharp
contrasts of ruin and leafy growth, it is the Roman counterpart of the castle-
crowned medieval German landscapes evoked by so many of Koch's compatriots.

The etching shows the east end of the Palatine, still its wildest section, with a
view into the arches of the great substructures built by Septimius Severus (Plates
77–80). To the right, rather freely treated, are ruins of the Stadium of Domitian and
the Baths of Severus (Plates 81–84).

In the foreground is one of those scenes which gave so much colour to papal
Rome. What appears to be a funeral procession wends its way from the hillside.
At the left a woman has laid her child upon the ground to receive a blessing; at the
right another women drops a coin into the box of a man, presumably a member
of the secular confraternity of the White Penitents, founded in the thirteenth
century for the care of the sick and poor. Saint Bonaventura, whose name is borne
by the convent still standing on the Palatine above, gave the confraternity its rule
and its white robe with the pointed, mask-like hood.

35. OVERBECK AND HIS GROUP OF GERMAN ARTISTS
IN THE CAFFÈ GRECO, 1818

Drawing by Karl Philipp Fohr (German). Frankfurt-am-Main, Staedel Institute

The renown of the German national group within the cosmopolitan artists' society of Rome inspired Fohr to plan an engraving showing them in this popular café. The young artist, who came to the city in 1818, did not, however, live to complete his composition. He was drowned in the Tiber within the year, leaving three sketches and a number of individual portrait studies.

Overbeck, moving spirit of the ascetic band of German artists known as the Nazarenes, sits in the centre. At the left are Theodor Rehbenitz and Peter Cornelius; at the right, Johann Schaller and Philipp Veit. Though the artists are absorbed in a game, their seriousness, especially that of Overbeck, suggests the religious fervour that gave them their name, rather than the pleasant conversation and excellent coffee for which the Greco was noted.

36. DANISH ARTISTS IN THE OSTERIA OF LA GENSOLA, ROME, 1837
Painting by Detlev Blunck (Danish). Copenhagen, Thorwaldsen Museum

The Danish artists who centred about Thorwaldsen are assembled here in the *osteria* or tavern of La Gensola at the Piazza Gensola in Trastevere. The contrast between their relaxed enjoyment in a tavern patronized by ordinary Romans and the silent concentration shown in the drawing of the German group need not be taken as typical. There is no doubt, however, that Blunck's picture suggests more of the carefree atmosphere of artists' life in nineteenth-century Rome.

The silver-haired Thorwaldsen sits at the end of the table in the right foreground; next him is Ernst Meyer (Plate 37); then Detlev Blunck himself. The others are, from right to left: Jørgen Sonne; Constantin Hansen entering the doorway; Michael Bindesbøll seated at the near side of the table behind the waiter; the waiter himself, facing the table; and Albert Küchler at the far end opposite Thorwaldsen.

Küchler is busy sketching something that attracts his attention in the Italian group opposite, where women and children are gathered at another table and other children, accompanied by a dog and several cats, play upon the floor.

37. A PUBLIC WRITER IN A ROMAN STREET WRITING A LETTER
FOR A YOUNG GIRL, 1829

Painting by Ernst Meyer (Danish). Copenhagen, Thorwaldsen Museum

Here, before the retaining wall of Augustus' Forum, is one of those picturesque groups that appealed alike to artists and writers. Story described just such a scene:

'At the corner of the piazza, in the open air, with a rickety table before him, on which are a few sheets of paper and an inkstand, sand and pens, is the *scrivano* or letter-writer, who makes contracts and writes and reads their letters for them . . . Ah! into his ear how many confessions have been made, how many a declaration of passionate love has been whispered, how many a tender and affectionate phrase has been uttered for the ears of distant friends and lovers! Italian letters are almost invariably expressions of feeling or sentiment, and not, like English letters, filled with news and incidents, and descriptions of persons and places.'

Though the letter-writer has long been gone from Rome, the columns of the Temple of Mars Ultor and the forum's wall still stand. The street at the right, however, no longer runs under the low Arch of the Pantini, Arch of the Swamps, named from the backing up of water in this spot just north of the Roman Forum.

38. EVENING OF AN OCTOBER FESTIVAL OUTSIDE THE WALLS OF
ROME, 1839

Painting by Wilhelm Marstrand (Danish). Copenhagen, Thorwaldsen Museum

The October festivals, survivals of the final harvest celebrations of ancient Rome, were among the scenes of popular merrymaking that fascinated visitors. Story wrote of them: 'After the vintage is over, come the October festivals, the *ottobrate* as they are called, when the Romans twice a week during the whole month are in the habit of going out to the villas and vineyards about Rome in companies to dance, sing, and picnic under the trees.'

The celebrations outside the Porta Angelica, opening out of the papal city on the right bank of the Tiber toward Monte Mario, were especially well known. The artist may have had this location in mind—the building silhouetted against the sky at the right is thought to be a great *osteria* outside this gate. But the walls shown here are not those built by the popes to defend their city, as these had no towers. Probably Marstrand, wishing a picturesque background, substituted the towered walls built by Aurelian in the third century A.D., most of which still stand on the left bank of the river. Despite centuries of rebuilding and repair these are essentially the walls constructed when Rome first began to feel the need for defence on her own territory.

39

40

41

42

39. THE SO-CALLED 'TOMB OF NERO' NEAR ROME

Drawing by Henry Wadsworth Longfellow in a notebook dated December, 1828.
Cambridge, Massachusetts, Longfellow House

This tomb on the Via Cassia near Rome is still Nero's in popular belief, in spite of its inscription, which clearly states that it was erected by Vibia Maria Maxima in memory of her parents.

40. THE COLOSSEUM FROM THE PALACE OF THE CAESARS ON THE PALATINE, WITH THE ENTRANCE TO NERO'S GOLDEN HOUSE IN THE DISTANCE

Pencil sketch, dated March 11, 1836, by Frances Elizabeth Appleton.
Cambridge, Massachusetts, Longfellow House

Like Longfellow's sketch of the 'Tomb of Nero' eight years earlier, this drawing represents the work of amateurs who, in the days before photography, wished to record the scenes they had admired.

In Switzerland, a little later in the same year, Miss Appleton met Longfellow, then on his second European journey. She was the heroine of his prose romance, *Hyperion*, published in 1839, and became his wife in 1843.

41. THE THREE CORNER COLUMNS OF THE TEMPLE OF VESPASIAN, 1832

Drawing by Thomas Cole (American). Detroit Institute of Arts

Inscribed 'Temple of Jupiter Tonans, R. Forum. This ruin is marble but stained yellowish and blackish.'

42. RUINS AT THE BATHS OF CARACALLA, 1869

Drawing by Frederic E. Church (American). New York, Cooper Union Museum
of the Arts of Decoration

43. ROMAN AQUEDUCT, 1832
Painting by Thomas Cole (American). New York, Metropolitan Museum of Art

The Roman Campagna, with its enclosing mountains and lines of aqueduct, had a special charm for landscape painters. The scene here is in the Sabine Hills, east and slightly north of Rome, between Tivoli and Subiaco, where a ruined medieval tower crowns a fragment of the Claudian Aqueduct. This group, popularly known as the 'Arch of Nero', was a favourite with artists, and was painted by Inness, among others.

In his journal for October 11, 1869, Sanford Gifford noted: 'Walked a couple of miles out on the road to Subiaco (from Tivoli) to the picturesque "Arch of Nero". This is a fragment of the great Claudian Aqueduct, forty-six miles long, which at this point went through the mountains and reappeared on the Campagna near Rome. This was the subject of one of Cole's finest pictures [the one shown here]. He relieved the arch magnificently against a great white cumulus cloud.'

44. ITALIAN LANDSCAPE: ROMAN CAMPAGNA, 1858
*Painting by George Inness (American). New Britain, Connecticut,
Art Museum of the New Britain Art Institute*

Here the Claudian Aqueduct and the arches of Pope Sixtus' Acqua Felice stretch south toward the Alban Hills, with Monte Cavo, their highest point, on the horizon. In the middle distance rises one of the exquisite stone pines that are the most characteristic of Roman trees. Nothing could harmonize more perfectly with Henry James' description of the Campagna in *Transatlantic Sketches*, 1875—'the long, gentle swell of the Alban Mountains' with 'the broken line of the Claudian Aqueduct, carrying its broad arches far away into the plain'. An almost identical view, painted by Thomas Cole in 1843, is in the Wadsworth Atheneum, Hartford.

45. THE TEMPLES IN THE FORUM BOARIUM IN THE LATE
NINETEENTH CENTURY

Water-colour by Ettore Roesler-Franz (Italian). Rome, Museo di Roma

Roesler-Franz's interest lay in the whole Roman scene; its buildings, its life, its atmosphere, the very stones of its walls and streets. The rainy season was especially congenial to his mood; here the grey light of a clearing rain has turned into mirrors of the silvery sky the old paving blocks over which donkeys plod their way.

At the left is a corner of the rectangular temple dating from the ancient Roman Republic, popularly called the 'Temple of Fortuna Virilis', although its true name is unknown. Beyond it is an equally mysterious round temple, long, but mistakenly, called the 'Temple of Vesta'.

46. THE TEMPLES IN THE FORUM BOARIUM

From an old photograph

This photograph was taken from the direction opposite to that in Roesler-Franz's painting. The 'Temple of Vesta' is in the left foreground. The 'Temple of Fortuna Virilis' is at the right, half-hidden by a building long since demolished. Beyond appears the medieval House of Crescentius (Plates 188–189).

47. THE PORTICO OF OCTAVIA, 1858
Painting by Albert Bierstadt (American). Boston Athenaeum

This painting shows only a small part of the remaining ruins of the portico built by Augustus in honour of his sister but reconstructed after a fire in the reign of Septimius Severus (A.D. 193–211). A medieval brick arch replaces two of the portico's Corinthian columns. The artist painted this view inside the portico, then used as a fish market, his back toward the church of Sant'Angelo in Pescheria, looking toward the old Ghetto down a vista of narrow streets long since cleared away. The fish market was removed and some excavation done in the 1870's, but the present tidy appearance of the portico is of more recent date. Story described this portico in 1862:

'Stone slabs, broken and grappled by iron hooks, stretch out on either side into the street, and usurp it so as to leave no carriageable way between them. If it be market-day you will see them covered with every kind of fishes. Green crusty lobsters, squirming crawfish all alive, heaps of red mullet, baskets of little shining sardines. . . . Great dark holes open into the houses behind, begrimed with dirt and smoke. Above stretches an arch supported by black beams, over which is reared a series of chambers; here juts out on its iron arm the lantern which illuminates feebly the street at night; and here, in a grimed corner, is placed a Madonna shrine with an onion-shaped lamp burning before it.'

William Wetmore Story, *Roba di Roma.*

48. THE PORTICO OF OCTAVIA BEFORE ITS CLEARING IN THE 1870'S
From an old photograph

This photograph testifies to the literal exactness of Bierstadt's painting. The view is nearly the same as that in his picture, except that it begins a little closer to the outer arch. About the time the photograph was taken Jean Jacques Ampère wrote of the portico:

'It is one of the most remarkable ruins of Rome; it offers one of those piquant contrasts between the past and the present that are a perpetual delight to the imagination in this city of contrasts. The Portico of Octavius is today a fish market. Its columns and pediment rise in the middle of the dirtiest place in Rome. Their effect is rendered even more picturesque, perhaps, by their setting. The site is made for a water colour. When bright sunshine lights up the ancient debris, the sombre old walls, and the narrow streets where fish are sold from straw mats spread across white marble slabs, you have, besides the Roman monument, the spectacle of a medieval market place and even something like the memory of an Oriental bazaar.'

Jean Jacques Ampère, *L'Empire Romain à Rome*, Paris, 1867.

49. THE FORUM BOARIUM AND EAST BANK OF THE TIBER
BEFORE 1891

From an old photograph

Here, between time-scarred walls that were rebuilt and straightened in the late nineteenth century, the Tiber flows peacefully, as is its wont except in its swift and unpredictable floods. In front of the round 'Temple of Vesta' the ancient Cloaca Maxima, Rome's oldest sewer, empties into the river. The triple arch may date from the first century B.C. or earlier; the sewer itself, built not to carry off refuse but to drain the Roman Forum and other low-lying sites, is much older. The photographer was evidently standing on the Ponte Palatina.

Behind the retaining wall runs the Lungotévere Aventino, thronged now with hurtling traffic. The 'Temple of Fortuna Virilis' and House of Crescentius (Plates 188–189) are hidden from view. The medieval clock tower is that of Santa Maria in Cosmedin (Plate 186), which still wears its eighteenth-century baroque façade, removed between 1891 and 1899.

In the background, behind the 'Temple of Vesta', rise the ruined arches of the substructures of the palace of Septimius Severus on the Palatine (Plates 77–80).

50. THE HOUSE OF CRESCENTIUS NEAR THE TEMPLES OF THE
FORUM BOARIUM

From an old photograph

The House of Crescentius, a museum today, is the most elaborate remaining example of a type of medieval domestic architecture once common in Rome. It is the lower part of a tower erected by a member of the Crescenzi family to control the traffic of the adjoining bridge across the Tiber, the now ruined *Ponte Rotto* or Broken Bridge. In its medieval brickwork are set assorted fragments of carved stone from the buildings of ancient Rome.

In the foreground a street leads to the temples in the Forum Boarium or cattle market; at right angles, another street in the foreground runs toward the Tiber.

51. THE PORTA SAN SEBASTIANO AND ARCH OF DRUSES,
LOOKING TOWARD THE APPIAN WAY

From an old photograph

The Arch of Druses, which stands just inside the Porta San Sebastiano, cannot be identified with the Druses whose name it has long borne. Actually, it was one of the arches built in the reign of Caracalla, early in the third century A.D., to carry the branch of the Aqua Marcia that supplied the water for the new imperial baths.

The present Porta San Sebastiano, through which visitors pass to travel the Appian Way and see the catacombs, is the old Roman Porta Appia, named from the famous ancient road. Like the city walls that extend here on both sides, the gate was originally built by Aurelian late in the third century A.D., and restored by Honorius in the fourth. Most of the present structure is probably that of Honorius. It bears a Greek inscription thanking God for saving Rome from the Goths in A.D. 402, and another in Latin recording a Roman victory over Robert, king of Naples, in 1327.

52. THE SUBSTRUCTURES OF SEPTIMIUS SEVERUS ON THE PALATINE

From an old photograph

This photograph shows, walled up for use as storage, the lower tier of arches of the great substructure of one of the Palatine's last imperial buildings. Beginning with the Middle Ages these arches, then the property of the monks of San Gregorio, were rented out for various purposes. Eventually they came to be used exclusively as haylofts. 'The abuse was suppressed,' wrote Lanciani, 'in 1862 after the terrific fire which consumed in one night thousands of bales of hay, and threatened to destroy the whole mass of buildings.'

Rodolfo Lanciani, *Ruins and Excavations of Ancient Rome*, 1897.

53. VIEW TOWARD THE ARCH OF TITUS AND THE TEMPLE OF VENUS
AND ROME FROM THE COLOSSEUM

From an old photograph

This view is almost identical with Turner's painting of 1819 (Plate 31), except for the appearance of the Arch of Titus. The medieval buildings at its sides had been removed and the arch itself renovated soon after the painter's visit to Rome. At the left is the Arch of Constantine; a little farther away, at the right, is one coffered apse of the ruined Temple of Venus and Rome. The other apse of this double temple was hidden then, as now, within the group of buildings comprising the church of Santa Francesca Romana and its adjoining convent.

In the background at the left is the Palatine hill, with the eastern end of the Farnese Gardens marked by two square towers. Beyond the Arch of Titus in the distance stretches the Roman Forum with the Capitol at its western end.

The costume of the visitors dates the photograph about 1860–1865.

54. THE TEMPLE OF ANTONINUS AND FAUSTINA AND A GLIMPSE
OF THE NORTH SIDE OF THE ROMAN FORUM

Photographed before 1876

Except for a difference in angle this photograph closely resembles Turner's drawing of 1819 (Plate 112). Most of the Forum as it appears in the photograph still retains the high level of ground accumulated through centuries. The small excavation about the temple's steps was made early in the nineteenth century; the main body of the steps and the sides close by were excavated in 1876. The old houses beyond, which covered the site of the Basilica Aemilia, were demolished in 1899 for the basilica's excavation.

The photograph shows, also, what is hidden by the luxuriant oleanders in Plate 111, the temple's exquisite frieze carved with griffins and garlands.

55. THE WEST END OF THE ROMAN FORUM ABOUT 1858
From an old photograph

The view above shows this part of the Forum still the half-excavated *Campo Vaccino*, or Cow Pasture, as it looked during the last period of papal rule before the achievement of Italian independence. Excavations near the Capitol had been carried on intermittently, and the section west of the circling carriage drive had been dug deeply, but the general level of the ground was still much higher than today.

In the background is the Senator's Palace, built above the old Tabularium. At the right the medieval church of Santa Maria in Aracoeli shares the Capitol hill. The monuments clustered here, reading from left to right, are: three columns of the Temple of Castor; eight of the Temple of Saturn; three corner columns of the Temple of Vespasian, which, owing to the angle, appear to be only two; the Column of Phocas, standing alone; the Arch of Septimius Severus; and the church of San Giuseppe de' Falegnami, erected over the Mamertine Prison at the foot of the Capitoline slope.

56. THE NORTHWEST ANGLE OF THE PALATINE WITH A VIEW
EASTWARD ALONG THE ROMAN FORUM

Photographed before 1881

On the Palatine hill, in the upper centre, the square tower of the Farnese Gardens, laid out in the sixteenth century, still stands above the buried Palace of Tiberius, which had been partially excavated by Napoleon III; its massive retaining wall runs down into the Forum through the site of the House of the Vestals, still hidden beneath the earth. At the foot of the hill is the church of Santa Maria Liberatrice, demolished in 1900–1901 for purposes of excavation. It was erected in the Middle Ages on the site of the abandoned church of Santa Maria Antiqua, which had been built into part of an ancient Roman structure usually called the Temple of Augustus, but perhaps a monumental entrance to the Palatine. The baroque façade and cupola of the church were added in the seventeenth century. Houses which appear in eighteenth-century engravings still nestle against the towering walls of the so-called Temple of Augustus.

Toward the left, rows of trees still run down the centre of the Forum to the Arch of Titus in the distance, though they had been removed long since from the western end of the Forum. In the foreground is the broken surface of this excavated western section.

57. THE CAPITOL HILL

Aeroplane view looking east, 1949

The Capitol hill is in the centre foreground. Beyond it the Roman Forum stretches toward the Colosseum, with the Palatine hill at the right.

In ancient times the hill had two distinct summits; the northern or Arx and the southern or Capitolium. The lower ground between was called the Asylum because Romulus was said to have made it a refuge for fugitives. Erosion and filling have made this part, now the Capitol piazza, look almost level with the rest of the hill, as seen from the air.

1. Corner of monument of Victor Emmanuel II, built 1885–1911.
2. Medieval church of Santa Maria in Aracoeli.

3. Ruins of Roman apartment house or insula, first century A.D.
4. Capitoline Museum, seventeenth century.
5. Senator's Palace, built from the twelfth to the seventeenth century on the lower floors of the old Roman Tabularium of 78 B.C.
6. Conservatori Museum, formerly the Palace of the Conservators or City Councillors, built fifteenth and sixteenth century.
7. *Museo Nuovo* (New Museum), once the sixteenth-century Caffarelli Palace, then the German Embassy; later, after considerable change, the *Museo Mussolini*.

The foundations of the Temple of Jupiter Capitolinus, dating from the sixth century B.C., lie beneath 6 and 7. The fragment of podium wall shown in Plate 59 stands among the trees behind 7.

8. The Salita delle Tre Pile, beside which lie fragments of Domitian's Temple of Jupiter Capitolinus (Plate 60), built first century A.D.

58. SOUTHEAST CORNER OF THE PLATFORM OF JUPITER'S TEMPLE
OF THE SIXTH CENTURY B.C., VIA DEL TEMPIO DI GIOVE

Photographed 1947

This corner of the temple's platform has been visible a comparatively short time. It and two other corners have been known at least since 1875, having been discovered when the site was definitely located on this peak of the hill, but they were uncovered only during excavations from 1919 to 1921. Dionysius of Halicarnassus relates the legendary events that accompanied the founding of this temple by the elder Tarquin, last king of ancient Rome (traditional date 616–579 B.C.):

'It was at this time, they say, that a wonderful prodigy appeared under ground; for when they were digging the foundations and the excavation had been carried down to a great depth, there was found the head of a man newly slain with the face like that of a living man and the blood which flowed from the severed head warm and fresh. Tarquinius, seeing this prodigy, ordered the workmen to leave off digging, and assembling the native soothsayers, inquired of them what the prodigy meant.' These men being unable to explain it, Tarquin sent out ambassadors, who, with considerable difficulty, obtained an explanation from the Tyrrhenian soothsayers:

' "Romans, tell your fellow citizens it is ordained by fate that the place in which you found the head shall be the head of all Italy." Since that time the place is called the Capitoline Hill from the head that was found there; for the Romans call heads *capita*. . . . The temple that was built in the time of our fathers after the burning of this one [Dionysius referred to a fire of 83 B.C.] was erected upon the same foundations, and differed from the ancient structure in nothing but the costliness of the materials, having three rows of columns on the front, facing the south, and a single row on each side. The temple consists of three parallel shrines, separated by party walls; the middle shrine is dedicated to Jupiter, while on one side stands that of Juno and on the other that of Minerva, all three being under one pediment and one roof.'

Dionysius of Halicarnassus, *Roman Antiquities*, Book IV, Chapters LIX–LXI.

59. A WALL OF THE PODIUM OF JUPITER'S SIXTH-CENTURY TEMPLE
Photographed 1949

This stretch of masonry, laid about twenty-five centuries ago, has probably always stood exposed to view. Incorporated in the garden wall of the Caffarelli Palace in the sixteenth century, it is located behind (7) on the aeroplane view (Plate 57). A parallel wall of the same structure is built into the link between the old Conservatori Museum and its extension, the New Museum, and may be seen in the Gallery of the Roman Wall.

60. FRAGMENT OF THE CORNICE OF THE LAST TEMPLE OF JUPITER
ON THE CAPITOL

Photographed 1949

This fragment of a cornice belongs to the rebuilding of the temple by Domitian after a fire in A.D. 80. With several similar pieces it now lies beside the Salita delle Tre Pile, on the hill below the Conservatori Museum, roughly in the location marked (8) on the aeroplane view. The annules or little rings carved between the tooth-shaped blocks, or dentils, which project beneath the cornice, are characteristic of Domitian's time.

Plutarch described Domitian's temple as well as those built before:

'The fourth temple, which is now standing on the same site as the others, was both completed and consecrated by Domitian. It is said that Tarquin expended upon its foundations forty thousand pounds of silver. But the greatest wealth now attributed to any private citizen of Rome would not pay the cost of the gilding alone of the present temple, which was more than twelve thousand talents. [A classical scholar in 1914 reckoned the talent as about $1,200.] Its pillars are of Pentelic marble, and their thickness was once most happily proportioned to their length; for we saw them at Athens. But when they were recut and scraped at Rome, they did not gain as much in polish as they lost in symmetry and beauty, and they now look too slender and thin.'

Plutarch, *Life of Publicola*, early second century A.D.

61. THE TEMPLE OF JUPITER ON THE CAPITOL

Roman relief, second century A.D. Rome, Conservatori Museum

The fragment of cornice opposite came from this temple of Domitian's time. The temple is at the left; the wall surrounding the enclosure is at the right. The temple's portico actually had six columns across its front, although only four appear here. In the foreground the emperor Marcus Aurelius, acting as Pontifex Maximus with covered head, is making solemn sacrifice.

At the top of this detail is the medieval Senator's Palace, a battlemented fortress. Below it, upside down, stands the Colosseum, shown with a dome in accordance with the tradition recorded in the *Mirabilia*. Between the two buildings stretches the Roman Forum. At the left is the Palatine hill, labelled *Palacium Maius*, Greater Palace, with rows of conventionalized arches which suggest its massive substructures. The medieval tower at the right, labelled *turris comitis,* is probably that of the Conti, which actually stands beside the imperial forums to the north.

This oldest known medieval view of the Capitol shows it roughly as it must have looked to the writer of the *Mirabilia*; to Master Gregory in the twelfth century; to the pilgrims who thronged Rome for the first papal Jubilee in 1300; and to Dante, who wrote: 'I am of the firm opinion that the stones that remain in her walls are deserving of reverence, and that she is worthy, beyond all that is praised and glorified of men.'

63. THE CAPITOL HILL LOOKING NORTH, 1532–1535
Detail of a drawing by Marten van Heemskerck (Dutch). Berlin, Print Room

'Behold the rich and ancient Capitol
That was my crown, and men have called
The pride and summit of the world!'
Fazio degli Uberti, *Dittamondo*, fourteenth century.

The desolate site of Jupiter's temple is in the left foreground, partly covered by racks for drying dyed cloth. Just beyond them is the back of the Conservators' Palace. The Caffarelli Palace was begun only a few years later, where the drying racks stand here.

Toward the right, in the Asylum, rises the Senator's Palace with its tall bell tower. The face toward the Forum, shown in Plate 62, cannot be seen in this drawing. Beyond the palace, to the left, is the church of Santa Maria in Aracoeli on the northern summit of the hill. Between it and the Senator's Palace is the medieval tower of the Milizie or city militia, wrongly labelled. The drawing shows a feature of the hill no longer there: the obelisk standing beside Santa Maria in Aracoeli, removed in 1582 to the Villa Mattei on the Caelian hill.

To the right is the Roman Forum, with the Temple of Saturn just below the brow of the hill; in the background is the tower of the Conti, which has been labelled 'tower of the Milizie'.

64. THE ANCIENT ROMAN TABULARIUM WITH THE SENATOR'S PALACE
ABOVE IT, SEEN FROM THE ROMAN FORUM

Photographed 1949

Directly in front of the Tabularium are three corner columns (one hidden behind its companion in this view) which belong to the Temple of Vespasian. The eight columns at the left formed part of the Temple of Saturn. The ledge in the foreground marks the top of a restoration of the rostrum from which the emperors and other dignitaries spoke.

Roman masonry of 78 B.C. reaches above the open archways of the Tabularium. Once all the arches were open; that at the right has always remained so. The others were closed from some time unknown until a few years ago, when two more were opened.

The square tower at the right still stands much as it was reconstructed in the fourteenth century. Above the back wall of the Senator's Palace rises the sixteenth-century bell tower of the Capitol.

It was of these massive Tabularium walls, supporting such a weight of later history, that Hawthorne wrote in his *French and Italian Notebooks* in 1858:

'Night before last, my wife and I took a moonlight ramble through Rome. . . . We ascended the Capitoline Hill, and I felt a satisfaction in placing my hand on those immense blocks of stone, the remains of the ancient Capitol, which form the foundation of the present edifice, and will make a sure basis for as many edifices as posterity may choose to rear upon it, till the end of the world. It is wonderful, the solidity with which those old Romans built; one would suppose they contemplated the whole course of Time as the only limit of their individual life.'

Vestigi d'una parte del Campidoglio che guarda verso il fori Romano che oggi si dice campo vaccino, doue di tanti edificii antichi che ui erano non si vede altro che nel segno A ch'era l'archiueria e castelli d'un portico d'ordine Dorico della triua
Castra. Nel segno B si uede parte del portico del tempio della Concordia restaurato da fraticino. Nel segno C si uedeuo un colme d'un portico d'un tempio di bellis.maniera d'Architettura, qu'al per esserui pochi vestigij non si sà di chi fusse

65. THE TABULARIUM AND SENATOR'S PALACE BEFORE 1575

Etching from Du Pérac's Vestigi, *Rome, 1575. New York, Metropolitan Museum of Art*

From the one open archway men are carrying salt, a state monopoly which was stored in the Tabularium until the seventeenth century and which has seriously eroded its masonry. The tower is still the medieval campanile, taken down in 1578, to be replaced by Martino Longhi's present structure.

Through the debris of centuries, the level of the Forum had risen until the columns of Vespasian's temple were half buried in Du Pérac's day. This accumulation was removed by nineteenth-century excavations, which were carried down to the early imperial level and, in some places, even lower.

66. THE CAPITOL PIAZZA ABOUT 1760–1765

Drawing by Hubert Robert (French). Valence, Museum

At the left are the Capitoline Museum and the statue of Marcus Aurelius which Pope Paul III moved to the piazza from the Lateran in 1538. At the right is the front of the Senator's Palace with the staircase planned by Michelangelo sharply foreshortened. In the distance is the staircase leading to the church of Santa Maria in Aracoeli.

In or near this church Gibbon, in 1764, conceived the idea of his monumental *Decline and Fall of the Roman Empire*.

67. THE CAPITOL PIAZZA IN MODERN TIMES. VIEW LOOKING NORTH
ALONG THE STAIRWAY OF THE SENATOR'S PALACE

Above the fountain at the foot of the stairway to the Senator's Palace is the staff
from which the city flag flies when the Council is in session. In the distance is the
tower of the Milizie.

68. THE CAPITOL ILLUMINATED
IN CELEBRATION OF THE PROCLAMATION OF THE ROMAN REPUBLIC,
FEBRUARY 9, 1849

Illustrated London News, *February 24, 1849. New York Public Library*

To the Italian revolutionaries who illuminated the Capitol in celebration of the Republic of 1849, Rome and her ancient centre symbolized at once a heroic past and a hopeful future. Their leader, Garibaldi, wrote of this feeling:

'What else was this city to me, a fervent lover of antiquity, but the capital of the world? A dethroned queen! Yes; but from her ruins, immense, sublime, gigantic, there emerges a luminous spectre—the memory of all that was great in the past. . . . But also the Rome of the future, bearing within her heart the passion of regeneration for a people pursued by the jealous enmity of the Powers, because that people was born great and has marched in the van of the nations. . . . Rome to me is the one and only symbol of Italian unity.'

69. CELEBRATION OF THE BIRTHDAY OF ROME
IN THE CAPITOL PIAZZA,
APRIL 21, 1951

Since the establishment of Rome as the nation's capital in 1870, the Capitol hill itself has played a less prominent part in national and international affairs. It was from the Palazzo di Montecitorio, seat of the Italian Parliament, that the vote in favour of the present republic was announced June 10, 1948; but when the delayed proclamation was made on June 16, the flag of the old republic of 1848 was displayed above the staircase Michelangelo had planned for the Senator's Palace.

As Rome the city is older than Italy the state, it is fitting that the Capitol should remain essentially the city's centre, the symbol, as in Vergil's day, of her enduring strength; as such, it is the most fitting of all places, in this city of historic legend, for the yearly celebration of Rome's legendary beginnings more than twenty-seven centuries ago.

70. SANTA MARIA IN ARACOELI AND THE SENATOR'S PALACE
Photographed 1936

At the left is a corner of the monument of Victor Emmanuel II, with the ruins of the ancient Roman apartment house below it. Above the broad staircase, built in 1348 of marble taken from the ruined Temple of the Sun or Serapis on the Quirinal (Plates 174–5), rises the bare brick façade of the church. At the right of the stairway is the Capitoline Museum. The Conservatori Museum is too far to the right to be seen. In the background is the Senator's Palace. The façade of the church was to have been faced with mosaic, but after six hundred years the raw brick-work still waits to be concealed. At the left of the central window, there appears very faintly a walled-in outline marking the location of the clock which regulated the city life of Rome for centuries before its removal to the bell tower of the Capitol. The shallow staircase called the Cordonata, toward the right, leads up to the Capitol Piazza.

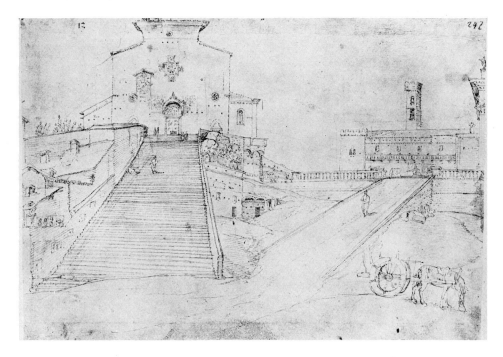

71. SANTA MARIA IN ARACOELI AND THE SENATOR'S PALACE
IN THE SIXTEENTH CENTURY

Drawing by the Anonymus Fabriczy (Netherlandish). Stuttgart, Print Room

In this sixteenth-century drawing the Capitol Piazza is not yet completed in accordance with Michelangelo's plans, although the statue of Marcus Aurelius stands in its centre, where Paul III placed it in 1538.

The Conservators' Palace, a corner of which appears at the extreme right, had been given part of its new façade, but the Capitoline Museum, now opposite, was as yet unbuilt and the statues have not yet been placed on the edge of the Capitol Piazza. The clock, which was later transferred to the Capitol bell tower, is shown still on the front of Mary's church.

In general, however, the piazza and Senator's Palace have begun to lose their medieval aspect of a fortified place and to take on their present ordered appearance.

72. RUINS OF A ROMAN APARTMENT HOUSE OF THE FIRST CENTURY A.D.
AT THE FOOT OF THE CAPITOL

Photographed 1933

At the left is a corner of the Victor Emmanuel monument; behind it, a glimpse of Santa Maria in Aracoeli, a corner of the Capitoline Museum, and the bell tower of the Senator's Palace. The great stairway to the church leads up above the ruined house, which was once six stories high. The belfry rising from the ancient building belonged to the medieval church of San Biagio di Mercatello, built into the apartment house.

73. THE SITE OF THE ROMAN APARTMENT HOUSE IN 1665
Engraving by Giovanni Battista Falda (Italian). Rome, Library of the American Academy

The baroque church of Santa Rita da Cascia which covers part of the site was demolished in 1927 and re-erected near the Theatre of Marcellus. Parts of the church of San Biagio lay beneath and behind this later church.

Between the date of this engraving and that of the sixteenth-century drawing (Plate 71) the Piazza has been completed according to Michelangelo's plans, though with some alterations. The Capitoline Museum confronts the Palace of the Conservators; the shallow staircase of the Cordonata has been finished; and the statues are in place on the balustrade at its top.

74. THE PALATINE HILL

Aeroplane view from the southeast, about 1935

The Palatine is seen here across the barren site of the ancient Circus Maximus.

1. Top of the substructures of Septimius Severus (Plates 77–80).
2. Baths of Severus and exedra of box built by Domitian to overlook his sunken garden, the Stadium (Plates 81–82).
3. Convent of San Bonaventura.
4. Convent of San Sebastiano.
5. Stadium or garden of Domitian (Plates 83–84).
6. Residential palace of Domitian (Plate 85).

7. Gateway of residential palace.

8. Palatine Museum, built on part of the site of this palace. The villa begun here by the Mattei family in the sixteenth century has been known from its various owners as Villa Spada or Villa Mills (Plate 86) as well as Villa Palatina from its site. In 1856 it became a convent of the nuns of the Visitation, who added the wing which is now the museum.

9. Ruins of Domitian's official or Flavian palace. The ruin which looks like two columns is the corner wall of its basilica (Plate 187).

10. Small casino built by Cardinal Alessandro Farnese, with frescoes of the school of Raphael.

11. Farnese Casino in the Farnese Gardens, on the site of the Palace of Tiberius, overlooking the Forum.

75. THE SOUTH SIDE OF THE PALATINE HILL

View from the Aventine across the site of the Circus Maximus. Photographed 1949

The side of the hill overlooking the circus faces roughly southwest; that overlooking the Forum, northeast; but for the sake of simplicity they are usually referred to as the south and north sides.

At the right and centre are the great arched substructures begun by Domitian and completed by Severus to increase the building surface of the hill. Above them is the Belvedere; nearer the centre the ruined walls of the baths and perhaps of other structures built by Severus, and the exedra of Domitian overlooking the east side of the Stadium. The Stadium's south end rises just beyond the round tower in the centre foreground.

In the background, beyond a clump of cypresses, is a corner of the Palatine Museum, marking the site of part of the Villa Palatina-Mills. The square dark doorway to the left is an entrance to the courtyard of Domitian's recently excavated residential palace.

Some distance to the left is the small sixteenth-century casino with a loggia decorated in the manner of Raphael. Farther to the left rises the monument of Victor Emmanuel.

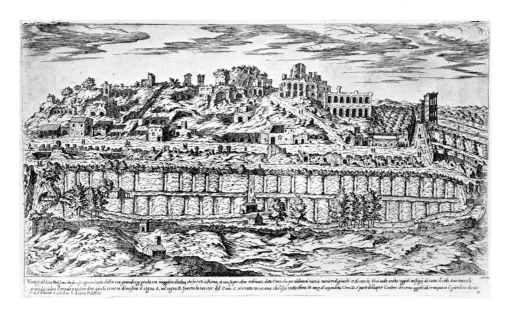

76. THE SOUTH SIDE OF THE PALATINE HILL
IN THE SIXTEENTH CENTURY

Etching from Du Pérac's Vestigi, *Rome, 1575. New York, Metropolitan Museum of Art*

At the extreme right, beyond the substructures of Severus, stand the remains of the Septizonium, built by Severus and demolished soon after this etching was made.

The site of the Circus Maximus is here planted with vegetables. A lengthwise path marks the line of the old *spina*, or low wall along its centre. The caption that Du Pérac adds to the etching notes that an obelisk lies buried here.

There were, in fact, two obelisks here, both excavated in 1587 by Pope Sixtus V. The first, the smaller one, had been brought by Augustus from Heliopolis and set up in the circus. Sixtus moved it to its present position in the Piazza del Popolo. The other, the last and largest brought to Rome, came from Egypt in A.D. 357 in a galley with three hundred oars. It was set up by Sixtus in front of the basilica of Saint John Lateran.

77. THE SUBSTRUCTURES OF SEPTIMIUS SEVERUS AND THE
SEPTIZONIUM SEEN FROM THE EAST, 1532–1535
Drawing by Marten van Heemskerck (Dutch). Berlin, Print Room

The inscription on the drawing, 'Her very ruins show how great Rome was', is found in almost the same form in Francesco Albertini's *Opusculum de Mirabilibus novae et veteris urbis Romae*, first published in 1510 and re-printed three times in the next few years. It seems to be quoted there from some earlier source, similar to but not identical with the famous lament of Hildebert of Tours. Sebastiano Serlio used it, as phrased by Van Heemskerck, on the title-page of his *Third Book of Architecture* in 1540. Since then it has been a common inscription on publications of Roman monuments. Fifty years after this drawing was made Sixtus V decreed the destruction of the Septizonium to provide a quarry for his great building projects.

78. LOOKING OUT EASTWARD FROM THE SECOND FLOOR OF THE
ARCHES SHOWN IN VAN HEEMSKERCK'S DRAWING

From an old photograph

'Beneath the terrace is a fine range of lofty chambers on arches, framing lovely glimpses
of the Alban Hills.'

Augustus Hare, *Walks in Rome*, 1882.

A view of the Palatine Hill, the Aqueduct of the Aqua Claudia, the Amphitheatre & the Arch of Constantine. Veduta del Monte Palatino, dell'Acquedotto dell'Acqua Claudia, del l'Anfiteatro Flavio e dell'Arco di Costantino.

79. THE SUBSTRUCTURES OF SEVERUS AND THE AQUEDUCT OF
DOMITIAN, WITH THE ARCH OF CONSTANTINE AT THE
END OF THE VIA DI SAN GREGORIO

Etching, first half of the nineteenth century. Rome, National Library

Few of Rome's imperial remnants appealed more strongly to the nineteenth century's love of the picturesque than these great substructures at the edge of the Palatine. George Hillard's description of the 'Palace of the Caesars' suited equally the etching and the reality:

'. . . One hardly knows whether to call the scene a landscape or a ruin. It is a labyrinth of vaults, arches, broken walls, and fragments of columns; a mighty maze of desolation without a plan.'

George Hillard, *Six Months in Italy*, 1853.

80. LOOKING OUTWARD FROM THE ARCHES IN THE ETCHING
OPPOSITE TOWARD THE VIA DI SAN GREGORIO

From an old photograph

The arches of these substructures, whether seen from within, as here, or from without, as in the etching opposite, fully justified the comment by Augustus Hare:

'Few compositions can be finer than those formed by the huge masses of stately brick arches, laden with a wealth of laurustinus, cytisus, and other flowering plants.'

Augustus Hare, *Walks in Rome*, 1882.

81. RUINS OF THE BATHS OF SEVERUS AND THE STADIUM BOX
Photographed 1949

The ruins of the baths are at the left, those of the Stadium at the right.

82. RUINS OF THE BATHS OF SEVERUS AND THE STADIUM BOX
SEEN FROM THE GARDEN OF THE CONVENT OF SAINT BONAVENTURA
Lithograph, early nineteenth century. Rome, National Print Collection, Palazzo Corsini

'Imagine a hill, upwards of a mile in circuit, and less than two hundred feet high, strewn with shapeless ruins and yawning with excavations, to such an extent that the original soil is almost displaced by fragments of brick and mortar; intersperse it with kitchen gardens for the growing of such matter-of-fact vegetables as cauliflower, artichokes, and lettuce; throw in occasionally the vine, the laurel, the cypress, and the ivy; overshadow it with here and there a stately oak; crown the whole with a smart, modern villa [the Villa Palatina-Mills] and you will have some notion of the Palace of the Caesars.'

George Hillard, *Six Months in Italy*, 1853.

83. LOOKING SOUTH ALONG THE STADIUM OR SUNKEN GARDEN
Photographed 1949

At the left is the curved wall of Domitian's exedra, overlooking the Stadium, with a glimpse of the Baths of Severus.

The stumps of brick columns parallel to the enclosure walls mark the outline of the ancient portico of Domitian. The cross-wall in the foreground shows the line of a portico added later. The oval enclosure at the far end was probably constructed by Theodoric.

84. LOOKING NORTHWEST ALONG THE STADIUM TOWARD
DOMITIAN'S RESIDENTIAL PALACE: THE LAST OF THE VILLA MILLS
Photographed May, 1936

This view is taken from the opposite end of the Stadium to that shown in the preceding plate. The small square building embedded in the ancient Roman walls
near the left centre is one of the last remnants of the Villa Palatina-Mills, which
had stood on the site of this palace for centuries. It was in the final stages of demolition when this photograph was taken.

85. THE LOWER PERISTYLE OF DOMITIAN'S RESIDENTIAL PALACE,
LOOKING NORTH

Photographed about 1938

This peristyle is one of the two open, colonnaded courtyards about which the palace was built. The main living rooms were grouped about a second, higher peristyle, farther north, entered from this upper level.

Until 1926–1927 much of the northern part of the palace was covered by the building and grounds of the Villa Palatina-Mills, begun by the Mattei family in the sixteenth century and added to at various periods. In 1868 the nuns of the Order of the Visitation, which had bought the property, added a new wing to their convent. To the left of the tree appears a corner of this wing, which has been considerably remodelled, and is now used as the Palatine Museum.

86. THE VILLA PALATINA-MILLS RISING BEHIND THE LOWER
PERISTYLE OF DOMITIAN'S RESIDENTIAL PALACE
IN THE NINETEENTH CENTURY

From an old photograph, courtesy of the Director of the Forum and Palatine

The point of view here is essentially the same as in the photograph opposite (Plate 85). Between 1818 and 1843 Charles Mills had covered, with the sham Gothic façade, which appears here, part of the old villa begun by the Mattei family in the sixteenth century. When this was removed in 1926 and the comparatively modern structures demolished, it was discovered that these later walls often enclosed those of the ancient imperial palace.

In the foreground lie some of the half-buried ruins about the lower peristyle, including the 'three underground rooms' which Lanciani described in the 1890's as mantled with ivy and 'very picturesque'. At the left is the new wing, added by the nuns in 1868 and now forming the Palatine Museum, which still marks the ground level of the Villa Palatina-Mills.

87. A CORNER WALL OF THE BASILICA OF THE FLAVIAN PALACE
FROM THE SOUTH

Photographed 1949

At the right is the corner of the basilica with fragments of marble columns belonging to the portico which surrounded the western and northern sides of Domitian's
state palace. The 'Hall of Isis', painted in Caligula's day (A.D. 37–41), lies beneath
the floor of the basilica. This official section of Domitian's palace was once part of
the Farnese estate on the Palatine.

At the left are the present Farnese Gardens, laid out above the Palace of Tiberius
in the sixteenth century. The shady modern road leading up from the Forum
roughly parallels the dividing line between the Palace of Tiberius and the rest of
the hill. The half-subterranean Cryptoporticus lies beyond the hedge at the left.

88. THE CRYPTOPORTICUS BUILT BY NERO TO CONNECT THE
PALATINE WITH HIS GOLDEN HOUSE

From a modern photograph

The arched openings at the right through which the sunlight sifts, rise above the ground in the present Farnese Gardens. The steps at the left lead up into the gardens themselves.

In the distance at the northern end of the Cryptoporticus a stairway leads up to an opening on the landing of the Farnese casino (Plate 93).

Part of the low vault in this shadowed passageway still retains its delicate stucco ornament in low relief.

89. THE SITE OF THE FARNESE GARDENS ABOVE THE PALACE OF
TIBERIUS AS SEEN FROM THE TOP OF THE ARCH OF TITUS

Photographed 1949

The roof of the old Farnese casino rises at the left among the thick trees which now mask the hillside. Past it the *Clivus Victoriae*, excavated now to its ancient level, runs beneath the partially excavated substructures of the Palace of Tiberius.

The ruins of the House of the Vestals, on the near or eastern side of the Temple of Castor, now lie uncovered where Vignola's wall ran until the early 1880's.

90. THE FARNESE GARDENS IN THE EIGHTEENTH CENTURY
Engraving by Carlo Antonini after a drawing by Francesco Pannini (Italian)
New York, Metropolitan Museum of Art

At the left in the engraving is the Farnese casino built by Rainaldi in the seventeenth century at about the level of the old Roman *Clivus Victoriae* or Street of Victory, named from the temple of Victory which it passed. Considerably remodelled, this casino remains today, its central fountain dripping into a basin on the lowest terrace. On the first landing of the casino's right-hand stairway a niche with a statue hides the present opening (Plate 93) into Nero's Cryptoporticus. An open door in the high supporting façade of the upper terrace, to the right, suggests at least some communication with the buried substructures.

At the far end of the garden the arched substructures of the Palace of Tiberius cross the upper terrace like flying buttresses to end against a square tower built by the Farnese and torn down between 1881 and 1884 (Plate 95). Beyond this tower more of the palace substructures rise above the Forum. At their foot is the cupola of the church of Santa Maria Liberatrice in the Forum; beyond, just below the Capitol, the columns of the temples of Saturn and Vespasian are faintly shown. At the extreme lower right is a suggestion of Vignola's sixteenth-century wall and gateway, demolished between 1881 and 1882, running through practically the middle of the ruined and buried House of the Vestal Virgins.

91. THE FARNESE GARDENS FROM THE FORUM ABOUT 1880

92. THE CARTOUCHE WITH THE
FARNESE ARMS FROM VIGNOLA'S GATE
LYING NEAR THE BATHS
OF CARACALLA, 1951

Above are the gardens when excavation of the Palace of Tiberius was fairly well advanced but many of the ancient walls along the slope were still covered. The wall with Vignola's gate still stood at its foot. Below is the gate's cartouche as it now lies with other fragments, including the inscription.

By 1880 the central group in the gardens, consisting of the casino with its double staircase and fountains on two levels had been reduced almost to its present condition (Plate 89). The niche on the first landings of the staircase had been opened and from the one at the right it was possible to enter the Cryptoporticus (Plate 88). Behind the casino to the left rises the corner of the Flavian basilica (Plate 87). Left of this lies the new wing added to the Villa Palatina-Mills (Plate 85) by the Order of the Visitation. At the extreme left are the pinnacles of the Gothic façade added to the old villa by Charles Mills

93. A CORNER OF THE FARNESE CASINO WITH THE ENTRANCE TO
NERO'S CRYPTOPORTICUS

Photographed 1949

At the left, the upper fountain still drips upon moss and ferns to splash softly into
the basin on the lower terrace. Beside the fountain, where in the eighteenth-
century engraving of the gardens (Plate 90) a statue filled the niche, the way is
open now into the cool, shadowy labyrinth of Nero's Cryptoporticus. At the right a
stairway leads up, past honey-coloured walls where traces of old fresco still remain,
to the remnants of the gardens lying above the Palace of Tiberius. From this
terrace there is a delightful view of the Forum.

94. THE FARNESE CASINO, WITH THE EXCAVATED SUBSTRUCTURES
OF THE TIBERIAN PALACE IN THE DISTANCE

Photographed 1949

In the foregound is the left-hand stairway leading up beside the casino to the top of the hill. The fleurs-de-lis which decorate it are from the Farnese coat-of-arms. The entrance (Plate 93) to the Cryptoporticus of Nero (Plate 88) is from the landing of the right-hand stairway beyond, under the arch whose top is barely visible here. Beneath the great central arch, shaded by oleanders and stone pines, is the fountain of the upper terrace.

In the distance, the *Clivus Victoriae* (Plate 96) runs beneath the substructures of the Palace of Tiberius, whose arches, still half-filled with earth, appear in Pinelli's painting, opposite.

95. ROMA SPARITA, VANISHED ROME: HALF-BURIED SUBSTRUCTURES
OF THE PALACE OF TIBERIUS IN THE EARLY NINETEENTH CENTURY
Painting by Bartolommeo Pinelli (Italian). Rome, Museo di Roma

In Pinelli's painting the great arches supporting the palace are buried almost to
their springing, as they continued to be until the excavations carried on by
Napoleon III in the 1860's. The Farnese tower, against which they abut, was not
demolished until 1881–1882. It is impossible to see the Capitol's bell tower through
these arches as the artist has shown it here.

96. BENEATH THE SUBSTRUCTURES OF THE PALACE OF TIBERIUS

Photographed 1949

In the foreground is the ancient Roman paving of the *Clivus Victoriae*, which passes here under the arches shown in the preceding picture. Above them, what remains of the Farnese Gardens is still supported by the massive vaults of the 'Palace of the Caesars'.

Through the now dark archways facing on this street there was once a fine view across the Forum. Emperors later than Tiberius flung these arches across the *Clivus Victoriae* like a bridge, making it a tunnel-like passage through the interior of the palace. In some of the hidden rooms opening off it and now inaccessible to visitors, there are still traces of paintings done almost two thousand years ago. Before the excavations of the 1860's these arches were filled with earth above the level of the balcony marked by the restored marble rail. There is much restoration also in the upper part of the great foreground pier.

97. THE CHURCH OF SANTA MARIA ANTIQUA
BUILT ABOUT THE SIXTH CENTURY INTO AN ANCIENT STRUCTURE.
BETWEEN THE PALATINE AND THE FORUM
Photographed 1949

From the *Clivus Victoriae* a double ramp leads down into Santa Maria Antiqua. Here, on the walls and ancient Roman columns, are Christian paintings, done from the sixth to the eighth century, and renewed about every fifty years owing to the damage caused by dampness in this area. The frescoes of the seventh century show Greek influence; they were done by artists who were refugees in Rome from the Arab invasion of the Easten Roman provinces.

98. THE SUBSTRUCTURES OF THE PALACE OF TIBERIUS AND THE SITE
OF SANTA MARIA LIBERATRICE, BUILT IN THE MIDDLE AGES ON
ALMOST THE SAME SITE AS THE CHURCH OF SANTA MARIA ANTIQUA

Photographed 1949

The entrance to the church of Santa Maria Antiqua is through a low arch just to the right of the little pent-roof.

The Forum has been excavated and many buried ruins have been discovered since the etching opposite was made. One of the notable landmarks is the site of the Regia, the official residence of the Pontifex Maximus, which lies in the immediate foreground.

99. THE SUBSTRUCTURES OF THE PALACE OF TIBERIUS AND THE
CHURCH OF SANTA MARIA LIBERATRICE, 1753

Etching from Giuseppi Vasi's Magnificenze di Roma, *Rome, 1753*
Rome, Library of the American Academy

In the foreground is the north side of the Forum, known at this time as the *Campo Vaccino* or Cow Pasture from its common use. The Farnese Gardens, at the upper left, show the neglect that overtook them after they passed in 1731 to the Bourbons of Naples.

The medieval church of Santa Maria Liberatrice, standing almost upon the site of Santa Maria Antiqua abandoned in the ninth century, shows the baroque façade which it retained until it was demolished in 1900–1901 for the excavation of the older building and of the ramp leading to the Palatine.

The mass of ruins to the right of the church belongs to the ancient structure into which it was built.

Behind the fountain are the three columns of the Temple of Castor.

100. THE ROMAN FORUM

Looking west along the Forum to the Capitol, 1949

The Forum runs about northwest and southeast but for simplicity the right side, as one faces the Capitol, is usually called the north, the other the south. The Sacred Way runs lengthwise along the north side. The Palatine hill is at the left. The view was taken from the top of the Arch of Titus.

1. Temple of Castor.
2. Basilica Julia, named for Julius Caesar who began it.
3. Small round Temple of Vesta, partially restored.
4. Temple of Saturn.
5. Temple of Vespasian, past which triumphal processions moved to the Capitol.
6. Column of Phocas.

7. Arch of Severus. The open space between it and the Temple of Castor is the heart of the ancient Forum.
8. Foundations of rostrum begun by Caesar, from which dignitaries spoke.
9. Spot where Caesar's body was burned in 44 B.C., where the Senate erected an altar and temple in his honour, and near which Antony made his famous speech.
10. Senate House, begun by Caesar, last restored by Diocletian (A.D. 284–305).
11. Church of Saints Martina and Luca built in ruins of an annex to the Senate House on part of the ancient Comitium or open place of assembly.
12. Temple of Antoninus and Faustina, with church of San Lorenzo in Miranda built into it. The Basilica Aemilia lies between this and the Senate House.
13. Ancient building long used as vestibule of church of Saints Cosmas and Damian.
14. Ancient building belonging to the Forum of Peace, now church of Saints Cosmas and Damian. On its north wall the Marble Plan was fastened.
15. Western apse of Basilica of Constantine or Maxentius. The column in the distance is that of Trajan in his forum.

101. THE SOUTHWEST END OF THE ROMAN FORUM
Photographed 1949

At the left are the columns of the Temple of Castor excavated to show the chambers within its foundations. A few reconstructed arches of the Basilica Julia rise beyond it to the right. At the foot of the Capitol stand the columns of the temples of Saturn and Vespasian.

The row of restored columns on tall bases that border the Forum's open space at the right probably once supported statues. One of these columns hides the Column of Phocas, on which once stood that emperor's bronze statue.

At the right is the Arch of Septimius Severus, which remained partially buried until the beginning of the nineteenth century.

102. THE SOUTHWEST END OF THE ROMAN FORUM, 1532–1535
Drawing by Marten van Heemskerck (Dutch). Berlin, Print Room

This drawing is the left-hand side of a panoramic view of the Forum from the Palatine, the other half of which appears as Plate 110. Here, at the left, the three columns of Castor's temple are buried to their bases. Just in front of them the House of the Vestals lies beneath the earth, where cattle graze between low enclosing walls. A few almost buried arches may belong to this or to some other ancient building.

In the distance, but seeming closer because of the artist's foreshortening, are the eight columns of Saturn's temple and the three of the Temple of Vespasian. Beside the Column of Phocas rises a small medieval tower later used as licence office for the cattle market. Behind it, very sketchily drawn, is the church of Saints Sergius and Bacchus, deconsecrated in the sixteenth century.

The Senator's Palace, in its medieval form, rises above the eastern face of the Capitol hill in the background; the famous palm and the obelisk stand beside Santa Maria in Aracoeli toward the right.

The drawing probably shows the Forum just before it was cleared for the procession of Charles V in 1536. There are no traces as yet of the trees planted to border the triumphal way to the Arch of Severus at the right.

, 1582. libro che io fato
Claudio Gillee 26

103. COLUMNS OF THE TEMPLE OF CASTOR, 1682

Drawing by Claude Lorrain (French). London, British Museum

Few of the Forum's monuments have been drawn more often than these three columns of Castor's temple. When Claude sketched them with his characteristic springing line, he knew them by the name common to his time, as remnants of the Temple of Jupiter Stator. The founding of this temple, as related in Livy's *Roman History*, was connected with a victory by Romulus over the Sabines, and was a thank offering to Jupiter rather than to Castor and Pollux.

104. THE FORUM, 1743
Painting by Antonio Canaletto (Italian). Windsor Castle, Royal Collection
Reproduced by gracious permission of H.M. The Queen.

The columns of Castor's temple rise prominently here in the foreground; beyond them are those of the Temple of Saturn; on the hill above is the Senator's Palace. The painting is signed and dated XXIV Octobris, MCCXLIII (1243), the artist having omitted the D that should have followed the Roman numeral M.

105. THE TEMPLE OF VESTA IN THE FORUM, PARTIALLY RESTORED
IN THE 1930's

Photographed 1949

In the partial reconstruction of the Temple of Vesta, illustrated above, the
darker portions are the original marble fragments. Behind the oleanders at the left
is the little round building which formed the vestibule of the church of Saints
Cosmas and Damian, with the broken vaulting of the Basilica of Constantine rising
high beyond it. At the right are the baroque façade and medieval bell tower of
the church of Santa Francesca Romana, at the east end of the Forum.

106. THE TEMPLE OF VESTA IN THE FORUM (?)
Roman relief, perhaps of the first century A.D. Florence, Uffizi

The relief shown above and pictures of the temple on coins were used in the partial reconstruction of the 1930's; some believe, however, that this relief may represent the temple of Vesta on the Palatine. The capitals here are Ionic instead of Corinthian like those found in the Forum and used in the present reconstruction, but this may simply mean that the relief shows an older form of the building than the fragments preserved today, which date from a restoration by the wife of Septimius Severus late in the second century A.D. Ancient coins show the space between the columns filled with grill-work as here.

107. THE NORTHWEST CORNER OF THE FORUM
Photographed 1949

At the left is the triumphal Arch of Septimius Severus, erected in A.D. 203; next to it, the church of Saints Martina and Luca, first founded in the seventh century in the remains of an annex of the Senate House, and rebuilt in 1640. The height of its floor above the Forum is striking evidence of the general rise in ground-level from the paving of Augustus' time, in front of the arch, to that of the seventeenth century.

Beside the church, on the old low level, is the Senate House begun by Julius Caesar shortly before his death in 44 B.C., to replace an older building. It was completed by Augustus, rebuilt by Domitian, and again restored in the time of Diocletian (A.D. 284–305). Originally, its lower walls were faced with marble slabs and the upper part was covered with stucco painted in imitation of marble. It was first converted into a church, dedicated to Saint Adrian, in the seventh century; it seems never to have had an elaborate baroque façade like those added to so many ancient churches. In 1935 it was restored as nearly as possible to the form of Diocletian's time.

In front of the Senate House, under a slanting roof, is one of Rome's mysterious relics—a black marble paving covering a much older buried stone carved with an incomplete inscription, still a mystery as to meaning, but the oldest monument we have of the Latin language. The ancient Romans themselves were divided as to whether this marked the grave of Romulus or that of another hero of ancient times.

108. THE NORTHWEST CORNER OF THE FORUM BEFORE 1575
Etching from Du Pérac's Vestigi, *Rome, 1575. New York, Metropolitan Museum of Art*

The etching shows clearly the depth to which the Senate House had been buried by the sixteenth century; it had then to be entered by a flight of steps leading down rather than up as originally built. Later, the ground rose still more and a new door had to be opened on a higher level.

The low group of buildings in the centre, with a medieval bell-gable, is labelled the church of Saint Martina in the inscription below the etching, which adds that 'inside it is a much ruined temple of Mars'. The Senate House, with a bell tower, is there called the Temple of Saturn, or church of Sant'Adriano.

At the far end of the Arch of Severus stands the battlemented tower remaining from the days when this northern section formed part of a baronial fortification. Van Heemskerck evidently did not choose to emphasize such medieval remnants in his drawing (Plate 102).

109. THE TEMPLE OF ANTONINUS AND FAUSTINA AND THE VESTIBULE
OF THE CHURCH OF SAINTS COSMAS AND DAMIAN ON THE
NORTH SIDE OF THE FORUM

Photographed 1949

At the left is a corner of the Senate House; next to it, the site of the Basilica
Aemilia. Behind this rise the Column of Trajan and the domes of the two churches
in Trajan's Forum.

Next to the basilica is the Temple of Antoninus and Faustina, with the seventeenth-century church of San Lorenzo in Miranda within it.

To the right is a round pagan building of weathered brick, called by various
names and long used as the vestibule of the church of Saints Cosmas and Damian.
The two isolated columns in front were part of a portico belonging to a side niche.
The bronze doors are the originals, more than 1,600 years old.

Behind the little building is the main body of the church, an ancient hall, con-
siderably reconstructed, which had some connection with Vespasian's Forum of
Peace to the north. To the back wall of this hall was attached the Marble Plan of
Rome.

110. THE TEMPLE OF ANTONINUS AND FAUSTINA AND THE VESTIBULE
OF THE CHURCH OF SAINTS COSMAS AND DAMIAN, 1532–1535

Drawing by Marten van Heemskerck (Dutch). Berlin, Print Room

This drawing, the other half of that shown in Plate 102, may have been done just before the 'tidying up' of the Forum early in 1536 for the triumph of Charles V. The sketchy outlines of the old church of San Lorenzo between the temple's columns, for instance, may be due to the fact that it was in bad repair; to the artist's comparative lack of interest in medieval remains; or to the efforts being made to clear it away in order to give a better view of the portico itself. One of the changes recorded in clearing out the Forum for Charles V's procession is the removal of the three chapels of the Apothecaries' Guild which stood within the portico. These chapels are not shown here, but as the artist has left out other structures that should appear in this view, their absence cannot be attributed with certainty to the preparations for this triumphal entry.

Van Heemskerck included not only the Column of Trajan but also that of Marcus Aurelius, moved somewhat closer to the Forum than it actually stands. The towering ruin shown on the top of the Quirinal hill in the background is that of the Temple of the Sun or of Serapis, destroyed in the next century. This ruin is the *Frontispizio di Nerone*, 'Emperor's Table', or 'Tower of Maecenas', which appears in Taddeo di Bartolo's view of Rome (Plate 8), and again in Plates 175 and 177.

At the foot of the hill are the ruins of the Temple of Minerva in the Forum of Nerva, most of which have also disappeared.

III. VIEW ALONG THE NORTH SIDE OF THE FORUM
LOOKING TOWARD THE CAPITOL

Photographed 1949

112. VIEW ALONG THE NORTH SIDE OF THE FORUM
LOOKING TOWARD THE CAPITOL, 1819

Drawing by J. M. W. Turner (English). London, British Museum

Turner's drawing gives a sharply foreshortened view along the north side of the Sacred Way, looking toward the Capitol and the western sky. The late afternoon sun gilds the columns and façade of the Temple of Antoninus and Faustina and spills over to the baroque front which still rose above the little round vestibule. The shadowy distant columns of the temples at the Capitol's foot are almost indistinguishable from the trees which still line the centre of the Forum; only the lone Column of Phocas and the Arch of Severus are recognizable. Light and delicate, as Turner's topographical drawings always were, this is precise for all its impressionistic lightness of touch. It has caught to perfection the fleeting moment when excavation and restoration had just begun, when the Forum was still essentially a landscape. The artist has merely indicated the litter of ruins which Shelley had described the year before in a letter to his friend, Peacock:

'The Forum is a plain in the midst of Rome, a kind of desert full of heaps of stones and pits; and though so near the habitations of men, is the most desolate place you can conceive. The ruins of temples stand in and around it, shattered columns and ranges of others complete, supporting cornices of exquisite workmanship and vast vaults of shattered domes distinct with regular compartments, once filled with sculptures of ivory and brass.'

113. VIEW OF THE FORUM FROM THE FARNESE GARDENS, 1826

Painting by J. B. C. Corot (French). Paris, Louvre

114. VIEW OF THE FORUM FROM THE FARNESE GARDENS

Photographed 1949

Corot, to whom the Italian sunlight came as a revelation, represented the Forum by broad masses of light and shade rather than by delicate line. The flow of light which he so loved he used to create harmony and unity in a scene which must have presented many disparate elements of trench and gaping hole. He took few liberties with his subject; he needed only to follow the guidance of nature to achieve the unifying effect of light.

The buildings are those already seen at the west end and north side of the Forum. The columns of the temples of Saturn and of Vespasian blend indistinguishably from this point of view. The artist purposely showed the dome of the church of the Holy Name of Mary in Trajan's Forum more widely separated from that of Saints Martina and Luca in the Roman Forum than they really are, in order to silhouette them both more clearly against the sky.

There is a sense of movement here, from the Capitol down into the Forum and towards its eastern end, paralleled closely in Longfellow's description, as he saw it two years later:

'It is now past midnight. The moon is full and bright, and the shadows lie so dark and massive in the streets that they seem a part of the walls that cast them. I have just returned from the Coliseum. . . . On my way to the Coliseum, I crossed the Capitoline hill, and descended into the Roman Forum by the broad stairway that leads to the triumphal arch of Septimius Severus. Close upon my right hand stood the three remaining columns of the Temple of the Thunderer [the Temple of Vespasian] and the beautiful Ionic portico of the Temple of Concord [the Temple of Saturn], their bases in shadow, and the bright moonbeams striking aslant upon the broken entablatures above. Before me rose the Phocian column—an isolated shaft, like a thin vapour hanging in the air scarce visible, and far to the left the three colossal arches of the Temple of Peace [the Basilica of Constantine]—dim, shadowy, indistinct—seem to melt away and mingle with the sky. I crossed the Forum to the foot of the Palatine and ascending the Via Sacra passed beneath the Arch of Titus.'

Henry Wadsworth Longfellow, *Rome in Midsummer*, in *Outre-Mer*, 1835.

Since Corot painted this scene in 1826, the monument of Victor Emmanuel has risen to dwarf the Capitol. Otherwise little has changed except for the addition of a few modern buildings in the distance or along the edges and the general lowering of the ground level by excavations. The removal of old buildings north of the Forum gives a clearer view of the dome of the church of Santa Maria di Loreto (left centre) and that of its sister church of the Holy Name of Mary, both in Trajan's Forum. The dome of the latter almost overlaps that of Saints Martina and Luca facing the Forum.

115. THE ROMAN FORUM LOOKING EAST TOWARD THE
COLOSSEUM AND THE ARCH OF TITUS, 1735
Painting by Giovanni Paolo Pannini (Italian). Detroit Institute of Arts

This view looking east along the Forum is almost photographic except for a slight inclination of the long axis to give a fuller view into the interior of the great arches of the Basilica of Constantine at the far left. Santa Francesca Romana, with the Colosseum behind it, rises as today. The space between it and the Arch of Titus is here entirely filled by low buildings and the arch itself still has its medieval additions. At the right rise the Farnese Gardens on the Palatine, with a glimpse of the church of Santa Maria Liberatrice at their foot, behind the three columns of the Temple of Castor.

To Plate 116

In the etching opposite, Vasi has swept the environs of Rome into a daringly foreshortened panoramic view eastward from the Capitol. He has shown not only all the familiar monuments of the Forum and many of those on the Palatine in his day, but also the lines of ruined aqueducts which carried the bountiful water supply of ancient Rome, and the outlying hill towns from Palestrina (left) at the southern end of the Sabine Mountains, to Castel Gandolfo and Albano (right) in the Alban Hills.

In the foreground are two structures which seem to be used in connection with the cattle exchange, since Vasi has named one the licence-office of the market. The one to the right of the column of Phocas may have held some remnants of the old church of Saints Sergius and Bacchus.

Beyond the Forum are such landmarks of later Rome as the basilica of Saint John Lateran (above the Colosseum) and the church of Santo Stefano Rotondo (above the Palatine). In the deep foreground emerges the entablature of the Temple of Vespasian, carved with implements of sacrifice, and identified as the 'Temple of Jupiter Tonans' in Vasi's caption.

116. THE FORUM OR CAMPO VACCINO, 1765

Etching by Giuseppi Vasi (Italian). New York, Metropolitan Museum of Art

117. EVENING IN THE FORUM, 1949

Eleanor Clark's phrase, 'the Forum, that lovely lake of time', aptly characterizes this low, quiet, sunny spot between the hills. Here, half the Forum's length apart, pagan ruins and a Christian church span the centuries. The marble fragments in the foreground probably belong to the Arch of Augustus of 19 B.C. Found in 1872, they were heaped here on the site of the Regia, official residence of the ancient kings and of the Pontifex Maximus, opposite the Temple of Antoninus and Faustina. The church is that of Santa Francesca Romana, on the ruins of the Temple of Venus and Rome. Its bell tower is medieval; its baroque façade was added by Carlo Lombardi in 1615.

118. A CAT AMONG THE RUINS
ON THE REGIA

119. LATE SUNLIGHT GILDS THE WEST SIDE OF THE ARCH OF TITUS
NEAR SANTA FRANCESCA ROMANA ON THE SUMMIT OF THE
SACRED WAY

Photographed 1949

120. THE EAST SIDE OF THE ARCH OF TITUS LOOKING TOWARD
THE FORUM AND THE CAPITOL

Photographed 1949

The inscription on the attic at this side is the original, almost nineteen hundred years old. It reads: SENATVS · POPVLVSQVE · ROMANVS · DIVO · TITO · DIVI VESPASIANI · F(ILIO) · VESPASIANO · AVGVSTO 'The Senate and People of Rome to the deified Titus Vespasian Augustus, son of the deified Vespasian.' The capitals of the lateral columns are the earliest existing example of the hybrid composite order, combining the acanthus-bell of the Corinthian order with Ionic volutes. The inscription on the west side of the arch (Plate 119) is modern.

To Plate 121
The view through the arch has changed little in the centuries since Van Heemskerck's drawing opposite. The Forum has been excavated, the Senator's Palace remodelled, and the monument of Victor Emmanuel built. The obelisk which the artist shows beside the church of Santa Maria in Aracoeli has been removed and its upper part is now in the garden of the Villa Celimontana (Mattei) on the Caelian hill.

Van Heemskerck copied the inscription fairly carefully, partly in Roman and partly in cursive lettering. The relief on the inside of the arch is that opposite the famous 'Seven Lamps', and shows Titus riding in triumph in a four-horse chariot led by the goddess Roma and crowned by a Victory.

121. THE EAST SIDE OF THE ARCH OF TITUS LOOKING TOWARD
THE FORUM AND THE CAPITOL, 1532–1535
Drawing by Marten van Heemskerck (Dutch). Berlin, Print Room

122. THE SPOILS OF THE TEMPLE OF JERUSALEM CARRIED IN
THE TRIUMPHAL PROCESSION OF TITUS

Relief on the south jamb of the Arch of Titus

The seven-branched candlestick and the other sacred utensils taken from the Temple of Jerusalem by Titus were deposited by Vespasian in his Temple of Peace. In 455 the Vandals carried them off to Carthage, whence they were rescued and sent to Constantinople by Justinian's general Belisarius when he conquered the Vandal kingdom in North Africa. According to Procopius, the Emperor Justinian sent the candlestick back to Jerusalem, where it finally disappeared, possibly when the Persians sacked the city in 614.

To Plate 123

Though Healy's painting opposite was not completed and dated until 1872, the preliminary work was done and photographs taken of the whole composition and of the various groups during Longfellow's last brief visit to Rome in 1869. The girl is the 'Edith with golden hair' of *The Children's Hour*. Of all American authors, he was probably the most widely loved and honoured in Europe. Lowell had written from Paris some years earlier: 'Over here it is more of reputation to *know* Longfellow than to have written various immortal works.' There still exists in Rome a Society of the Friends of Longfellow.

The other figures here are representative of the American colony of residents and visitors who enjoyed the pleasures of the artist's life as well as the ruins of antiquity in nineteenth-century Rome. Seated at the right, sketching, is the landscape painter, Stanford Glifford; behind him is the sculptor, Launt Thompson. Healy himself stands at the right, watching the progress of the sketch. Traces of a figure beside Longfellow are still visible beneath the paint; the photograph of this group on the spot, though rather indistinct, suggests that this was probably Jervis McEntee, American landscape painter.

123. LONGFELLOW AND HIS DAUGHTER EDITH UNDER THE
ARCH OF TITUS, 1869

*Painting by George Peter Augustus Healy (American). Newark, New Jersey,
Newark Museum Association*

124. THE ARCH OF CONSTANTINE WITH THE ARCH OF TITUS
IN THE DISTANCE

Photographed 1949

The round medallion on the near end of the arch, contemporary with the monument itself, represents the moon in her chariot sinking into the sea. The band of narrow relief below is also of the fourth century A.D., but the larger panel above and the free-standing figures, considerably restored, which stand above the columns are of earlier date.

The circle on the paving toward the right shows the place where, until 1934, there stood the remains of the ancient fountain, which marked the meeting-point of four of the fourteen regions into which Augustus divided the city (regions II, III, IV, X). This fountain, the *Meta Sudans*, was removed to widen the street and parts of it were placed in the Municipal Antiquarium.

At the extreme left, on the Palatine, is a glimpse of the convent church of San Bonaventura and, at the right of the arch, of that of San Sebastiano.

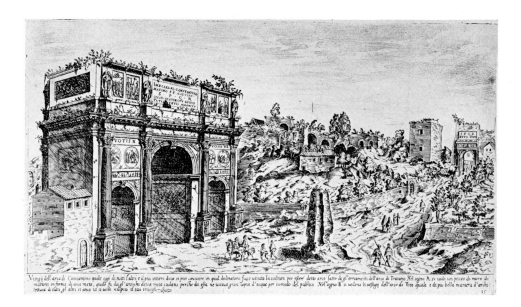

Vengo dell'arco di Constantino quale ogi di tutti l'altri e il piu intiero doue si puo conoscere in qual dolinatione fusse uenuta la scultura per esser detto arco fatto de gl'ornamenti dell'arco di Traiano. Nel segno A si uede un pezzo di muro di mattone in forma di una meta, quale fu da gl'antichi detta meta sudans perche da essa ne uscuia gran copia d'acqua per comodo del publico. Nel segno B si uedeno le uestigy dell'arco di Tito quale e di piu bella maniera d'archi tettura di tutti gl'altri et anco til si uede il spirito il suo triumfo.

15

125. THE ARCH OF CONSTANTINE WITH THE ARCH OF TITUS IN THE DISTANCE AND REMAINS OF THE META SUDANS IN THE FOREGROUND

Etching from Du Pérac's Vestigi, *Rome, 1575. New York, Metropolitan Museum of Art*

The etching shows clearly the inscription which still remains on both faces of the arch: IMP · CAES · FL · CONSTANTINO · MAXIMO · P · F · AVGVSTO S · P · Q · R · QVOD · INSTINCTV · DIVINITATIS · MENTIS · MAGNITVDINE · CVM EXERCITV · SVO · TAM · DE · TYRANNO · QVAM · DE · OMNI · EIVS · FACTIONE VNO TEMPORE · IVSTIS · REMPVBLICAM · VLTVS · EST · ARMIS · ARCVM · TRIVMPHIS · INSIGNEM · DICAVIT

'To the Emperor and Caesar Flavius Constantinus the Great, the Pious, the Fortunate, Augustus—inasmuch as through the inspiration of Deity, and the greatness of his mind, he, with his army, avenged the State, with righteous arms both on the Tyrant and on all the partisans of his faction—the Senate and People of Rome dedicated the Arch adorned with Triumphs.'

126. RELIEFS OVER A SIDE OPENING OF THE ARCH OF CONSTANTINE

The circular medallions above, of much finer workmanship than the band of relief, were taken from some earlier monument, perhaps one of Hadrian's time (A.D. 117–138). The head of the emperor in the boar-hunting scene seems to have been replaced by one of Constantine; that in the sacrifice to Apollo may be an older head reworked.

The band of relief below, executed with fourth-century carelessness, shows a unique ancient view of the west end of the Roman Forum. In the centre is the rostrum (Plate 100, No. 8) on which Constantine, surrounded by his court, stands to address the people. The emperor's head has been broken off, perhaps during one of the revolts against Christianity. Statues of seated emperors are at each end of the rostrum.

At the right is the triple opening of the Arch of Septimius Severus; at the extreme left are arches of the Basilica Julia, several of which have been restored. Between them and the rostrum is the single Arch of Tiberius of which only the foundation and a few fragments remain.

127. DETAILS OF FOURTH-CENTURY SCULPTURE ON THE EAST END OF
THE ARCH OF CONSTANTINE

All the sculpture of this central section of the arch's eastern end belongs to the time of Constantine. In the round medallion the artist has tried to follow the earlier roundels opposite. The design of this scene, in which the moon sinks into a sea represented by the reclining god, Oceanus, is delightful, but its execution, in comparison with the older medallions, is coarse.

The narrow band of relief below may represent Constantine's army setting out from Milan in 312 for victory over Maxentius. Two trumpeters lead the way. They are followed by soldiers bearing statues of the gods most venerated by the army—Victory and the Mithraic deity, Sol Invictus, the Invincible Sun. This relief, from Constantine's own century, demonstrates even more forcefully than the re-used medallions of sacrificial scenes shown opposite the strong pagan element of the time. The Roman army then, and for years afterward, was a stronghold of Mithraism, Christianity's most formidable rival; the representation of these gods evidently seemed a matter of course on the eve of Constantine's recognition of the Christian faith.

128. THE REMAINING ARCHES OF THE NORTH AISLE OF THE BASILICA
OF CONSTANTINE OR MAXENTIUS

Photographed 1949

The last remaining column which stood beneath the vault between the first and second bays was removed in 1613 to stand in front of Santa Maria Maggiore and to bear a statue of the Virgin. The overhanging masonry is unaffected, testifying both to the purely decorative function of these huge columns and to the strength of Roman concrete.

In the right pier the remains of an ancient circular stair lead upward toward the roof of the nave; there may once have been several similar staircases. A part of one is embedded in a great fragment of pier and vaulting which fell northward into the Forum of Peace some time in the Middle Ages.

129. THE REMAINING ARCHES OF THE NORTH AISLE OF THE BASILICA
IN THE SIXTEENTH CENTURY

Etching from Du Pérac's Vestigi, *Rome, 1575. New York, Metropolitan Museum of Art*

The column is still in place between the first and second bays. The caption of the etching tells us that this 'temple' was the repository of 'all the riches and ornaments of the temple of Solomon which Titus brought in triumph to Rome'. It makes the old mistake of identifying the basilica with Vespasian's Temple of Peace.

The artist has shown the roof covered with the conventionalized foliage like that in his etching of the Baths of Diocletian (Plate 158). Rodolfo Lanciani states that this roof was granted in 1547 to Eurialo Silvestri, who laid out a garden there and filled it with antiques.

130. THE COLOSSEUM SEEN THROUGH THE ARCHES OF MAXENTIUS'
PORTICO OF THE BASILICA OF CONSTANTINE, 1825
Painting by J. B. C. Corot (French). Paris, Louvre

Here the basilica's eastern portico forms a monumental foreground for the Colosseum's mighty bulk. This painting, dated December, 1825, was one of the first Corot did in Rome, to which he came late in that year. He wrote early in the month: 'I cannot say much for the climate of Rome; since I have been here it has done nothing but rain. That does not affect me, however, for I expected it.' He put to good use, however, the winter's golden moments, for the arches of Maxentius glow in the light of the setting sun.

More than any of his spring-time pictures, showing Rome softened and veiled by feathery trees, this painting embodies the artist's feeling for the city's incomparable severity and grandeur of mass. There is an emphasis here on solid form absent from *The Forum from the Farnese Gardens* (Plate 113) and *The Colosseum from the Farnese Gardens* (Plate 135), both painted in March of 1826.

131. VIEW IN THE BASILICA OF CONSTANTINE LOOKING TOWARD
THE COLOSSEUM: PREPARATIONS FOR A CONCERT

Photographed 1949

At the extreme left is the basilica's central apse into which the concert shell has
been built. Toward the right are the ruined brick piers of the fallen southern
aisle. On these adventurous boys find seats for night concerts, when floodlights
illuminate the Colosseum beyond the portico and the church of Santa Francesca
Romana beside it.

132. THE SOUTHWEST SIDE OF THE COLOSSEUM AND THE
ARCH OF CONSTANTINE

Photographed 1949

This view was taken from the top of the Arch of Titus. In the foreground appear ruins of part of the Temple of Venus and Rome; between the Colosseum and the Arch of Constantine a circle in the paving marks the site of the *Meta Sudans*, removed in 1934. The buttresses which support the broken edges of the Colosseum were built by Pope Leo XII, the outer one being completed in 1825.

133. THE SOUTHWEST SIDE OF THE COLOSSEUM AND THE
ARCH OF CONSTANTINE
Drawing by the Anonymus Escurialensis, about 1491. Madrid, Escorial Collection

Here the walls of the outer arcades are broken and crumbling and a stump-like
core marks the *Meta Sudans*.

134. THE SOUTHWEST SIDE OF THE COLOSSEUM, 1819
Painting by J. M. W. Turner (English). London, British Museum

Here the outer and inner arcades of this side next the Forum are still crumbling and unsupported, as they were when Byron visited the Colosseum in 1817.

135. THE COLOSSEUM FROM THE FARNESE GARDENS ON THE PALATINE,
MARCH, 1826

Painting by J. B. C. Corot (French). Paris, Louvre

This painting was done shortly after the buttress of the Colosseum's western wall
had been completed by Leo XII in 1825. At the left is the Arch of Titus as it had
been reconstructed by Valadier in 1822. The frame of trees and flowering shrubs in
the foreground gives the painting a more picturesque effect than most of Corot's
Roman works; by its very nature the scene lent itself to such a presentation.

136. THE COLOSSEUM, 1820
Drawing by Friedrich Olivier (German). Dresden, Print Collection

Though only eight years had elapsed since the French weeding of the Colosseum in 1812, this drawing reveals a luxuriant growth upon its ancient walls. The American painter, Rembrandt Peale, describing the ruin as he saw it in 1829, suggests that some greenery had been spared purposely. 'Some spots,' he says, '. . . are left neglected and covered with plants and shrubs, as a sample of its former guise. My old friend, as an artist, is among those who regret the change; for he remembers seeing the Colosseum a beautiful wilderness of ruins, vines, and shrubbery.'

Olivier spent most of the years 1818 to 1825 in and about Rome and filled several notebooks with drawings of Italian scenes. The one to which this drawing belonged has been divided among several collections; another, entire, is now in the Albertina in Vienna.

137. IN THE UPPER CORRIDORS OF THE COLOSSEUM
Engraving after a drawing by J. P. Cockburn, in Views of the Colosseum, Rome
London, W. B. Cooke, 1841

Fourteen years after the engraving of this romantic view in a shrub-decked corridor of the ruined amphitheatre, Richard Deakin published his memorable *Flora of the Coliseum*. Nothing could express more aptly the popular sentiments regarding this aspect of the Colosseum than a passage from his Introduction:

'The object of the present little volume is to call the attention of the lover of the works of creation to those floral productions which flourish, in triumph, upon the ruins of a single building. Flowers are perhaps the most graceful and most lovely objects of the creation but are not, at any time, more delightful than when associated with what recalls to the memory time and place, and especially that of generations long passed away. They form a link in the memory, and teach us hopeful and soothing lessons, amid the sadness of bygone ages.'

Veduta dell' interno dell' Anfiteatro Flavio
detto el Colosseo

138. INTERIOR OF THE COLOSSEUM LOOKING NORTHEAST, 1766
Etching by Giovanni Battista Piranesi (Italian). New York, Metropolitan Museum of Art

The most widely known views of the Colosseum in Byron's day were still those of
Piranesi. Before long, however, the poet's descriptions of moonlight in the Colosseum led to such engravings as Cockburn's view opposite, which is so completely
Byronic in inspiration that it might serve as an illustration for one of the famous
passages in *Childe Harold*:

> '. . . when the rising moon begins to climb
> Its topmost arch and gently pauses there;
> When the stars twinkle through the loops of time,
> And the low night-breeze waves along the air
> The garland forest, which the gray walls wear
> Like laurels on the bald first Caesar's head:
> When the light shines serene but doth not glare,
> Then in the magic circle raise the dead:
> Heroes have trod this spot—'tis on their dust ye tread.'

139. MOONLIGHT VIEW IN THE UPPER CORRIDORS OF THE COLOSSEUM

Engraving after a drawing by J. P. Cockburn, published in Views of the Colosseum, Rome
W. B. Cooke, London, 1841

140. A CONCERT IN THE COLOSSEUM, SUNDAY AFTERNOON,
OCTOBER 7, 1951

For this concert, a memorial of the fiftieth anniversary of Verdi's death, the building was illuminated by flares at the intermission, when dusk was coming on.
Orchestra and singers from the opera were directed by Oliviero de Fabritis; the
audience numbered about five thousand.

141. THE SOUTHWEST SIDE OF THE COLOSSEUM FLOODLIT
Photographed 1938

Though the floodlit southwestern side of the Colosseum hangs like a silver bubble upon the blue Italian night, the lighting penetrates very little into its deep interior. That the moonlight here is no longer the all-enveloping radiance of Byron's day is due not so much to this illumination as to the reflection in the sky of the city's countless other lights, which cluster so thickly now that they pale the moon's rays upon Byron's 'topmost arch'.

142. AN ARCHED CORRIDOR IN THE EASTERN WING OF NERO'S
GOLDEN HOUSE, DISCOVERED LATE IN THE FIFTEENTH CENTURY

Here Raphael's assistant Giovanni da Udine and other artists wrote their names
high up near the arch. Motifs from the paintings in this corridor influenced the
decoration of the Vatican loggie done under Raphael's supervision (Plate 145),
and many other works as well.

143. PAINTING ON THE CEILING VAULT OF THE ARCHED CORRIDOR
SHOWN OPPOSITE, FIRST CENTURY A.D.

Slender-columned pavilions, such as appear here, furnished a recurring motif for decorative painting of the Renaissance and later periods.

The small scale and fine detail of this style were appropriate to the modest rooms of Roman villas such as those of Pompeii and Herculaneum. Here in the vast halls of Nero's palace it is difficult not only to appreciate but even to see their delicate fantasy.

144. A PAINTED CORRIDOR IN THE EASTERN WING OF THE
GOLDEN HOUSE NEAR 'THE HALL OF THE GILDED CEILING'

Vasari describes the early excavations of these rooms and their effect on artists:

'Excavations were made at San Piero in Vincula [*sic!*], and among the ruins of the
Palace of Titus [the name by which the Baths of Trajan were then known] with the hope of
finding statues, when certain subterranean chambers were discovered, and these were
decorated all over with minute *grottesche*, some figures, stories, and ornaments, executed
in stucco in very low relief. These discoveries Raffaello was taken to see, and Giovanni
[Udine] accompanied his master, when they were both seized with astonishment at the
freshness, beauty, and excellent manner of these works.'

Giorgio Vasari, *Lives of the Most Eminent Painters, Sculptors, and Architects*, 1550.

145. ONE OF THE VATICAN LOGGIE PAINTED ABOUT 1517–1519
BY RAPHAEL'S PUPILS, SHOWING THE INFLUENCE OF THE
DECORATIONS IN THE GOLDEN HOUSE

Though it is probable that Giulio Romano did much of the painting in this loggia,
Vasari credited considerable of the work to Giovanni Udine, the assistant who
wrote his name on the walls of the arched corridor (Plate 142):

'These grottesche (for they were called *grottesche* because they had first been found in
these grottoes or subterranean places), executed with so much care . . . did so deeply
enter into, and take possession of the mind and heart of Giovanni, that he devoted
himself wholly to the study thereof. . . .'

146. THE LAOCOÖN,
DISCOVERED IN 1506 ON THE SITE OF NERO'S GOLDEN HOUSE
Rome, Vatican Museum

The missing parts of this statue have been restored several times. The present restorations, made in the early nineteenth century after it was returned from France, followed those of the eighteenth century; they are now believed to be incorrect.

MRCVS·RAVENAS·

·LAOCHOON·

·ROMAE·IN·PALATIO·PONT·IN·
·LOCO·QVI·VVLGO·DICITVR·
·BEIVEDERE·

147. THE LAOCOÖN SOON AFTER IT WAS FOUND

Engraving by Marco Dente of Ravenna, died 1527. New York, Metropolitan Museum of Art

The statue was found broken in several pieces, with some parts missing, chiefly the right arm and shoulder of Laocoön, the right arm of the younger son, and the right hand of the elder.

148. LOOKING THROUGH THE SIDE ARCHES OF THE CENTRAL HALL
OF THE BATHS OF CARACALLA TOWARD ITS
FRIGIDARIUM OR COLD BATH

Photographed 1937

These great brick and concrete walls, built more than seventeen centuries ago, are bleak and bare today, their marble columns gone, their painted stucco facings destroyed, their immense vaults fallen, their halls open to the sky. Quiet reigns now, except for tourists and the summer opera throng, in what was once one of the city's largest and most luxurious bathing establishments.

149. THE BATHS OF CARACALLA: FROM THE CENTRAL HALL
TOWARD THE FRIGIDARIUM, 1560–1569

Drawing by Giovanni Antonio Dosio (Italian). Florence, Uffizi

When this drawing was done two of the eight immense grey granite columns still remained against the piers of the central hall. The one at the right was taken to Florence between 1561 and 1565 and set up there in the Piazza of Santa Trinità. The fate of the other is unknown.

The wall of the cold bath still had some of its original colonnettes and pedimented niches, but this marble decoration was probably removed soon after the drawing was made.

150. VIEW IN THE SOUTHERN PERISTYLE OR GYMNASIUM
OF THE BATHS OF CARACALLA

Gaping holes in the brick and concrete walls show where the marble decorations
have been torn away. Part of the mosaic floor is still in place, though considerably
sunken; other mosaic fragments lean against the walls.

151. COMPOSITE CAPITAL FOUND
IN THE BATHS OF CARACALLA IN
1868

Rome, Baths of Caracalla

This capital, with a figure of Hercules resembling the famous statue (Plate 152), was found in the central hall, not far from where it stands today. It forms one of the supports for the lighting of the opera.

152. STATUE OF HERCULES
FOUND IN THE 1540'S IN THE
BATHS OF CARACALLA

Naples, National Museum

This statue, signed Glycon of Athens and probably based on a work by the Greek Lysippos, was carved in the first century B.C. Found in the central hall of the baths, it was almost immediately acquired by the family of the reigning pope, Paul III Farnese, and is often known as the Farnese Hercules.

153. LOOKING NORTHWEST ALONG THE CENTRAL HALL OF THE BATHS
OF CARACALLA

Photographed 1936

In 1819, when Shelley was working on *Prometheus Unbound* among the trees and
flowers on the tops of these ruins, he described them in a letter to his friend,
Peacock:

'In one of the buttresses that supports an immense and lofty arch, "which bridges the
very winds of heaven", are the crumbling remains of an antique winding staircase, whose
sides are open in many places to the precipice. This you ascend, and arrive on the summit
of these piles. There grow on every side thick entangled wildernesses of myrtle, and the
myrletus, and bay, and the flowering laurustinus, whose white blossoms are just
developed, the white fir, and a thousand nameless plants sown by the wandering winds.
These woods are intersected on every side by paths, like sheep-tracks through the
copse-wood of steep mountains, which wind to every part of the immense labyrinth.
From the midst rise those pinnacles and masses, themselves like mountains, which you
have seen from below. In one place you wind along a narrow strip of weed-grown ruin:
on one side is the immensity of earth and sky, on the other a narrow chasm, which is
bounded by an arch of enormous size, fringed by the many-coloured foliage and
blossoms and supporting a lofty and irregular pyramid, overgrown like itself with the
all-prevailing vegetation.'

154. THE TOPS OF THE PIERS IN THE CENTRAL HALL OF THE
BATHS OF CARACALLA, 1857

Drawing by Elihu Vedder (American). Author's Collection

The arched opening in the pier shown in the drawing is the same as that which appears, considerably restored, in the second pier of the photograph opposite. It is probably the door through which the American painter, Elihu Vedder, entered the staircase to climb the piers thirty-eight years after Shelley had written there his *Prometheus Unbound*. Vedder's sketch of 1857 and his description in *Digressions of V*, written many years later, suggest that time had brought few changes to the ruins in these intervening years.

As an older man, in his *Digressions*, Vedder dwelt wistfully upon 'the twilight passed on the great piers of the Baths of Caracalla. The fallen masonry formed such great heaps that the door of the staircase by which we ascended is now halfway up one of these piers. The levels above were one mass of flowers, and the mosaic pavement up there could have been gathered by the bushel.' In these later years he pencilled on the drawing's mount: 'This was some time in June 1857. . . . The ruins were wonderfully beautiful before they were "slicked up". This view from the top can no longer be had.'

It was from this same spot that Jean Jacques Ampère looked out at this same view, with the dome of Saint Peter's rising against the sky, 'the sole work of man that has something of the grandeur of the works of God'.

Jean Jacques Ampère, *L'Empire Romaine à Rome*, Paris, 1867.

155. THE BATHS OF CARACALLA: THE TWO REMAINING PIERS OF
THE CALIDARIUM SEEN FROM THE SOUTH

Photographed before 1937

The first of the popular summer opera series was given in these baths in July, 1937. The steel scaffolding erected to support the stage is so constructed as not to harm the building and to be easily removable. It is, however, left in place between the seasons, so that a photograph such as appears above is not now possible.

156. THE BATHS OF CARACALLA: THE STAGE BUILT BETWEEN
THE PIERS OF THE CALIDARIUM SET FOR PUCCINI'S OPERA, *La Tosca*

Photographed 1937

The setting for the last act of *La Tosca*, as presented in the opening season of 1937, is shown above. The action takes place in one of Rome's most famous monuments, Hadrian's Tomb, or the Castle of Sant' Angelo, used as a prison fortress at the time in which the opera is set. From its battlements, over which the statue of the Archangel Michael sheathes his sword in token of the ending of a plague centuries before, the heroine throws herself to death after the villainous chief of police has executed her lover on the castle platform.

157. THE CENTRAL HALL OF THE BATHS OF DIOCLETIAN,
NOW THE CHURCH OF SANTA MARIA DEGLI ANGELI
Photographed 1949

Most of the vaulting and eight of the red granite columns are ancient Roman work. This view, lengthwise along the central hall of the baths, follows the orientation used by Michelangelo in remodelling the ancient hall as a church in 1563–1566. In 1749 Vanvitelli changed it, making the entrance in the south side, through a little chamber opening into the old *calidarium* (to the left). The present church is therefore considerably wider than it is long.

158. THE CENTRAL HALL OF THE BATHS OF DIOCLETIAN BEFORE
MICHELANGELO REMODELLED IT AS THE CHURCH OF
SANTA MARIA DEGLI ANGELI

Etching from Du Pérac's Vestigi. *Rome, 1575. New York, Metropolitan Museum of Art*

The etchings in Du Pérac's book were often based on drawings considerably
older. In this case the hall had been completely converted into a church some
years before the book was published.

   The view is taken along the main axis of the hall, facing in the same direction
as the photograph of the church shown opposite.

159. SIR MOSES EZEKIEL ON THE BALCONY OF HIS UPPER STUDIO
IN THE BATHS OF DIOCLETIAN
Photograph from a contemporary painting

Moses Jacob Ezekiel (1844–1917), whose studio in Diocletian's baths was renowned in Rome, was born of a cultivated Jewish family in Richmond; fought in the Confederate army during the Civil War; then took up painting and soon afterward sculpture. He studied in Berlin and in the 1860's won a scholarship which took him to Rome, his residence for most of his life. The title of *cavaliere* was conferred upon him by King Victor Emmanuel II; that of Officer of the Crown of Italy by Humbert I.

160. THE UPPER STUDIO OF SIR MOSES EZEKIEL IN THE
BATHS OF DIOCLETIAN
Photographed 1886

Writing in 1909, the year before the Italian Government took over the studio as part of the present National Museum, one author described the gatherings in this studio, where Liszt often visited and played:

'Once a week throughout the winter season, Sir Moses lays aside his white buckskin coat and receives his guests, and there is music on these afternoons . . . by the first pianist and the four finest string-musicians in Rome. . . . Artists, musicians, and poets are drawn there by the sympathy of a like earnestness of life and its purpose. The vaulted roof of the studio, lined with the time-tinted garlands of leaves, is the same roof that has sheltered the generations . . . of the fluctuating populations of "the Eternal City".'

Katharine B. Wrenshall in *The World's Work*, vol. 19 (November, 1909).

161. THE BATHS OF DIOCLETIAN AND THE ENTRANCE TO THE
CHURCH OF SANTA MARIA DEGLI ANGELI SEEN FROM THE
PIAZZA DELL'ESEDRA

Photographed 1938

The entrance to the church looks, as Hawthorne said, 'like a confused pile of ruined brickwork', for it is simply the naked brick curve of a small apse opening from the now vanished *calidarium* into a little chamber of the baths which forms the vestibule of the church. Above it rise the clerestory windows which light the church from above as they did the great hall in ancient days. All exterior beauty of finish had long been gone before Michelangelo transformed the hall into a church, and little has been added since. Yet nothing in Rome suggests more immediately the continuity of pagan and Christian city than this ancient entrance curtained with the changing colours of the Church's seasons.

The cross marks the central vault of the great hall into which the vestibule opens. At the right, toward the railway station, lies the entrance to the National or *Terme* Museum, which stretches away behind the church. Moses Ezekiel's studio was located among the ruins at the extreme right, close to the Museum's entrance.

162. THE COLONNACCE, LAST REMNANT OF THE ENCLOSING
WALL AND PORTICO OF THE FORUM OF NERVA, AT THE CORNER
OF THE VIA DEI FORI IMPERIALI AND THE VIA CAVOUR
Photographed 1949

Drawing by the Anonymus Escurialensis. Madrid, Escorial Collection

At the left is the temple of Minerva; at the right, the *Colonnacce*, with the medieval tower of the Conti rising behind it. The arch to the right, through which the ancient street called Argiletum continued to the Esquiline, is sometimes said to have been called 'Noah's Ark' in the Middle Ages, from a contraction of *arcus Nervae*, Arch of Nerva, into *arco Noe*. Some, however, believe that the name was applied to the temple, which, according to Master Gregory, was used as a storehouse for grain and might have suggested Noah's laying in of provisions for the Flood.

164. RUINS OF THE FORUM OF NERVA: THE COLONNACCE ABOUT 1770
Etching by Giovanni Battista Piranesi (Italian). New York, Metropolitan Museum of Art

The street opening at the right in Piranesi's etching is the Via Alessandrina, built in the sixteenth century, and recently destroyed to make way for the broad Via dei Fori Imperiale, formerly the Via dell' Impero.

To Plate 165:

The photograph opposite shows the ruins of the Forum of Nerva as Hawthorne wrote of them in *The Marble Faun* in 1859:

'They passed the portico of a Temple of Minerva, most rich and beautiful in architecture, but woefully gnawed by time and shattered by violence, besides being buried midway in the accumulation of soil that rises over dead Rome like a flood-tide. Within this edifice of antique sanctity, a baker shop was now established, with an entrance on one side; for everywhere, the remnants of old grandeur and divinity have been made available for the meanest necessities of today.'

The baker's shop appears at the right, with the sign *Forno* 'oven' or 'bakery' above its doorway; the paving of small lava blocks still rises to the level on which Hawthorne's party walked.

165. THE COLONNACCE BEFORE EXCAVATION
From an old photograph

166. THE NORTHEASTERN HEMICYCLE OF THE FORUM OF TRAJAN
BUILT EARLY IN THE SECOND CENTURY A.D.

Photographed 1949

The arches of the ground floor remained almost buried from some time in the early Middle Ages until the excavations which were begun in the 1920's, while those of the upper stories were almost completely hidden by later buildings.

The medieval buildings uncovered when these later structures were cleared away belonged largely to the Priory of the Knights of Malta, established in the twelfth century. The square medieval tower in the right background is the Torre del Grillo.

167. PART OF THE NORTHEASTERN HEMICYCLE OF THE
FORUM OF TRAJAN, 1560–1569
Drawing by Giovanni Antonio Dosio (Italian). Florence, Uffizi

Only the tops of the ground-floor arches are here visible above the earth.

168. PART OF THE NORTHEASTERN HEMICYCLE OF TRAJAN'S FORUM
BEFORE THE EXCAVATIONS BEGUN IN THE 1920'S

From an old photograph

Though the lower arches have been somewhat cleared, those of the upper stories are more completely hidden by later buildings than in Dosio's drawing. The Via Biberatica, named from the pepper (*pipera*) sold here in ancient times, runs above the upper arches. The scene as a whole probably looks much the same as when John Dennie described it in the 1890's:

'The custode of the Forum is much pleased to show what he calls "The Baths of Paulus Aemilius", but neither are they baths, nor had the great general of Republican times any connection with the place. A door in a wall is unlocked for the visitor, in a narrow street called Campo Carleo. It is a singular ruin, a brick building in three stories, following the huge curve; half of this is open, a length of over two hundred feet; the rest is partly visible over high walls of a garden. There is the ancient pavement of Trajan's time, of which the lava blocks are solid as ever; on to this road open, on the lower floor, a row of the usual tiny Roman shops or offices, about ten feet square, paved with mosaic of grey and white *tesserae*; inside there are the remains of stucco on the walls. There are no windows, but each little room opens upon the road, with a tall archway into which is set a kind of architrave of travertine, and the doorsill is in place, with its groove to hold the wooden front, and the groove also in the travertine jambs. If one could see the shop, with its ancient silver ware, or its rugs and woollen stuffs, it would bring the old time a little nearer certainly; yet the imagination readily supplies the details. Hardly anything in Rome makes the everyday life of that age more distinct before the mind than this row of little shops. A flight of ancient stairs, laid in tiles not very much broken, leads from the level on which the modern street passes by this fragment of antiquity; here was the second floor, of rooms less important evidently; and a great staircase, now all broken away, led to upper rooms, ending at the very top of Trajan's excavation of the hill. All about this little ruin of the second century modern life goes on very briskly. Part of the ancient brick building itself serves as a blacksmith's shop, facing outward on the Via di Campo Carleo.'

John Dennie, *Rome of Today and Yesterday*, New York, 1897.

169. LOOKING ALONG THE ANCIENT SHOPS ON THE VIA BIBERATICA
AT THE UPPER LEVEL OF THE HEMICYCLE

Photographed 1936

The view above, including part of the Priory of the Knights of Malta (left), shows the opposite end of the exedra from that illustrated in Plate 168.

170. THE COLUMN OF TRAJAN AND A CORNER OF THE EIGHTEENTH-
CENTURY CHURCH OF THE HOLY NAME OF MARY

Photographed 1933

This column, erected in A.D. 113, commemorates Trajan's successful campaigns
from 101 to 107 against the threatening Dacians, inhabitants of a region north of
the Danube toward the Black Sea.

171. THE COLUMN OF TRAJAN AND THE SITE OF HIS FORUM'S
LIBRARIES IN THE SIXTEENTH CENTURY

Etching from Du Pérac's Vestigi, *Rome, 1575. New York, Metropolitan Museum of Art*

The church at the left is that of Santa Maria di Loreto, which lies above part of the site of the temple built by Hadrian in honour of the deified Trajan. Its dome has been completed since this etching was made; in the eighteenth century the church of the Holy Name of Mary was built at the right to balance it.

The sunken pit about the column, first excavated by the French early in the nineteenth century, has been famed for years as the central feeding place for Rome's homeless cats.

In the view opposite, the steep Via Magnanapoli leads down from the Quirinal to the column. The name of this street is of uncertain origin, coming from that evolved during the Middle Ages for Trajan's hemicycle itself—Balnei Neapolis. A later name was the Balnea Pauli, or 'Baths of Paulus Aemilius', which Dennie noted as erroneous (Plate 168).

172. TRAJAN'S ARMY CROSSING THE DANUBE, READY FOR AN
IMPERIAL REVIEW

Detail from the lower part of the Column of Trajan

The spiral reliefs of the column give a magnificent picture, in continuous narrative form, of the Roman army on parade, in daily routine, and in combat. The lower row begins with the army setting out from a walled city to pass in review before Trajan. The soldiers cross the Danube toward Dacia on a bridge of boats, while the reed-crowned god of the river looks on. The last to leave the city are the regular legionaries. They wear the conventional dress of the Roman regulars, with kilted tunics that show below cuirasses made of metal strips fastened on leather jackets. Their swords are belted on; their crestless helmets are hung over their right shoulders; their oblong shields are on their left arms. Over their left shoulders they carry stakes from which hang their kits, including cooking and eating pots and bags that probably held food and tools. The standard bearers appear at the extreme right, following the officers who are out of sight around the column.

The action continues in the upper spirals, showing the army pitching camp, building communication stations and permanent bases, fighting and caring for the wounded.

173. SOLDIERS BRINGING TRAJAN THE HEADS OF DACIANS

Detail of a relief on the Column of Trajan

The soldiers who appear here show the differences in dress that were already foretelling the gradual change from the classic to the medieval world. The cavalrymen wear trousers, such as were the common garb in most non-Mediterranean lands and were adopted by the Roman army as useful for service in cold climates. Eventually they were worn in Rome itself, in spite of laws prohibiting them. The soldiers holding the Dacian heads may be cavalrymen who fought dismounted.

174. FRAGMENTS OF THE TEMPLE OF THE SUN OR SERAPIS AND
PERHAPS OF THE BATHS OF CONSTANTINE, LYING IN THE
COLONNA GARDENS

Photographed 1949

At the right is the giant corner from the cornice of a temple of the third century A.D., 'the largest block of marble in Rome', lying upside down as it fell more than three hundred years ago. The part embedded in the ground is the pedestal of its acroterium or angle ornament, which appears in the etching opposite.

The fragments grouped at the left may have come from this temple, from the Baths of Constantine, or from both.

Pia ve del monte Quirinale che guarda verso Ponente, dove si vede nel segno A. gli vestigij di due grandissi scalle per salire, del piano nella sommita del monte, d'ove eranno diversi edificij, nel segno B. vi si vede vestigij del Tempio del Sole qual credo alcuni, su da
Imperatore Aurelio edificato alla grande, si come anco ne dimostrano i suoi fragmenti, tra lequali si como trovanti communo questo di marchi ha xvi di colonne grandi, d'onde de luna di esse si ne fatto il vaso della fontana del popolo, il volgi chiamo questo edificio il frontese di Neroni

1 7 5 . THE RUINS OF THE TEMPLE OF THE SUN OR SERAPIS AND THE
STAIRCASE RAMPS ENCLOSING MEDIEVAL BUILDINGS OF THE
COLONNA FAMILY IN THE SIXTEENTH CENTURY

Etching from Du Pérac's Vestigi, Rome, 1575. *New York, Metropolitan Museum of Art*

Here the corner of the pediment still crowns the fragment of temple wall, against
which rises a fortified tower of the Colonna. Colonna structures also lie between the
ruins of the two double stairways of imperial times.

176. LOOKING DOWN ONE OF THE COLONNA GARDENS' ALLEYS
TOWARD THE SUBSTRUCTURES OF A STAIRCASE RAMP AT ITS
NORTHWESTERN END

Photographed 1949

177. SUBSTRUCTURES OF THE STAIRCASE RAMPS
IN THE SIXTEENTH CENTURY
Anonymous drawing. Berlin, Print Room

Above the southeastern ramp of the staircase rises the remnant of the temple, with the section of cornice and its supporting modillions still in place.

The stone from these staircases furnished the material for the stairway to Santa Maria in Aracoeli on the Capitol in 1348.

178. THE COLONNA GARDENS IN THE EIGHTEENTH CENTURY
Engraving by Carlo Antonini after a drawing by Francesco Pannini (Italian).
New York, Metropolitan Museum of Art

The fragment of the temple cornice lies out of sight at the right on the upper terrace. In the distance at the end of the garden are the staircase ramps (Plates 175–177), topped by buildings which still stand today.

At the left are the bridges which cross the Via della Pilotta from the gallery of the Colonna Palace to the box parterre of the lower terrace.

179. A CORNER OF THE UPPER TERRACE OF THE COLONNA GARDENS
IN THE EARLY NINETEENTH CENTURY
Painting by an anonymous artist. Rome, Museo di Roma

Here the fragments of ancient architecture are placed farther apart than they actually lie, probably in order to give a better view of the tower of the Milizie in the background. A tall building hides this tower now.

So the gardens and their ruins looked when Charlotte Eaton wrote in *Rome in the Nineteenth Century*: 'It was just such a combination that a painter would have wished. It was more than picturesque. It was what his fancy could never have formed, but his taste must at once have selected.'

180. THE BRONZE BOXER FOUND IN THE QUIRINAL RUINS AND
NOW IN THE TERME MUSEUM

The statue is at present thought to be a Roman copy of a Hellenistic work done
about the second century B.C.

181. THE BRONZE BOXER AS DISCOVERED IN 1885 AMONG THE RUINED
SUBSTRUCTURES OF THE TEMPLE ON THE QUIRINAL OR THE
ADJOINING BATHS OF CONSTANTINE

Photographed 1885

This is the 'photograph taken at the moment of the discovery' to which Lanciani refers in his *Ancient Rome in the Light of Recent Excavations*, after the 'semi-barbaric athlete' had been uncovered 'as if awakening from a long repose'. See Text, (page 111).

182. THE THEATRE OF MARCELLUS
Photographed 1949

The columns at the right, discovered during the clearing of the neighbourhood in the 1930's and re-erected in 1940, are believed to belong to the Temple of Apollo restored by C. Sosius in the first century B.C. and called after him the Temple of Apollo Sosianus. This temple enjoys the reputation of being the earliest important marble structure that has survived from antiquity in Rome.

183. THE THEATRE OF MARCELLUS IN THE SIXTEENTH CENTURY

Etching from Du Pérac's Vestigi, *Rome, 1575. New York, Metropolitan Museum of Art*

The colonnaded hall to the left with the arched passageway through it was part of the ancient theatre. The archway was called the 'Arch of the Savelli' during this family's occupancy of the theatre; it disappeared, with the medieval construction above it, in the seventeenth century.

184. PIFFERARI PLAYING BEFORE A SHRINE OF THE MADONNA
AT THE THEATRE OF MARCELLUS, 1830
Etching by Bartolommeo Pinelli (Italian). Rome, National Library

Here, as elsewhere in Rome, the customs of the papal city blended harmoniously with their ancient settings. Pinelli's etching shows a scene loved and described and painted often in the nineteenth century but vanished almost entirely now. The *pifferari*, peasants from the mountains of southern Italy, made pilgrimages to the cities during the Christmas season, picking up welcome cash from householders who employed them to sing and play before their shrines. 'Their song', wrote William Wetmore Story in *Roba di Roma*:

'is called a *novena* from its being sung for nine consecutive days,— first, for nine days previous to the Festa of the Madonna, which occurs on the 8th of December, and afterward for the nine days preceding Christmas. The same words and music serve, however, for both celebrations. The *pifferari* always go in couples, one playing on the *zampogna*, or bagpipe, the bass and treble accompaniment, and the other on the *piffero*, or pastoral pipe, which carries the air; and for the month before Christmas the sound of their instruments resounds through the streets of Rome, wherever there is a shrine,— whether at the corners of the streets, in the depths of the shops, down little lanes, in the centre of the Corso, in the interior courts of the palaces, or on the stairways of private houses.'

The lamps kept burning before such shrines were almost the only illumination of Rome's streets until modern times.

185. SHOPS IN THE THEATRE OF MARCELLUS BEFORE 1927
From an old photograph

This photograph shows the theatre as it remained until after 1927, much as Hawthorne had described it in his *French and Italian Notebooks*, 'closely linked in, indeed identified with, the shops, habitations, and swarming life of modern Rome'.

186. THE 'TEMPLE OF FORTUNA VIRILIS' AND 'TEMPLE OF VESTA' WITH
THE CHURCH OF SANTA MARIA IN COSMEDIN IN THE BACKGROUND

Photographed 1949

At the left is the corner of the 'Temple of Fortuna Virilis'; at the right, the 'Temple of Vesta', so called from its round shape. The Tiber lies out of sight at the right.

The church of Santa Maria in Cosmedin, facing on the Piazza Bocca della Verità, is closely interwoven with the pagan past. Built in the sixth century in part of a hall used as a distributing centre for grain, it also rests partly on the foundations of an altar and temple which may have been dedicated to Hercules. These structures probably dated from the days of the Republic; they must have been very large, since Pope Hadrian I, when he destroyed them to enlarge the church at the end of the eighth century, took a year to dispose of their remains. The ancient columns embedded in the walls of the church are those of the grain hall built in the fourth century A.D. as a centre for distributing free grain to the populace. As the imperial administration decayed, this function was taken over by the Church in *diaconiae*, or 'deaneries' established in churches on the sites of the old granaries. Santa Maria in Cosmedin was one of these and Santa Maria Antiqua in the Forum another. The bell tower and extensions of the church are medieval.

In the early Middle Ages the church was used by Greek refugees from the Arab conquerors and was known as Saint Mary's in *Schola Graeca*.

187. THE 'TEMPLE OF FORTUNA VIRILIS' AND 'TEMPLE OF VESTA'
WITH THE CHURCH OF SANTA MARIA IN COSMEDIN
IN THE SIXTEENTH CENTURY
Drawing by Matthaeus Brill (Flemish). Vienna, Albertina

Matthaeus Brill's drawing shows, somewhat indistinctly, the sixteenth-century location of one of the church's popular curiosities. Leaning against the façade, to the right of the porch, is the round stone known as the *Bocca della Verità*, which was placed where it now stands, inside the portico, in 1637.

188. THE HOUSE OF CRESCENTIUS

Photographed 1949

Carved marbles from buildings of ancient Rome decorate the medieval brickwork of this house, the remnant of a once tall tower. The inscription which bears the names of its twelfth-century builder, 'the First among the First, the great Nicholas', and of his father, mother, and son is upon the archivolt above the doorway. A Latin couplet still marks the place where a bust of Crescentius originally stood near the entrance.

189. THE HOUSE OF CRESCENTIUS IN THE SEVENTEENTH CENTURY
Drawing by Claudio Coello (Spanish). Vienna, Albertina

This seventeenth-century artist, chiefly known for his religious paintings and portraits, has drawn with loving care the classic ornamentation of this ruinous building. The medieval brickwork seems to have interested him less, for the structure is left incomplete.

There are few medieval records of this building in pictures or even in words, except for those which deal with its use in the processional Passion Plays, when it was called 'the House of Pilate', and those which associate it wrongly with Cola di Rienzi. It was left for the nineteenth century's revival of interest in the Middle Ages to bring it to the attention of visitors.

190. THE EXTERIOR OF THE PANTHEON

Photographed 1949

The inscription below the Pantheon's pediment bears mute evidence to the pre-
cautions Hadrian took when he rebuilt the temple in order not to claim for his own
the structure first built by Agrippa. It reads:

M (ARCVS) AGRIPPA · L (VCIVS) · F · COS · TERTIVM · FECIT

'Marcus Agrippa, son of Lucius, built this in his third consulship.' The empty
matrices of this inscription, which had kept the names of Agrippa and his father
visible through the centuries, were refilled with bronze in 1894. Holes in the stones
of the pediment itself show where bronze ornaments were once affixed.

Originally the Pantheon was approached by a flight of steps, but the surrounding earth has risen until the entrance is now at street level. The sunken area around
its sides and back was excavated in 1881–1882.

191. SIDE VIEW OF THE PANTHEON IN THE SIXTEENTH CENTURY
Etching from Du Pérac's Vestigi, *Rome, 1575. New York, Metropolitan Museum of Art*

Du Pérac's etching shows clearly the relieving arches of the brick facing and gives as well a glimpse of the ruined Baths of Agrippa behind the temple.

In front of the building stands a collection of ancient sarcophagi and other sculptured objects, to which Master Gregory referred as early as the twelfth century: 'baths and other marvellous receptacles of porphyry, and lions and other figures of the same material'.

In this etching one bell tower rises from the centre of the pediment. Other pictures show such towers on the gable ends as well.

192. THE EXTERIOR OF THE PANTHEON BEFORE 1881

From an old photograph

By the seventeenth century the medieval bell towers had become unsafe, and Bernini erected the two shown here. Known later as the 'asses' ears', these were finally demolished in 1883. The photograph also shows the empty matrices of the inscription.

The excavations of 1881 about the sides and back of the great rotunda had not yet begun when this view was taken. Some time since then the now sunken area has become one of Rome's many sanctuaries for homeless cats.

'Thousands of cats', writes Eleanor Clark in *Rome and a Villa*, 'a city of cats, as of fountains and churches, and as naturally. . . . The cats are drawn for some reason to one place or another, which may remain the haunt of their descendants for centuries, and people come and feed them. . . . One of the smaller ancestral centres that remains is in back of the Pantheon, where there is a colony of twenty or thirty.'

The photograph opposite shows most of this colony in the deep trench now opening off the narrow street beside the Pantheon.

193. CATS IN THE EXCAVATIONS AROUND THE PANTHEON
Photographed 1949

'But thou, of temples old and altars new,
Standest alone, with nothing like to thee.'
Byron, *Childe Harold*, Canto IV, 1817.

There was nothing like it in the Empire when it was built, at least not of comparable size; it stands out in the history of architecture as the first of existing ancient buildings that was composed as an interior.

This view was taken between the columns of the central niche at the right on entering. The entrance is at the left; the high altar faces it at the right.

195. THE INTERIOR OF THE PANTHEON

Painting by Giovanni Paolo Pannini (Italian). Washington, National Gallery of Art, Samuel H. Kress Collection

Above the central opening the clouds, noted by so many visitors, move across the brilliant sky. The artist here faced the portico, looking out to the Piazza delle Rotonda, with his back to the high altar. Raphael's tomb is out of sight at the right.

196. THE PYRAMID OF CESTIUS WITH THE PORTA SAN PAOLO
Photographed 1949

This tomb, raised almost two thousand years ago and built into the walls when Aurelian fortified the open city in the third century A.D., has seen siege after siege and defence after desperate defence. One of Rome's few monuments to be scarred by bombardment in World War II, it survived this peril as well. First a Roman citizen's tomb and now a guardian of the dead from alien lands, it stands today a symbol of Rome's timeless endurance. Of it, as of the city itself, it may fittingly be said:

'In this perspective a year is not epochal and no event is final. Before such a record of indestructibility it is impossible to despair.'

Anne O'Hare McCormick, *New York Times Magazine*, December 30, 1951.

197. THE INNER FACE OF THE PYRAMID AND THE PORTA SAN PAOLO
IN THE SIXTEENTH CENTURY

Drawing attributed to Bartolommeo Ammanati (Italian). Cambridge, Harvard University, Fogg Museum of Art

The setting of the pyramid has changed much since Ammanati's day, but the pyramid scarcely at all, except for the excavation of its base in the seventeenth century, when the doorway of the burial chamber was found. The drawing above suggests a wild and desolate spot; today the pyramid faces inward toward soft green grass and flowers shadowed by pines and cypresses, beneath which the dead of two centuries lie asleep.

198. THE GRAVE OF SHELLEY BY THE AURELIAN WALL
NEAR THE PYRAMID OF CESTIUS

Engraving after a drawing by W. B. Scott, 1873

In the engraving an acanthus grows before the flat and simple slab which marks the grave of Shelley. Just beyond lies his friend, Trelawney, who, with Byron, claimed and burned the drowned poet's body when it was washed ashore along the Gulf of Spezia in 1822 and placed this slab above the ashes. In the light of his own untimely end and final resting place, Shelley's Preface to *Adonais* the year before seems prophetic: 'It might make one in love with death to think that one should be buried in so sweet a place.'

199. VIEW OF THE PROTESTANT BURYING-GROUND, 1832–1834

Painting by Thomas Cole (American). Collection of Mrs. Louis P. Church, Hudson, N.Y.

Cole's fondness for romantic indefiniteness, together with the fact that the cemetery walls have been changed considerably since his time, give the scene an unfamiliar appearance. The Old Cemetery, where Keats is buried, is in the left foreground, almost hidden by trees. The New Cemetery, with the grave of Shelley close by the Aurelian wall, lies to its right. These two graves are maintained now by the Keats-Shelley Association, whose headquarters is the house in the Piazza di Spagna where Keats died.

'As we approached the walls', wrote Bayard Taylor, 'the sepulchre of Caius Cestius came in sight—a single solid pyramid one hundred feet in height. The walls are built against it, and the light apex rises far above the massive gate beside it which was erected by Belisarius. But there were other tombs at hand for which we had more sympathy than that of the forgotten Roman, and we turned aside to look for the graves of Shelley and Keats.

'They lie in the Protestant burying-ground, on the side of a mount that slopes gently up to the old wall of Rome beside the pyramid of Cestius. The meadow around is still verdant and sown thick with daisies, and the soft green of the Italian pine mingles with the dark cypress above the slumberers.'

Bayard Taylor, *Views Afoot*, 1846.

200. HADRIAN'S TOMB, OR CASTLE OF SANT'ANGELO, AND THE BRIDGE
OF SANT'ANGELO SEEN FROM DOWNSTREAM

Photographed 1949

Hadrian himself completed the original bridge as an approach to his tomb; its
ancient name, *Pons Aelius*, came from that of the emperor, T. Aelius Hadrianus.
Only the three centre arches belong to the old Roman bridge, as one arch was
added at each end when the Tiber banks were straightened and strengthened in
1892–1894.

The ten colossal statues of angels were done by pupils of Bernini, after his designs, in the seventeenth century.

In the background is the Palazzo di Giustizia, or Courts of Justice, built in the
nineteenth and twentieth centuries; in the foreground, a group of river bath houses.

The photograph was taken from the Ponte Vittorio Emanuele, first bridge
downstream from that of Sant'Angelo.

201. THE CASTLE AND BRIDGE OF SANT'ANGELO FROM DOWNSTREAM,
ABOUT 1491

Drawing by the Anonymus Escurialensis. Madrid, Escorial Collection

The drawing shows the monument just before the extensive alterations carried out by the Borgia Pope Alexander VI, at the end of the fifteenth century. The bridge-head across the Tiber is heavily fortified by towers and walls; once across the bridge one was already in the Castle.

202. THE CASTLE AND BRIDGE OF SANT'ANGELO AND THE DOME OF
SAINT PETER'S SEEN FROM UPSTREAM

Painting by J. B. C. Corot (French). San Francisco, California Palace of the Legion of Honor

Corot, the painter of light, was characteristically uninterested in the baroque angels on the bridge or, indeed, in any part of the scene which did not present surfaces suitable for broad massing of light and shade.

This painting and the photograph opposite show the scene of which George Hillard wrote:

'The most familiar view of Rome embraces the castle and the bridge of St. Angelo and the church of St. Peter's. A thousand times had I seen it in engravings, and it was with a peculiar feeling—half recognition and half surprise—that I beheld the real group in the smokeless air of a Roman December. The combination is so happy and picturesque that they appear to have arranged themselves for the especial benefit of artists, and to be good-naturedly standing, like models, to be sketched. They make a picture inevitable.'

George Hillard, *Six Months in Italy*, 1853.

203. THE CASTLE AND BRIDGE OF SANT'ANGELO AND DOME OF
SAINT PETER'S SEEN FROM UPSTREAM

From an old photograph

The photograph of the castle and bridge was taken before the change in the Tiber's banks and the addition of the new arches to the bridge in 1892–1894.

204. THE GIRANDOLA AT THE CASTLE OF SANT'ANGELO
CELEBRATING THE ANNIVERSARY OF THE ELECTION OF A POPE
From an engraving by Ambrogio Brambelli in Lafreri's Speculum, *1579.*
New York, Metropolitan Museum of Art

The text engraved below this plate, made about a hundred years after the first
recorded display of the *girandola*, describes it as 'a sign of joy which is performed in
Rome, and which is called "the whirling one". . . . It would seem that all the stars
in heaven are falling to earth, a thing verily most amazing, and vastly marvellous
to see. . . . That it may be understood by all, this drawing of it is newly published
with every diligence.'

205. THE GIRANDOLA AT THE CASTLE OF SANT'ANGELO, 1884
Painting by Franz Theodor Aerni (Swiss). Rome, Museo di Roma

Sharply foreshortened and dramatically lighted, the angels of the bridge show clearly the baroque restlessness which led to their being called Bernini's 'breezy Maniacs'. The *girandola* of this painting, done during the long reign of Leo XIII, was one of the last displays of fireworks to be given at Castle Sant'Angelo.

206. THE VATICAN OBELISK IN THE PIAZZA IN FRONT OF SAINT PETER'S

Photographed 1937

At the left is a corner of the Vatican Palace; the sweep of colonnade is part of that erected by Bernini. The fountain at the right is by Carlo Maderna, who completed the façade of the church; the other was constructed to match it some years later.

212. THE STATUE OF MARCUS AURELIUS
AND THE HEAD AND HAND OF THE BRONZE COLOSSUS
BESIDE THE LATERAN

Enlarged detail of an early fourteenth-century manuscript. Venice, Library of St. Mark's

In this detail from the oldest known medieval view of Rome the statue, then generally believed to represent the Emperor Constantine, is pictured between the basilica and palace of the Lateran, above the little building erected over the *Scala Santa*, the Sacred Steps said to have been brought from the palace of Pilate in Jerusalem.

The head and hand, together with the orb indicated here by the circle in the hand, were believed in the Middle Ages to have belonged to the sun-god which stood before the Colosseum; they are now in the Conservatori Museum.

213. THE STATUE OF MARCUS AURELIUS BESIDE THE LATERAN,
1532–1535
Drawing by Marten van Heemskerck (Dutch). Berlin, Print Room

Part of the old Lateran Palace, before which the statue is shown, had been badly damaged by fire during the absence of the popes in Avignon in the fourteenth century. It stood until late in the sixteenth century, when it was pulled down and rebuilt on small scale. The Sacred Steps, entered from the arcade at the left, were re-erected close to their old location. The four columns in the foreground supported a slab of marble that was thought to mark the height of Christ.

214. THE STATUE OF MARCUS AURELIUS IN THE CAPITOL PIAZZA
IN 1565

Engraving from Lafreri's Speculum. *Rome, second half of the sixteenth century*
New York, Metropolitan Museum of Art

Under the arcade of the Conservators' Palace at the right is the same colossal head which appeared beside the statue in the early plan of Rome (Plate 212).

In the background, beside the staircase to the Senator's Palace, are two river gods, also among Rome's unburied statues, brought here in the sixteenth century from their old location on the Quirinal. A Jupiter which in Michelangelo's design was destined for the central niche between them was never executed, and its place was taken, twenty years after this print was made, by an unimposing figure of Minerva, found in the Aurelian walls and transformed by an altered detail or two into a personification of Rome.

The staircase at the left leads to the church of Santa Maria in Aracoeli.

215 · HEAD OF THE BRONZE COLOSSUS
IN THE CONSERVATORI MUSEUM

This head, which lay for centuries beside the statue of Marcus Aurelius at the Lateran, has borne many names. The Middle Ages believed it to be the head of that 'wondrous colossus . . . girt with rays', described by Martial, which Nero erected near his Golden House, close by the later site of the Colosseum, but it is now believed to represent one of the sons and successors of Constantine the Great.

The crown of the head is missing, as though a diadem had been removed. This agrees with the *Graphia's* description of the colossus as 'having on his head a crown of gold dight with jewels'.

216. THE HEAD OF THE BRONZE COLOSSUS AND THE RIVER GODS
TIBER AND NILE FROM THE QUIRINAL, LYING ON THE CAPITOL,
1532–1535
Van Heemskerck (Dutch). Berlin, Print Room

In the drawing itself, the outline of the arcade of the Conservators' Palace is
visible behind the head, which was evidently standing about where it appears in
the engraving of 1565 (Plate 214). The arcades disappear in reproduction.

The river gods, which had been brought to the Capitol in 1517, had not yet been
placed before the staircase of the Senator's Palace, but were still in front of the
dimly drawn arcade of the Conservators' Palace.

217. THE RIVER GODS FROM THE QUIRINAL BESIDE THE STAIRCASE
OF THE SENATOR'S PALACE IN 1949

Between the gods stands an ancient red porphyry figure of Minerva, disguised as the goddess Roma and providing by its too-small scale the one jarring note in the generally harmonious composition of the Capitol.

218. THE RIVER GODS FROM THE QUIRINAL IN FRONT OF THE
ARCADE OF THE CONSERVATORS' PALACE, 1532–1535
Drawing by Marten van Heemskerck (Dutch). Berlin, Print Room

Beyond, toward the right, is the façade of the Senator's Palace, lightly sketched in.
At the left are the obelisk and famous palm beside the church of Santa Maria in
Aracoeli.

219. THE HORSE TAMERS OR 'MARBLE HORSES'
ON THE QUIRINAL PIAZZA
TODAY

OPVS PRAXITELIS

OPVS FIDIAE

HEVS TV QVI PRAETERIS MORARE PAVLVM AC INSPICE
IN QVO INALI HI SVNT EQVI MARMOREI MVTILI ATQ GRANDES
ARTE VICTA NATVRA PARIDIS SPIRITVM CVR ERIPIT
QVID PRAXITELES ET FIDIAS EFFINXERE ISTOS AEMVLAMVR
SAT DIXI ABEI VALE SALVE MISCE BIBE DA MI
ROMAE ᴐ ᴐ XLVI

ANT LAFRERI
SEQVANI FORMIS

220. THE HORSE TAMERS OR 'MARBLE HORSES' ON THE QUIRINAL
IN THE SIXTEENTH CENTURY

Engraving from Lafreri's Speculum, *Rome, 1546. New York, Metropolitan Museum of Art*

The engraving, after an earlier example by Salamanca, is printed in reverse.

Restored and moved slightly from their original positions in the late sixteenth century, these statues were arranged in the late eighteenth century as they appear today, grouped about the obelisk from the Mausoleum of Augustus.

221. THE COLOSSAL RIVER GOD MARFORIO IN THE COURTYARD
OF THE CAPITOLINE MUSEUM TODAY

This river god's remote, withdrawn, but watchful countenance still conveys something of the feeling of unease which such images must have inspired when the pagan world was dying and the Christian not yet firmly established. To Christians such 'idols' were both dangerous and detestable; to Julian the Apostate, Constantine's nephew, seeking to restore paganism, they were reassuring. 'He who loves the gods delights to gaze on the images of the gods, and their likenesses' he wrote, in a fragmentary *Letter to a Priest*, 'and he feels reverence and shudders with awe of the gods who look at him from the unseen world.'

Ammianus Marcellinus, who knew and admired Julian, noted that ill-fated emperor's special devotion to Mercury. 'He secretly prayed to Mercury,' the historian wrote, 'whom the teaching of the theologians showed to be the swift intelligence of the universe, arousing the activity of men's minds.' According to one tradition, Julian was tempted to renounce Christianity by a statue of Mercury which he had raised from the bed of the Tiber. According to the *Mirabilia*, the tempter was a statue of Faunus, god of fields and rural life, 'that spake to Julian and beguiled him'. The stories are natural outgrowths of the Christian distrust of images of the ancient gods (with an unconscious tribute, perhaps, to the power of the arts) coupled with Julian's own feeling for the gods who look on 'from the unseen world'.

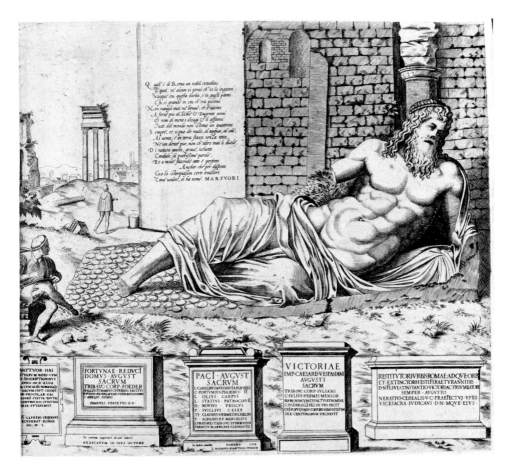

222. THE RIVER GOD MARFORIO LYING IN THE VIA DI MARFORIO
IN THE SIXTEENTH CENTURY

Engraving from Lafreri's Speculum, *Rome, 1550.*
New York, Metropolitan Museum of Art

The three columns of the Temple of Castor in the background suggest the nearness of the Roman Forum. An artist sketches the statue; Latin inscriptions indicate both the popularity of classical studies and the battle of dialogue and wit carried on by *pasquinades*, or lampoons, posted near Marforio and his opponent Pasquino.

Conceived in the tone of the *pasquinades*, these verses tell of Marforio's birth 'in these clothes and with this beard', his age, 'perhaps more than twelve hundred years', his indifference to circumstance and weather, 'for which he cares not one cent,' and the quiet, grave, and earnest character of 'this noble Roman citizen, Marforio'.

NOTES

SINCE there are no footnotes it is necessary to indicate in each case the exact
portion of the text to which it refers. The numbers are those of pages when
referring to the text, or of plates when referring to the latter. The notes are arranged
in order of appearance under chapter headings, Notes on Text first, followed by
Notes on Plates for the same chapter.

FOREWORD

The closing quotation is from an anonymous sonnet on the ruins of Ninfa found
in a guest book there.

INTRODUCTION

TEXT

Page 1

The opening quotation is a variation on a theme which may be traced through
Hildebert de Lavardin of Tours in the 12th century at least back to Alcuin in the
eighth. It appears in the Latin *Roma quanta fuit ipsa ruina docet* as an inscription,
believed to be by the artist's own hand, on Marten van Heemskerck's drawing of
the Substructures of Severus (Plate 77), done between 1532 and 1535. The closest
known source is a passage in Francesco Albertini's *Opusculum de Mirabilibus Novae
et Veteris Urbis Romae*, Rome, 1510, 1515, 1522, and 1523, near the end of the first
paragraph of the third book. *Quanta* and *ipsa* are transposed in Albertini's volume.

For the Marble Plan and the *Curiosum* and *Notitia* see Jerome Carcopino's *Daily
Life in Ancient Rome*, translated by Henry T. Rowell, New Haven, 1940, pp. 285–
286. The texts of the *Curiosum* and *Notitia* are published in Ludwig Urlichs' *Codex
Topographicus Urbis Romae*, Würzburg, 1871, vol. I.

Page 2

Chesterton's quotation is from his *Resurrection of Rome*, New York, 1930,
pp. 166–167.

The quotation from Rutilius Namatianus appears in his *Voyage Home to Gaul*,
Book I, 195–198.

Page 3

The quotation from Alcuin is translated by Eva Matthews Sanford in *The Classical Weekly*, vol. 40, No. 16 (March 3, 1947), p. 126.

The description of Charlemagne's round picture is from Einhard, *Early Lives of Charlemagne by Eginhard and the Monk of St Gall*. London, 1926, p. 54.

Page 4

"These and many more temples" etc. is from the *Mirabilia* as translated in *The Marvels of Rome* by Francis Morgan Nichols, London, 1889, p. 117. All quotations from the *Mirabilia* and most from the *Graphia* are from this edition. Latin texts may be found in Karl Ludwig Urlichs' *Codex Topographicus Urbis Romae*, Würzburg, 1871; in H. Jordan, *Topographie der Stadt Rom im Altertum*, vol. 2, Berlin, 1871; and in *Mirabilia Romae e Codicibus Vaticanis Emendata*, edited by Gustav Parthey, Berlin, 1869.

For discussions of the *Mirabilia*, the *Graphia*, and the works of Master Gregory and Ranaulf Higden, see Ferdinand Gregorovius, *History of the City of Rome in the Middle Ages*, translated by Annie Hamilton, vol. IV, part II, 2nd edition revised, London, 1905, pp. 476–477, 653 ff; Charles H. Haskins, *The Renaissance of the Twelfth Century*, Cambridge (Mass.), 1928, pp. 121–124; G. McN. Rushforth, *Magister Gregorius de Mirabilibus Urbis Romae* in *Journal of Roman Studies*, vol. IX (1919), pp. 14–58.

Page 5

Master Gregory's Latin text has recently been published in George B. Parks' *The English Traveler to Italy*, California, Stanford University Press (n.d.), pp. 254–268.

The early medieval plan of Rome in the Library of St. Mark's (H. S. Zan. lat. 399) is discussed by Walther Holtzmann in *Der älteste mittelalterliche Stadtplan von Rom* in *Jahrbuch des Deutschen Archäologischen Instituts*, Band XLI (1926), Berlin, 1927, pp. 55–66.

For discussion of the seal of Ludwig of Bavaria see William Erben, *Rombilder auf kaiserlichen und päpstlichen Siegeln des Mittelalters*, Vienna, 1939, pp. 39–45.

Dante, "Come and behold thy Rome" from *The Divine Comedy*, Purgatory, Canto VI, translated by H. F. Cary, London, 1908, p. 172 (Everyman ed.).

Page 6

The passage from Petrarch's letter to Charles IV, 1350, is quoted from Jane Robinson's *Petrarch, the First Modern Scholar and Man of Learning*, New York, 1904, p. 366.

Quotations from Fazio degli Uberti are from the first printed edition of the *Ditta Mundi*, Venice, 1474. 'Come hither and thou shalt see,' Book II, ch. 33; 'I saw her face' etc., Book I, ch. 11. Translations by Walter Hauser.

Page 8

The division of history into periods is well treated in Wallace K. Ferguson, *The Renaissance in Historical Thought*, Boston, 1948, pp. 73–77.

Petrarch's discussion of the divisions of history in *Letters to His Friends*, VI, 2, is quoted from Frances Eleanor Trollope, *The Homes and Haunts of the Italian Poets*, London, 1881, vol. I.

Page 10

For Carel van Mander's description of Van Heemskerck's Italian journey, see his *Dutch and Flemish Painters*, translated by Constant van de Wall, New York, 1936, p. 211.

Pages 10–11

For the quotation from Montaigne, see *The Essays of Montaigne* translated by E. J. Trechmann, London, 1927, vol. II, Of Vanity.

Page 13

Girolamo Franzini (flourished 2nd half of the 16th century) was the author of *Le Cose maravigliose dell'alma città di Roma*; Giovanni Franzini (flourished first half of the 17th century) wrote the *Descrittione di Roma antica e moderna*.

Page 14

Among societies founded in Rome by various nationalities are: the German Archaeological Institute, founded 1829; the Spanish School, 1874; the British School at Rome, 1901; the Netherlandish Institute, 1904; the *Biblioteca Hertziana*, 1911; the Swedish Institute, 1926; and the American Academy in Rome, formed in 1913 by combining the American School of Architecture and the American School of Classical Studies, founded respectively in 1894 and 1895.

Page 15

Goethe's remarks on engravings of Rome are from Johann Wolfgang Goethe, *Travels in Italy*, translated by Rev. A. J. W. Morrison and Charles Nisbet, London, 1892, p. 114.

Page 16

The reference to *Truth and Poetry* is from Johann Wolfgang Goethe, *Truth and Poetry*, ed. by Parke Godwin, New York, 1850, vol. I, p. 5.

Smollett's comment on Piranesi is from Tobias George Smollett, *Travels through France and Italy*, *Collected Works*, Edinburgh, vol. 5, p. 459.

De Valenciennes on Piranesi is quoted from Lionello Venturi, *Pierre Henri de Valenciennes* in *The Art Quarterly*, Detroit Institute of Arts, vol. IV (1941), p. 90.

Page 17

Cassiodorus, 'A city unfriendly to none' is from Cassiodorus, *Variae Epistolae*, Book I, Letter 39, in *The Letters of Cassiodorus, a Condensed Translation of the Variae Epistolae* by Thomas Hodgkin, London, 1886, p. 165.

All references to Cassiodorus and most translations are from this volume. Here, however, the translation is from Grant Showerman's *Eternal Rome*, New Haven, 1925, p. 352. The Latin reads: *Nulli fit ingrata Roma, quae dici non potest aliena.*

Anecdotes concerning Benjamin West are from John Galt, *The Life, Studies, and Works of Benjamin West*, London, 1820.

Page 18

The quotation on artists at the Caffè Greco is from James E. Freeman, *Gatherings from an Artist's Portfolio*, New York, 1877, p. 15.

Irving's reminiscences of seeing Rome with Allston is from *Spanish Papers and Other Miscellanies*, New York, 1855, vol. II, pp. 144–145.

Pages 18–19

On the absence of Roman sketches by Irving: 'While sketches of people and landscapes in England and Wales and on the Continent outside of Italy appear on the leaves of his [Irving's] diaries, it seems quite certain that he made no drawings while in Rome.' Letter of June 16th, 1952, from George S. Hellman, editor of Irving's Journals.

Page 21

Mary Shelley's description of her husband's enjoyment of Rome is from the Introductory Note by Mrs. Shelley to *Prometheus Unbound* in the Cambridge edition of the poet's works.

Page 22

The quotation from Hillard is from George Stillman Hillard, *Six Months in Italy*, Boston, 7th edition, 1863, p. 552. All quotations used are from this edition. The first was published in 1853. It records a visit in 1847–1848.

Page 24

The quotation from Ludwig Friedländer is from his *Views in Italy in the Years 1815 and 1816*, London, 1821, p. 77, translated from his *Ansichten von Italien*, Leipzig, 1819–1820.

Pages 24–25

The description of the Caffè Greco is from James E. Freeman, *Gatherings from an Artist's Portfolio*, New York, 1877, pp. 11–12.

Page 25

Hans Christian Andersen's descriptions are from *The Improvisatore*, translated from the Danish by Mary Howitt, New York, 1891. First published 1835.

Page 26

The comment to Hawthorne concerning the success of *The Marble Faun* is from a letter of Henry Bright in 1860 quoted in Julian Hawthorne's *Nathaniel Hawthorne and His Wife*, Boston, 1885, vol. II, p. 240.

Page 28

Henry James' quotation, 'golden air', is from his *William Wetmore Story and His Friends*, Boston, 1903, vol. II, p. 131.

Pages 28–29

Thomas Cole's comments on Italy and Rome are from Louis L. Noble, *The Course of Empire* etc., New York, 1853. All quotations from Cole are from this volume.

Page 29

Quotation from William Wetmore Story is from his *Roba di Roma*, Boston, 4th edition, 1864. All quotations from *Roba di Roma* are from this edition.

Page 31

John Murray's comment on the lack of guidebooks is from the article under his name in *The Dictionary of National Biography*.

Page 33

The quotation from Gregorovius concerning Rome after 1870 is from *The Roman Journals of Ferdinand Gregorovius, 1852–1874*, edited by F. Althaus and translated by Mrs. Gustavus W. Hamilton, London, 1911, p. 437. All quotations from the *Journals* are from this volume.

Page 34

Verses of Louis I of Bavaria are quoted from Christian Hülsen, *The Roman Forum*, translated by Jesse Benedict Carter, Rome, 1906, p. 48.

Page 36

'. . . all moments of history confront us.' Edward Kennard Rand, *The Building of Eternal Rome*, Cambridge (Mass.), 1943, Preface, p. vii.

PLATES

Indispensable references for drawings of Roman scenes are: *Codex Escurialensis, ein Skizzenbuch aus der Werkstatt Domenico Ghirlandaios*, by Christian Hülsen and Adolf Michaelis, Vienna, 2 vols. (1905–1906); *Die Römischen Skizzenbücher von Marten van Heemskerck*, by Christian Hülsen and Hermann Egger, Berlin, 2 vols. (1913–1916); and *Römische Veduten; Handzeichnungen aus dem XV. bis XVIII. Jahrhundert*, by Hermann Egger, Vienna and Leipzig, 2 vols. (1911–1931).

Figure 1

The Roman coins are illustrated and described in Harold Mattingly's *Coins of the Roman Empire in the British Museum* as follows: sestertius of Vespasian, Temple of Jupiter, vol. II, London, 1930, pl. 29, No. 6 and text p. 168; sestertius of Trajan, Circus Maximus, vol. III, London, 1936, pl. 32, No. 2 and text p. 180; sestertius of Titus, Colosseum, vol. II, London, 1930, pl. 50, No. 2 and text p. 262.

Figure 2

The circular view of Rome in the Hours of the Duke of Berry is discussed in Paul Durrieu's *Les Très Riches Heures de Jean de France, Duc de Berry*, Paris, 1904, text accompanying Plate XLIX.

Plate 2

The relief of Marcus Aurelius passing a triumphal arch is discussed in H. Stuart Jones, *Catalogue of Ancient Sculptures Preserved in the Municipal Collections of Rome*, by Members of the British School at Rome, *The Sculptures of the Palazzo dei Conservatori*, Oxford, 1926, pp. 25–26.

Plates 3–4

The Marble Plan is described in Rodolfo Lanciani's *Ruins and Excavations of Ancient Rome*, Boston and New York, 1897, pp. 94–97; 214–215.

Plate 5

For the early medieval plan of Rome see note to page 5.

Plate 6

For the seal of Ludwig of Bavaria see note to page 5.

Plate 7

The view of Rome in Fazio degli Uberti's *Dittamondo* (Bibl. Nat. *fonds. ital.* 81) is described in Giovanni di Rossi's *Piante iconografiche e prospettiche di Roma*, Rome, 1879, text, pp. 87–89; 142–143.

Plate 8

For the topography of Taddeo di Bartolo's view of Rome in the Palazzo Pubblico, Siena, see Enrico Stevenson, *Di una pianta di Roma dipinto da Taddeo di Bartoli* in *Bolletino della commissione archaeologica comunale di Roma*, ser. 2, vol. IX (1881), pp. 74–105.

Plate 11

The drawing of the Forum by the Anonymus Escurialensis is discussed by Hermann Egger in *Römische Veduten*, vol. II, p. 11 and pl. 8 and by Egger, Hülsen, and Michaelis in *Codex Escurialensis: ein Skizzenbuch aus der Werkstatt Domenico Ghirlandaios*, Vienna, 1905–1906, fol. 20 and text, p. 79.

Plate 12

Van Heemskerck's drawing of the Garden of the Casa Galli is discussed in Hülsen and Egger's *Die Römischen Skizzenbücher von Marten van Heemskerck*, Berlin, 1913, vol. I, fol. 72, pl. 74 and text pp. 39–40.

Plate 13

The Mantua painting is discussed in Giovanni di Rossi's *Piante Iconografiche*, text, pp. 104–111; 149–151.

Plate 25

Goethe's remark on Tischbein's portrait is from Goethe's *Travels in Italy*, translated by the Rev. A. J. W. Morrison and Charles Nisbet, London, 1892, p. 141.

Plate 26

Goethe's comment on the picturesque views in Rome is from the *Travels* as above, p. 119; on the Palatine, p. 123.

Plate 30

Shelley's description of the Baths of Caracalla is from *The Letters of Percy Bysshe Shelley*, collected and edited by Roger Ingpen, London and New York, 1909, vol. II, p. 677.

Plate 36

The location of La Gensola is given in a letter of March 9, 1955, from the Director of the Thorwaldsen Museum. It is referred to in *Römische Briefe von einer Florentiner*, 1837–1838, vol. I, Leipzig, 1840, pp. 184–185. The Danish artists are identified in a numbered chart in the Thorwaldsen Museum's illustrated guide, Copenhagen, 1931, p. 50.

Plate 38

The building outside the walls in *October Festival* is identified by Karl Madsen in *Wilhelm Marstrand*, Copenhagen, 1905, p. 60.

Plate 43

Sanford Gifford on Cole's *Roman Aqueduct* is quoted from *Travelers in Arcadia*, Detroit, 1951, p. 27.

Plates 47-48

The excavation of the Portico of Octavia is discussed by Rodolfo Lanciani in the *Bollettino dell' Istituto di corrispondenza archeologica*, 1878, p. 209 ff. Murray's *Handbook of Rome* for 1881 states that it is no longer a market.

Plate 49

For the date of the Cloaca Maxima see Marion E. Blake, *Ancient Roman Construction in Italy from the Prehistoric Period to Augustus*, Washington, Carnegie Institution, No. 570, 1947, pp. 38, 159–160.

Plate 54

Rodolfo Lanciani in *Ruins and Excavations of Ancient Rome*, New York, 1897, p. 249, gives the date 1876 for the excavations of the steps of the Temple of Antoninus and Faustina. Christian Hülsen in *The Forum and the Palatine*, New York, 1926, plate 39, shows a photograph dated 1881 in which the steps have been excavated but the old houses still stand, though the centre of the Forum had been excavated in 1878–1880 as noted on p. 57 of the same volume. The date 1899 for the destruction of the houses preparatory to excavating the Basilica Aemilia is given in a letter from Pietro Romanelli, Superintendent of Antiquities in the Forum and Palatine.

THE CAPITOL

TEXT

Page 37

Opening quotation is from Vergil's *Aeneid*, Book VIII, 351 ff.

Page 38

The September Games, or *Ludi Romani*, with their procession of the gods are discussed by Dionysius of Halicarnassus, *The Roman Antiquities*, Book VII, 71 ff.: 'Before beginning the games, the principal magistrates conducted a procession in honour of the gods from the Capitol through the Forum to the Circus Maximus. . . . Last of all in the procession came the images of the gods. . . . Not only of Jupiter,

Juno, Minerva . . . but also those still more ancient.' Translation by Earnest Cary in the Loeb Classical Library, *Dionysius*, vol. IV, London, 1943, pp. 361–373.

For a general discussion of Roman religious festivals see Warde Fowler, *The Roman Festivals of the Period of the Republic*, London, 1908.

Quotation from Ammianus Marcellinus is from his *History*, Book XVI, 10, 14.

'The Capitol's unshaken rock.' Vergil, *Aeneid*, Book IX, 448.

Vandal plundering of the roof of Jupiter's temple, Procopius, *History of the Wars: the Vandalic War*, Book III, V, 4.

Cassiodorus on the Capitol, Cassiodorus, *Variae Epistolae*, VII, 6.

Page 39

Flaminio Vacca on the fragments of the temple found near the Conservatori is quoted from Lanciani, *Ruins and Excavations of Ancient Rome*, p. 299.

Page 40

'The Capitol . . . head of the world.' *Mirabilia*, pp. 86–87.

The legends of the Salvation of Rome are treated by E. Rodocanachi in *The Roman Capitol*, translated by Frederick Lawton, New York, 1906, pp. 58–63. Vergil as a magician is discussed by Domenico Comparetti in *Vergil in the Middle Ages*, translated by E. F. M. Benecke, London, 1895, and by John Spargo, *Virgil the Necromancer* in *Harvard Studies in Comparative Literature*, Vol. X, Cambridge (Mass.), 1934.

The *Mirabilia* describes the images, pp. 46–47.

For drying racks on the Capitol see note to plate 63.

Page 42

Poggio Bracciolini's description of the Capitol is from his *Historiae de Varietate Fortunae* (Paris), 1723, Book I, pp. 5 and 21. Translated by Marjorie J. Milne.

The coronation of Corilla on the Capitol is discussed in E. Rodocanachi's *The Roman Capitol*, pp. 233–238.

Page 43

Gibbon's differing versions of the spot on which he conceived the idea of his *History* are discussed in *The Autobiographies of Edward Gibbon*, ed. by John Murray, London, 1896, pp. 270, 302, 405–406.

The establishment of the Republic of 1849 and its proclamation on the Capitol are discussed by Margaret Fuller Ossoli in *At Home and Abroad*, Boston, 1856, pp. 357–359. The letter quoted is dated Rome, February 20, 1849.

Page 45

'Where high Moneta lifts her steps sublime.' Ovid, *Fasti*, Book I, 638.

Pages 45–46

The story of Augustus (Octavian) and the Sibyl is told in the *Mirabilia*, pp. 35–38.

Page 46

The quotation from Leo I is Grant Showerman's translation of a passage in Leo's Sermon LXXXII, *On the Feast of the Apostles Peter and Paul*. See *A Select Library of Nicene and Post-Nicene Fathers of the Christian Church*, 2nd series, New York, 1895, vol. 12, p. 195.

Pages 46–47

For Roman apartment houses in general and that at the foot of the Capitol in particular see Philip Harsh, *The Origins of the Insulae at Ostia*, in *Memoirs of the American Academy in Rome*, vol. XII (1935), p. 61; Jerome Carcopino, *Daily Life in Ancient Rome*, translated by E. O. Lorimer, ed. by H. T. Rowell, New Haven, 1940, pp. 22–51; Antonio Muñoz, *Campidoglio*, Rome (1930), p. 45 ff.

Page 47

Juvenal describes life in Roman apartment houses in Satire III, 190–199; 232–239.

Page 48

For the church of S. Biagio see Mariano Armellini, *Le Chiese di Roma*, Rome, vol. I, 1942, p. 672.

PLATES

Plate 58

The discovery and excavation of the s.e. corner of the Temple of Jupiter as well as the other parts of the platform are discussed by Rodolfo Paribeni in *Notizie degli Scavi* vol. 46 (1921), pp. 38–49.

Plate 60

The fragments of the cornice of Jupiter's temple are discussed by Giuseppi Lugli in *The Classical Monuments of Rome and Its Vicinity*, translated by Gilbert Bagnani, Rome (1929), p. 36 and by Rodolfo Lanciani in *Ruins and Excavations of Ancient Rome*, Boston, 1897, p. 299. Distinguishing marks of Domitian's time visible in these cornice carvings are the annules or rings between the dentils, the small rectangular blocks projecting like teeth beneath the cornice.

Plate 61

The relief of Marcus Aurelius Sacrificing before the Temple of Jupiter is discussed in H. Stuart Jones' *Catalogue of the Ancient Sculpture Preserved in the Municipal Collections of Rome*, by Members of the British School at Rome, *The Sculptures of the Palazzo dei Conservatori*, Rome, 1926, pp. 22–25.

Plate 62

For the Capitol and Senator's Palace in H. S. Zan. lat. 399 see note to page 5.

The quotation from Dante is from Book IV, Chapter V of the *Convito* ; the translation is from Jane H. Robinson's *Petrarch, The First Modern Scholar and Man of Learning*, New York, 1904.

Plate 63

The drying racks shown in Van Heemskerck's drawing are discussed in Rodolfo Lanciani's '*Lo Monte Tarpeio*' *nel secolo XVI* in *Bollettino della Commissione Comunale di Roma*, vol. 29 (1901), pp. 243–269.

Plates 72–73

The date of the first century A.D. for the insula at the foot of the Capitol is given in Muñoz, *Campidoglio*, Rome (1930), p. 46.

THE PALATINE

TEXT

Page 50

Claudian's description of Rome: Claudian, *Panegyric on the Sixth Consulship of Honorius*, 35–52.

The place and approximate time of Narses' death are given in the *Liber Pontificalis* compiled by the ninth-century priest of Ravenna, Agnellus, which is printed in Muratori, *Rerum italicarum scriptores*, vol. II, Part III,[3] p. 232: *Narsisque patricius obiit Rome . . . in palacio quievit; nonagesimo quinto vite sue anno mortuus est*—'Narses the patrician died in Rome . . . where he ended his days in the palace; he died in the ninety-fifth year of his age.'

The campaigns of Narses and details of his life are discussed by Procopius in his *Gothic Wars*, Book II, 13 and Books III and IV.

Page 51

The story of Numa and the brazen shield is told in Ovid's *Fasti*, III, 361–392. Propertius describes the temple of Apollo in his Elegies, Book II, 31.

Page 52

The *Graphia*'s description of the Palatine and the Greater Palace is incorporated in Nichols' translation of the *Mirabilia*, p. 19.

Page 54

Frances Elizabeth Appleton's description of the Palatine is quoted from her unpublished Journal for March 11, 1836, at Craigie House, Cambridge, by courtesy of the late Henry Wadsworth Longfellow Dana.

Page 55

The history of the site of the House of Augustus, later the Villa Palatina-Mills, is discussed in English in Giuseppi Lugli's *Classical Monuments of Rome and its Vicinity*, translated by Gilbert Bagnani, Rome, 1929, p. 286, and in great detail, including an account of the demolition of the Villa Mills, by Alfonso Bartoli in *Scavi del Palatino, Notizie degli Scavi*, vol. VII (1929), pp. 3–29. Additional details concerning the changes made in the convent of the Order of the Visitation when it was transformed into the Palatine Museum were given in a letter of June 21, 1952, from Pietro Romanelli.

Pages 55–56

Rodolfo Lanciani describes the underground rooms visible at the Villa Mills in the 1890's in his *Ruins and Excavations of Ancient Rome*, p. 142.

Page 56

Marguerite, Countess of Blessington, describes the ruins in the gardens of the Villa Mills and her meeting with Napoleon's mother there in her *Idler in Italy: the Journal of a Tour*, Philadelphia, 1839, pp. 276, 325.

The buried rooms beneath the Flavian Palace are described by Giuseppe Lugli in his *Classical Monuments of Rome and Its Vicinity*, Rome (1929), pp. 274–285; *Roma Antica*, Rome, 1946, pp. 493–508; and *I Monumenti antichi di Roma e suburbio, Supplemento*, Rome, 1940, pp. 109–118.

Pages 56–57

The paintings in the buried 'Hall of Isis' are described and illustrated by Emanuele Rizzo in *Monumenti della pittura antica scoperti in Italia*, vol. 3, *La pitture Ellenistico-Romano*, Part 2, *Le pitture dell'Aula Isiaca di Caligola*, Rome, 1936, and in Lugli as given above.

Page 57

For Turnbull's engravings from these buried paintings see George Turnbull, *Treatise on Ancient Painting*, London, 1740, and *A Curious Collection of Ancient Paintings*, London, 1741.

Page 58

Bernard de Montfauçon's comment on the Palatine's subterranean passages is from *The Antiquities of Italy, Being the Travels of the Learned and Reverend Bernard De Montfauçon from Paris through Italy in the Years 1698 and 1699*, translated from the Paris edition of the Latin original by John Henley, London, 1725, p. 130.

For the extent of the Farnese Gardens see Rodolfo Lanciani, *Ruins and Excavations*, plate facing p. 110; G. B. Falda, *Li Giardini di Roma*, Rome (1683?); and Luigi Dami, *The Italian Garden*, translated by L. Scopoli, New York (1925), p. 36 and Plates XLVI–XLVIII. Also inscriptions in place among the ruins of the Flavian Palace excavated by the dukes of Parma.

The location of the lower retaining wall of the Farnese Gardens is discussed by Rodolfo Lanciani in *R. Accademia nazionale dei Lincei, Notizie degli Scavi di Antichità*, 1883, pp. 486–487 and *Ruins and Excavations*, pp. 156–158.

Page 59

The quotation from Ludwig Hermann Friedländer is to be found in his *Views in Italy*, translated from the *Ansichten von Italien während einer Reise in der Jahren 1815 und 1816*, and published in London in 1821.

Pages 59–60

The excavation of the substructures of the Palace of Tiberius over the *Clivus Victoriae* is discussed by Esther van Deman, *The House of Caligula*, in *The American Journal of Archaeology*, 2nd series, vol. XXVIII (1924), No. 4, p. 372 ff.

Page 60

Helen Hunt Jackson's description of the Palatine is from *Bits of Travel* by H. H. Boston, 1891, pp. 189–191.

Page 61

For the church of S. Maria Antiqua see Wladimir de Grüneisen, *Sainte Marie Antique*, Rome, 1911; and G. McN. Rushforth, *S. Maria Antiqua* in *Papers of the British School at Rome*, Vol. I (1902), pp. 1–119.

Livy's story of Marcus Curtius is related in his *Roman History*, Book VII, 6.

Page 62

Cassiodorus' plans concerning a university and a monastery are discussed by Edward Kennard Rand in *Founders of the Middle Ages*, Cambridge (Mass.), 1929, p. 241, and by Thomas Hodgkin, *Letters of Cassiodorus*, London, 1886, Introduction, p. 56 and note.

PLATES

Plate 77

The inscription on Marten van Heemskerck's drawing of the Palatine and Septizonium has been discussed in the note to page 1.

Plates 85–86

Notes concerning the history of this site and changes in the Villa Palatina-Mills have been given in connection with the text on page 55.

Plate 90

The date of the destruction of the lower retaining wall of the Farnese Gardens and the Farnese tower is discussed by Rodolfo Lanciani in *Ruins and Excavations*, p. 156, and in *Notizie degli Scavi* (1882), p. 413.

THE ROMAN FORUM

TEXT

Page 63

Opening quotation is from Propertius, *Elegies*, Book IV, II, 4–7.

Page 64

'The Forum in which all justice is preserved.' Cicero, Fourth Oration against Catiline, I, 3–4.

For Poggio's description of the Forum see Poggio Bracciolini, *Historiae de Varietate Fortunae* (Paris), 1723, Book I, p. 21. Translated by Marjorie J. Milne.

Page 65

'The *Campo Vaccino* was heretofore the *Forum Romanum*.' From *An Itinerary Contayning a Voyage Made through Italy in the Years 1646 and 1647* by Jo. Raymond, London, 1648, p. 110.

Page 66

The inscription on the column of Phocas is given in *Corpus Inscriptionum Latinarum*, Berlin, 1863, vol. VI, 1200. It is partially translated in Christian Hülsen's *The Roman Forum*, p. 94.

Cicero's reference to the Temple of Castor is in his Second Oration against Verres, XLIX, 129.

Page 67

Ovid speaks of the traditional shape of the Temple of Vesta in his *Fasti*, Book VI, 261–270.

Plutarch mentions the shape of the temple in his *Parallel Lives*, *Life of Numa*, XI.

Page 68

Dionysius of Halicarnassus tells the story of Castor and Pollux in his *Roman Antiquities*, Book VI, XIII. Livy describes the battle, with less emphasis on the supernatural, in his *Roman History*, Book II, XIX–XX.

Page 69

Thomas Babington Macaulay's story of Castor and Pollux is told in his *Battle of Lake Regillus* in *Lays of Ancient Rome*, first published in 1842.

Page 70–71

The battle in the Senate over the Altar of Victory is discussed in Edward Gibbon's *History of the Decline and Fall of the Roman Empire*, London, 1881, vol. III, pp. 406–413. Quotation is from p. 410.

Pages 72–73

The church of Saints Cosmas and Damian and the structure into which it was built are discussed by Philip Barrows Whitehead in *The Church of SS. Cosma e Damiano in Rome* in *The American Journal of Archaeology*, vol. XXXI (1927), pp. 1–18. An interesting earlier photograph, taken when the excavations were less advanced and the ground-level of the Forum considerably higher, is discussed in Rodolfo Lanciani's *The Roman Forum*, Rome, 1910, Fig. XLVI and caption.

PLATES

Plate 102

This left half of Van Heemskerck's panoramic drawing of the west end and part of the north side of the Forum is reproduced and discussed in Hülsen and Egger's *Die Römischen Skizzenbücher von Marten van Heemskerck*, Berlin, vol. I, 1913, fol. 6, pl. 7 and text, pp. 5–6; also in Egger's *Römische Veduten*, Vienna, vol. II, 1931, pl. 11 and pp. 12–13.

Plate 103

Livy tells the story of the founding of the Temple of Jupiter Stator in his *Roman History*, Book I, XII.

Plate 110

This right half of Van Heemskerck's panoramic view is discussed in Hülsen and Egger, *Skizzenbücher*, as above, fol. 9 and pp. 5–6 and in Egger's *Römische Veduten*, pl. 11, pp. 12–13.

Plate 117

The identity of the fragments piled on the site of the Regia is discussed by Christian Hülsen in *The Forum and the Palatine*, translated by Helen H. Tanzer, New York, 1928, p. 15, and by Fritz Toebelmann in *Römische Gebälke*, Heidelberg, 1923, pp. 13–26.

TRIUMPHAL ARCHES

TEXT

Page 76

The date of the restoration of the Arch of Titus and Valadier's account of the work are given in Giuseppe Valadier's report presented to the *Accademia Romana di Archeologia*, December 10th, 1821, and published in the *Atti della Pontificia accademia romana di archaeologia*, vol. I, Part 2 (1823), pp. 275–286.

PLATES

Plate 122

Procopius (*History of the Wars: The Vandalic War*, Book IV, IX, 5–10) refers to the removal from Carthage to Byzantium of 'the treasures of the Jews, which Titus, the son of Vespasian . . . had brought to Rome after the capture of Jerusalem'.

Plate 123

For Lowell's reference to Longfellow's European reputation see Henry James, *William Wetmore Story and His Friends*, Boston, 1903, vol. I, p. 327.

The information concerning the artists shown in Healy's painting of Longfellow and his daughter beneath the Arch of Titus is due to the courtesy of Mrs. Marie de Mare, Healy's granddaughter.

Plates 124–127

The sculpture of the Arch of Constantine is discussed by Ludwig Curtius in *Das Antike Rom*, Vienna (1944), pp. 49–51. The identification of the Forum's buildings, now commonly accepted, is given on p. 50. H. Stuart Jones discusses more fully, with some differences in attribution, the medallions and attic reliefs in *Notes on Roman Historical Sculpture, Papers of the British School at Rome*, vol. III (1906), pp. 229–271.

THE BASILICA OF CONSTANTINE OR MAXENTIUS

TEXT

Page 78

The names associated with the basilica are discussed by Philip Barrows Whitehead, *The Church of SS. Cosma e Damiano in Rome*, in *American Journal of Archaeology*, vol. XXXI (1927), pp. 1–5. Theodore Dwight's description of the Basilica of Constantine is from his *Journal of a Tour in Italy in the Year 1821*, New York, 1824, p. 229.

Plate 130

Corot's comment on the rainy season in Rome is from Etienne Moreau-Nélaton, *Corot raconté par lui-même*, Paris, 1924, vol. I, p. 14.

THE COLOSSEUM

TEXT

Page 80

Martial's description of the Colosseum is from his *Epigrams on the Spectacles*, II, 5–6.
Suetonius' estimate of Titus is from the *Lives of the Caesars, The Deified Titus*, VII.

Page 82

For the last mention of the Colossus in antiquity see note to page 136 under Statues that were never buried.

Page 83

Suetonius' description of Nero's Golden House is from his *Lives of the Caesars, Nero*, XXXI.
The quotation from Arnold of Harff is taken from Alessandro d'Ancona's *Origini del Teatro in Italia*, Florence, 1877, vol. I, p. 282.
The story of the bull sacrificed in the Colosseum in the sixteenth century is noted by Gregorovius in his *History of the City of Rome in the Middle Ages*, vol. VI, Part II, p. 708.

Pages 83–84

Cellini's adventures in the Colosseum are related in *Benvenuto Cellini: Autobiography*, translated by John Addington Symonds, New York, 1906, vol. I, pp. 252 ff.

Page 84

The dates of the erection of the various buttresses of the Colosseum are given on tablets erected on the buttresses.

Page 85

Goethe's description of moonlight in Rome is from Johann Wolfgang Goethe's *Travels in Italy*, London, 1892, p. 159.

Pages 86–87

Longfellow's description of the Colosseum by moonlight is from the essay 'Rome in Midsummer,' in *Outre-Mer*, first published in 1835.

Page 87

Hawthorne's opinion of the Colosseum by moonlight is from *The Marble Faun*, begun in Rome in 1859, first published in England in 1860 under the title of *Transformation*.

Quotations on the Colosseum from Henry James are from *Daisy Miller*, first published 1878.

Page 88

Gregorovius' reference to the weeding of the Colosseum is from his *Roman Journals*, p. 402.

Cole's description of the Colosseum is from Thomas Cole, *The Course of Empire, Voyage of Life* etc., by Louis L. Noble, New York, 1853, p. 159-160.

PLATES

Plate 136

Peale's description of flowers in the Colosseum is from Rembrandt Peale, *Notes on Italy*, Philadelphia, 1831, p. 105.

Plate 137

The quotation from Deakin is to be found in Richard Deakin, *Flora of the Colosseum in Rome*, London, 1855, pp. vi–vii.

THE GOLDEN HOUSE OF NERO

TEXT

Page 90

Martial comments on the works replacing the Golden House in his *Epigrams on the Spectacles*, II, 5–6.

For Suetonius on Nero's Golden House, see note to page 83.

Pliny refers to the painter Fabullus and the Golden House in his *Natural History*, XXXV, XXXVIII.

Page 91

The paintings and inscriptions of the Golden House and reproductions of the Baths of Trajan from the sixteenth to the eighteenth century are discussed by

Fritz Weege, *Das goldene Haus des Nero* in *Jahrbuch des kaiserlich deutschen archäologischen Instituts*, vol. XXVIII (1913), pp. 127–244 and pls. 4–21. Weege's illustrations are invaluable not only because they show details of the paintings but also because of photographs taken while some of the rooms were still buried almost to their vaulting.

Page 92

Pliny refers to the Laocoön in his *Natural History*, XXXVI, IV.

For the present dating of the Laocoön see Gisela M. A. Richter, *Three Critical Periods in Greek Sculpture*, Oxford, 1951, pp. 66–70.

The discovery of the Laocoön is discussed by Lanciani in *Storia degli Scavi*, vol. I (1902), pp. 139 ff.

Page 93

Michelangelo's opinion of the Laocoön is quoted from Margarete Bieber's *Laocoön*, New York, 1942, pp. 1–2. Sadoleto's poem is quoted from the same book, p. 2.

Canova's letter concerning the return of the Laocoön and other works to Rome is from Dorothy Mackay Quynn's *The Art Confiscations of the Napoleonic Wars* in *The American Historical Review*, vol. L, No. 3 (April, 1945), p. 456.

PLATES

Plates 144–145

The quotations concerning artists in the Golden House are from Giorgio Vasari's life of Giovanni da Udine, in *Lives of the Most Eminent Painters, Sculptors, and Architects*, translated from the Italian by Mrs. Jonathan Foster, vol. V, London, 1852, pp. 19–20.

THE BATHS OF CARACALLA

TEXT

Page 94

The relationship between the central halls of Roman baths and the main waiting room of the Pennsylvania Station in New York is noted in *The American Architect* for May 26, 1906, p. 175 and plates, and the same for October 5, 1910, pp. 113–118.

Page 95

Cassiodorus on the aqueducts is quoted from the *Variae Epistolae*, VII, 6.

Page 96

The discovery of the statues and capitals in the Baths of Caracalla is discussed by Sergius Iwanoff, in *Architektonische Studien*, translated from the Russian by Michael Rostovtsev, part III, *Aus den Thermen des Caracalla*, Berlin, 1898, pp. 15–16; 72–79.

THE BATHS OF DIOCLETIAN

TEXT

Page 98

Petrarch on the Baths of Diocletian is quoted from Frances Eleanor Trollope, *The Homes and Haunts of the Italian Poets*, London, 1881, vol. I.

Page 99

Roberto Paribeni refers to the documents granting the Carthusians a foundation within the Baths of Diocletian in 1091 and additional funds in 1313, in *Le Terme di Diocleziano*, Rome, 1928, pp. 33–34, but considers it doubtful that the work was carried out. However, the illustration from Fazio degli Uberti's *Dittamondo* (Plate 7) and Taddeo di Bartolo's painting in Siena (Plate 8) seem to show monastic cells constructed within the baths.

Page 100

Moses Ezekiel and his studio in the Baths of Diocletian are discussed by Henry K. Bush-Brown, *Sir Moses Ezekiel*, in *Art and Archaeology*, vol. XI (June 1921), pp. 227–234. For much information concerning the location of Ezekiel's studio and its appearance the author is deeply indebted to Salvatore Aurigemma, Director of the National Museum in Rome, and to Signora Virginia Vacca of Rome.

The reference to the Baths of Diocletian when Ezekiel had his studio there is from *An American Sculptor in Rome*, by Katharine B. Wrenshall, in *The World's Work*, vol. 19 (November, 1909), p. 12255.

THE FORUM OF NERVA

TEXT

Page 102

Master Gregory's description of the forum and temple of Minerva is discussed by G. McN. Rushforth, *Magister Gregorius*, etc., in *Journal of Roman Studies*, vol. IX (1919), pp. 30–31. The translation of Master Gregory's description, from page 53, is due to the kindness of Marjorie Milne, Research Fellow in the Museum's Department of Greek and Roman Art.

Plate 163

Lanciani in *Ruins and Excavations*, p. 308, calls the arch 'Noah's Ark'. Rushforth, however, in *Journal of Roman Studies*, vol. IX, p. 31, feels that the name belonged to the temple.

THE FORUM AND COLUMN OF TRAJAN

TEXT

Page 104

Ammianus Marcellinus discusses the magnificence of the Forum of Trajan in his *History*, Book XVI, 10, 15–16.

For Cassiodorus on the Forum of Trajan see his *Variae Epistolae*, VII, 6.

The legend of Gregory and the soul of Trajan and Venantius Fortunatus on the use of Trajan's forum in the eighth century are discussed by Ferdinand Gregorovius in his *History of the City of Rome in the Middle Ages*, vol. II, pp. 81–85.

Page 105

Gregorovius refers to the Senate's resolution concerning the Column of Trajan in his *History*, vol. IV, Part II, pp. 685–687.

PLATES

Plates 172–173

A selection of scenes from the column is discussed by I. A. Richmond in *Trajan's Army on Trajan's Column, Papers of the British School at Rome*, vol. XIII (1935), pp. 1–40.

RUINS IN THE COLONNA GARDENS

TEXT

Page 108

Columns from the Temple of the Sun are mentioned in a list of antiquities in Constantinople early in Justinian's reign, compiled by an anonymous author and included in Anselmo Banduri's *Imperium orientale sive antiquitates constantinopolitanae*, Paris, 1711, vol. I, Book IV, 185, p. 66.

The women's senate house is described in the *Life of Antonius Elagabalus* attributed to Aelius Lampridius in *Scriptores Historiae Augustae*, IV, 3.

A typical Renaissance discussion of the ruined temple is that of Andrea Fulvio in *L'Antichità di Roma*, Venice, 1588, pp. 61–62. First Latin edition published 1517.

Page 109

Quotation on the Colonna Gardens by Joseph Forsyth is from his *Remarks on Antiquities, Arts, and Letters during an Excursion in Italy*, 2nd edition, London, 1816, pp. 190–191.

Page 110

For Charles Platt's description of the gardens see his *Italian Gardens*, New York, 1893, pp. 51–55.

PLATES
Plates 180–181

For the dating of the bronze boxer in the Terme Museum see Gisela M. A. Richter, *Three Critical Periods in Greek Sculpture*, Oxford, 1951, p. 48.

THE THEATRE OF MARCELLUS

TEXT
Page 112

For Vergil's lament for Marcellus, see the *Aeneid*, Book VI, 883–884. The history of the Theater of Marcellus in the Middle Ages and Renaissance is discussed by Rodolfo Lanciani in *Ruins and Excavations*, pp. 490–492 and by Umberto Gnoli in *Topographia e Toponomastica di Roma medioevale e moderna*, Rome (1939), p. 125.

Page 113

Niebuhr's letter describing life in the interior of the theatre, dated February 16, 1817, is quoted from *The Life and Letters of Barthold George Niebuhr, with Essays on His Character and Influence*, by the Chevalier Bunsen and Professors Brandis and Lorbell, New York, 1852, p. 347.

UNIDENTIFIED TEMPLES BY THE TIBER

TEXT
Page 115

The derivation of the name Santo Stefano delle Carozze is discussed by Umberto Gnoli in *Topografia e toponomastica di Roma medioevale e moderna*, p. 64.

The date of the renaming of the church Santa Maria del Sole is discussed by Gnoli, as above, pp. 282–283.

PLATES
Plates 186–187

For the history of Santa Maria in Cosmedin see G. B. Giovenale, *La basilica di S. Maria in Cosmedin*, Rome, 1927, one of a series of *Monografie sulle Chiese di Roma*, edited by the *Associazione Artistica fra i cultori di architettura in Roma*.

The altar and temple of Hercules and the grain hall into which S. Maria in Cosmedin was built are discussed by Giuseppe Lugli in *The Classical Monuments of Rome and Its Vicinity*, translated by Gilbert Bagnani, Rome, 1929, pp. 340–344.

HOUSE OF CRESCENTIUS

TEXT

Page 116

The House of Crescentius is discussed and its inscription translated in Ferdinand Gregorovius' *History of the City of Rome in the Middle Ages*, translated by Annie Hamilton, London, 1905, vol. IV, pt. II, pp. 687–690.

Page 117

The quotation from Benjamin of Tudela is included with Nichols' translation of the *Mirabilia*, in *The Marvels of Rome*, London, 1889, pp. 153–154.

PLATE

Plate 189

Coello's drawing of the House of Crescentius is published in Hermann Egger's *Römische Veduten*, Vienna and Leipzig, vol. I, pp. 34–35 and pl. 55.

THE PANTHEON

TEXT

Page 118

Dio Cassius' description of the Pantheon is from his *Roman History*, Book LIII, 27, 3.

Pliny tells the story of Cleopatra's pearls in his *Natural History*, Book IX, LVIII.

PLATES

Plate 190

For the excavations about the sides of the Pantheon see *Notizie degli Scavi*, 1881, p. 294.

Plate 191

Master Gregory's description of the sculpture in front of the Pantheon is given in G. McN. Rushforth's *Magister Gregorovius*, etc., in *Journal of Roman Studies*, vol. IX (1919), pp. 37, 53.

Plate 192

The date of the demolition of the two bell towers is given as 1883 in the *Enciclopedia Italiana*, vol. 26, 1935, p. 213.

Plate 193

The description of cats by the Pantheon is from Eleanor Clark's *Rome and a Villa*, New York, 1955, pp. 128–129, c. 1950, 51, 52, and reprinted by permission of Doubleday and Co., Inc.

THE PYRAMID OF CESTIUS

TEXT

Page 122

Boccaccio refers to the pyramid called 'tomb of Remus' in his *Della genealogia degli dei*, Venice, 1627, Book IX, p. 149.

Poggio Bracciolini comments on the pyramid in his *Historiae de Varietate Fortunae*, Paris, 1723, p. 7.

Page 123

For the history of the Protestant Cemetery see Keats-Shelley Memorial Association *Bulletin and Review No. 2* (1913).

Page 124

The grave of Charles Mills in the Protestant Cemetery is number 17, 12th row, Old Zone. Letter of March 15, 1955, from the Superintendent of the Cemetery.

HADRIAN'S TOMB

TEXT

Page 125

The famed Seven Hills of Rome are the Capitol, Palatine, Aventine, Caelian, Esquiline, Viminal, and Quirinal, all on the east bank of the Tiber. The hills on the west bank were never included in the number. Sometimes spurs of the same hill have been called by different names, thus increasing the number, and in early times the names were not all the same as in the famous later list.

The description of the Janiculum is from Martial, *Epigrams*, Book IV, LXIV.

Page 126

Procopius' description of the tomb and the Gothic siege is from his *History of the Wars, The Gothic War*, Book V, XXII.

Page 127

The legend of the angel bowing to the Madonna is told in Mariano Borgatti's *Castel Sant'Angelo in Rome*, Rome (1931), p. 119; the angel erected by Nicholas V is discussed on p. 165; the history of the Girandola is treated on pp. 187, 198–199, Note 277–278, 321, 413, 457, 474, 512–513. But in spite of the fact that Borgatti states that it was not shown at the castle from 1798 until 1870, Mrs. Eaton saw it there during her visit in 1817–1818. (*Rome in the Nineteenth Century*, New York, 1827, vol. II, pp. 274–276.

THE VATICAN OBELISK

TEXT

Page 129

The neighbourhood of St. Peter's and its ancient cemeteries from antiquity to the present are discussed by B. M. Apollonj-Ghetti and others in *Esplorazione sotto la confessione de San Pietro in Vaticano*, Rome, Vatican City, 2 vols., 1951, vol. I, pp. 9–21. The rest of the text volume considers in detail early graves discovered in the excavations of 1940–1949.

Page 132

The characterization of Sidonius Apollinaris of Rome as 'the city unique upon earth' is from his *Letters*, Book I, Letter VI. *To His Friend Eutropius*, A.D. 467.

STATUES THAT WERE NEVER BURIED

TEXT

Page 133

The quotation from Cassiodorus in the opening sentence is from his *Variae Epistolae*, Book VII, 15.

The quotation from Lactantius Firmianus on images is from the Ante-Nicene Christian Library, *The Works of Lactantius*, vol. 21, p. 136, translated by William Fletcher, London, 1861.

Page 134

Wace's lines on the statue of Marcus Aurelius are quoted from E. Rodocanachi, *The Roman Capitol*, p. 135.

Benjamin of Tudela's description of the statue is given at the end of Nichols' translation of the *Mirabilia*.

Page 135

For the date of the new pavement of the Campidoglio see Armando Schiavo, *Michelangelo Architetto*, Rome, 1949, p. facing Plate 57. Du Pérac's etching after Michelangelo's design appears in Lafreri's *Speculum*, Rome, 1569. It is shown in various books, including Schiavo's *Michelangelo Architetto*, Fig. 56, and *Il Campidoglio nel cinquecento* by Pio Pecchiai, Rome, 1950, fig. 4.

'. . . wondrous colossus . . . girt with rays' from Martial, *Epigrams*, Book I, II.

Master Gregory's description of the Colossus is published in G. McN. Rushforth's *Magister Gregorovius*, etc., in *Journal of Roman Studies*, vol. IX (1919), p. 23. A fifteenth-century English translation of the description by Ranaulf Higden in his *Polychronicon* is published in *Chronicles and Memorials of Great Britain and Ireland during the Middle Ages*, London, Public Record Office No. 41, vol. I, pp. 233–235.

Page 136

The last reference to the Colossus of Nero appears in the *Corpus Inscriptionum Latinarum*, I, in a note on the *Fasti*, or calendar of Philocales, and seems to refer to the custom of crowning this colossus on June 6 as an annual event in memory of its dedication by Vespasian as a sun god. The statue and its connection with the name Colosseum is discussed by Howard Canter in *The Venerable Bede and the Colosseum* in *Transactions and Proceedings of the American Philological Association*, vol. LXI (1930), pp. 150 ff.

Page 137

The positions of the river gods on the Capitol are discussed by Pio Pecchiai in *Il Campidoglio nel cinquecento*, Rome, 1950, pp. 70–85.

For the names 'Solomon and Bacchus' used of the river gods by Master Gregory see Rushforth in *Journal of Roman Studies*, vol. IX (1919), pp. 26 and 51.

Page 138

For Master Gregory's description of the Marble Horses see Rushforth as above, pp. 26 and 51.

Page 139

The story that the Marble Horses were sent to Nero by the king of Armenia is told by Andrea Fulvio in *L'Antichità di Roma*, Venice, 1588, p. 62; that concerning their association with Alexander, by Giovanni Franzini in his *Descrittione di Roma antica e moderna*, Rome, 1640, pp. 578–579.

Marforio used as a fountain with the bronze ball from the Vatican obelisk is discussed by Pio Pecchiai in *Il Campidoglio nel cinquecento*, p. 73.

Page 140

The story of Master Gregory and the statue of Venus is told by Rushforth in *Journal of Roman Studies*, vol. IX (1919), pp. 24–26 and 51. The unproved tradition that the Capitoline Venus was discovered walled up is given, p. 25, note 5. An additional account of the discovery of this statue is in H. Stuart Jones, *Catalogue of the Ancient Sculptures Preserved in the Municipal Collections of Rome*, by Members of the British School in Rome, vol. I, *The Sculptures of the Museo Capitolino*, p. 183. This states that the statue was found in a garden near the church of S. Vitale.

Pages 140–141

The story of Venus and the ring is found in William of Malmesbury, *History of the Kings of England and the Modern History*, translated from the Latin by the Rev. John Sharpe, London, 1815, Book II, ch. 13, pp. 266–269.

Page 141

The quotation from Cassiodorus on statues is from his *Variae Epistolae*, Book VII, 15.

PLATES

Plate 221

The quotation from Julian the Apostate is from his *Fragment of a Letter to a Priest*. Julian's prayer to Mercury is quoted from Ammianus Marcellinus' *History*, Book XVI, 4, 5. The story that Julian was beguiled by a statue of Mercury taken from the Tiber is told by Arturo Graf in *Roma nella memoria e nelle immaginazoni del medio evo*, Turin, 1888, vol. II, p. 136.

It is perhaps superfluous to note the author's continual indebtedness to *A Topographical Dictionary of Ancient Rome*, by Samuel Ball Platner, completed and revised by Thomas Ashby, Oxford, 1929.

CHRONOLOGICAL LIST

Dates of emperors, popes, and kings are those of their reigns; dates of emperors in ( ) are those in which they became co-rulers

B.C.

753 Traditional date of the founding of Rome by Romulus.

509 Traditional date of the expulsion of the kings and the founding of the Republic.

390 Approximate date of the sack of Rome by the Gauls.

312 Construction of the first aqueduct of Rome, the Aqua Appia.

264–241 First Punic War between Rome and Carthage.

218–201 Second Punic War; Hannibal crossed the Alps from France to Italy.

149–146 Third Punic War; destruction of Carthage.

146 Sack of Corinth; Rome assumed control of Greece and Macedonia.

102–101 Victories of Marius and Catulus over the Cimbri.

88–84 Civil wars in Rome.

82–79 Dictatorship of Sulla in Rome.

70–48 Rise and rule of Pompey in Rome.

64–63 Conspiracy of Catiline; Cicero's orations against Catiline, 63 B.C.

58–51 Julius Caesar's conquest of Gaul.

54 Caesar's conquest of Britain.

48–44 Caesar, dictator.

44 Assassination of Caesar.

43 Octavian, Caesar's heir (later Augustus) assumed power.

31 Octavian's fleet defeated Antony and Cleopatra at the Battle of Actium.

27 Octavian given title of Augustus by the Senate.

27 B.C.–14 A.D. Reign of Augustus*.

A.D.

14–37 Tiberius, emperor*.

37–41 Caligula, emperor*.

41–54 Claudius, emperor*.

42?–67? St. Peter, pope.

54–68 Nero, emperor*.

64 Fire of Nero.

67? Death of St. Peter.

67–79? Linus, pope.

68–69 Galba, emperor.

69 Otho, emperor.

69 Vitellius, emperor.

69–79 Vespasian, emperor†.

70 Capture of Jerusalem by Titus.

79–81 Titus, emperor†.

79–90? Anacletus I, pope.

81–96 Domitian, emperor†.

90–99? Clement I. pope.

96–98 Nerva, emperor.

98–117 Trajan, emperor.

99–107? Evaristus, pope.

101–107 Trajan's Dacian wars; frontiers of empire greatly enlarged.

107–116? Alexander I, pope.

113–117 Trajan's Parthian wars; frontiers of empire enlarged still more to the east.

116–125? Sixtus I, pope.

117–138 Hadrian, emperor; eastern boundary of empire withdrawn from Tigris to Euphrates.

125–136? Telesphorus, pope.

136–140? Hyginus, pope.

138–161 Antoninus Pius, emperor‡.

140–154? Pius I, pope.

154–165? Anicetus, pope.

---

* Julio-Claudian emperors.

† Flavian emperors.

‡ Antonine emperors.

(395)

161–180
(147)   Marcus Aurelius, emperor‡.
165–174?   Soter, pope.
174–189?   Eleutherius, pope.
180–192
(176)   Commodus, emperor‡.
189–198?   Victor I, pope.
193   Pertinax, emperor.
193   Didius Julianus, emperor.
193–211   Septimius Severus, emperor; Roman frontiers in Britain retracted.
198–217?   Zephyrinus, pope.
209–211   Geta, emperor.
211–217
(198)   Caracalla, emperor.
212   Edict of Caracalla extended Roman citizenship to practically all free inhabitants of empire, probably to increase taxes.
217–218   Macrinus, emperor.
217–222?   Calixtus I, pope.
218–222   Elagabalus, emperor.
220–230?   Urban I, pope.
222–235   Alexander Severus, emperor.
230–235   Pontianus, pope.
235–238   Maximinus, emperor (proclaimed by Rhine legions).
235–236   Anterus, pope.
236–250   Fabianus, pope.
237–238   Gordian I, emperor (proclaimed by African legions).
238   Pupienus, emperor.
238   Balbinus, emperor
238–244   Gordian III, emperor.
244–249   Philip the Arabian, emperor.
249–251   Decius, emperor.
251–253   Cornelius, pope.
251–253   Gallus, emperor.
252–253   Aemilian, emperor.
253–254   Lucius I, pope.
253–259   Valerian, emperor.
254–257   Stephen I, pope.
257–258   Sixtus II, pope.
259–268   Dionysius, pope.

259–268
(255)   Gallienus, emperor.
268–270   Claudius II, emperor.
269–274   Felix I, pope.
270–275   Aurelian, emperor. Began the existing walls of Rome after repulsing the Alemanni from Italy.
275–283   Eutychianus, pope
275–276   Tacitus, emperor.
276–282   Probus, emperor.
282–283   Carus, emperor.
283–296   Caius, pope.
284–305   Diocletian, emperor. Reorganized empire into eastern and western sections.
286–305   Maximianus, emperor.
296–304   Marcellinus, pope.
305–306   Constantius I, emperor.
(293)
305–311
(293)   Galerius, emperor.
311–324
(307)   Licinius, emperor.
311–337
(306)   Constantine I, the Great, emperor (proclaimed by troops in Britain).
306–312   Maxentius, emperor (proclaimed by praetorian guard in Rome).
308–309   Marcellus, pope.
310   Eusebius, pope.
311–314   Melchiades, pope.
312   Constantine defeated Maxentius at the Milvian bridge near Rome, and soon after recognized Christianity.
313   Constantine's proclamation of equal rights for all religions and restoration of confiscated Christian property.
314–335   Sylvester I, pope.
324   Constantine reunited the empire under one emperor.
330   Constantine dedicated Constantinople as capital of the empire.
336   Marcus, pope.

‡ Antonine emperors.

337–352 Julius I, pope.
337–361 Reigns of Constantine's sons: Constantine II, Constantius II and Constans.
341 Edict prohibiting pagan sacrifice in public and permitting confiscation of temples.
352–366 Liberius, pope.
355–358 Felix II, pope (more properly, anti-pope).
356 Visit of Constantius II to Rome, chronicled by Ammianus Marcellinus.
361–363 Julian the Apostate, Constantine's nephew, emperor; attempted to revive paganism.
363–364 Jovian, emperor.
364–375 Valentinian I, emperor (in the west).
364–378 Valens, emperor (in the east).
366–384 Damasus I, pope.
375–383 (367) Gratian, emperor (in the west).
375–392 (367) Valentinian II, emperor (in the west).
376 Visigoths (West Goths) crossed the Danube and ravaged the Balkans.
379–395 Theodosius I, the Great, emperor (in the east; after 392, in the west also).
392–394 Eugenius, emperor (in the west).
382 Gratian refused title of *pontifex maximus*; withdrew state support from pagan rites and enacted severe edicts against pagan worship.
384–398 Siricius, pope.
395–408 (383) Arcadius, elder son of Theodosius, emperor (in the east).
395–423 (393) Honorius, younger son of Theodosius, emperor (in the west; capital at Ravenna. Beginning of permanent separation of eastern, or Byzantine, and western empires).

398–401 Anastasius I, pope.
402 Stilicho, Vandal general of Honorius, defeated attempt of Alaric and the Visigoths to invade Italy. Gaul overrun by Vandals, Alans, Suevi, and Burgundians.
402–417 Innocent I, pope.
407 Roman legions withdrawn from Britain.
408–450 (402) Theodosius II, emperor (in the east).
410 Sack of Rome by Alaric and the Visigoths.
417–418 Zosimus, pope.
418–422 Boniface I, pope.
422–432 Celestine I, pope.
423–425 Interregnum in the west after death of Honorius.
425–455 Valentinian III, emperor (in the west).
432–440 Sixtus III, pope.
440–461 Leo I, the Great, pope.
450–457 Marcian, emperor (in the east).
455 Petronius Maximus, emperor (in the west).
455 Sack of Rome by Genseric and the Vandals, called in after murder of Petronius Maximus.
455–457 Avitus, emperor (in the west).
457–461 Majorian, emperor (in the west).
457–474 Leo I, emperor (in the east).
461–465 Severus, emperor (in the west).
461–468 Hilarius, pope.
465–467 Interregnum in the west.
467–472 Anthemius, emperor (in the west).
468–483 Simplicius, pope.
472 Olybrius, emperor (in the west).
473–474 Glycerius, emperor (in the west).
473–475 Julius Nepos, emperor (in the west).
473–474 Leo II, emperor (in the east).
474–491 Zeno, emperor (in the east).
475–476 Romulus Augustulus, emperor (in the west).

476   Odoacer deposed Romulus: traditional date of the 'Fall of the Roman empire'. Theoretically, Rome was reunited with the eastern (Byzantine) empire; actually, Odoacer ruled Italy as king, and eastern connections practically ceased.

483–492   Felix III, pope.

489–526   Theodoric the Ostrogoth ruled Italy from his capital at Ravenna and attempted to continue the Roman tradition.

492–496   Gelasius I, pope.

496–498   Anastasius II, pope.

498–514   Symmachus, pope.

514–523   Hormisdas, pope.

523–526   John I, pope.

526–530   Felix IV, pope.

526–535   Struggle in Italy among the successors of Theodoric.

527–565   Justinian, Byzantine emperor.

530–532   Boniface II, pope.

533–535   John II, pope.

535–536   Agapetus I, pope.

535–554   Reconquest of Italy by Justinian the Great, Byzantine emperor, and his generals, Belisarius and Narses.

536?–538   Silverius, pope.

537–538   Siege of Rome by Witiges and the Ostrogoths; city held by Belisarius, but aqueducts cut.

538?–555   Vigilius, pope.

539   Capture of Ravenna by Belisarius.

546   Capture and sack of Rome by Totila the Ostrogoth. Recaptured and abandoned by Belisarius, it eventually came into Justinian's hands.

556–561   Pelagius I, pope.

561–574   John III, pope.

568–774   Lombard conquest and kingdom in northern Italy.

575–579   Benedict I, pope.

579–590   Pelagius II, pope.

c.582–756   Rome and most of Italy not occupied by Lombards organized as Exarchate of Ravenna and ruled by official responsible to Byzantine emperor at Constantinople.

590–604   Gregory the Great, pope.

604–606   Sabinianus, pope.

607   Boniface III, pope.

608–615   Boniface IV, pope.

615–618   Deusdedit, pope.

619–625   Boniface V, pope.

625–538   Honorius I, pope.

638–640   Severinus, pope.

640–642   John IV, pope.

642–649   Theodore I, pope.

649–655   Martin I, pope. (Died in exile.)

654–657   Eugenius I, pope.

657–672   Vitalianus, pope.

663   Constans II, Byzantine emperor, visited Rome and robbed her of much remaining metalwork, including the bronze tiles of the Pantheon.

672–676   Adeodatus, pope.

676–678   Donus, pope.

678–681   Agatho, pope.

682–683   Leo II, pope.

684–685   Benedict II, pope.

685–686   John V, pope.

686–687   Conon, pope.

687–701   Sergius, pope.

701–705   John VI, pope.

705–707   John VII, pope.

708   Sisinnius, pope.

708–715   Constantine, pope.

715–731   Gregory II, pope.

731–741   Gregory III, pope.

741–752   Zacharias, pope.

752   Stephen, pope.

752–757   Stephen II, pope.

756   Pepin, king of the Franks, granted to the papacy much of the Exarchate of Ravenna.

757–767   Paul I, pope.

768–772   Stephen III, pope.

772–795   Adrian I, pope.

774 Charlemagne absorbed Lombard kingdom of northern Italy into his empire and confirmed Pepin's grant to the papacy.

795–816 Leo III, pope.

800 Revival of the Roman Empire in the west. Charlemagne crowned in Rome by Leo III.

816–817 Stephen IV, pope.

817–824 Paschal I, pope.

824–827 Eugenius II, pope.

827 Valentinus, pope.

827–844 Gregory IV, pope.

844–847 Sergius II, pope.

846 Saracen raid on outskirts of Rome.

847 Earthquake damaged many Roman monuments.

847–855 Leo V, pope; built the first walls about the Vatican section as protection against further Saracen invasions.

855–858 Benedict III, pope.

858–867 Nicholas I, pope.

867–872 Adrian II, pope.

872–882 John VIII, pope.

882–884 Martin II, pope.

884–885 Adrian III, pope.

885–891 Stephen V, pope.

891–896 Formosus, pope.

896 Boniface VI, pope.

896–897 Stephen VI, pope.

897 Theodore II, pope.

898–900 John IX, pope.

900–903 Leo V, pope.

903–904 Christopher, pope.

904–911 Sergius III, pope.

913–914 Lando, pope.

914–928 John X, pope.

928 Leo VI, pope.

928–931 Stephen VII, pope.

931–936 John XI, pope.

936–939 Leo VII, pope.

939–942 Stephen VIII, pope.

942–946 Martin III, pope.

946–955 Agapetus II, pope.

955–963 John XII, pope.

962 Coronation of Otto I, the Great (936–973) of Saxony, marked revival of Charlemagne's Roman Empire in the west.

963– 965 Leo VIII, pope.

965 Benedict V, pope.

965– 972 John XIII, pope.

973– 974 Benedict VI, pope.

974– 983 Benedict VII, pope.

983–1002 Otto III, Holy Roman emperor: revival of interest in ancient Rome.

983– 984 John XIV, pope.

984– 985 Boniface VII, pope.

985– 996 John XV, pope.

996– 999 Gregory V, pope.

999–1003 Sylvester II, pope.

1003 John XVII, pope.

1003–1009 John XVIII, pope.

1009–1012 Sergius IV, pope.

1012–1024 Benedict VIII, pope.

1024–1032 John XIX, pope.

1032–1045 Benedict IX, pope.

1045–1046 Gregory VI, pope.

1046–1047 Clement II, pope.

1048 Damasus II, pope.

1049–1054 Leo IX, pope.

1054–1057 Victor II, pope.

1057–1058 Stephen IX, pope.

1058–1059 Benedict X, pope.

1059–1061 Nicholas II, pope.

1061–1073 Alexander II, pope.

1073–1085 Gregory VII, pope.

1084 Destructive sack of Rome by Normans from Sicily.

1087 Victor III, pope.

1088–1099 Urban II, pope.

1099–1118 Paschal II, pope.

1118–1119 Gelasius II, pope.

1119–1124 Calixtus II, pope.

1124–1130 Honorius II, pope.

1130–1143 Innocent II, pope.

1143 Romans proclaimed their city a republican commune and restored the Senate. Arnold of Brescia became a leader.

Conflict between the popes and the emperor, Frederick Barbarossa.

1143–1144 Celestine II, pope.
1144–1145 Lucius II, pope.
1145–1153 Eugene III, pope.
1153–1154 Anastasius IV, pope.
1154–1159 Adrian IV, pope.
1155 Death of Arnold of Brescia.
1159–1181 Alexander III, pope.
1181–1185 Lucius III, pope.
1185–1187 Urban III, pope.
1187 Gregory VIII, pope.
1187–1191 Clement III pope.
1188 Papal recognition of the principle of the Roman commune and the Senate effects working compromise between Church and city. Senators usually appointed by the pope.
1191–1198 Celestine III, pope.
1198–1216 Innocent III, pope.
1216–1227 Honorius III, pope.
1227–1241 Gregory IX, pope.
1241 Celestine IV, pope.
1243–1254 Innocent IV, pope.
1254–1261 Alexander IV, pope.
1261–1264 Urban IV pope.
1265–1268 Clement IV, pope.
1271–1276 Gregory X, pope.
1276 Innocent V, pope.
1276 Adrian V, pope.
1276–1277 John XXI, pope.
1277–1280 Nicholas III, pope.
1281–1285 Martin IV, pope.
1285–1287 Honorius IV, pope.
1288–1292 Nicholas IV, pope.
1294 Celestine V, pope.
1294–1303 Boniface VIII, pope.
1300 First Holy Year of Jubilee in Rome.
1303–1304 Benedict IX, pope.
1305–1314 Clement V, pope.
1305–1378 Popes withdraw to Avignon ('Babylonian Captivity'); Rome 'the widowed city'.

1316–1334 John XXII, pope.
1334–1342 Benedict XII, pope.
1341 Petrarch crowned poet laureate on the Capitol.
1342–1353 Clement VI, pope.
1347 Revolution under Cola di Rienzi.
1352–1362 Innocent VI, pope.
1354 Cola di Rienzi appointed Senator by the pope, but killed in the same year by opposing nobles.
1362–1370 Urban V, pope.
1370–1378 Gregory XI, pope.
1378 Return of the popes from Avignon to Rome.
1378–1389 Urban VI, pope.
1389–1404 Boniface IX, pope.
1404–1406 Innocent VII, pope.
1406–1415 Gregory XII, pope.
1417–1431 Martin V, pope; early humanists (Poggio Bracciolini).
1431–1447 Eugenius IV, pope; humanists: Poggio and Flavio Biondo.
1447–1455 Nicholas V, pope: humanistic interest in Roman antiquities increased.
1455–1458 Calixtus III, pope.
1458–1464 Pius II (Aeneas Sylvius Piccolomini), pope; a brilliant humanist.
1464–1471 Paul II (Pietro Barbo), pope.
1471–1484 Sixtus IV (Francesco della Rovere), pope.
1484–1492 Innocent VIII (Giovanni Battista Cibo), pope.
1492–1503 Alexander VI (Roderigo Borgia), pope.
1503 Pius III (Antonio Tedeschini Piccolomini), pope.
1503–1513 Julius II (Giuliano della Rovere), pope.
1513–1521 Leo X (Giovanni de' Medici) pope.
1522–1523 Adrian VI (Adrian Florent), pope (the last non-Italian pope).

1523–1534	Clement VII (Giulio de' Medici), pope.	1670–1676	Clement X (Giovanni Battista Alfieri), pope.
1527	Sack of Rome by armies of the emperor, Charles V, under the Constable of Bourbon.	1676–1689	Innocent XI (Benedetto Odescalchi), pope.
		1689–1691	Alexander VIII (Pietro Ottoboni), pope.
1534–1549	Paul III (Alessandro Farnese), pope; beginning of Counter-Reformation.	1691–1700	Innocent XII (Antonio Pignatelli), pope.
1536	Triumphal procession of Charles V through the Roman Forum after his victory in Tunis the year before.	1700–1721	Clement XI (Giovanni Francesco Albani), pope.
		1721–1724	Innocent XIII (Michelangelo Conti), pope.
1550–1555	Julius III (Giovanni Maria Ciucchi del Monte), pope.	1724–1730	Benedict XIII (Pietro Francesco Orsini), pope.
1555	Marcellus III (Marcello Cervini), pope.	1730–1740	Clement XII (Lorenzo Corsini), pope.
1555–1559	Paul IV (Giovanni Pietro Caraffa), pope.	1740–1758	Benedict XIV (Prospero Lambertini), pope.
1559–1565	Pius IV (Giovanni Angelo de' Medici), pope.	1758–1769	Clement XIII (Carlo Rezzonico), pope.
1566–1572	Pius V (Michele Ghislieri), pope.	1769–1774	Clement XIV (Lorenzo Francesco Ganganelli), pope.
1572–1585	Gregory XIII (Ugo Boncompagni), pope.	1775–1799	Pius VI (Angelo Braschi), pope.
1585–1590	Sixtus V (Felice Peretti), pope.	1796	French army under Napoleon invaded Italy.
1590–1591	Gregory XIV (Nicolo Sfrondati), pope.	1798	Rome proclaimed a republic.
1591	Innocent IX (Giovanni Antonio Facchinetti), pope.	1799	Fall of republic and restoration of papal power.
1592–1605	Clement VIII (Ippolito Aldobrandini), pope.	1800–1823	Pius VII (Gregorio Barnaba Chiaramonti), pope.
1605	Leo XI (Alessandro Ottaviano de' Medici), pope.	1805	Napoleon declared king of Italy.
1605–1621	Paul V (Camillo Borghese), pope.	1806	End of Holy Roman Empire with Francis II (Francis I of Austria).
1621–1623	Gregory XV (Alessandro Ludovisi), pope.	1809	Napoleon annexed Rome and other papal states to French Empire.
1623–1644	Urban VIII (Matteo Barberini), pope.		
1644–1655	Innocent X (Giovanni Battista Pamfili), pope.	1814	Napoleon exiled to Elba; papal power restored in Rome by Austria.
1655–1667	Alexander VII (Fabio Chigi), pope.	1823–1829	Leo XII (Annibale della Genga), pope.
1667–1669	Clement IX (Giulio Rospigliosi), pope.	1829–1830	Pius VIII (Francesco Saverio Castiglioni), pope.

1831–1846 Gregory XVI (Mario Cappellari), pope.

1846–1878 Pius IX (Giovanni Maria Mastai-Ferretti), pope.

1848–1849 Revolution in Rome and throughout Italy; Garibaldi and Mazzini among the leaders.

1849 Rome declared a republic (9th February).

1849 Surrender of Rome to French army (30th June), after defence by Garibaldi. Papal power nominally restored by French.

1849–1870 Unification of Italy by the king of Piedmont and Count Cavour.

1861 Victor Emanuel II of Piedmont proclaimed king of Italy (17th March).

1870 French withdrew from Rome (19th August) because of Franco-Prussian War.

1870 Rome became capital of Italy (2nd October), after a plebiscite.

1878–1900 Humbert I, king of Italy.

1878–1903 Leo XIII (Gioacchino Pecci), pope.

1900–1946 Victor Emmanuel III, king of Italy.

1903–1914 Pius X (Giuseppe Melchiorre Sarto), pope.

1914–1922 Benedict XV (Giacomo della Chiesa), pope.

1916 Italy declared war on Austro-Hungary and Germany.

1918 End of World War I.

1922–1939 Pius XI (Achille Ratti), pope.

1922 Fascist 'March on Rome' (27th–31st October); beginning of Mussolini's government.

1939 Pius XII (Eugenio Pacelli), pope).

1940 Italy declared war on France and Great Britain (10th June).

1943 Mussolini forced to resign (25th July).

1943 Rome declared open city.

1944 Anglo-American troops entered Rome (4th June).

1945 Mussolini killed (29th April).

1946 Victor Emmanuel III abdicated (9th May), in favour of Humbert II.

1946 Italy voted to establish a republic (2nd June); declaration of republic 10th June; Humbert II left Italy (13th June); republic proclaimed (16th June).

1948 Constitution of the republic went into effect (1st January).

SOURCES OF PHOTOGRAPHS

PLATE 104. By gracious permission of Her Majesty the Queen.

FRONTISPIECE. Courtesy of the Victoria and Albert Museum, London.

PLATE 1. German Archaeological Institute, Rome.

PLATES 2, 18, 55, 80, 88, 145, 150, 205. Anderson, Rome.

PLATE 3. Courtesy of the Municipal Antiquarium, Rome.

PLATES 4, 59, 64, 75, 81, 83, 87, 89, 94, 96, 97, 98, 100, 101, 105, 107, 109, 111, 114, 117, 120, 124, 128, 132, 143, 157, 162, 166, 168, 182, 188, 190, 200, 211, 217. *Gabinetto Fotografico Nazionale*, Rome.

PLATES 5, 62, 212. P. Fiorentini, Venice.

PLATES 6, 7, 8, 10, 11, 12, 14, 19, 20, 21, 22, 23, 24, 26, 43, 57, 63, 65, 66, 71, 76, 77, 90, 102, 108, 110, 113, 116, 121, 125, 129, 133, 136, 137, 138, 139, 147, 149, 154, 158, 163, 164, 167, 171, 175, 177, 178, 181, 183, 187, 189, 191, 194, 198, 201, 204, 207, 208, 209, 213, 214, 215, 216, 218, 220, 222. Metropolitan Museum of Art.

PLATES 9, 49, 61, 67, 70, 72, 78, 106, 122, 126, 127, 151, 152, 172, 173, 180, 185, 196, 221. Alinari, Florence.

PLATE 13. Courtesy Philadelphia Free Library, Philadelphia.

PLATES. 15, 16, 32, 130, Fig. 2. Giraudon, Paris.

PLATES 17, 30, 31, 103, 112, 134, Fig. 1. Courtesy of the Trustees of the British Museum, London.

PLATES 25, 35. Courtesy of Staedel Art Institute, Frankfurt.

PLATE 27. Courtesy of the Museum of Fine Arts, Boston.

PLATE 28. Courtesy of Edward Coykendall, Kingston, New York.

PLATES 29, 85. Vasari, Rome.

PLATE 33. Courtesy Bristol City Art Gallery, Bristol, England.

PLATES 34, 45, 73, 79, 82, 95, 99, 179, 184. Sansaini, Rome, for Metropolitan Museum.

PLATES 36, 37, 38. Courtesy Thorwaldsen Museum, Copenhagen.

PLATES 39, 40. Courtesy Henry Wadsworth Longfellow Dana.

PLATES 41, 115. Courtesy Detroit Institute of Arts, Detroit.

PLATE 42. Courtesy Cooper Union Museum for the Arts of Decoration, New York.

PLATE 44. Courtesy Art Museum of the New Britain Art Institute, New Britain, Connecticut.

PLATES 46, 48, 51, 56, 165, 192. Photographer unknown.

PLATE 47. Courtesy Boston Athenaeum.

PLATES 50, 52, 53, 54, 91. Mang.

PLATE 58. Laura Voelkel.

PLATES 60, 92, 93, 131, 174, 176, 186. John Bayley.

PLATE 68. Courtesy New York Public Library.

PLATES 69, 140, 210. Wide World Photos, New York.

PLATE 74. Courtesy *Militaria aeronautica Italiana*, Rome.

PLATES 84, 118, 119, 141, 148, 153, 161, 169, 206. Ernest Nash.

PLATE 86. Courtesy Director of Excavations in the Forum and Palatine, Rome.

PLATE 123. Courtesy Newark Museum Association, Newark, New Jersey.

PLATE 135. *Archives Photographiques*, Paris.

PLATES 142, 144. Brunner and Company, Como.

PLATE 146. I. Schneider-Lengyel.

PLATE 155. E. Richter, Rome.

PLATE 156. Courtesy *Commissione Reale*, Rome.

PLATE 159. Courtesy Virginia Vacca, Rome.

PLATE 160. Courtesy Valentine Museum, Richmond, Virginia.

PLATE 170. Anna Holman.

PLATE 193. Ralph Crane, Courtesy Life Magazine (c) Time, Inc.

PLATE 195. Courtesy National Gallery of Art, Washington.

PLATE 197. Courtesy Fogg Art Museum, Cambridge (Mass.).

PLATE 199. Courtesy Mrs. Louis P. Church, Hudson, New York.

PLATE 202. Courtesy California Palace of the Legion of Honor, San Francisco.

PLATE 203. Brogi, Florence.

PLATE 219. Courtesy M. Hürlimann, Zürich.

LIST OF PLATES

FRONTISPIECE: Prout (English): *The east end of the Arch of Constantine.* Water-colour. Courtesy of the Victoria and Albert Museum, London

INTRODUCTION

FIGURE 1. *Monuments shown on Roman coins.* British Museum, London

FIGURE 2. *Circular view of Rome.* From the *Très Riches Heures* of the Duke of Berry. Chantilly, Musée Condé.

1. *The Temple of Magna Mater on the Palatine.* Roman relief. Rome, Villa Medici

2. *Marcus Aurelius passing a temple.* Roman relief. Rome, Conservatori Museum

3. *Fragment of the Marble Plan of Rome.* Rome, Municipal Antiquarium

4. *Reproduction of the Marble Plan of Rome.* Rome, Conservatori Museum

5. *The oldest known medieval view of Rome,* 1320–28. From a manuscript in the Library of St. Mark's, Venice. HS. Zan. lat. 399, fol. 98

6. *Circular view of Rome on the golden seal of the Emperor Ludwig of Bavaria,* 1328. Dresden, State Archives

7. *Rome bewailing her widowed state:* From a manuscript of Fazio degli Uberti's *Dittamondo.* Paris, National Library, *fonds italien* 81

8. Taddeo di Bartolo (Italian): *Circular view of Rome,* 1413–14. Siena, Chapel of the Palazzo Pubblico

9. Benozzo Gozzoli (Italian): *Panoramic view of Roman 'marvels',* 1465. Detail from *The Departure of Saint Augustine from Rome for Milan.* San Gimignano, Church of Saint Augustine

10. Raphael (Italian): *Giuliano de' Medici, with Hadrian's Tomb in the background.* Detail. About 1514–1515. New York, Metropolitan Museum of Art

11. Anonymus Escurialensis (Italian): *The Roman Forum from the Capitol,* about 1491. Drawing. Madrid, Escorial Collection

12. Van Heemskerck (Dutch): *Garden of the Casa Galli, Rome,* 1532–35. Berlin, Print Room

13. *The earliest known printed view of Rome,* Venice, 1490. Philadelphia, Free Library, P. A. B. Widener Collection

14. *Map of Rome,* 1557. Engraving from Lafreri's *Speculum.* New York, Metropolitan Museum of Art

15. Poussin (French): *The Ponte Molle.* Drawing. Paris, École des Beaux-Arts

16. Poussin (French): *Orpheus and Eurydice.* Paris, Louvre

17. Claude Lorrain (French): *The Roman Forum.* Drawing. Courtesy of the Trustees of the British Museum, London

18. Claude Lorrain (French): *Ruins of Ancient Rome with the Burial of Santa Serapia.* Madrid, Prado Museum

19. Pannini (Italian): *Landscape with Roman Ruins,* 1735. Berlin, Kaiser Friedrich Museum

20. Pannini (Italian): *A gallery of views of Ancient Rome,* 1757. New York, Metropolitan Museum of Art

21. Robert (French): *Arches of the Colosseum.* Drawing. Besançon, Library

22. Robert (French): *Portico with statue of Marcus Aurelius.* Paris, Louvre

23. Piranesi (Italian): *The Pyramid of Cestius.* Etching. New York, Metropolitan Museum of Art

24. Piranesi (Italian): *Fragments of Roman ruins in the Colonna Gardens.* Etching. New York, Metropolitan Museum of Art

25. Tischbein (German): *Goethe in the Roman Campagna,* 1787. Frankfurt-am-Main, Staedel Institute

26. Goethe (German): *The Palatine from the Via di San Sebastiano,* 1787. Drawing. Weimar, Goethe Museum

27. Copley (American): *Mr. and Mrs. Ralph Izard, with the Colosseum in the background,* 1774. Boston, Museum of Fine Arts

28. Vanderlyn (American): *The Arch of Titus,* about 1805. Kingston, N.Y., Collection of Edward Coykendall

29. Severn (English): *Shelley in Rome.* Rome, Keats-Shelley Memorial

30. Towne (English): *The tops of the piers of the Baths of Caracalla*, 1781. Courtesy of the Trustees of the British Museum, London

31. Turner (English): *The Arches of Constantine and Titus*. Courtesy of the Trustees of the British Museum, London

32. Corot (French): *The Castle and Bridge of Sant' Angelo*, 1826–27. Paris, Louvre.

33. Prout (English): *View in the Forum, Rome*. Bristol City Art Gallery

34. Koch (German, Tyrolese): *Ruins of the Palace of the Cæsars*. Etching. Rome, Library of the American Academy in Rome

35. Fohr (German): *Overbeck and his group in the Caffè Greco*. Drawing. Frankfurt-am-Main, Staedel Institute

36. Blunck (Danish): *Danish Artists in the Osteria of La Gensola, Rome*, 1837. Copenhagen, Thorwaldsen Museum

37. Meyer (Danish): *A Public Writer in a Roman Street Writing a Letter for a Young Girl*, 1829. Copenhagen, Thorwaldsen Museum

38. Marstrand (Danish): *Evening of an October Festival Outside the Walls of Rome*, 1839. Copenhagen, Thorwaldsen Museum

39. Longfellow (American): *The so-called 'Tomb of Nero'*. Drawing. Cambridge, Massachusetts, Longfellow House

40. Appleton (American): *The Colosseum from the Palace of the Cæsars*, 1836. Drawing. Cambridge, Massachusetts, Longfellow House

41. Cole (American): *The three corner columns of the Temple of Vespasian*, 1832. Drawing. Detroit Institute of Arts

42. Church (American): *Ruins at the Baths of Caracalla*, 1869. Drawing. New York, Cooper Union Museum of the Arts of Decoration

43. Cole (American): *Roman Aqueduct*, 1832. New York, Metropolitan Museum of Art

44. Inness (American): *Italian Landscape: Roman Campagna*, 1858. New Britain, Art Museum of the New Britain Art Institute.

45. Roesler-Franz (Italian): *The temples in the Forum Boarium*. Water-colour. Rome, Museo di Roma

46. *The temples in the Forum Boarium*, 19th century photograph.

47. Bierstadt (American): *The Portico of Octavia*, 1858. Boston Athenaeum

48. *The Portico of Octavia*. 19th century photograph.

49. *The Forum Boarium and the east bank of the Tiber before* 1891. 19th century photograph

50. *The House of Crescentius*. 19th century photograph

51. *The Porta San Sebastiano and the Arch of Druses*. 19th century photograph

52. *The Substructures of Septimius Severus on the Palatine*. 19th century photograph

53. *View toward the Arch of Titus and the Temple of Venus and Rome from the Colosseum*. 19th century photograph

54. *The Temple of Antoninus and Faustina and north side of the Forum before* 1876. 19th century photograph

55. *The west end of the Forum about* 1858. 19th century photograph

56. *The north-west angle of the Palatine before* 1881. 19th century photograph

THE CAPITOL

57. *The Capitol hill*. Airplane view, 1949

58. *The south-east corner of the platform of Jupiter's temple of the sixth century B.C.* 1947

59. *A wall of the podium of Jupiter's sixth-century temple*. 1949

60. *Fragment of the cornice of the last Temple of Jupiter on the Capitol*. 1949

61. *Domitian's Temple of Jupiter on the Capitol*. Roman relief. Rome, Conservatori Museum

62. *The Capitol and Senator's Palace about* 1300. Enlarged detail from a manuscript in the Library of Saint Mark's, Venice, HS. Zan. lat. 399, fol. 98

63. Van Heemskerck (Dutch): *The site of Jupiter's temple*, 1532–35. Drawing. Berlin, Print Room

64. *The Tabularium and Senator's Palace from the Forum*. 1949

65. Du Pérac (French): *The Tabularium and Senator's Palace from the Forum*, before 1575. Etching. New York, Metropolitan Museum of Art

66. Robert (French): *The Capitol Piazza*, about 1760–65. Drawing. Valence, Museum

67. *The Capitol Piazza in modern times*

68. *The Capitol illuminated in celebration of the proclamation of the Roman Republic, February 9, 1849. Illustrated London News, February 24, 1849.* New York Public Library

69. *Celebration of the Birthday of Rome in the Capitol Piazza, April 21st, 1951*

70. *Santa Maria in Aracoeli and the Senator's Palace, 1936*

71. Anonymus Fabriczy (Netherlandish): *Santa Maria in Aracoeli and the Senator's Palace in the 16th century.* Drawing. Stuttgart, Print Room

72. *Ruins of a Roman apartment house at the foot of the Capitol. 1933*

73. Falda (Italian): *Site of the Roman apartment house in 1665.* Engraving. Rome, Library of the American Academy in Rome

THE PALATINE HILL

74. *The Palatine hill.* Airplane view from the south-east, about 1935

75. *The south side of the Palatine hill, 1949*

76. Du Pérac (French): *The south side of the Palatine hill in the 16th century.* Etching. New York, Metropolitan Museum of Art

77. Van Heemskerck (Dutch): *The Substructures of Septimius Severus and the Septizonium, 1532–35.* Drawing. Berlin, Print Room

78. *Looking out from the arches shown in Van Heemskerck's drawing*

79. *The Substructures of Severus and the Aqueduct of Domitian in the 19th century.* Etching. Rome, National Library

80. *Looking outward from the arches shown in the etching toward the Via di San Gregorio*

81. *Ruins of the Baths of Severus and the Stadium Box, 1949*

82. *Ruins of the Baths of Severus and the Stadium Box from the garden of Saint Bonaventura.* 19th century lithograph. Rome, National Print Collection

83. *Looking south along the Stadium, 1949*

84. *Looking north-west along the Stadium: the last of the Villa Mills, 1936*

85. *The lower peristyle of Domitian's residential palace, looking north,* about 1938

86. *The Villa Mills in the 19th century*

87. *A corner wall of the basilica of the Flavian Palace from the south, 1949*

88. *The Cryptoporticus of Nero*

89. *The site of the Farnese Gardens above the Palace of Tiberius, 1949*

90. Antonini (Italian): *The Farnese Gardens in the 18th century.* Engraving. New York, Metropolitan Museum of Art

91. *The Farnese Gardens from the Forum,* about 1880

92. *The cartouche with the Farnese arms from Vignola's gate to the gardens, lying near the Baths of Caracalla, 1951*

93. *A corner of the Farnese casino with the entrance to Nero's Cryptoporticus, 1949*

94. *The Farnese casino with the substructures of the Tiberian palace in the distance, 1949*

95. Pinelli (Italian): *Roma Sparita: half-buried substructures of the Palace of Tiberius,* early 19th century. Rome, Museo di Roma

96. *Beneath the substructures of the Palace of Tiberius, 1949*

97. *The church of Santa Maria Antiqua, 1949*

98. *The substructures of the Palace of Tiberius and the site of Santa Maria Liberatrice, 1949*

99. Vasi (Italian): *The substructures of the Palace of Tiberius and the church of Santa Maria Liberatrice, 1753.* Etching. Rome, Library of the American Academy in Rome

THE ROMAN FORUM

100. *The Roman Forum, looking west toward the Capitol, 1949*

101. *The south-west end of the Forum, 1949*

102. Van Heemskerck (Dutch): *The south-west end of the Forum, 1532–35.* Drawing. Berlin, Print Room

103. Claude Lorrain (French): *Columns of the Temple of Castor, 1682.* Drawing. London, British Museum

104. Canaletto (Italian): *The Forum, 1743.* Windsor, Royal Collection

105. *The Temple of Vesta in the Forum, 1949*

106. *The Temple of Vesta in the Forum(?).* Roman relief. Florence, Uffizi

107. *The north-west corner of the Forum, 1949*

108. Du Pérac (French): *The north-west corner of the Forum before 1575.* Etching. New York, Metropolitan Museum of Art

109. *The Temple of Antoninus and Faustina and vestibule of the church of Saints Cosmas and Damian on the north side of the Forum,* 1949

110. Van Heemskerck (Dutch): *The Temple of Antoninus and Faustina and vestibule of the church of Saints Cosmas and Damian,* 1532–35. Drawing. Berlin, Print Room

111. *View along the north side of the Forum looking toward the Capitol,* 1949

112. Turner (English): *View along the north side of the Forum looking toward the Capitol,* 1819. Drawing. London, British Museum

113. Corot (French): *View of the Forum from the Farnese Gardens,* 1826. Paris, Louvre

114. *View of the Forum from the Farnese Gardens,* 1949

115. Pannini (Italian): *The Roman Forum looking east toward the Colosseum and Arch of Titus,* 1735. Detroit Institute of Arts

116. Vasi (Italian): *The Forum or Campo Vaccino,* 1765. Etching. New York, Metropolitan Museum of Art

117. *Evening in the Forum,* 1949

118. *A cat among the ruins on the Regia*

119. *Late sunlight gilds the west side of the Arch of Titus,* 1949

TRIUMPHAL ARCHES

120. *The east side of the Arch of Titus,* 1949

121. Van Heemskerck (Dutch): *The east side of the Arch of Titus,* 1532–35. Drawing. Berlin, Print Room

122. *The spoils of the Temple of Jerusalem.* Relief on the south jamb of the Arch of Titus

123. Healy (American): *Longfellow and his daughter Edith under the Arch of Titus,* 1869. Newark Museum Association

124. *The Arch of Constantine with the Arch of Titus in the distance,* 1949

125. Du Pérac (French): *The Arch of Constantine with the Arch of Titus in the distance,* 1575. Etching. New York, Metropolitan Museum of Art

126. *Constantine speaking from the rostrum in the Forum; Constantine hunting; a sacrifice to Apollo.* Reliefs over a side opening of the Arch of Constantine

127. *The setting moon; Constantine's army on the march.* Details of 4th-century sculpture on the east end of the Arch of Constantine

THE BASILICA OF CONSTANTINE OR MAXENTIUS

128. *The remaining arches of the north aisle of the basilica of Constantine or Maxentius,* 1949

129. Du Pérac (French): *The remaining arches of the north aisle of the basilica in the 16th century.* Etching. New York, Metropolitan Museum of Art

130. Corot (French): *The Colosseum seen through the arches of Maxentius' portico of the basilica,* 1825. Paris, Louvre

131. *View in the Basilica of Constantine or Maxentius: preparations for a concert,* 1949

THE COLOSSEUM

132. *The south-west side of the Colosseum and the Arch of Constantine,* 1949

133. Anonymus Escurialensis (Italian): *The south-west side of the Colosseum and the Arch of Constantine,* about 1491. Madrid, Escorial Collection

134. Turner (English): *The south-west side of the Colosseum,* 1819. London, British Museum

135. Corot (French): *The Colosseum from the Farnese Gardens,* 1826. Paris, Louvre

136. Olivier (German): *The Colosseum,* 1820. Drawing. Dresden, Print Collection

137. *In the upper corridors of the Colosseum.* Engraving after Cockburn, London, 1841

138. Piranesi (Italian): *Interior of the Colosseum looking north-east,* 1766. Etching. New York, Metropolitan Museum of Art

139. *Moonlight view in the upper corridors of the Colosseum.* Engraving after Cockburn, London, 1841

140. *A concert in the Colosseum,* 1951

141. *The south-west side of the Colosseum floodlit,* 1938

THE GOLDEN HOUSE OF NERO

142. *An arched corridor in the eastern wing of Nero's Golden House*

143. *Painting on the ceiling vault of the arched corridor,* 1st century A.D.

144. *A painted corridor in the eastern wing of the Golden House, near the Hall of the Gilded Ceiling*

145. *One of the Vatican loggie painted by Raphael's pupils about 1517–19 and showing the influence of the decorations of the Golden House*

146. *The Laocöon to-day.* Rome, Vatican Museum

147. Dente (Italian): *The Laocoön soon after it was found on the site of the Golden House.* Engraving. New York, Metropolitan Museum of Art

THE BATHS OF CARACALLA

148. *Looking through the side arches of the central hall of the Baths of Caracalla, 1937*

149. Dosio (Italian): *Looking through the side aisles of the central hall of the Baths of Caracalla, 1560–69. Drawing.* Florence, Uffizi. Arch. 2563

150. *View in the southern peristyle of the Baths of Caracalla*

151. *Composite capital found in the Baths of Caracalla in 1868.* Rome, Baths of Caracalla

152. *Statue of Hercules found in the 1540's in the Baths of Caracalla.* Naples, National Museum

153. *Looking north-west along the central hall of the Baths of Caracalla, 1936*

154. Vedder (American): *The tops of the piers in the central hall of the Baths of Caracalla, 1857. Drawing.* Author's collection

155. *The two remaining piers of the calidarium seen from the south* before 1937

156. *The stage set between the piers for Puccini's opera, La Tosca, 1937*

THE BATHS OF DIOCLETIAN

157. *Central hall of the Baths of Diocletian, now the church of Santa Maria degli Angeli, 1949*

158. Du Pérac (French): *Central hall of the Baths of Diocletian before its conversion by Michelangelo into the church of Santa Maria degli Angeli.* Etching. New York, Metropolitan Museum of Art

159. Unknown artist: *Moses Ezekiel on the balcony of his upper studio in the Baths of Diocletian*

160. *The upper studio of Moses Ezekiel in the Baths of Diocletian*

161. *The Baths of Diocletian and entrance to the church of Santa Maria degli Angeli, 1938*

THE FORUM OF NERVA

162. *The Colonnacce, last remnant of the enclosing wall and portico of the Forum of Nerva, 1949*

163. Anonymus Escurialensis (Italian): *Ruins of the Forum of Nerva, about 1491.* Madrid, Escorial Collection

164. Piranesi (Italian): *Ruins of the Forum of Nerva: The Colonnacce, about 1770.* Etching. New York, Metropolitan Museum of Art

165. *The Colonnacce before excavation*

THE FORUM AND COLUMN OF TRAJAN

166. *The north-east hemicycle of the Forum of Trajan, 1949*

167. Dosio (Italian): *Part of the north-east hemicycle of the Forum of Trajan, 1560–69. Drawing.* Florence, Uffizi. Arch. 2565

168. *Part of the north-eastern hemicycle of the Forum of Trajan before excavations begun in the 1920's*

169. *Looking along the ancient shops on the Via Biberatica on the upper level of the hemicycle, 1936*

170. *The Column of Trajan and a corner of the 18th-century church of the Holy Name of Mary, 1933*

171. Du Pérac (French): *The Column of Trajan and the site of his forum's libraries in the 16th century.* Etching. New York, Metropolitan Museum of Art

172. *Trajan's army crossing the Danube, ready for an imperial review.* Detail from the lower part of the Column of Trajan.

173. *Soldiers bringing Trajan the heads of Dacians.* Detail of a relief on the Column of Trajan

THE TEMPLE OF THE SUN OR OF SERAPIS

174. *Fragments of the Temple of the Sun or Serapis and perhaps of the Baths of Constantine lying in the Colonna Gardens, 1949*

175. Du Pérac (French): *Ruins of the Temple of the Sun or Serapis and the staircase ramps enclosing medieval buildings of the Colonna in the 16th century*. Etching. New York, Metropolitan Museum of Art

176. *Looking down one of the Colonna Gardens' alleys toward the substructures of a staircase ramp at its north-western end*, 1949

177. Anonymous artist: *Substructures of the staircase ramps in the 16th century*. Drawing. Berlin, Print Room.

178. Antonini (Italian): *The Colonna Gardens in the 18th century*. Engraving. New York, Metropolitan Museum of Art

179. Anonymous artist: *A corner of the upper terrace of the Colonna Gardens in the early 19th century*. Rome, Museo di Roma

180. *The bronze boxer found in the Quirinal ruins and now in the Terme Museum*

181. *The bronze boxer as discovered among the ruined substructures of the temple on the Quirinal or the adjoining Baths of Constantine in 1885*

THE THEATRE OF MARCELLUS

182. *The Theatre of Marcellus*, 1949

183. Du Pérac (French): *The Theatre of Marcellus in the 16th century*. Etching. New York, Metropolitan Museum of Art

184. Pinelli (Italian): *Pifferari playing before a shrine of the Madonna at the Theatre of Marcellus*, 1830. Etching. Rome, National Library

185. *Shops in the Theatre of Marcellus before 1927*

UNIDENTIFIED TEMPLES BY THE TIBER

186. *The 'Temple of Fortuna Virilis' and 'Temple of Vesta' with the church of Santa Maria in Cosmedin in the background*, 1949

187. Brill (Flemish): *The 'Temple of Fortuna Virilis' and 'Temple of Vesta' with the church of Santa Maria in Cosmedin in the 16th century*. Drawing. Vienna, Albertina

THE HOUSE OF CRESCENTIUS

188. *The House of Crescentius*, 1949

189. Coello (Spanish): *The House of Crescentius in the 17th century*. Vienna, Albertina

THE PANTHEON

190. *The exterior of the Pantheon*, 1949

191. Du Pérac (French): *Side view of the Pantheon in the 16th century*. Etching. New York, Metropolitan Museum of Art

192. *The exterior of the Pantheon before 1881*

193. *Cats in the excavations around the Pantheon*, 1949

194. Piranesi (Italian): *The interior of the Pantheon*, 1768. Etching. New York, Metropolitan Museum of Art

195. Pannini (Italian): *The interior of the Pantheon*. Washington, National Gallery of Art (Samuel H. Kress Collection)

THE PYRAMID OF CESTIUS

196. *The Pyramid of Cestius with the Porta San Paolo*, 1949

197. Ammanati (Italian): *The inner face of the pyramid and the Porta San Paolo in the 16th century*. Drawing. Cambridge, Fogg Museum of Art

198. *The grave of Shelley by the Aurelian Wall near the Pyramid of Cestius*. Engraving after Scott, 1873

199. Cole (American): *View of the Protestant Burying-ground*, 1832–34. Hudson, New York, Collection of Mrs. Louis P. Church

HADRIAN'S TOMB

200. *Hadrian's Tomb or the Castle of Sant'Angelo, and the Bridge of Sant' Angelo seen from downstream*, 1949

201. Anonymus Escurialensis (Italian): *The Castle and Bridge of Sant' Angelo seen from downstream*, about 1491. Madrid, Escorial Collection

202. Corot (French): *The Castle and Bridge of Sant' Angelo and dome of Saint Peter's seen from upstream*. San Francisco, California Palace of the Legion of Honor

203. *The Castle and Bridge of Sant' Angelo and dome of Saint Peter's seen from upstream before 1892*

204. Brambelli (Italian): *The Girandola at the Castle of Sant' Angelo celebrating the anniversary of the election of a pope.* Engraving from Lafreri's *Speculum*, 1579. New York, Metropolitan Museum of Art

205. Aerni (Swiss): *The Girandola at the Castle of Sant' Angelo*, 1884. Rome, Museo di Roma

THE VATICAN OBELISK

206. *The Vatican obelisk in the piazza in front of Saint Peter's*, 1937

207. Van Heemskerck (Dutch): *The Vatican obelisk in its old location by the sacristy south of Saint Peter's*, 1532–35. Drawing. Berlin, Print Room

208. *The moving of the Obelisk in* 1586. Engraving from Lafreri's *Speculum*, 1586. New York, Metropolitan Museum of Art

209. *A papal blessing from the front of old Saint Peter's before the obelisk was moved to the piazza.* Engraving from Lafreri's *Speculum*, between 1564 and 1586. New York, Metropolitan Museum of Art

210. *Saint Peter's Piazza*, 1950, *with the crowd awaiting a papal announcement*

STATUES THAT WERE NEVER BURIED

211. *The equestrian statue of Marcus Aurelius in the Capitol Piazza*, 1949

212. *The statue of Marcus Aurelius and the head and hand of the bronze colossus beside the Lateran.* Enlarged detail from an early 14th century manuscript in the Library of St. Mark's, Venice. HS. Zan. lat. 399, fol. 98

213. Van Heemskerck (Dutch): *The statue of Marcus Aurelius beside the Lateran.* Drawing. Berlin, Print Room

214. *The statue of Marcus Aurelius in the Capitol Piazza.* Engraving from Lafreri's *Speculum*, 1565. New York, Metropolitan Museum of Art

215. *The head of the bronze Colossus in the Conservatori Museum*

216. Van Heemskerck (Dutch): *The head of the bronze Colossus and the river gods Tiber and Nile from the Quirinal lying on the Capitol*, 1532–35. Drawing. Berlin, Print Room

217. *The river gods from the Quirinal beside the staircase of the Senator's Palace*, 1949

218. Van Heemskerck (Dutch): *The river gods from the Quirinal in front of the arcade of the Conservators' Palace*, 1532–35. Drawing. Berlin, Print Room

219. *The Horse Tamers or 'Marble Horses' on the Quirinal Piazza to-day*

220. *The Horse Tamers or 'Marble Horses' on the Quirinal in the 16th century.* Engraving from Lafreri's *Speculum*, 1546. New York, Metropolitan Museum of Art

221. *The colossal river god Marforio in the courtyard of the Capitoline Museum to-day*

222. *The colossal river god Marforio lying in the Via di Marforio in the 16th century.* Engraving from Lafreri's *Speculum*, 1550. New York, Metropolitan Museum of Art

INDEX

Acqua Felice, pl. 44.

Acqua Paolo, 102.

Adonais, Shelley, 21; quoted, 124. Preface to pl. 198.

Aedificiorum illustrium reliquiae, 12.

Aeneid, Vergil, quoted, Capitol, 37, 38; lament for Marcellus, 112.

Aerni, Franz Theodor (1853–1918), *La Girandola*, painting, pl. 205.

Agnellus of Ravenna (ninth century), 50.

Agrippa, M. Vipsanius (63 B.C.–12 B.C.), victor over Antony and Cleopatra, 118.

— builds Pantheon, 118.

— in legend of Pantheon, 119–120.

— and Pyramid of Cestius, 122.

Agrippina (d. A.D. 59), 129.

Alaric the Visigoth (A.D. c. 370–410), sack of Rome, 50, 71.

Alban Hills, in painting by Inness, pl. 44.

Albertini, Francesco (d. 1520), pl. 77.

Alcuin (735–804), quoted, 3.

Alessandro I, Farnese, cardinal (b. 1468–d. 1549), pl. 74. See also Paul III, Farnese, Pope.

Alessandro II, Farnese, cardinal (sixteenth century), 58.

Alexander VI, Borgia, pope (1492–1503), pl. 201.

Allston, Washington (1779–1843), 17–18.

Altar of Victory, 70–71.

Ammanati, Bartolommeo (1511–1592), drawing, pl. 197.

Ammianus Marcellinus (fourth century A.D.), quoted, on temples of Jove, 38; on Trajan's Forum, 104; on Julian the Apostate, pl. 221.

Ampère, Jean Jacques (1800–1864), quoted, 30, 131, pls. 48, 154.

Ancient Rome in the Light of Recent Excavations, Lanciani, quoted, 55–56, 111.

Andersen, Hans Christian (1805–1875), 25.

Angel's Castle. See Castle of Sant' Angelo.

Angelico, Fra (1387–1455), 7.

Annius Verus (second century A.D.), 134.

Anonymus Escurialensis (fifteenth–sixteenth century), sketchbook, 9–10.

Anonymus Escurialensis, value of drawings of, 11.

— sketches from painting in Nero's Golden House, 91.

— drawings, pls. 11, 133, 201.

Anonymus Fabriczy (sixteenth century), pl. 71.

Ansichten von Italien, Friedländer, 20, quoted, 24, 59.

Antiquarian, Dalmazonni, quoted, 19–20.

Antiquities of Rome, The, du Bellay, tr. by Spenser, quoted, 10.

Antiquities of Rome, Fulvio, 12.

Antonine Baths. See Baths of Caracalla.

Antonine Column (Column of Marcus Aurelius), in Fazio's view of Rome, pl. 7.

Antonini, Carlo (late eighteenth–nineteenth century), engravings, pls. 90, 178.

Antoninus Pius, Roman emperor (A.D. 138–161), 72.

Antony, or Marc Antony (c. 82 B.C.–30 B.C.), site of funeral oration in Forum, 63, pl. 100.

— defeated at Actium by Agrippa, 118.

Apartment house of first century A.D., 46–47.

— aeroplane view of ruins of, pl. 57.

— in photographs, pls. 70, 72.

— site of, in engraving, pl. 73.

Apollo Belvedere (statue), West on, 17.

— Canova on, 93.

Apollodorus of Damascus (d. A.D. 129), 103.

Appian Way, 29, pl. 51.

Appleton, Frances Elizabeth (Mrs. Henry Wadsworth Longfellow; 1817–1861), 26.

— quoted, 54.

— drawing of Colosseum, pl. 40.

— heroine of Longfellow's *Hyperion*, pl. 40.

Aqua Marcia (aqueduct), destruction of, 95–96.

— supplies water for public baths, 95, 98, pl. 51.

— in view of Rome, pls. 7, 8.

— carried by Arch of Druses, pl. 51.

Aqueduct of Domitian, nineteenth century etching, pl. 79.

Aqueducts, Cassiodorus on care of, 95.

— in etching by Vasi, pl. 116.

Aqueducts. See also Acqua Felice, Aqua Paolo, Aqua Marcia, Claudian Aqueduct.

Arachne, legend of, 101.

Arch of Augustus, marble fragments of, in Forum, photograph, pl. 117.

Arch of Constantine, description, 76.

— later names of, 76.

— *Mirabilia* on, 76.

— painting by Prout, Frontispiece.

— in painting by Pannini, pl. 19.

— painting by Turner, pl. 31.

— photograph, pl. 53.

— in aeroplane view, pl. 74.

— in nineteenth-century etching, pl. 79.

— photograph, pl. 124.

— inscription on, pl. 125.

— sixteenth-century etching, pl. 125.

— reliefs from, pls. 126, 127.

— in photograph, pl. 132.

— fifteenth-century drawing, pl. 133.

Arch of Druses, photograph, pl. 51.

'Arch of Nero' (of Claudian Aqueduct), painting by Cole, pl. 43.

— Gifford on, pl. 43.

Arch of the Pantini, in painting by Meyer, pl. 37.

Arch of Septimius Severus, erected by Senate, 69.

— inscription mentioned, 69.

— in fifteenth-century drawing, pl. 11.

— in painting by Prout, pl. 33.

— in photographs, pls. 55, 100, 101, 111.

— in drawing by Heemskerck, pl. 102.

— in sixteenth-century etching, pl. 108.

— in drawing by Turner, pl. 112.

— in eighteenth-century etching, pl. 116.

— in relief on Arch of Constantine, pl. 126.

'Arch of the Swamps' (Arch of the Pantini), in painting by Meyer, pl. 37.

Arch of Tiberius, in relief on Arch of Constantine, pl. 126.

Arch of Titus, 75–76.

— painted by Turner, 22, pl. 31.

— painted by Healy, 30, pl. 123.

— building of, 75.

— various names of, 75.

— *Mirabilia* on, 75.

Arch of Titus, rebuilt by Valadier, 76.
— in Ludwig's Golden Seal, pl. 6.
— as part of Frangipani fortress, 76, pl. 28.
— painting by Vanderlyn, pl. 28.
— photographs, pls. 53, 56, 119, 120, 124.
— in painting by Pannini, pl. 115.
— inscription on, pl. 120.
— relief from, pl. 122.
— in sixteenth-century etching, pl. 125.
— reconstructed by Valadier, 76, pls. 31, 135.
Archive Tower (of Frangipani fortress), in painting by Turner, pl. 31.
Arnold of Brescia (d. 1155), 5.
Arnold von Harff (fifteenth-sixteenth century), quoted, 83.
Asylum, origin of name, 37.
— in aeroplane view, pl. 57.
— in drawing by Heemskerck, pl. 63.
Atrium Vestae (House of the Vestals), 68.
'Augustan Palace'. See Flavian Palace.
Augustine, Saint (A.D. 354–430).
— cited, 71.
Augustus, title conferred on Octavius, Roman Emperor (27 B.C.– d. A.D. 14), vision of Virgin and Child, 46.
— housing controls of, 47.
— birthplace, 49.
— finishes Caesar's new Senate House, 70, pl. 107.
— builds theatre in memory of Marcellus, 112.
— portico of Octavia built by, pls. 47, 48.
— obelisk placed in Circus Maximus by, pl. 76.
— divides Rome into regions, pl. 124.
Aurelian, Roman emperor (A.D. 270–275), and Forum of Trajan, 103.
— builds Temple of the Sun, 107.
— restores Temple of the Sun at Palmyra, 108.
— builds fortifications of Rome, 122, 126.
— builds Porta San Sebastiano, pl. 51.
Aurelian wall, building of, 122, 126.
— damaged in World War II, 123.
— Shelley buried near, 124.
— in etching by Piranesi, pl. 23.
— in painting by Marstrand, pl. 38.
— in photograph, pl. 51.
Aventine Hill, shown on Marble Plan, pls. 3, 4.

Ave Roma Immortalis, Crawford, 27.
Bacchus, Michelangelo, in drawing by Heemskerck, pl. 12.
Baedeker, Karl (1801–1859), 31.
Basilica Aemilia, 71.
— corner of, in fifteenth-century drawing, pl. 11.
— location of, in photographs, pls. 54, 100, 109.
Basilica Julia, part uncovered in 1788, 33.
— in photograph of Forum, pl. 100.
— reconstructed arches of, in photograph, pl. 101.
— in relief on Arch of Constantine, pl. 126.
Basilica of Constantine or Maxentius, 77–79, pls. 128–131.
— called "Temple of Romulus", 72.
— begun by Maxentius, 77.
— plan changed by Constantine, 72, 77.
— building described, 77–78.
— ruined, 78.
— later names for, 78.
— Evelyn on, 78.
— Dwight on, 78–79.
— concerts in, 79, pl. 131.
— in Fazio's view of Rome, pl. 7.
— western apse, in photograph, pl. 100.
— arches, in painting by Pannini, pl. 115
— arches, photograph, pl. 128.
— Lanciani on roof of, pl. 129.
— arches of, sixteenth-century etching, pl. 129.
— arches of, in painting by Corot, pl. 130.
Basilica of St. John Lateran, pls. 7, 8, 116, 212, 213.
Baths, Mirabilia on, 96.
Baths of Agrippa, ruins, in sixteenth-century etching, pl. 191.
Baths of Caracalla, 94–97, pls. 148–156.
— drawing by Dosio, 12, pl. 149.
— facilities of, 94.
— description of, 94–95.
— water supply for, 95.
— decline of, 95–96.
— excavations in, 96.
— sculpture in. 96.
— Charlotte Eaton on, 96–97.
— weeding of, 96–97.
— opera in, 97, pls. 151, 155, 156.
— Shelley on, 21, 97, pls. 30, 153.
— drawing by Towne, pl. 30.
— drawing by Church, pl. 42.
— cartouche of Vignola's gate lying near, pl. 92.
— frigidarium, photograph, pl. 148.
— drawing by Dosio, looking toward frigidarium, pl. 149.

Baths of Caracalla, marble column placed in Piazza Santa Trinità, pl. 149.
— gymnasium interior, photograph, pl. 150.
— capital found in, photograph, pl. 151.
— statue of Hercules found in, pl. 152.
— central hall, photograph, pl. 153.
— tops of piers in central hall, drawing by Vedder, pl. 154.
— Vedder on, pl. 154.
— calidarium piers, photograph, pl. 155.
Baths of Constantine, location of, 107.
— ruins of, confused with temple ruins, 110–111.
— fragments possibly from, 107, 174, 179.
Baths of Diocletian, 98–100, pls. 157–161.
— sixteenth-century etching, 12, 98, pl. 158.
— Michelangelo designs Church of Santa Maria degli Angeli in, 12, 99, pl. 157.
— building of, 98.
— Mirabilia on, 98.
— Church of San Bernardo in, 98.
— Terme Museum in, 98.
— Carthusian monks in, 99, pl. 7.
— Hawthorne on, 99.
— later uses of, 99, 100.
— in Fazio's view of Rome, pl. 7.
— central hall, in sixteenth-century etching, pl. 158.
— studio of Ezekiel in, 100, photographs, pls. 159, 160, 161.
'Baths of Livia', 57, 59.
'Baths of Paulus Aemilius', so-called, pls. 168, 171.
Baths of Severus, 53, 54.
— in etching by Koch, pl. 34.
— aeroplane view, pl. 74.
— photographs, pls. 81, 83.
— nineteenth-century lithograph, pl. 82.
Baths of Trajan, built above ruins of Nero's Golden House, 90, 91.
— model for Baths of Caracalla, 94.
Bede, the Venerable (c. 672–735), quoted, on Colosseum, 81–82.
Belisarius (A.D. 505–565), defends Rome against Goths, 126.
Belvedere Museum, in sixteenth-century engraving, pl. 208.
Benedict XIV, pope (1740–58), and Colosseum, 84.
Benjamin of Tudela (twelfth century), 117, 134.
Bernini, Giovanni Lorenzo (1598–1680), creates Piazza of St. Peter's, 131.

Bernini, bell towers on Pantheon, pl. 192.
— angels on Castle of Sant' Angelo, pls. 200, 205.
Berry, Duc de, 7, Fig. 2.
Beyle, Henri-Marie. See Stendhal.
Bibiena, Ferdinando Galli (1657–1743), 15.
Bierstadt, Albert (1830–1902), 30, 31, pl. 47.
Bindesbøll, Michael (1800–1856), in painting by Blunck, pl. 36.
Biondo, Flavio (c. 1388–1463), 8, 12.
Blessington, Marguerite, Countess of (1789–1849), quoted, 56.
Blue Guide, Muirhead, 31.
— quoted, on Forum of Trajan, 104–105.
Blunck, Detlev (1799–1853), 25.
— painting of Danish artists in La Gensola, pl. 36.
Bocca della Verità, drawing by Brill, pl. 187.
Boccaccio, Giovanni (1313–1375), quoted, 122.
Bonaparte, Mme Marie-Letitia (1750–1836), 56.
Bonaventura, St., garden of, 54, pl. 82.
Boni, Giacomo (1859–1925), 34.
Boniface IV, pope (608–615), 210.
Book of Hours, Duc de Berry, 7, Fig. 2.
Bourbon family, inherits Farnese gardens, 58, pl. 99.
Bourbon, Charles, duke of, constable of France (1490–1527), 127.
Boxer, bronze statue, found near Colonna Gardens, 111.
— Lanciani on, 111, pl. 181.
— photographs, pls. 180, 181.
Boy Extracting a Thorn from His Foot (statue), 140.
Bramante (Donato da Urbino; c. 1444–1514), plan for St. Peter's, 130.
Brambelli, Ambrogio (sixteenth century), *La Girandola*, engraving, pl. 204.
Bridge of Sant' Angelo, in Poussin's painting, pl. 16.
— paintings by Corot, pls. 32, 202.
— photographs, pls. 200, 203.
— fifteenth-century drawing, pl. 201.
— Hillard on, pl. 202.
Brill, Paul (1554–1626), 14.
Brill, Matthaeus (1550–83), 14.
Brosses, Charles de (1709–77), 14, pl. 187.
Brown, George Loring (1814–89), 30.
Byron, George Gordon, Lord (1788–1824), visits Rome (1817) 21, 52–53.

Byron *Manfred*, 21.
— *Childe Harold*, 21.
— on Palatine, 53.
— on Column of Phocas, 66.
— on Colosseum, 82, 85–86, pl. 138.
— on Pantheon, 120, pl. 194.

Caesar, Julius (102 or 101 B.C.–44 B.C.), and Roman Forum, 63.
— begins new Senate House, 70, pl. 107.
— plans Theatre of Marcellus, 112.
— statue of, in Pantheon, 118.
— gardens on west bank of Tiber, 125.
— and Vatican Obelisk, 129–130.
— monuments in Forum associated with, pl. 100.
Caffarelli Palace, built on site of Temple of Jupiter Capitolinus, 39.
— transformed into New Museum, 39.
— becomes Museo Mussolini, and Museo Nuovo, pl. 57.
— site of, in drawing by Heemskerck, pl. 63.
Caffarelli Palace, gardens of, wall from Jupiter's Temple built into wall of, 39, pl. 59.
Caffè Greco, gatherings at, 18, 24.
— Fohr's drawing of German artists at , 24, pl. 35.
Caligula, Roman emperor (A.D. 37–A.D. 41), 56, 129.
Campagna, Roman, Tischbein's painting of Goethe in, 17, pl. 25.
— painting by Inness, 29, pl. 44.
— described by James, 29, pl. 44.
— described by Story, 29.
— Ponte Molle in (drawing), pl. 15.
— painting by Cole, 29, pl. 43.
Campo Vaccino, (Roman Forum), 65, pls. 31, 55.
— drawing by Claude Lorrain, pl. 17.
— etchings by Vasi, pls. 99, 116.
Campus Martius, 101, 118.
Canaletto, Antonio (Antonio Canale; 1697–1768), 15.
— painting of the Forum, pl. 104.
Canova, Antonio (1757–1822), 16, 93.
Capitol, 37–48, pls. 57–73.
— Senate established in ruins of, 4, 41.
— Gibbon conceives *Decline and Fall* among ruins, 14.
— origin of name, 37, pl. 58.
— Vergil on, 37, 38.
— in Middle Ages, 40–41.
— ranked among Seven Wonders of the World, 40.

Capitol, *Mirabilia* on, 40.
— drawing by Heemskerck, 42, pl. 63.
— poets crowned on, 42.
— Poggio Bracciolini on, 42.
— Republics proclaimed from, 4, 43, 44.
— in views of Rome, pls. 5, 7, 8.
— in Gozzoli's panoramic view, pl. 9.
— aeroplane view showing monuments on, pl. 57.
— fourteenth-century manuscript, pl. 62.
— Fazio on, pl. 63.
Capitoline Museum, aeroplane view, pl. 57.
— in drawing by Robert, pl. 66.
— in engraving by Falda, pl. 73.
— in photograph, pl. 70.
Capitoline Venus (statue), 140.
Capitol Piazza, drawing by Robert, 42–43, pl. 66.
— statue of Marcus Aurelius moved to, 135, pls. 211, 214.
— aeroplane view, pl. 57.
— photograph, pl. 67.
— illuminated, pl. 68.
— photograph, pl. 69.
— sixteenth-century drawing, pl. 71.
— completed according to Michelangelo's plans, 42, pl. 73.
Caracalla, Roman emperor (211–217), and restoration of Temple of Vespasian, 66.
— and inscription on Arch of Severus, 69.
— murder of Geta, 69.
— opens baths, 94.
— builds Temple of Serapis, 107.
— buried in Hadrian's Tomb, 126.
— See also Baths of Caracalla.
Carstens, Asmus Jakob (1754–94), 23.
Carthusian monks, in Baths of Diocletian, 99, pls. 7, 8.
Casa Galli, garden of, drawing by Heemskerck, pl. 12.
Cassiodorus (A.D. c. 490–c. 583), on Rome, 17.
— plans for university, 62.
— quoted, on Capitol, 38.
— on care of aqueducts, 95.
— on Forum of Trajan, 104.
— on statues, 133, 141.
Castle of Sant' Angelo (Hadrian's Tomb), 125–128, pls. 200–205.
— scene of *la girandola*, 128, 204, 205.
— in Fazio's view of Rome, pl. 7.
— in Gozzoli's panoramic view, pl. 9.
— in painting by Poussin, pl. 16.
— paintings by Corot, pls. 32, 202.

Castle of Sant' Angelo, setting of Puccini's *Tosca*, pl. 156.
— photographs, pls. 200, 203.
— fifteenth-century drawing, pl. 201.
— Hillard on, pl. 202.
Castor and Pollux, legend of, 67, 68–69.
— thought represented by Marble Horses, 138.
Catel, Franz (1778–1856), 24.
Catiline (d. 62 B.C.), 49.
Cats, in excavations around Pantheon, pl. 193.
— Eleanor Clark on, pl. 192.
— in Forum, 74, pl. 118.
Cavour, Camillo Benso, Count (1810–61), 32, 44.
Cellini, Benvenuto (1500–71), quoted, 83–84.
— at defence of Castle of Sant' Angelo, 127.
Cenci, The, Shelley, 21.
Cestius, Caius (first century B.C.), 122. See also Pyramid of Cestius.
Chapel of the Virgin at Subiaco, Morse, 28.
Charlemagne (b. 771; Holy Roman emperor, 800–814), 2.
— circular view of Rome of, 3, 6.
Charles IV, Holy Roman emperor (1355–1378), 6.
Charles V, Holy Roman emperor (1519–1556), war with Francis I, 9.
— Forum cleared for triumphal procession of, 9, 11, 64, 75, pls. 102, 110.
— siege of Castle of Sant' Angelo, 127.
— sack of Rome in 1527, 9.
Chesterton, Gilbert K. (1874–1936), 2.
Church, Frederic E. (1826–1900), 30, pl. 42.
Church of Saint Andrew, pl. 207.
Church of Saint John Lateran. See Basilica of Saint John Lateran.
Church of Saint Paul, pls. 7, 8.
Church of Saints Martina and Luca (in Secretarium senatus), 70.
— in photograph of Forum, pls. 100, 107, 114.
— in sixteenth-century etching, pl. 108.
— dome, in painting by Corot, pl. 113.
Church of Saints Cosmas and Damian, *Mirabilia* on, 72.
— unidentified building becomes vestibule of, 72.
— in building of Forum of Peace, 73, pl. 100.

Church of Saints Cosmas and Damian, vestibule of, in photographs, pls. 100, 105, 109, 111.
— vestibule, drawing by Heemskerck, pl. 110.
— in drawing by Turner, pl. 112.
Church of Saints Sergius and Bacchus, holds part of Arch of Severus, 69.
— in drawing by Heemskerck, pl. 102.
— remnants of, in eighteenth-century etching, pl. 116.
Church of San Bernardo, in Baths of Diocletian, 98.
Church of San Biagio in Mercatello, built into ruins of first-century apartment house, pl. 72.
Church of San Bonaventura, in photographs, pls. 74, 124.
Church of San Giuseppe de' Falegnami, in photographs, pls. 55, 74.
Church of San Lorenzo in Miranda, Temple of Antoninus and Faustina, 71.
— in photographs of Forum, pls. 100, 109, 111.
— outlines sketched, in Heemskerck drawing, pl. 110.
Church of San Pietro ad Vincula, pls. 7, 8.
Church of San Sebastiano, pls. 7, 8, 74, 124.
Church of Sancta Maria ad Martyres (Pantheon), 119.
Church of Sant' Adriano (former Senate House), 71, pls. 107, 108.
Church of Santa Cecilia, pl. 7.
Church of Santa Maria in Aracoeli, 39.
— thought to be on site of ruins of Temple of Jupiter on Capitol, 39.
— on site of Temple of Juno on Capitol, 45.
— origin of name, 45–46.
— staircase of, 109, pls. 70, 71, 72.
— in Gozzoli's panoramic view, pl. 9.
— in photographs, pls. 55, 57, 70, 72.
— aeroplane view, pl. 57.
— in drawings by Heemskerck, pls. 63, 71, 102, 121.
— Gibbon conceives *Decline and Fall* near, 43, pl. 66.
— clock from, moved to bell tower of the Capitol, pl. 70.
— in engraving by Falda, pl. 73.
Church of Santa Maria in Cosmedin, in drawing by Brill, pl. 187.
— medieval clock tower of, in photographs, pls. 49, 186.

Church of Santa Maria Libera nos a poenis inferni, Latin name for Santa Maria Liberatrice, 62.
Church of Santa Maria Liberatrice, built near site of Santa Maria Antiqua, 62, pl. 56.
— demolished, 62.
— location, near Temple of Vesta, 68.
— in painting by Pannini, pl. 115.
Church of Santa Maria Nova, built into ruins of Temple of Venus and Rome, 61, 73.
Church of Santa Croce in Gerusalemme, pls. 7, 8.
Church of Santa Francesca Romana, 61.
— rebuilt from Santa Maria Nova in ruins of Temple of Venus and Rome in seventeenth century, 61, 73.
— in painting by Turner, pl. 31.
— in photographs, pls. 53, 105, 117, 131.
— in painting by Pannini, pl. 115.
Church of Santa Maria Antiqua, 61, 62.
— built into ruins of "Temple of Augustus" on Palatine in Middle Ages, 61, pl. 56.
— Santa Maria Liberatrice built on site of, 62, pls. 98, 99.
— excavation of, 62, pls. 97–99.
Church of Santa Maria degli Angeli, (in Baths of Diocletian), designed by Michelangelo, 12, 99.
— photograph, pl. 157.
— entrance, photograph, pl. 161.
— Hawthorne on, 99.
Church of Santa Maria di Loreto, above ruins of temple built to Trajan, 105.
— in photograph, pl. 114.
— in sixteenth-century etching, pl. 171.
Church of Santa Maria Egiziaca, built in temple by Tiber, 115.
Church of Santa Maria Rotonda (the Pantheon), *Mirabilia* tells legend of, 119–120.
— in Fazio's view of Rome, pl. 7.
Church of Santa Rita da Cascia, built by Fontana on site of first-century apartment house, 48.
— engraving by Falda, pl. 73.
Church of Santa Sabina, on the Aventine, tradition concerning, pl. 18.
Church of Santo Stefano delle Carozze, in temple by Tiber, 115.
Church of the Holy Name of Mary, above ruins of Temple built to Trajan, 105.

Church of the Holy Name of Mary, dome, in painting by Corot, pl. 113.
— in photographs, pls. 114, 170.
— location of, pl. 171.
Cicero (106–43 B.C.), 49.
— on Forum, 64.
— on Temple of Castor, 66.
Cimabue (thirteenth–fourteenth century), 6, 127.
Circus of Gaius and Nero, 129.
Circus Maximus, 50.
— rebuilt by Trajan, on sestertius, Fig. 1.
— site of, in photographs, pls. 74, 75.
— obelisks buried in, pl. 76.
— site, of, in sixteenth-century etching, pl. 76.
City of God, St. Augustine, cited, 71.
Clark, Eleanor (1913–), quoted, pls. 117, 192.
Claude Lorrain (1600–1682), influences on, 14.
— Allston compared with, 18.
— Corot compared with, 23.
— influence on German painters in Rome, 23.
— landscapes attract Americans to Rome, 28.
— drawings, pls. 17, 103.
— painting, pl. 18.
Claudian (d. A.D. c. 404), quoted, 50.
Claudian Aqueduct, 29.
— in view of Rome, pl. 5.
— painting by Cole, pl. 43.
— in painting by Inness, pl. 44.
— James on, pl. 44.
Clement VII, Medici, pope (1523–1534), pl. 10.
Clement IX, pope, and Colosseum, 84.
Cleopatra (statue), Story, 27.
Cleopatra, queen of Egypt (c.69 B.C.–30 B.C.), 118.
Clivus Victoriae (Street of Victory), 60, 61, pls. 89, 90, 94, 96.
Cloaca Maxima, in photograph, pl. 49.
Cockburn, James Pattison (1779?–1847), illustrations, pls. 137, 139.
Codex Escurialensis, anonymous artist of. See Anonymus Escurialensis.
Coello, Claudio (1630–1693), drawing, pl. 189.
Cole, Thomas (1801–1848), quoted, 28–29, 88.
— painting of Colosseum, 88.
— drawing, pl. 41
— *Roman Aqueduct*, painting, pl. 43.
— *Protestant Cemetery*, painting, pl. 199.

Coleridge, Samuel Taylor (1772–1834), 18.
Colonna family, 107, pl. 175.
Colonna, Giovanni, cardinal, (d. 1348), letter of Petrarch to, quoted, 8–9, 98.
Colonna Gardens, substructures of staircase ramps, in photograph, pl. 176.
drawing, pl. 177.
etching, pl. 175.
Colonna Gardens, ruins in, 107–111, pls. 174–181.
— Forsyth on, 109.
— Mrs. Eaton on, 109, pl. 179.
— Platt on, 110.
— Hillard on, 110.
— etching by Piranesi, pl. 24.
— eighteenth-century engraving, pl. 178.
— nineteenth-century painting, pl. 179.
Colonna palace, 109.
Colonnacce, Le. See Forum of Nerva.
Colossal statue, head and hand of, now in Conservatori Museum, 136, 137.
— mistaken for Nero's Colossus, 135–136.
— in view of Rome, pl. 5.
— beside Lateran, 135–136, pl. 212.
— head, photograph, pl. 215.
— head, in sixteenth-century drawing, pl. 216.
— head, by Conservators' Palace, in sixteenth-century engraving, pl. 214.
Colosseum, 80–89, pls. 132–141.
— linked with fall of Rome, 3.
— in portrait by Copley, 17, pl. 27.
— painted by Turner, 22, pl. 134.
— Andersen on, 25.
— described by Hawthorne, 26.
— begun by Vespasian, 80.
— opened by Titus, 80.
— completed by Domitian, 80.
— built on site of Nero's lake, 80.
— Martial on, 80.
— games in, 80, 81.
— dimensions of, 80–81.
— construction of, 81.
— origins of name, 81.
— Bede on, 81–82.
— Byron on, 82.
— damaged by earthquake, 82.
— *Mirabilia* on, 82.
— plays in, 83.
— erroneously depicted with a dome, 83, pls. 5, 7, 62.
— Arnold von Harff on plays in, 83.
— Cellini on demons in, 83–84.
— later uses of, 84.
— Turner's drawings and paintings of, 84, pl. 134.

Colosseum, Corot's paintings of, 84, pls. 130, 135.
— buttressing in nineteenth century, 84, pls. 132, 135.
— excavations in, 84–85.
— Goethe on, 85.
— Byron on, 85–86, pl. 138.
— Longfellow on, 86–87.
— Hawthorne on, 87.
— James on, 87.
— flowers of, 87–88, pls. 136, 137.
— Longfellow on flowers of, 87–88.
— Gregorovius on flowers of, 88.
— Cole on, 88.
— concerts in, 89, pl. 140.
— on sestertius of Titus, Fig. 1.
— in Ludwig's Golden Seal, pl. 6.
— in painting by Claude Lorrain, pl. 18.
— in painting by Copley, 17, pl. 27.
— in painting by Pannini, pls. 19, 115.
— arches of, drawing by Robert, pl. 21.
— drawing by Frances Appleton, pl. 40.
— in aeroplane view, pl. 57.
— in eighteenth-century etching, pl. 116.
— photograph of, pl. 132.
— fifteenth-century drawing of, pl. 133.
— drawing of by Olivier, pl. 136.
— weeding of, 88, pl. 136.
— Peale on, pl. 136.
— Deakin on flora of, 87, pl. 137.
— Sebastiani on flora of, 87.
— interior of upper corridors, engraving, pl. 137.
— interior, etching by Piranesi, pl. 138.
— southwest side, floodlit, photograph, pl. 141.
Colossus of Nero, and Byron's lines on Colosseum, 82.
— changed to statue of sun god, 135.
— Martial on, 135.
— *Mirabilia* on, 136.
— Master Gregory on, 136.
— Higden on, 136.
— last mention of in antiquity, 136.
— dimensions, according to Pliny and Suetonius, 137.
Column of Hadrian. See Trajan's column.
Column of Marcus Aurelius, 106, pls. 7, 8, 110.
Column of Phocas, Byron on, 66.
— excavation of base, 66.
— inscription of, 66.
— painting by Prout, pl. 33.
— in photographs, pls. 55, 100.

Column of Phocas, in drawing by Heemskerck, pl. 102.
— in drawing by Turner, pl. 112.
— in eighteenth-century etching, pl. 116.
Column of Trajan, 103, 105–106. pls. 170–173.
— preservation of, 105.
— *Mirabilia* on, 105.
— description of, 105.
— St. Peter's statue placed on, 106.
— in Ludwig's Golden Seal, pl. 6.
— in Fazio's view of Rome, pl. 7.
— in Bartolo's panoramic view, pl. 8.
— in Gozzoli's panoramic view, pl. 9.
— in painting by Pannini, pl. 19.
— in drawing by Heemskerck, pl. 110.
— photograph, pl. 170.
— sixteenth-century etching, pl. 171.
— reliefs from, pls. 172, 173.
Comitium, church on site of, 70.
Conservatori Museum (formerly Palace of the Conservators), aeroplane view, pl. 57.
Conservators' Palace, in drawings, pls. 63, 71.
— in engravings, pls. 73, 214.
— now Conservatori Museum, q.v.
Constantine I, the Great, Roman emperor (A.D. 311–337), moves seat of imperial government from Rome, 38, 50.
— victory over Maxentius, pls. 15, 127.
Constantine, Basilica completed by, 77.
— colossal statue of, fragments found in basilica, 77.
— statue of Marcus Aurelius confused with, 133–134.
— in relief from arch, pl. 126.
Constantinople, becomes seat of imperial government, 38, 50.
Constantius II, Roman emperor (A.D. 337–361), and Forum of Trajan, 104.
Conti tower, in view of Rome, pl. 5.
— in fourteenth-century manuscript, pl. 62.
— in drawing by Heemskerck, pl. 63.
Copley, John Singleton (1737–1815), painting of Mr. and Mrs. Izard, 17, pl. 27.
Cordonata, staircase of, pls. 70, 73.
Corilla Olimpica (Maria Maddele Morelli; 1727–1800), 42.
Corinne, Mme. de Stael, 20, 42.
Cornelius, Peter (1783–1867), 24, pl. 35.

Corot, Jean Baptiste Camille (1796–1875), 22–23.
— paintings, 84, pls. 32, 113, 130, 135, 202.
Cosmas, Saint (third century A.D.), 72; see also Church of Saints Cosmas and Damian.
— See also Basilica of Constantine or Maxentius, Baths of Constantine, Forum of Peace.
Courts of Justice, pl. 200.
Crawford, F. Marion (1854–1909), 27.
Crawford, Thomas (1813–1857), 27.
Crescentius, Giovanni (d. 998), defence of Hadrian's Tomb, 126.
Crescentius, Nicholas (twelfth century). See House of Crescentius.
Crescenzi family, pl. 50.
Cropsey, Jasper (1823–1900), 30.
Cryptoporticus of Nero, 57–58, 60.
— location of, pl. 87.
— photograph of, pl. 88.
— one modern entrance to, pls. 90, 91, 93, 94.
Curiosum, 1, 8, pl. 3.
Cybele (Magna Mater) Temple of, 51, pl. 1.
— in legend of Pantheon, 119–120.

Dacians, Trajan's capaign against, 105.
— in relief from column, pls. 172, 173.
Dalmazonni, Angelo (eighteenth-nineteenth century), quoted, 19–20.
Damian, Saint (third century A.D.), 72; see Church of Saints Cosmas and Damian.
Dante Alighieri (1265–1328), quoted, 5, pl. 62.
Deakin, Richard (1808–1873), 87; quoted, pl. 137.
Decline and Fall, Gibbon. See *History of the Decline and Fall of the Roman Empire*.
Dennie, John (nineteenth century), quoted, pl. 168.
Dente, Marco (d. 1527), pl. 147.
De Varietate Fortunae, Poggio Bracciolini, 8.
Diarium Italicum, Montfaucon, 13.
— quoted, 58.
Diary, Evelyn, quoted, 78.
Digressions, Vedder, quoted, pl. 154.
Dio Cassius (second-third century A.D.), quoted, 118.
Diocletian, Roman emperor (A.D. 284–305), divides empire, 49–50.
— rebuilds Senate House, 70, pl. 107.
— See also Baths of Diocletian.

Dionysius of Halicarnassus, quoted, 68, pl. 58.
Dirce and Bull (statue), found in Baths of Caracalla, 96.
Dittamondo, Fazio degli Uberti, 5, 6.
— view of Rome from, pl. 7.
— quoted, on Capitol, pl. 63.
Domenichino (Domenico Zampieri; 1581–1641), 91.
Domitian, Roman emperor (A.D. 81–96), rebuilds Temple of Jupiter Capitolinus, 40, pl. 60.
— substructures of Severus begun by, 50, pl. 75.
— Stadium built by, 54, pls. 83, 84.
— extends Palace of Tiberius, 58.
— builds Temple of Vespasian, 66.
— rebuilds Senate House, 70, pl. 107.
— completes Colosseum, 80.
— Forum of Nerva begun by, 101.
Domitian, official palace of. See Flavian place.
Domitian, residential palace of, excavations in, 55–56, pl. 75.
— aeroplane view, pl. 74.
— lower peristyle, photograph, pl. 85.
— photograph, with Villa Palatina-Mills, pl. 86.
Domus Transitoria, 56–57.
Dosio, Giovanni Antonio (1533–after 1609), drawings, 12, pls. 149, 167.
Du Bellay, Joachim (c. 1522–1560), quoted, 10.
Du Pérac, Etienne (c. 1525–1604), 12.
— etchings of Palatine, 50–51, pl. 76.
— etching of Baths of Diocletian, 98–99, pl. 158.
— Tabularium and Senator's Palace, etching, pl. 65.
— northwest corner of Forum, etching, pl. 108.
— Arch of Constantine, etching of, pl. 125.
— arches of Basilica of Constantine or Maxentius, etching of, pl. 129.
— Column of Trajan, etching, pl. 171.
— ruins of Temple of the Sun or Serapis, etching, pl. 175.
— Theatre of Marcellus, etching, pl. 182.
— side view of Pantheon, etching, pl. 191.
Durand, Asher (1796–1886), 29.
Dwellings. See apartment house.
Dwight, Theodore (1796–1866), 25–26; quoted, 59, 78–79.
Dying Gaul, in paintings by Pannini, pls. 19, 20.

Eaton, Mrs. Charlotte (Waldie) (1788–1859), 22.
— quoted, on Palatine, 53.
— on Baths of Livia, 57.
— on Farnese Gardens, 59.
— on Nero's Golden House, 91–92.
— on Baths of Caracalla, 96–97.
— on ruins in Colonna Gardens, 109–110, pl. 179.
Eckersberg, Christoffer Wilhelm (1783–1853), 25.
Einhard, biographer of Charlemagne (c. 770–840), 3.
Einsiedeln Itinerary, 3, 4.
— inscription of Temple of Vespasian preserved in, 66.
Elagabalus, Roman emperor (218–222), 107–108, pl. 24.
Elsheimer, Adam (1578–1610), 14.
Empire Romain à Rome, L', Ampère, 30; quoted, 30, pls. 48, 154.
Emperor's Table. See Temple of the Sun or Serapis.
Eugenius, Roman emperor (A.D. 392–394), 71.
Eustace, John Chetwoode (1762–1815), 19.
Evelyn, John (1620–1706), quoted, 78.
Excavations, scientific, begun, 33.
— in Roman Forum, 33–34, 64–65, 72, pls. 54, 55, 56, 6.
— of Farnese Gardens, 34, 54, 56–60, pls. 89–91.
— on Palatine, 34, 54–60.
— under Mussolini's government, 34, 46.
— of Temple of Vejovis, 37.
— of Temple of Jupiter Capitolinus, 39.
— by dukes of Parma, 56, 58.
— by Farnese family, 58.
— of base of Column of Phocas, 66.
— in Colosseum, 84–85.
— in Baths of Caracalla, 96.
— in Forum of Trajan, 105, pls. 166, 168.
— of Basilica Aemilia, 71, pl. 54.
— on Palatine, pl. 56.
— of platform of sixth-century Temple of Jupiter, 39, pl. 58.
— by Napoleon III, 34, 59, pls. 56, 95.
— around columns of Vespasian temple, pl. 65.
— of *Clivus Victoriae*, 60, pls. 89, 94–96.
— of Palace of Tiberius, pls. 89, 91, 94, 95, 96.
— of Santa Maria Antiqua, 62, pls. 97–99.
— of Forum of Nerva, 102, pls. 162, 165.
— around Theatre of Marcellus, 114, pl. 182.

Excavations, around Pantheon, pls. 192, 193.
Ezekiel, Sir Moses (1844–1917), 27.
— studio in Baths of Diocletian, 100, pls. 159, 160, 161.

Fabullus (first century A.D.), 90.
Falda, Giovanni Battista (d. 1678), 15.
— etching by, pl. 73.
Farnese casino, built by Rainaldi, pl. 90.
— in Antonini's engraving, pl. 90.
— photographs, pls. 91, 93, 94.
Farnese family, excavations of, 58.
— arms of, in cartouche from Vignola's gate, pl. 92.
— arms of, decorating casino, pl. 94.
Farnese gardens, neglect of, 34.
— bought by Napoleon III, 34, 58–60.
— Friedländer on, 59.
— Charlotte Eaton on, 59.
— Dwight on, 59.
— passed to dukes of Parma, 58.
— Helen Hunt Jackson on, 60.
— in photographs, pls. 56, 74, 87–89, 91.
— engraving of, by Antonini, pl. 90.
— etching by Vasi, pl. 99.
Farnese tower, in engraving by Antonini, pl. 90.
— in photograph, pl. 91.
— in painting by Pinelli, pl. 95.
Fasti, Ovid, quoted, 45, 67.
Faunus, legend of, 115.
Faustina the Elder, Roman empress (d. A.D. 141), 72.
Faustina the Younger, Roman empress (d. A.D. 175), 72.
Fazio degli Uberti (d. c. 1368), *Dittamondo*, 5, 6; quoted, 6, pl. 63.
Fea, Carlo (1753–1836), excavations of, 33–34.
Fiorelli, Giuseppe (1823–1896), 34.
Fish market in Portico of Octavia, painting by Bierstadt, pl. 47.
— Story on, pl. 47.
Flavian Amphitheatre. See Colosseum.
Flavian emperors. See Vespasian, Titus, Domitian.
Flavian Palace, 51, 56, 57.
— ruins of, aeroplane view, pl. 74.
— basilica, photograph, pl. 87.
— basilica of, in nineteenth-century photograph, pl. 91.
Flora, colossal statue of, found in Baths of Caracalla, 96.
Flora Colisea, Sebastiani, 87.
Flora of the Colosseum, Deakin, 87; quoted, pl. 137.

Fohr, Karl Philipp (1795–1818), 23, 24.
— drawing of German artists at Cafè Greco, 24, pl. 35.
Fontana, Carlo (1634–1714), builds church of Santa Rita da Cascia, 48, pl. 73.
Fontana, Domenico (1543–1607), plans for turning Colosseum into factory, 84.
— supervises moving of Vatican Obelisk, 130, pl. 208.
Foresti, Giovanni Filippo (1434–1520), *Supplementum Chronicorum*, 11, pl. 13.
Forma Urbis. See Marble Plan.
Forsyth, Joseph (1763–1815), 19; quoted, 109.
Forum, Roman, 61, 62, 63–74, pls. 100–120.
— changes made for procession of Charles V, 9, 11, 64, 75, pls. 102, 110.
— dispute over site of, 13, 65.
— excavations in, 33–34, 65, 72, pls. 54–56.
— Zola on, 34, 74.
— Hillard on, 35.
— Propertius on, 63.
— home of the Senate, 63.
— legends set in, 63.
— deterioration of monuments in, 64.
— Cicero on, 64.
— Poggio on, 64.
— as cow pasture, (*Campo Vaccino*), 65, pls. 17, 31, 55, 116.
— swept by fire, 65.
— fifteenth-century drawing, pl. 11.
— drawing by Claude Lorrain, pl. 17.
— painting by Prout, pl. 33.
— in drawing by Heemskerck, pl. 63.
— north side, in eighteenth-century etching, pl. 99.
— photograph from Arch of Titus showing monuments in, pl. 100.
— southwest end, drawing by Heemskerck, pl. 102.
— painting by Canaletto, pl. 104.
— northwest corner, sixteenth-century etching, pl. 108.
— north side, with temples, drawing by Heemskerck, pl. 110.
— north side, drawing by Turner, pl. 112.
— Shelley on, pl. 112.
— Longfellow on, pl. 113.
— from Farnese Gardens, painting by Corot, pl. 113.
— looking east, painting by Pannini, pl. 115.
— Eleanor Clark on, pl. 117.

Forum, Roman, through Arch of Titus, drawing by Heemskerck, pl. 121.
— in relief on Arch of Constantine, pl. 126.
Forum Boarium, site of unidentified temples by Tiber, 115.
— painting by Roesler-Franz, pl. 45.
— photograph, pl. 49.
Forum Julium, 101.
Forum of Augustus, excavated, 35.
— wall of, in painting by Meyer, pl. 37.
Forum of Caesar, excavated, 35.
'Forum of Mars', 139.
Forum of Nerva, 101–102, pls. 162–165.
— excavated, 35, 102.
— Hawthorne on, pl. 164.
— ruins of, photographs, pls. 162, 165; drawing, pl. 163; etching, pl. 164.
— Colonnacce: 101, 102; photographs, pls. 162, 165; drawing, pl. 163; etching, pl. 164.
Forum of Peace, large hall of Saints Cosmas and Damian part of, 73, pls. 100, 109.
— Marble Plan attached to wall of, 73, pl. 100.
Forum of Trajan, 103–105, pls. 166–171.
— excavation of, 35, 105.
— location of, 103.
— monuments in, 103.
— ancient uses of, 103–104.
— Ammianus Marcellinus on, 104.
— Cassiodorus on, 104.
— Gregory the Great in, legend, 104.
— drawing by Dosio, pl. 167.
— Dennie on, pl. 168.
— sixteenth-century etching, pl. 171.
Forum Transitorium. See Forum of Nerva.
Fountain of Juturna, beside Temple of Vesta, 69.
France, claim of kings of, on Italian states, 9.
— occupies Rome under Napoleon, 20, 43.
— restores papal power over Rome in 1850, 32.
Francis, Saint, Upper Church of, paintings of Roman monuments in, 6, 127.
Francis I, king of France (1515–1547), 9.
Frangipani fortress incorporates Arch of Titus, 76, pl. 28.
— in painting by Turner, pl. 31.
Franzini, Giovanni Domenico (fl. first half of seventeenth century), 13.

Franzini, Girolamo (fl. second half of sixteenth century), 13.
Fredis, Felice de (fifteenth–sixteenth century), discovers Laocoön, 92.
Freeman, James E. (1808–1884), quoted, 18, 24–25, 26.
French Academy, founded, 14.
— in Villa Medici, pl. 1.
French and Italian Notebooks, Hawthorne quoted, on Tabularium, pl. 64.
— quoted, on Baths of Diocletian and Church of Santa Maria degli Angeli, 99.
— quoted, on Theatre of Marcellus, 113–114, pl. 185.
— quoted, on Pantheon, 121.
— quoted, on Marble Horses, 139.
French Revolution, 19, 20, 43.
Friedländer, Ludwig Herman (1790–1851), 20; quoted, 24, 59.
Friends of Longfellow, Society of, in Rome, pl. 123.
Frontispizio di Nerone. See Temple of the Sun or Serapis.
Fuller, Sarah Margaret (Ossoli) (1810–1850), quoted, 43–44.
Fulvio, Andrea (fl. 1510–1543), 12.

Galli, Jacopo (fifteenth–sixteenth century), pl. 12.
Galt, John (1779–1839), quoted, 17.
Garibaldi, Giuseppe (1807–1882), and Roman Republic, 32.
— defence of Rome, 44.
— quoted, on Rome, pl. 68.
Gatherings from an Artist's Portfolio, Freeman, 18, 24–25, 26.
Genealogy of the Gods, Boccaccio, quoted, 122
Gensola, La (tavern), painted by Blunck, 25, pl. 36.
Geta, Roman emperor (209–211), 69.
Ghetto, Roman, 113.
Giacomo della Porta (c. 1537–1602), 130.
Gibbon, Edward (1737–1794), conceives Decline and Fall, 14, pl. 66.
— quoted, 43
Gibson, John (1790–1866), 27.
Gifford, Sanford (1823–1880), 30.
— in painting by Healy, 30, pl. 123.
— quoted, pl. 43.
Giovanni da Udine, name inscribed in Nero's Golden House, 91, pl. 142.
— and decorations of Vatican loggie, 91, pls, 144, 145.
Girandola, la, 128, pls. 204, 205.

Giulio Romano (1499–1546). pl. 145.
Goethe, Johann Wolfgang von (1749–1832), visits to Rome, 15, 16.
— quoted, on Rome, 15–16, pls. 25, 26.
— quoted, on Colosseum, 85.
— Tischbein's portrait of, pl. 25.
— drawing of Palatine, pl. 26.
Golden House of Nero, 90–93, pls. 142–147.
— building of, 56.
— destruction of, 56, 90.
— Basilica of Constantine on site of portico of, 77.
— Suetonius on, 82–83, 90.
— Pliny on, 90.
— excavations in, 91.
— decorations of, 91.
— Charlotte Eaton on, 91–92.
— sculpture in, 92.
— entrance to, in drawing, pl. 40.
— corridors in, pls. 142, 143, 144.
— Vasari on paintings in, pls. 144, 145.
— paintings in, inspire decorations of Vatican loggie, 91, pls. 144–145.
Golden Seal of Ludwig of Bavaria, 5, pl. 6.
Goths, fight for Rome in sixth century, 2, 95–96, 126.
Gozzoli, Benozzo (1420–1497), 7, pl. 9.
Grand Tour, 17.
Graphia aureae urbis Romae, 5.
— on Palatine, 51–52.
— on colossal statue, pl. 215.
Gratian, Roman emperor (A.D. 375–383), 71.
'Greater Palace'. See Palatine Hill.
Gregorovius, Ferdinand (1821–1891), 30; Roman Journals, quoted, 33, 88.
Gregory I, the Great, pope (590–604), and recovery of Rome after Gothic Wars, 2.
— in Forum of Trajan, legend, 104.
— and Castle of Sant' Angelo, legend, 127.
— and destruction of colossal statue, 136.
Gregory XVI, pope (1831–1846), 84.
Gregory, Master (twelfth century), description of Rome, 5.
— on Temple of Minerva, 102, pl. 163.
— quoted, on colossal statue, 136.
— on statues of river gods, 137.
— on statue of Venus, 140.
— quoted, on sculpture before Pantheon, pl. 191.
Guidebooks, modern, 31, 53.

Hadrian I, pope, enlarges Santa Maria in Cosmedin, pl. 186.
Hadrian, Roman emperor (A.D. 117–138), and destruction of Nero's Golden House, 90.
— and Trajan's Forum, 103, 105.
— rebuilds Pantheon, 118.
— begins tomb, 125.
— builds bridge to Sant' Angelo, pl. 200.
— column of. See Column of Trajan.
Hadrian's Tomb, 125–128, pls. 200–205.
— alterations in, 126.
— various names of, 126–127.
— Caracalla buried in, 126.
— Procopius on, 126.
— *Mirabilia* on, 126–127.
— used as fortress by Belisarius, 126.
— in view of Rome, pl. 5.
— in Ludwig's Golden Seal, pl. 6.
— in Fazio's view of Rome, pl. 7.
— in Bartolo's view of Rome. pl. 8.
— in painting by Raphael, pl. 10.
— passage connecting with Vatican, pl. 10.
— in Poussin's painting, pl. 16.
— paintings by Corot, pls. 32, 202.
— fifteenth-century drawing, pl. 201.
Hall of Isis (under Flavian Palace), 56–57.
Handbook for Central Italy, Murray, 31; quoted, 53.
Hansen, Constantin (1804–1880), 25, pl. 36.
Hapsburg family, successors to Napoleon's power in Rome, 20.
Hapsburgs, Spanish, claim on Italian states, 9.
Hare, Augustus John (1834–1903), 31; quoted, pls. 78, 80.
Hawthorne, Nathaniel (1804–1864), influence of *Marble Faun*, 26.
— influence of Story on, 27.
— quoted, on Colosseum, 87.
— quoted, on Baths of Diocletian and Church of Santa Maria degli Angeli, 99.
— quoted, on Theatre of Marcellus, 113–114.
— quoted, on Pantheon, 121.
— quoted, on statue of Marcus Aurelius, 135.
— quoted, on Marble Horses, 139.
— quoted, on Tabularium, pl. 64.
— quoted, on Temple of Minerva and Nerva's Forum, pl. 164.
Healy, George Peter Augustus (1813–1894), 28, painting of Longfellow under Arch of Titus, 30, pl. 123.

Heemskerck, Marten van (1498–1574), sketchbook, 10.
Heemskerck, Rome as drawn by, 42, 52.
— garden of Casa Galli with Michelangelo's *Bacchus*, pl. 12.
— Capitol Hill looking north, pl. 63.
— substructures of Severus and Septizonium, pl. 77.
— statue of Marcus Aurelius beside Lateran, pl. 213.
— head of colossal statue and river gods, pl. 216.
— southwest end of Forum, pl. 102.
— Temple of Antoninus and Faustina, pl. 110.
— Arch of Titus, looking toward Forum and Capitol, pl. 121.
— Vatican Obelisk, pl. 207.
Henley, John (1692–1756), 13.
Herculaneum, 14.
Hercules Farnese, in paintings by Pannini, pls. 19, 20.
— found in Baths of Caracalla, 96, pl. 152.
— acquired by Paul III, pl. 152.
Higden, Ranaulf (d. 1364), 5, 136.
Hildebert de Lavardin (of Tours) (c. 1055–1133), 4, pl. 77.
Hillard, George Stillman (1808–1879), quoted, on writings of Charlotte Eaton, 22.
— *Six Months in Italy* discussed, 26.
— quoted, on Murray's *Handbook*, 31.
— quoted, on Roman Forum, 35.
— quoted, on ruins in Colonna Gardens, 110.
— quoted, on 'Palace of the Caesars', pls. 79, 82.
— quoted, on Castle and Bridge of Sant' Angelo and dome of St. Peter's, pl. 202.
Hippolytus (third century A.D.), legend of, 102.
Histoire romaine à Rome, Ampère, 30.
Historiarum ab inclinato Romano Imperio Decades III, Biondo, 8, 12.
History of the City of Rome in the Middle Ages, Gregorovius, 30, 33.
History of the Decline and Fall of the Roman Empire, Gibbon, 14, pl. 66.
— quoted, 43.
History of the Wars, Procopius, quoted on roof of Jupiter's temple, 38.
— quoted on Hadrian's Tomb, 126.
Hodgkin, Thomas (1831–1913), *Italy and Her Invaders*, 30–31.

Holy Roman Empire, beginning of, 2.
— as continuation of imperial Rome, 8.
— ended by Napoleon, 20.
Honorius, Roman emperor (A.D. 393–423), Claudian's welcoming poem to, 50.
— restores Porta San Sebastiano, pl. 51.
Hörny, Franz (1798–1824), 23.
Horse Tamers. See Marble Horses.
Hosmer, Harriet (1830–1908), 27.
Hotson, Leslie (1897–), pl. 208.
House of Crescentius, 116–117, pls. 188–189.
— inscription on, 116.
— used in Passion plays, 117, pl. 189.
— photographs of, pls. 46, 50.
— drawing by Coello, pl. 189.
'House of Pilate'. See House of Crescentius.
'House of Rienzi'. See House of Crescentius.
House of the Vestals, 56, 68, pls. 89, 90.
Hudson River School, 28, 29–30.
Huntington, Daniel (1816–1906), 28.

Improvisatore, The, Andersen, 25.
Inness, George (1825–1894), 29, 30, pl. 44.
Insula. See apartment houses.
Irving, Washington (1783–1859), friendship with Allston, 18.
— notebooks, 18–19.
Italian Journey, Goethe, 16, 25.
Italy, history of. See Chronological list.
Italy, Rogers, 23.
Izard, Ralph (1741/2–1804), 17, pl. 27.

Jackson, Helen Hunt (Mrs. Edward Hunt; 1830–1885), quoted, 60.
James, Henry (1843–1916), 2.
— quoted, on 'golden air' of Rome, 2, 28.
— quoted, on Roman Campagna, 29, pl. 44.
— quoted, on Colosseum, 87.
Janiculum, in view of Rome, pl. 5.
— Martial on, 125.
Jerusalem, capture by Titus, 75.
— sacked by Persians, pl. 122.
Journal, Goethe, quoted, pl. 25.
Journal, Lady Blessington, quoted, 56.
Journal, Gibbon, quoted, 43.
Journal, Gregorovius, quoted, 33, 88.
Journal d'Italie, Stendhal, 20.

Journal of a Classical Tour through Italy, Eustace, 19.
Journal of a Tour in Italy, Dwight, 25–26; quoted, 59, 78–79.
Julia Domna, Roman empress (d. A.D. 217), 107.
Julia Maesa (d. A.D. 223), 107–108.
Julia Soamias (d. A.D. 222), 108.
Julian the Apostate, Roman emperor (A.D. 361–363), restores Altar of Victory, 71.
— Faunus and, legend, 115.
— quoted, pl. 221.
— Ammianus Marcellinus on, pl. 221.
— *Mirabilia* on, pl. 221.
Julius II, pope (1503–1513), 9, 92–93, 130.
Jupiter, speaks to Numa, 51.
Justinian I, the Great, Byzantine emperor (527–565), reconquers Italy, 2, 62.
— reduces Rome to dependency of East, 62.
— and spoils from Temple of Jerusalem, pl. 122.
Juvenal (active A.D. c. 96–after 127), *Satires;* quoted, 47, 48.

Keats, John (1795–1821), 20, 21, pl. 199.
Keats-Shelley Association, pl. 199.
Keats-Shelley Memorial, 21.
Knights of Malta, Priory of, pls. 166, 169.
Koch, Joseph Anton (1768–1839), 23–24, pl. 34.
Kotzebue, August von (1761–1818), 20.
Kuchler, Albert (1803–1845), pl. 36.

Lactantius Firmianus (A.D. c. 247–after 317), quoted, 133.
Lafreri, Antonio (1512–1577), *Speculum Romanae Magnificentiae*, 12; map from, 12, pl. 14; engravings from, pls. 204, 208, 209, 214, 220, 222.
Lament for Rome, Alcuin, quoted, 3.
Lament for Rome, Hildebert, quoted, 4.
Lanciani, Rodolfo (1847–1929), takes over excavations in Rome, 34.
— quoted, on Villa Palatina, 55–56.
— on Bronze Boxer, 111, pl. 181.
— on substructures of Severus as haylofts, pl. 52.
— on ruins of Domitian's residential palace, pl. 86.
— on roof of Basilica of Constantine or Maxentius, pl. 129.

Laocoön, discovery in Nero's Golden House, 92–93, pl. 146.
— Pliny on, 92.
— Goethe's essay on, 93.
— Michelangelo on, 93.
— Napoleon and, 93.
— poem by Sadoleto on, 93.
— in painting by Pannini, pl. 20.
— restored, photograph, pl. 146.
— before restoration, engraving, pl. 147.
Laokoön, Lessing, 14, 93.
Lateran Palace, site of statue of Marcus Aurelius, 133–134, 135.
— colossal head and hand found near, 135.
— in views of Rome, pls. 5, 7, 212, 213.
— in drawing by Heemskerck, pl. 213.
Latin language, oldest monument of, in Forum, pl. 107.
Lays of Ancient Rome, Macaulay, quoted, on Temple of Vesta, 69.
Leo I, the Great, pope (440–461), quoted, 46.
Leo X, Medici, pope (1513–1521), 8, 9, pl. 10.
Leo XII, pope (1823–1829), builds buttresses for Colosseum, 84, pls. 132, 135.
Lessing, Gotthold Ephraim (1729–1781), 14, 93.
Life, Studies, and Works of Benjamin West, Galt, quoted, 17.
Ligorio, Pirro (1510–1583), 65.
Limbourg, Pol de (fourteenth-fifteenth century), view of Rome in Hours of Duc de Berry, 6, 7, Fig. 2.
Liszt, Franz (1811–1886), pl. 160.
Lives of the Most Eminent Painters, Sculptors, and Architects, Vasari, quoted, pls. 144, 145.
Livia, wife of Augustus (58 B.C.–A.D. 29), 57.
Livy (c. 59 B.C.–A.D. 17), version of Marcus Curtius legend quoted, 61.
— on founding of Temple of Castor, pl. 103.
Lombardi, Carlo (1554–1620), pl. 117.
Longfellow, Henry Wadsworth (1807–1882), 26.
— notebooks, 26.
— sketches, 26, pls. 39, 40.
— painted by Healy beneath Arch of Titus, 30, pl. 123.
— quoted, on flowers in Colosseum, 87–88.
— quoted, on Forum, pl. 113.
— reputation in Europe, according to Lowell, pl. 123.

Longfellow, Society of Friends of, Rome, pl. 123.
Longhi, Martino, the Elder (d. 1591), pl. 65.
Louis I, king of Bavaria (1768–1868), quoted, 34.
Louis XIV, king of France (1643–1715), founds French Academy in Rome, 14.
Lowell, James Russell (1819–1891), quoted, on Longfellow's reputation, pl. 123.
Ludwig of Bavaria, Holy Roman emperor (1328–1347), Golden Seal of, 5, 6, pl. 6.
Lungotevere Aventino, pl. 49.

Macaulay, Thomas Babington (1800–1859), quoted, 69.
Maderna, Carlo (1556–1629), 131, pl. 206.
Magnana family, 55.
Mamertine Prison, Church of San Giuseppe de' Falegnami erected over, 139, pl. 55.
Mander, Carel van (1548)–1606), quoted, 10.
Marble Faun, Hawthorne, 26.
— importance of, 26.
— quoted, on Colosseum, 87.
— quoted, on statue of Marcus Aurelius, 135.
— — on Temple of Minerva and Nerva's Forum, pl. 164.
Marble Horses or Horse Tamers, *Mirabilia* on, 137, 138.
— stand on Quirinal, 137.
— many names for, 137–138, 139.
— Master Gregory on, 138.
— Hawthorne on, 139.
— in Fazio's view of Rome, pl. 7.
— in Bartolo's view of Rome, pl. 8.
— photograph, pl. 219.
— sixteenth-century engraving, pls. 2, 20.
Marble Plan of Rome, significance of, 1.
— fragments attached to wall in Forum of Peace, 73, pls. 100, 109.
— fragment showing temple of Minerva, pl. 3.
— reproduction in Courtyard of Conservatori Museum, pl. 4.
Marcellus, M. Claudius (c.43 B.C.–23 B.C.), 112.
Marcus Aurelius Antoninus, Roman emperor (A.D. 161–180), and Temple of Antoninus and Faustina, 72.
— and Trajan's Forum, 103.
— in reliefs, pls. 2, 61.
— imitates Trajan.s column, 106.
— column of, in medieval view of Rome, pls. 5, 7, 8, 212.

Marcus Aurelius Antoninus, column, in drawing by Heemskerck, pl. 110.
— equestrian statue of, as centre of Rome's birthday celebrations, 45, 69.
— — identity of, 133–134.
— — position near Lateran, 133.
— — Wace on, 134.
— — *Mirabilia* on, 134–135.
— — popular beliefs concerning, 135.
— — moved to Capitol Piazza, 135.
— — Hawthorne on, 135.
— — in manuscript view of Rome, pl. 5.
— — in Fazio's view of Rome, pl. 7.
— in Bartolo's view of Rome, pl. 8.
— in Hours of Duc de Berry, Fig. 2.
— — in painting by Robert, pl. 22.
— — in drawing by Robert, pl. 66.
— — in sixteenth-century drawing, pl. 71.
— — in Capitol piazza, photograph, pl. 211.
— — beside Lateran, drawing by Heemskerck, pl. 213.
— — in Capitol piazza, in sixteenth-century engraving, pl. 214.
— described by Hawthorne, 135.
Marcus Curtius, legend of, 61, 63.
Marforio (river god), colossal statue, moving of, 139–140.
— *Mirabilia* on, 139.
— in Capitoline Museum, photograph, pl. 221.
— in Via di Marforio, sixteenth-century engraving, pl. 222.
Marliani, Giovanni Bartolommeo (c. 1490–c. 1560), 12–13.
Marrana (brook), 96, pls. 7, 8.
Marstrand, Wilhelm (1810–1873), 25, pl. 38.
Martial (A.D. c. 40–c. 104), *Epigrams*, quoted, on Colosseum, 80, 90.
— quoted, on Janiculum, 125.
— quoted, on Nero's Colossus, 135.
Martin V, Colonna, pope (1417–1431), 109.
Marvels of Rome, Nichols, 13.
Mattei family, Villa Palatina begun by, 55, pl. 86.
Mausoleum of Augustus, no longer concert hall, 35.
Maxentius, Roman emperor (A.D. 306–312), begins basilica, 77.
— defeat by Constantine, pl. 15.

Maxentius, death, pl. 15.
Mazzini, Giuseppe (1805–1872), 32.
McCormick, Anne O'Hare (1882–1954), quoted, pl. 196.
McEntee, Jervis (1828–1901), pl. 123.
Medici, Giuliano de', duke of Nemours (1479–1516), pl. 10.
Mérimée, Prosper (1803–1870), 141.
Meta Sudans, on sestertius of Titus, Fig. 1.
— site of, pls. 124, 132.
— remains of, in sixteenth-century etching, pl. 125.
— in fifteenth-century drawing, pl. 133.
Meyer, Ernest (1797–1861), 25, 31.
— in painting, pl. 36.
— painting by, pl. 37.
Michael (Archangel), and Castle of Sant' Angelo, 127.
Michelangelo Buonarroti (1475–1564), ceiling of Sistine Chapel, 8.
— *The Last Judgement*, 10.
— remodels central hall of Baths of Diocletian as Church of Santa Maria degli Angeli, 12, 99, pls. 157, 158.
— and Senator's Palace, 42.
— on Laocoön, 93.
— and *la girandola*, 128.
— put in charge of plans for St. Peter's, 130.
— directs moving of statue of Marcus Aurelius, 135.
— *Bacchus*, in sixteenth-century drawing, pl. 12.
— new dome for St. Peter's, on map, pl. 14.
— — in sixteenth-century engraving, pl. 209.
Milizie Palace, in view of Rome, pl. 5.
Milizie Tower. See Tower of the Milizie.
Mills, Charles Andrew (d. 1846), builds Gothic façade on Villa Palatina, on site of Domitian's residential palace, 55, pl. 86.
— buried in Protestant Cemetery, 124.
Milvian Bridge. See Ponte Molle.
Minerva, statue of, as Roma, before Senator's Palace, photograph, pl. 217.
Mirabilia Romae, described, 4.
— printed, 12.
— excerpts in Montfaucon's diary, 13.
— quoted, on Capitol, 40.
— quoted, on vision of Augustus, 46.

Mirabilia Romae, on Palatine, 52.
— on site of Old Saint Mary's church, 61.
— on Temple of Saturn as Senate treasury, 65.
— on church of Saints Cosmas and Damian, 72.
— on triumphal arches, 75.
— on Arch of Titus, 75.
— on Arch of Constantine, 76.
— on Colosseum, 82.
— on baths, 96.
— Baths of Diocletian, 98.
— on Forum of Nerva, 102.
— on Column of Trajan, 105.
— on Temple of the Sun or Serapis, 108.
— on Rome, 111.
— on legend of Faunus, 115.
— on Pantheon, 119–120.
— on Hadrian's Tomb, 126–217.
— on Vatican Obelisk, 129–130.
— on statue of Marcus Aurelius, 134–135.
— on colossal statue, 136.
— on statues of river gods, 137.
— on Marble Horses, 137, 138.
— on statue of Marforio, 139.
— on Julian the Apostate, pl. 221.
Mirri, Ludovico (1747–1824), 91.
Mithraism, pl. 127.
Mommsen, Theodor (1817–1903), 30.
Mons Aventinus. See Aventine Hill.
Montaigne, Michel de (1533–1592), quoted, 10–11.
Monte Cavallo, 138.
Monte Cavo, in painting by Tischbein, pl. 25.
— in painting by Severn, pl. 29.
— in painting by Inness, pl. 44.
Monte Testaccio, 117.
Montfaucon, Bernard de (1655–1741), 13; quoted, 58.
Morris, William (1834–1896), 141.
Morse, Samuel F. B. (1791–1872), 28.
Muirhead Fundlay (1860–1935), 31, quoted; 104–105.
Murray, John (1808–1892), 31; quoted, 53.
Museo Mussolini. See Museo Nuovo; Caffarelli Palace.
Museo Nuovo, transformed from Caffarelli Palace, 39.
— in aeroplane view, pl. 57.
Mussolini, Benito (1883–1945), excavations during government of, 34, 46.

Napoleon Bonaparte (1769–1821), and end of Holy Roman Empire, 20.
— incorporates Rome with France, 20.

Napoleon Bonaparte, takes sculptures from Italy, 93.
Napoleon III (1808–1873), buys Farnese Gardens, 34, 59–60.
— excavations of, pls. 56, 95.
Napoleonic Wars, 19, 20.
Nash, Ogden (1902–), 141.
National Museum. See Terme Museum.
Nazarenes (group of German artists), 24–25, pl. 35.
Neptune, in legend of Pantheon, 119.
Nero, Roman emperor (A.D. 54–68), Domus Transitoria of, 56, 57.
— lake drained for site of Colosseum, 80, 90.
— colossal statue of. See Colossus of Nero.
— Cryptoporticus of. See Cryptoporticus of Nero.
— Golden House of. See Golden House of Nero.
Nerva, Roman emperor (A.D. 96–98). See Forum of Nerva.
New Basilica. See Basilica of Constantine or Maxentius.
New Museum. See Museo Nuovo.
Nibby, Antonio (1792–1839), 34.
Nicholas V, pope (1447–1455), plan to rebuild Old Saint Peter's, 130.
Nichols, Francis Morgan (1826–1915), 13.
Niebuhr, Barthold Georg (1776–1831), 30; quoted, 113.
Nile, possibly represented by statue of river god, 137.
'Noah's Ark', arch or temple in Forum of Nerva, pl. 163.
Notitia, 1, 8, pl. 3.
Numa, king of Rome (trad. date 715–673 B.C.), 51.

Oceanus, in relief from Arch of Constantine, pl. 127.
Octavius. See Augustus.
October Festival, Marstrand, 25, pl. 38.
Odoacer (c. 434–493), 2.
Olivier, Friedrich (1791–1859), 24, pl. 136.
One Touch of Venus, Nash and Perelman, 141.
Opusculum de Mirabilibus novae et veteris urbis Romae, Albertini, cited, pl. 77.
Orestes and Electra, in painting by Copley, pl. 27.
Orpheus and Eurydice, Poussin, pl. 16.
Outre-Mer, Longfellow, 26; quoted, pl. 113.
Overbeck, Friedrich (1798–1869), 24, pl. 35.
Ovid (43 B.C.–A.D. c. 18), Fasti, quoted, 45, 67.

Page, William (1811–1885), 28.
'Palace of Nero'. See Lateran Palace.
'Palace of the Caesars' (vague term for monuments on Palatine), meaning of, 52.
— Charlotte Eaton on, 53.
— Frances Appleton on, 54.
— etching by Koch, pl. 34.
— Hillard on, pls. 79, 82.
Palace of the Conservators. See Conservators' Palace.
Palace of the Popes, in Gozzoli's panoramic view, pl. 9.
Palace of Tiberius, location of, 51.
— description of, 57–58.
— in aeroplane view, pl. 74.
— Farnese Gardens laid out above, 58, pls. 87, 93.
— excavated substructures of, photographs, pls. 94, 96, 98.
— substructures, painting by Pinelli, pl. 95.
— substructures, eighteenth-century etching, pl. 99.
'Palace of Titus' (Baths of Trajan) above Nero's Golden House, 91.
Palatine, 49–62, pls. 74–99.
— Andersen on, 25.
— excavations on, 34, 54, 56, 58, 60, pl. 56.
— residence of Cicero and Catiline, 49.
— birthplace of Augustus, 49.
— fortified by Romulus, 49.
— palaces of, 49–51.
— residence of Narses, 50.
— appearance today compared with past, 50.
— temples of, 51.
— Byron on, 53.
— in view of Rome, pl. 5.
— drawing by Goethe, pl. 26.
— etching by Koch, pl. 34.
— aeroplane view showing monuments on, pl. 74.
— — sixteenth-century etching, pl. 76.
Palatine Museum, 55, pls. 74, 85, 86.
Palatium, ancient name of Palatine, q.v.
'Palazzo Maggiore' (vague term for ruins on Palatine) 51–52.
Palazzo Pubblico (Siena), view of Rome in, by Bartolo, 6–7.
Palazzo Venezia, 35.
Palladium, 67.
Palmyra, Temple of the Sun at, 108.
Pannini, Francesco (eighteenth century), engraving after, pls. 90, 178.
Pannini, Giovanni Paolo (1691 or 1692–1765), 15.

Pannini, Giovanni Paolo, Landscape with Roman Ruins, pl. 19.
— Gallery of Views of Ancient Rome, pl. 20.
— Roman Forum Looking East, pl. 115.
— Interior of Pantheon, pl. 195.
Pantheon, 118–121, pls. 190–195.
— Hawthorne on, 26, 118, 121.
— burned, 118.
— rebuilt by Hadrian, 118.
— dedicated Church of Sancta Maria ad Martyres, 119.
— as Church of Santa Maria Rotonda, 119.
— repaired by Septimius Severus, 119.
— stripped of marble and metal, 119.
— Mirabilia on, 119–120.
— burial place of Raphael, 120.
— Byron on, 120.
— Shelley on, 120–121.
— in view of Rome, pl. 5.
— in Ludwig's Golden Seal, pl. 6.
— in Fazio's view, pl. 7.
— in Bartolo's view, pl. 8.
— in Gozzoli's panoramic view, pl. 9.
— inscription on, pl. 190.
— Master Gregory on sculpture before, pl. 191.
— side view, sixteenth-century etching, pl. 191.
— with Bernini's towers, photograph, pl. 192.
— Eleanor Clark on cats around, pl. 192.
— interior, etching by Piranesi, pl. 194.
— painting by Pannini, pl. 195.
Parisio, Prospero (fl. first half of sixteenth century), 13.
— illustrated guide of 13.
Parma, dukes of, excavations by, 56, 58.
Pasquino (statue), mentioned, 140 pl. 222.
Paul III, Alessandro Farnese, pope (1534–1549), 9, 58, 83, pl. 66.
Paul V, pope (1605–1621), demolishes ruins of Temple of Minerva, 102.
— changes St. Peter's, 131.
Paul, Saint (d. A.D. 67?), statue of, on column of Marcus Aurelius, 106.
Paulinus the Minorite (Paolino; d. 1344), 5, pl. 5.
Peacock, Thomas Love (1785–1866), letter of Shelley to, quoted, on Pantheon, 120–121.
— on Baths of Caracalla, pls. 30, 153.

Peacock, Thomas Love, on Forum, pl. 112.
Peale, Rembrandt (1778–1860), quoted, pl. 136.
Perelman, Sidney J. (1904–), 141.
Peruzzi, Baldassare (1481–1536), 113.
Peter, St. (d. A.D. 67?), death and burial of, 129.
— statue placed on Column of Trajan, 106.
— See also St. Peter's basilica and church.
Petrarch (Francesco Petrarca; 1304–1374), quoted, 6, 8, 98.
— crowned in Senator's Palace, 41.
— refers to Pyramid of Cestius as 'Tomb of Remus', 122.
Pforr, Franz (1788–1812), 24.
Phocas I, Byzantine emperor (602–610), gives Pantheon to Church, 120.
— See also Column of Phocas.
Piazza dell'Esedra, before Baths of Diocletian, 100.
Piazza del Popolo, obelisk placed in, by Sixtus V, pl. 76.
Pierleoni family, fortify Theatre of Marcellus, 113.
Pifferari, pl. 184.
Pincian Hill, Villa Medici on, pl. 1.
Pinelli, Bartolommeo (1781–1835), painting of substructures of Palace of Tiberius, pl. 95.
— pifferari before shrine at Theatre of Marcellus, etching, pl. 184.
Piranesi, Giovanni Battista (1720–1778), 16.
— The Pyramid of Cestius, etching, pl. 23.
— Ruins in Colonna Gardens, etching, pl. 24.
— Interior of the Colosseum, etching, pl. 138.
— Ruins of Forum of Nerva, etching, pl. 164.
— Interior of Pantheon, etching, pl. 194.
Pius IV, pope (1559–1565), 99.
Pius VII, pope (1800–1823), and Colosseum, 84.
Pius IX, pope (1846–1878), and Colosseum, 84.
Pius XII (Eugenio Pacelli; 1876–), pl. 210.
Platt, Charles (1861–1933), quoted, on Colonna Gardens, 110.
Pliny the Elder (A.D. c. 23–A.D. 79), Natural History on Basilica Aemilia, 71.
— on Nero's Golden House, 90.
— on Laocoön, 92.
— on statue of Venus in Pantheon, 118.

Plutarch (A.D. 46–after 120), Lives quoted, on temples of Jupiter on Capitol, pl. 60.
— on Temple of Vesta, 67.
Poggio Bracciolini (1380–1459), books on Roman monuments, 8.
— quoted, on Capitol, 42.
— quoted, on Forum, 64.
— on identification of Pyramid of Cestius, 122.
Polychronicon, Higden, Master Gregory source for, 5.
— on colossal statue, 136.
Pompeii, excavations at, 14.
Pons Aelius (Bridge of Sant. Angelo), pl. 200.
Pons Aemilius (Bridge of Santa Maria), pl. 8.
Ponte Molle (Pons Milvius), drawing of, pl. 15.
— resemblance of bridge in Poussin painting to, pl. 16.
Ponte Rotto, pl. 50.
Pontifex Maximus, residence of. See Regia.
Porta Appia. See Porta San Sebastiano, pl. 51.
Porta Ostiensis. See Porta San Paolo.
Porta San Paolo, Pyramid of Cestius near, 122.
— in view of Rome, pl. 5.
— in etchings by Piranesi, pl. 23.
— photograph, pl. 196.
— drawing by Ammanati, pl. 197.
Porta San Sebastiano, photographs, pls. 8, 51.
Portico of Octavia, painting by Bierstadt, 30, pl. 47.
— as fish market, Story on, pl. 47.
— — Ampère on, pl. 48.
— photograph, pl. 48.
Portunus, guardian of Tiber port, 115.
Poussin, Nicolas (1593 or 1594–1665), 14, pls. 15, 16.
Prints, introduction in fifteenth century, 11.
Procopius (sixth century A.D.), quoted, 38, 126.
Promenades dans Rome, Stendhal, 20.
Propertius (active 29 B.C.–c. 15 B.C.), Elegies, 51, quoted, 63.
Protestant Cemetery, 21.
— location near Pyramid of Cestius, 123.
— Keats buried in, 21, 123.
— Shelley buried in, 21, 123–124.
— Severn buried in, 123.
— Shelley on, 123–124, pl. 198.
— Mills buried in, 124.
— grave of Shelley, engraving, pl. 198.
— painting by Cole, pl. 199.
— Taylor on, pl. 199.

Prout, Samuel (1783–1852), 23, Arch of Constantine, Frontispiece.
— View in the Forum. pl. 33.
Public Letter Writer, Meyer, 25, pl. 37.
Puccini, Giacomo (1858–1924), pl. 156.
Pyramid of Cestius, 122–124, pls. 196–199.
— described by Shelley, 21.
— Boccaccio on, 122.
— Petrarch on, 122.
— called 'Tomb of Remus', 122.
— inscription on, 122.
— in views of Rome, pls. 5, 7, 8.
— in Ludwig's Golden Seal, pl. 6.
— in painting by Pannini, pl. 19.
— etching by Piranesi, pl. 23.
— photograph, pl. 196.
— drawing by Ammanati, pl. 197.
— in engraving, pl. 198.
— in painting by Cole, pl. 199.
— Taylor on, pl. 199.

Quirinal, Temple of the Sun or Serapis on, 107–109, pls. 174, 179.
— Marble Horses on, 137, pls. 7, 8, 13, 219.
— statues of river gods on, 137, pl. 13.
— ruins on, in drawing by Heemskerck, 110.

Rainaldi, Carlo (1611–1691), pl. 90.
Rancoureuil, Abbé (eighteenth century), 55.
Raphael (Raffaele Sanzio; 1483–1520), frescoes of Vatican apartments, 8, 13.
— architect of St. Peter's, 9.
— painting by, pl. 10.
— decorations of Vatican loggie, inspired by those in Nero's Golden House, pl. 142.
— buried in Pantheon, 120.
Raymond, John (seventeenth century), on Forum, 65.
Recke, Elisa von der (1754–1833), 20.
Regia, site of, pls. 98, 117, 118.
Regio Transtiberina, 125.
Rehbenitz, Theodor (1791–1861), in drawing by Fohr, pl. 35.
Remarks on Antiquities, Arts, and Letters During an Excursion in Italy, Forsyth, 19; quoted, 109.
Remus, co-founder of Rome, pl. 49, see also Pyramid of Cestius.
Richter, Ludwig (1803–1884), 24.
Rienzi, Cola di (c. 1313–1354), revolution, 5, 41.
— statue of, 39.
Rinehart, William H. (1825–1874), 27.

Rinehart scholarships, 27.
Ring Given to Venus, Morris, 141.
River gods, colossal statues of, on Quirinal, 137.
— moved to Capitol piazza, 137.
— *Mirabilia* on, 137.
— Master Gregory on, 137.
— in *Supplementum Chronicorum*, pl. 13.
— beside staircase of Senator's Palace, in sixteenth-century engraving, pl. 214.
— in drawing by Heemskerck, pl. 216.
— beside staircase of Senator's Palace, photograph, pl. 217.
— in front of Conservators' Palace, drawing by Heemskerck, pl. 218.
Roba di Roma, Story, 26, 27–28.
— quoted, on Claudian Aqueduct, 29.
— quoted, on changing Rome, 31–32.
— quoted, on public letter writer, pl. 37.
— quoted, on October Festivals, pl. 38.
— quoted, on fish market in Portico of Octavia, pl. 47.
— quoted, on *pifferari*, pl. 184.
Robert, King of Naples (1309–1343), defeat of, pl. 51.
Robert I, duke of Normandy (d. 1035), 134.
Robert, Hubert (1733–1808), painter of ruins, 15.
— sketches Capitol piazza, 42–43, pl. 66.
— *Arches of the Colosseum*, pl. 21.
— *Portico with Statue of Marcus Aurelius*, pl. 22.
— *The Capitol Piazza*, pl. 66.
Roesler-Franz, Ettore (1845–1907), 31, 33, pl. 45.
Rogers, Samuel (1763–1855), 23.
Roma Instaurata, Biondo, 8.
Roma Triuumphans, Biondo, 8.
Roman Aqueduct, Cole, 29, pl. 43.
Roman Antiquities, Dionysius of Halicarnassus, quoted, on legend of Castor and Pollux, 68–69.
— quoted, on Tarquin's Temple of Jupiter, pl. 58.
Roman de Rou, quoted, 134.
Roman Elegies, Goethe, 16.
'Roman fever', 84–85.
Roman History, Dio Cassius, quoted, 118.
Roman History, Livy, on founding of Temple of Castor, pl. 103.
— quoted on Marcus Curtius, 61.
Roman Senate. See Senate.
Roman Journals, Gregorovius, 33, quoted, 88.

Rome, birthday of, 45, pl. 69.
— history of. See Chronological List.
— Holy Year of Jubilee, pls. 62, 210.
— Pilgrimage Centre, 2, 131, pls. 62, 210.
Rome, Zola, quoted, 34, 74.
Rome and a Villa, Clark, quoted, pls. 117, 192.
Rome in Midsummer, Longfellow, 26; quoted, pl. 113.
Rome in the Nineteenth Century, Eaton, 22.
— quoted, on Palatine, 53.
— on Baths of Livia, 57.
— on Farnese Gardens, 59.
— on Nero's Golden House, 91–92.
— on Baths of Caracalla, 96–97.
— on ruins in the Colonna Gardens, 109–110, pl. 179.
Rome, Naples, and Florence, Stendhal, 20.
Rome of Today and Yesterday, Dennie, quoted, pl. 169.
Romulus, founder of Rome (trad. date, eighth century B.C.), and Asylum, 37, 49, 63, pl. 57.
— vestibule of Saints Cosmas and Damian associated with, 72.
— victory over Sabines, pl. 103.
— and Remus Suckled by the Wolf (statue), 49, 140.
Romulus Augustulus, last Roman emperor (A.D. 475–476), 72.
Rosa, Pietro (1815–1891), directs excavations in Roman Forum, 34.
— in charge of excavating Farnese gardens, 59.
— excavates *Clivus Victoriae*, 60.
— weeds Colosseum, 88.
Rottmann, Karl (1797–1830), 24.
Round Saint Stephen's, in Temple of Vesta, Forum Boarium, 115, pl. 8.
Rousseau, Jean-Jacques (1712–1778), 19.
Rubens, Peter Paul (1577–1640), 13–14.
Ruins and Excavations of Ancient Rome, Lanciani, quoted, 55–56, pls. 52, 86.
Rutilius Namatianus, Gallo-Roman (third–fourth century A.D.), *Voyage Home from Gaul*, quoted, 2.

Sabina, Saint (first–second century A.D.), story of, pl. 18.
Sabine Hills, in painting by Cole, pl. 43.
— in etching by Vasi, pl. 116.
Sabine women, 63.

Sacred Steps, in medieval manuscript, pl. 212.
— in drawing by Heemskerck, pl. 213.
Sacred Way, spanned by Arch of Titus, 73, 75.
— in photograph, pls. 100, 111, 119.
— in drawing by Turner, pls. 111, 112.
Sadoleto, Jacopo, cardinal (1477–1547), quoted, 93.
Saint Mary in the Capitol, Church of. See Santa Maria in Aracoeli, Church of.
Saint Peter's, old basilica of, plundered by Saracens, 3.
— in view of Rome, pl. 5.
— in Ludwig's Golden Seal, pl. 6.
— in Fazio's view of Rome, pl. 7.
— in Bartolo's view of Rome, pl. 8.
— in Gozzoli's panoramic view, pl. 9.
— in *Supplementum Chronicorum*, pl. 13.
St. Peter's, present church of, conceived by Nicholas V, 130.
— begun by Julius II, 130.
— Bramante as architect, 130.
— Raphael changes design, 130.
— Michelangelo put in charge, 130.
— façade designed by Maderna, 131.
— dedicated by Urban VIII, 131.
— Ampère on dome of, 131.
— dome, in drawing by Vedder, pl. 154.
— dome, in painting by Corot, pl. 202.
— Hillard on, pl. 202.
— dome unfinished, in sixteenth-century engravings, pls. 14, 208, 209.
'St. Peter's needle'. See Vatican Obelisk.
St. Peter's Piazza, designed by Bernini, 131.
— photographs, pls. 206, 210.
Salita delle Tre Pile, aeroplane view, pl. 57.
— fragment of Jupiter's temple beside, pl. 60.
San Bonaventura, Convent of, aeroplane view, pl. 74.
Sangallo family, 12.
San Gregorio, monks of, and substructures of Severus, pl. 52.
San Paolo, Gate of. See Porta San Paolo.
San Sebastiano, Convent of, in aeroplane view, pl. 74.
Sant' Isidoro, monastery of, dwelling of Nazarenes, 24.
Savelli family, palace in Theatre of Marcellus, 113, pl. 183.

Schadow, Rudolph von (1786–1822), 24.

Schadow, Wilhelm von (1788–1862), 24.

Schaller, Johann (1777–1842), pl. 35.

Schnorr von Carolsfeld, Julius (1794–1872), 24.

Scott, William Bell (1811–1890), engraving after, pl. 198.

Sebastiani, Antonio (1782–1821), 87.

Senate House, consecrated to Victory, 63.

— new, begun by Caesar, 70, pl. 107.

— finished by Augustus, 70, pl. 107.

— rebuilt by Diocletian and Domitian, 70, pl. 107.

— struggle over Altar of Victory in, 71.

— becomes Church of Sant' Adriano, 71, pl. 107.

— restored in 1935, pl. 107.

— in photograph of Forum, pl. 100.

— Church of Saints Martina and Luca built into ruins of annex to, pl. 100.

— in sixteenth-century etching, pl. 108.

Senate, Roman, re-established in Middle Ages, 4, 40, 42.

— erects Arch of Severus, 69.

— erects temple to Faustina, 72.

— resolves to preserve Trajans' Column, 105.

Senator's Palace, called Capitol in Middle Ages, 40, 41.

— poets crowned in, 40.

— built in Middle Ages, 42.

— today, 44–45.

— in view of Rome, pl. 5.

— in Ludwig's Golden Seal, pl. 6.

— in painting by Bartolo, pl. 8.

— in painting by Prout, pl. 33.

— aeroplane view, pl. 57.

— in fourteenth-century manuscript, pl. 62.

— medieval tower replaced by Longhi's, pl. 65.

— in drawings by Heemskerck, pls. 63, 102.

— in sixteenth-century etching, pl. 65.

— in drawing by Robert, pl. 66.

— sixteenth-century drawing, pl. 71.

— in painting by Canaletto, pl. 104.

Septimius Severus, Roman emperor (A.D. 193–211), 50.

— and substructures on Palatine, 50–51.

— and restoration of Temple of Vespasian, 66.

Septimius Severus, wife reconstructs Temple of Vesta, 68, pl. 106.

— attaches Marble Plan in Forum of Peace, 73, pls. 3, 4.

— fire in reign of, pl. 47.

— substructures of. See Substructures of Severus.

— See also Baths of Severus.

Septizonium, 52, pl. 77.

Serapia, Santa (first–second century A.D.), pl. 18.

Serlio, Sebastiano (1475–1554), pl. 77.

Sestertii, of Vespasian, of Trajan, of Titus, Fig. 1.

Seven Hills of Rome, 125, note to 125.

Seven Wonders of the World, 40.

Severn, Joseph (1793–1879), painting of Shelley, pl. 29.

Severus, Roman emperor. See Septimius Severus.

Shakespeare, quoted, pl. 208.

Shelley, Mary Wollstonecraft (1797–1851), quoted, 21.

Shelley, Percy Bysshe (1792–1822), The Cenci, 21.

— Adonais, 21.

— Prometheus Unbound, 21.

— Keats-Shelley Memorial, 21.

— quoted, on Baths of Caracalla, 97, pls. 30, 153.

— quoted on Pantheon, 120–121.

— quoted, on Protestant Cemetery, 123–124, pl. 198.

— painting of, by Severn, pl. 29.

— grave of, engraving, pl. 198.

— quoted, on Forum, pl. 112.

Sidonius Apollinaris (fifth century A.D.), Letters, quoted, 131–132.

Sistine Chapel, 8 10.

Six Months in Italy, Hillard, 26.

— quoted on Charlotte Eaton, 22.

— on Murray's Handbook, 31.

— on Forum, 35.

— on ruins in Colonna Gardens, 110.

— on 'Palace of the Caesars', pls. 79, 82.

— on Castle and Bridge of Sant' Angelo and dome of St. Peter's, pl. 202.

Sixtus V, pope (1585–1590), and destruction of Septizonium, 52, pl. 77.

— and Colosseum, 84.

— has Vatican Obelisk moved to present position, 130.

— moves Marble Horses, 138.

— excavates obelisks in Circus Maximus, pl. 76.

Smollett, Tobias George (1721–1771), quoted, on Piranesi, 16.

Sol Invictus, pl. 127.

Solinus (third century A.D.?), 6, pl. 7.

Sønne, Jorgen (1801–1890), 25, pl. 36.

Sosius, C. (first century B.C.), pl. 182.

Spada family, 55.

Spanish Steps, Keats-Shelley Memorial by, 21.

Speculum Romanae Magnificentiae, Lafreri, discussed, 12.

— map of Rome, pl. 14.

— La Girandola, engraving, pl. 204.

— moving of Vatican Obelisk, engraving, pl. 208.

— old St. Peter's, engraving, pl. 209.

— statue of Marcus Aurelius in Capitol Piazza, engraving, pl. 214.

— Horse Tamers, engraving, pl. 220.

— Marforio in Via di Marforio, engraving, pl. 222.

Spenser, Edmund (1552?–1599), Ruines of Rome, translation of du Bellay quoted, 10.

Stadium, or Garden of Domitian, on Palatine, 54.

— in etching by Koch, pl. 34.

— aeroplane view, pl. 74.

— photographs, pls. 83, 84.

Stael, Mme de (Anna Louise Germaine Necker; 1766–1817), 20, 42.

Statues never buried, 133–141, pls. 211–222.

Stendhal, pseud. (Henri-Marie Beyle; 1783–1842), 20.

Stilicho (d. A.D. 408), 38.

Story, William Wetmore (1819–1895), influence on Hawthorne, 27.

— quoted, on Claudian aqueduct, 29.

— on Rome, 31–32.

— quoted, on public letter writer, pl. 37.

— on October festivals, pl. 38.

— on fish market in Portico of Octavia, pl. 47.

— on pifferari, pl. 184.

Street of Victory. See Clivus Victoriae.

Substructures of Septimius Severus on Palatine, 50, 52, pls. 74–80.

— Eaton on, 53.

— Murray on, 53.

— in etching by Koch, pl. 34.

— in painting by Severn, pl. 29.

— used as haylofts, pl. 52.

— drawing by Heemskerck, pl. 77.

— Hare on, pls. 78, 80.

— Hillard on, pl. 79.

Suetonius (first half of second century A.D.), quoted, on Titus, 80.

Suetonius, quoted, on Nero's Golden House, 82–83, 90.

Supplementum Chronicorum Orbis, Foresti, 11, pl. 13.

Symmachus, Q. Aurelius (A.D. c. 340–after 402), quoted, 71.

Tabularium, on Capitol Hill remains standing in Middle Ages, 39, 41.
— Senator's Palace built above, 41, 44, pls. 5, 6, 8, 9, 33, 55, 57, 62–71.
— Hawthorne on, pl. 64.

Taddeo di Bartolo (c. 1362–1422), 6, 11, pl. 8.

Tarquin the Elder, trad. king of Rome (c. 616–579 B.C.), founds temple of Jupiter on Capitol, legend, pl. 58.

Taylor, Bayard (1825–1878), quoted, pl. 199.

Temple of Antoninus and Faustina, 69, 71–72.
— houses Church of San Lorenzo in Miranda, 71, pls. 54, 100, 109–112.
— portico of, in fifteenth-century drawing, pl. 11.
— drawing by Heemskerck, pl. 110.

Temple of Apollo on Palatine, 51.

Temple of Apollo Sosianus, ruins of, in photograph, pl. 182.

'Temple of Augustus', so-called, site of, 61, pl. 56.

Temple of Castor, Cicero on, 66.
— remains described, 66.
— first built after Battle of Lake Regillus, 67.
— rebuilt by Tiberius, 67.
— columns of, in painting by Pannini, pl. 19.
— columns of, in etching by Vasi, pl. 99.
— columns partly buried, in drawing by Heemskerck, pl. 102.
— columns of, drawing by Claude Lorrain, pl. 103.
— identified as 'Temple of Jupiter Stator', 67, pl. 103.
— columns of, in painting by Canaletto, pl. 104.
— columns of, in painting by Pannini, pl. 115.
— columns of, in etching by Vasi, pl. 222.

'Temple of Concord', so-called. See Temple of Saturn.

'Temple of Fortune', so-called. See Temple of Saturn.

'Temple of Fortuna Virilis', so-called, described, 115.
— painting by Roesler-Franz, pl. 45
— drawing by Brill, pl. 187.

Temple of Jerusalem, spoils brought from by Titus, pl. 122.

Temple of Juno, 37, 43, 45.

Temple of Jupiter Capitolinus, called 'Capitol' in ancient times, 37.
— disappearance of, 38, 39.
— gold removed from doors and roof, 38.
— rebuilt by Domitian, 40.
— on Sestertius of Vespasian, Fig. 1.
— foundations beneath Palace of the Conservators and Caffarelli Palace, pls. 57, 63.
— fragment beside *Salita delle Tre Pile*, pl. 60.
— in relief, pl. 61.
— site of, in drawing, pl. 63.
— founded by Tarquin, pl. 58.
— platform excavated, 39, pl. 58.
— Dionysius of Halicarnassus on, pl. 58.
— wall incorporated into Caffarelli garden wall, 39, pls. 57, 59.
— Plutarch on, pl. 60.

Temple of Jupiter the Victorious, 51.

'Temple of Jupiter Stator'. See Temple of Castor.

'Temple of Jupiter Tonans', so-called. See Temple of Vespasian.

Temple of Magna Mater on Palatine, relief, pl. 1.

'Temple of Mater Matuta', so-called, 115.

Temple of Minerva, in Nerva's Forum, 101–102.
— Master Gregory on, 102.
— ruins, in drawing by Heemskerck, pl. 110.
— fifteenth-century drawing, pl. 163.
— Hawthorne on, pl. 164.

Temple of Minerva on the Aventine, shown in Marble Plan, pl. 3.

Temple of Pallas. See Temple of Minerva, in Forum of Nerva.

'Temple of Peace'. See Basilica of Constantine or Maxentius.

'Temple of Rome'. See Basilica of Constantine or Maxentius.

'Temple of Romulus'. See Basilica of Constantine or Maxentius.

Temple of Saturn, as Senate Treasury, *Mirabilia* on, 65.
— confusion as to identity of, 65.
— inscription on, 65.
— columns of portico, in fifteenth-century drawing, pl. 11.
— columns, in painting by Prout, pl. 33.
— in drawings by Heemskerck, pls. 63, 102.
— columns of, sixteenth-century etching, pl. 65.

Temple of Saturn, columns of, i painting by Canaletto, pl. 104

'Temple of the Sibyl', so-called, a Tivoli in painting by Robert pl. 22.

Temple of the Sun at Palmyra, 108.

Temple of the Sun or Serapis identity of, 107.
— decay and fall of, 108, 109.
— *Mirabilia* on, 108.
— names by which called, 108.
— marble from, in staircase of Santa Maria in Aracoeli, 109, pl. 70.
— in drawing by Heemskerck, pl. 110.
— fragments found in Colonna Gardens, 107, 109–110, pl. 174.
— ruins of, sixteenth-century etching, pl. 175.

Temple of Vejovis, 37.

Temple of Venus and Rome Santa Maria Nova built in ruins of, 61.
— Santa Francesca Romana on site of, 61, 73, pl. 117.
— ruins of, in painting by Turner, pl. 31.

Temple of Vespasian, built by Titus and Domitian, 65–66.
— inscription of, 66.
— restored by Severus and Caracalla, 66.
— corner of, in drawing by Anonymus Escurialensis, pl. 11.
— in painting by Prout, pl. 33.
— drawing by Cole, pl. 41.
— excavation of, pl. 65.
— in sixteenth-century etching, pl. 65.
— in drawing by Heemskerck, pl. 102.
— identified as 'Temple of Jupiter Tonans' 65–66, and in etching by Vasi, pl. 116.

Temple of Vesta in Forum, 51.
— Ovid on, 67.
— Plutarch on, 67.
— Palladium kept in, 67.
— described, 67–68.
— closed, 68.
— excavated and partially restored, 68.
— *Mirabilia* on, 68.
— Macaulay on, 69.
— relief, identity uncertain, pl. 106.
— restoration by wife of Septimius Severus, 68, pl. 106.

'Temple of Vesta', so-called, in Forum Boarium, 115.
— painting by Roesler-Franz, pl. 45.
— sixteenth-century drawing, pl. 187.

'Temple of Vesta', so-called, Tivoli, in painting by Pannini, pl. 19.

Terme Museum, in Baths of Diocletian, 98.

— entrance to, in photograph, pl. 161.

Theatre of Marcellus, 112–114, pls. 182–185.

— shops cleared from 35.

— planned by Julius Caesar, 112.

— built by Augustus, 112.

— plan of, 112.

— destruction of, 112–113.

— fortified by Pierleoni, 113.

— acquired by Savelli, 113

— shops in, 113–114, pl. 185.

— Niebuhr on, 113.

— Hawthorne on, 113–114.

— sixteenth-century etching, pl. 183.

— *pifferari* before, etching by Pinelli, pl. 184.

Theodoric (c. 455–526), 2.

— keeps Roman tradition, 2.

— repairs Roman palaces, 50.

— and aqueducts, 95.

— associated with Hadrian's Tomb, 126.

Third Book of Architecture, Serlio, cited, pl. 77.

Thompson, Launt (1833–1894), pl. 123.

Thorwaldsen, Bertel (1768?–1844), 16, 25, pl. 36.

Tiber, becomes source of Roman water supply, 96.

— in painting by Poussin, pl. 16.

— in paintings by Corot, pls. 32, 202.

— in fifteenth-century drawing, pl. 201.

Tiberius, Roman emperor (A.D. 14–37). See Palace of Tiberius.

Time, reckoning of, ancient, medieval, modern, 8.

Tischbein, Johann Wilhelm Heinrich (1751–1829), 17, pl. 25.

Titus, Roman emperor (A.D. 79–81), builds Temple of Vespasian, 66.

— capture of Jerusalem, A.D. 70, 75, pl. 122.

— opens Colosseum, 80.

— Suetonius on, 80.

— sestertius of, Fig. 1.

— riding in triumph, in drawing by Heemskerck, pl 121.

— triumphal procession of, pl. 122.

Tomb of Hadrian. See Hadrian's Tomb, Castle of Sant' Angelo.

'Tomb of Nero', so-called, drawing by Longfellow, pl. 39.

'Tomb of Remus', so-called. See Pyramid of Cestius.

'Tomb of Romulus', so-called, 122, pls. 9, 13.

Torre del Grillo, in photograph, pl. 166.

'Tower of Maecenas'. See Temple of the Sun or Serapis.

Tower of the Milizie, in drawing by Heemskerck, pl. 63.

— in nineteenth-century painting, pl. 179.

Towne, Francis (c. 1740–1816), drawing of Baths of Caracalla, pl. 30.

Trajan, Roman emperor (A.D. 98––117), destroys part of Nero's Golden House, 90.

— builds forum, 103.

— statue of, in Forum of Trajan, 103.

— temple in honour of, built by Hadrian, 105.

— sestertius of, Fig. 1.

— in relief from column, pl. 173.

— See also Column of Trajan, Forum of Trajan.

Transtiberine Section of Rome, 125.

Trastevere, 35–36, 125.

Trasteverini, Story on, 31–32.

Travels in Italy, Goethe, quoted, 15, 85, pl. 25.

Travels through Italy, Kotzebue, 20.

Trelawny, Edward J. (1792–1881), pl. 198.

Très Riches Heures de Jean de France, Duc de Berry, 7, Fig. 2.

Triumphal Arches, 75–76, pls. 120–127. See also Arch of Constantine; Arch of Septimius Severus; Arch of Titus. *Mirabilia* on, 75.

Truth and Poetry, Goethe, 16.

Turnbull, George (eighteenth century), 57.

Turner, Joseph Mallord William (1775–1851), 22–23, drawings and paintings of Colosseum, 84.

— *Arches of Constantine and Titus*, pl. 31.

— *View of north side of Forum*, drawing, pl. 112.

— *View of Forum from Farnese Gardens*, pl. 113.

— *Southwest Side of Colosseum*, pl. 134.

Turris Cartularia (of Frangipani fortress), in painting by Turner, pl. 31.

Turris comitis. See Conti tower.

Uberti, Fazio degli. See Fazio degli Uberti.

Udine, Giovanni da (1487–1564), inspired by decorations in Nero's Golden House, 91.

Urban II, pope (1088–1094), 99.

Urban V, pope in Avignon, settles Carthusian monks in Baths of Diocletian, pl. 7.

Urban VIII, pope (1623–1644), dedicates St. Peter's, 131.

Vacca, Flaminio (1538?–1600), 13, 39.

Valadier, Giuseppe (1762–1839), 76, pl. 135.

Vanderlyn, John (1775–1852), — *Arch of Titus*, painting, pl. 28.

Vanvitelli, Luigi (1700–1773), 99, pl. 157.

Vasari, Giorgio (1511–1574), quoted, on paintings in Nero's Golden House, Pls. 144, 145.

Vasi, Giuseppe (1710–1782), 15–16, 62; etchings, pls. 99, 116.

Vatican, connected by passage with Castle of Sant' Angelo, 127, pl. 10.

Vatican loggie, painted under Raphael's supervision, 91, pl. 145.

Vatican Naumachia, pl. 5.

Vatican Obelisk, 129–132, pls. 206–210.

— called 'St. Peter's needle', 129.

— *Mirabilia* on, 129–130.

— globe replaced with cross, 130.

— moved to present position, 130.

— by sacristy of St. Peter's, drawing by Heemskerck, pl. 207.

— moving of, engraving, pl. 208.

Vatican Palace, pls. 8, 9, 206, 208–210.

Vedder, Elihu (1836–1923), 28.

— quoted, pl. 154.

— drawing by, pl. 154.

Veit, Philipp (1793–1877), 24, pl. 35.

Venantius Fortunatus, Bishop of Poitiers (c. 530–c. 609), 104.

Venus, statue of, in Pantheon, 118.

Venus statue of, on Quirinal, Master Gregory on, 140.

Venus and ring, legend, 140–141.

Venus d'Ille, Mérimée, 141.

Verdi, Giuseppe (1813–1901), death commemorated in Colosseum concert, 89, pl. 140.

Vergil (70–19 B.C.), quoted, 37, 38, 112.

Vernet, Joseph (1714–1789), 15.

Vespasian, Roman emperor (A.D. 69–79), temple built by sons to, 66.

— wrongly associated with Basilica of Constantine or Mazentius, 78.

— Sestertius of, Fig. 1.

— deposits spoils from Temple of Jerusalem in Forum of Peace, pl. 122.

Vesta, 67.

Vestal Virgins, 67, 68.

Vestigi dell' Antichità di Roma, Du Pérac, 12.

Vestigi dell' Antichità di Roma, Tabularium and Senator's Palace, etching, pl. 65.
— south side of Palatine, etching, pl. 76.
— northwest corner of Forum, etching, pl. 108.
— Arch of Constantine, etching, pl. 125.
— arches of Basilica of Constantine or Maxentius, etching, pl. 129.
— central hall of the Baths of Diocletian, etching, pl. 158.
— ruins of Temple of the Sun or Serapis, etching, pl. 175.
— Column of Trajan, etching, pl. 171.
— side view of Pantheon, etching, pl. 191.
Via Alessandrina (now Via dei Fori Imperiali), in etching by Piranesi, pl. 164.
Via Biberatica, pls. 168, 169.
Via dei Fori Imperiali, 34, pl. 164.
Via dei Trionfi. See Via di San Gregorio.
Via di Marforio, 139, pl. 222.
Via di San Gregorio, 34, pl. 79.
Via Magnanapoli, pls. 170–171.
Via Sacra. See Sacred Way.
Vibia Maria Maxima, monument to parents thought to be tomb of Nero, pl. 39.

Vicissitudes of Fortune, Poggio Bracciolini, 8.
Victor Emmanuel II (b. 1820, king of Italy 1861–1878), becomes king of Italy, 32.
— monument of, 35, 48, pls. 57, 70, 72, 100, 114.
— unites Italian territories, 44.
Victory, goddess of, patron of Senate House, 63, 70.
Views in Italy, Friedländer, 20, quoted, 24, 59.
Vignola, Giacomo B. (1762–1839), wall of Farnese Gardens, pls. 89, 90, 91
— gate, 58, pls. 91, 92.
Villa Mattei on Caelian hill, obelisk moved to, from Santa Maria in Aracoeli, pl.63.
Villa Medici, pl. 1.
Villa Mills. See Villa Palatina-Mills.
Villa Palatina-Mills, history and description of, 55–56.
— Lady Blessington on, 56.
— site of, pls. 75, 85.
— Hillard on, pl. 82.
— last remnants of, in photograph, pl. 84.
— begun by Mattei family, pl. 85.
— with Gothic façade, photograph, pl. 86.
— wing added by nuns of the visitation, pls. 74, 75.
See also Palatine Museum.

Villa Spada. See Villa Palatina-Mills.
Virginius, legend of, 63.
Visitation, Order of, buys Villa Palatina-Mills, 55, pls. 74, 85.

Wace (twelfth century), quoted, 134.
Walks in Rome, Hare, 31; quoted, pls. 78, 80.
Wall of Aurelian. See Aurelian Wall.
Walls, papal, pls. 8, 38.
West, Benjamin (1738–1820), quoted, 17.
Wilhelm Meister, Goethe, 16.
William of Malmesbury (c.1080–1143), 140–141.
Winckelmann, Johann J. (1717–1768), pioneer art historian, 14.
— and excavations, 33.
— discusses Laocoön, 93.
'Women's senate house', so-called, said to have been built by Elagabulus, 108.
— etching by Piranesi, pl. 24.
World History, Paulinus, view of Rome from, 5, pls. 5, 62, 212.
Wrenshall, Katharine (nineteenth-twentieth century), quoted, 100, pl. 160.

Zenobia (third century A.D.), 107.
Zola, Emile (1840–1902), *Rome*, quoted, 34, 74.